To Liz & Jon

Delighted that 92 Redhatch Drive
is still being used for the
furtherance of the Kingdom!

Anne Valerie.

December 2017

THREADS OF DESTINY

THREADS OF DESTINY

by

John Smith

Bound Biographies

Dedication

This autobiography is dedicated to my wonderful family
who have been the inspiration to start it
and the encouragement to finish it.

The author in 1963

What can be done to preserve for the family the legacy of happy memories? Hilarious incidents, scary moments and even that rare pearl of wisdom, shared at a meal table may be forgotten next week, to say nothing of next year. The only remedy is to write it all down. This I have done to the best of my ability and memory!

John Smith

John is a master storyteller. His own eventful and compelling life story he tells with great insight and side-splitting humour; this book is truly inspirational.

Andrew Mowll

Challenging, entertaining and encouraging. Don't miss breakfast with the insurance salesman! A remarkable modern example of the way God works in a mysterious way!

Paul Wraight

I heartily recommend this book as a good, lively read.

Ann Thatcher

This is a "can't put down book" written with great lucidity, candour and humour causing the reader to question the ultimate purpose of life. A compelling read.

Douglas Austin

This is an historic, charming, challenging and spiritual journey across decades of war and peace, blessings and disappointments. It's a book to enjoy with a favourite glass and a snug corner.

Gerald Coates, speaker, author and broadcaster.

I love this book. One moment I was laughing out loud, the next I was weeping.

Fiona Oyekan

Contents

Foreword
by Roger Forster

For those not having the privilege of knowing John Smith, his name alone would not appear auspicious for launching into authorship – particularly not of an autobiography! He has had many dubious looks over the years when his name is mentioned, especially, as he recounts himself, when with his new bride he signed into their honeymoon hotel as Mr and Mrs John Smith.

However, this ordinary name belongs to an extraordinary person. John has an unusually developed gift for 'reading' people, and for making instant friends with unlikely persons. Added to this is his perception of the significance of ordinary events, his sense of destiny in his own life, and in the lives of others, and of the part that friendships and relationships play. His gift as a raconteur is undoubted – he tells the stories of his life with great humour, always drawing the reader into a relationship of friendship with him – the very gift which endears him to all he meets. Folk come away from an encounter with John Smith with a mysterious feeling that they have met a long-lost friend, one moreover whose friendship will last forever. My wife and I have been privileged to know him over many years and can testify to the warm generosity and charm of this amazing man.

In this book, John tells the story of his life in such a lively way that you feel you are there with him. You are there in the jungle of Malaya when a tiger leaps on his makeshift hut; and you are there with him when he encounters Jesus as he reads his little New Testament. The ordinary events of life – marriage, getting a job, buying a house or going on holiday – are never straightforward when John is at the centre of them, and his ability to tell a story, even against himself, with rollicking good humour and a sort of magical significance is what makes this book so very readable.

Life with the Smiths has never been dull, mundane or predictable. John turns his innovative mind to every area of his life. He built up the Reading Branch of the Sun Life Assurance Company of Canada to become the World Leader, finding it another glorious opportunity to share the good news of the Gospel! He ran a number of Children's Special Service Missions in and around Reading reaching many hundreds of children with the gospel during the summer holidays. He helped advance missionary work in Borneo by developing the UK Branch of the Borneo Evangelical Mission. All of these exploits should have been enough to keep him and Valerie on their toes (and the reader with them) but in addition there is huge involvement with their amazing family of children, grandchildren and elderly relatives.

Many of his contemporaries, like myself, will enjoy John's childhood reminiscences from World War II years followed by his escapades in the Palestine Police and the Army Intelligence. The Christian movement that swept through the ranks of young army apprentices when John was in the Army Education Corps, described by him here, and witnessed by many of us, were a complete contrast to the media picture portraying the UK as becoming increasingly pagan. John also depicts global events of the time with interesting and insightful observations on them. The book is a sort of historical sweep from a personal perspective.

But, in the end, life and history are really about people. John Smith's evident love of family life and his artless delight in, and reminiscences of, his wife and children, his friends and colleagues, and even complete strangers, is permeated with the love, respect, and prayer he shows for all human beings who are made 'in God's image' and therefore created for a destiny.

In these pages, you will meet a friend who will draw you into his life-story, inviting you to share and enjoy his friendship and destiny. This is John Smith, 'everyman extraordinaire'!

Roger Forster
Founder of the Ichthus Christian Fellowship
Vice-President of Tearfund
Chairman of the Council of the Evangelical Alliance

Foreword
by Jim Graham

John Smith of Reading sounds such a cliché, but nothing could be further from the truth so far as this John Smith from Reading is concerned. Loved by his family, respected by his colleagues, valued by his friends, and honoured in the business world for his diligence and integrity this John Smith has something to say that needs to be heard and something to write that needs to be read. In our celebrity-crazed culture where image is much more important than substance it is so refreshing to come to terms with the reality of a life that lacks pretentiousness and superficiality.

This book is about a man I know and whose friendship I have valued through the years. Although we have not spent all that much time together in the great span of a lifetime, our times together have always been memorable for me and I have come away from those times with a desire in my heart to be a better man. John's impact on my life has been about character - uncluttered, penetrating, godly character. This is the man you will undoubtedly meet in this book.

This man's life rings true because of its joys and its sorrows, its laughter and its tears, its successes and its failures, its certainties and its apprehensions, its hope and its despair, its pleasure and its pain, its mistakes and its accomplishments which he shares so openly. The whole journey of this life is under girded and sustained by a simple, childlike and yet informed trust and confidence in God. This is no simplistic, fantasy God but a God who unmistakably has no boundaries to His presence, His provision, and His power. This is not just a theologically-thought-through God but One who has been discovered and known in the fire of confronting reality in life.

Long ago the Apostle Paul wrote a letter to the Church at Ephesus which was to be read by the surrounding churches and in the very first Chapter he says:

'Because of Jesus we are now here on earth at this time not by chance but by choice (His choice) whatever the circumstances of our birth, heredity, or environment so that God might fulfill His agenda perfectly in us. He has done this so that all in heaven and on earth might lavishly and profoundly express their thankfulness for His comprehensive completeness and indescribable brilliance. So those of you who are reading this letter must realize that you, too, became part of this God-plan the moment you heard, grasped, and believed what God had done for you in His Son Jesus. He brought you into a living, vibrant relationship with Himself; setting your feet on a road that would bring pleasure to Him, and giving you a hope that not even death can destroy. God did something excitingly wonderful in that moment of honesty as you stubbornly faced the actual reality of your situation apart from God - He identified that you, indeed, were His and His life burst forth in you (His transforming, life-changing life that delivered you from religion and gave you reality). Something began in you in history that one day will be perfected in eternity - so that people and angels will worship this God for His comprehensive completeness and indescribable, shadowless light.'

John Smith can never be understood apart from this. You will be struck by the fact that though he never takes himself too seriously he certainly took others very seriously indeed. This was to be seen so clearly in his passionate concern to impact the market-place with integrity and truth and influence the world of business with good practice and God-based values. Only eternity will be able to testify to the effect this has had on so many lives.

All the while you will meet a man who struggles with his own imperfection, frailty and humanity yet constantly is drawn to something more and something better. I think life taught him that God is not looking for extraordinary people to do extraordinary things but rather that God is looking for ordinary people to do ordinary things in an extraordinary way with His resources.

I commend 'Threads of Destiny' to you.

Jim Graham, Director of External Ministries,
Gold Hill Baptist Church, Buckinghamshire

Acknowledgements

There are many people who have helped to make Threads of Destiny a reality. It is not possible to mention them all but to everyone goes my heartfelt appreciation. I would specifically mention my daughter Penny who goaded me into initial action and then immediately started asking when the book would be completed. To escape the pressure I had either to completely abandon the idea of writing an autobiography or to finish it quickly. In fact it was written in just eight weeks but it meant working at it for twelve hours a day.

It was only when it was finished and I started to read it that I discovered that the Spell Check on the computer is a snare and a delusion. It is unimaginable how many "mistakes" it can overlook. Proof reading your own work may save a veritable fortune but it is a minefield of concealed typographical traps. Far from being the rip-off that I imagined I now know the proof reader deserves every penny he gets. I have therefore been especially blessed in having a daughter who is an English teacher and has spent much of her professional life marking essays. Katie has laboured long and hard at proof reading the text and in the process found a humbling number of errors.

On the other side of the road, my neighbour Brian Turner has been a stern but kind critic while on the other side of the world my brother Fred in Australia has been able to bring me out of childhood fantasies into the accurate world of reality. It must be so much easier to write a novel where events are completely imaginary than to write an autobiography where accuracy is of the essence.

It is a privilege to have "Forewords" for the book written by two such eminent churchmen as Roger Forster and Jim Graham. My reaction on reading them was to ask whether they really were writing about me!

To enable us to take photographs of Riddlesworth Hall, Mr Paul Cochrane, the Headmaster of Riddlesworth Hall School gave us permission to wander all over the huge mansion. It was just like old times and fascinating to Valerie to see what hitherto had only been described from memory. The School cook was particularly thrilled that Riddlesworth Hall would feature in a book!

A special word of thanks goes to my friend Peter Cornforth who not only has been a great encouragement but also pointed out an advertisement that was headed Bound Biographies. This company specialises in helping ordinary people record the past for the future. Mike Oke and Tony Gray, the two men who run the company are stars. I had already written the book before learning of their existence but I quickly discovered that nothing was too much trouble for them and I was completely comfortable with placing my precious manuscript in their hands. Their skills and commitment would be a great encouragement to folk who are contemplating writing their biography but hardly know where to start.

Having dipped a tentative toe into the world of authors I have been enormously impressed by the all pervasive atmosphere of encouragement I have encountered. Numerous copyrights have been waived but in every case they were attended by a personal word of encouragement to persevere and, even though there was no vested interest, there have been follow-up enquiries regarding progress. It is certainly a great encouragement to explore further this friendly fraternity.

A portrait photograph of Valerie and me was urgently needed for the front cover and in a moment of inspiration we contacted our friend Paul Howard. Within a matter of hours he had taken the photographs and provided us with over 50 proofs from which to choose one for the cover. Without doubt he is Reading's Lord Snowdon!

It is all very well for Miss Prism, in "The Importance of being Ernest", to say to Cecily that "memory is the diary we carry about with us," but now that I have finished this book my capricious memory starts to recall amazing incidents that have been omitted and, what is more important, wonderful people I haven't mentioned. My heart fails me at the prospect of re-writing the book or producing a sequel so the less arduous alternative is to list at the back of the book as many of those "wonderful people" that my failing memory will recollect. I recognise the hazards inherent in such a list because of the inevitability of omitting a number of "bosom pals" but I am depending on their loving forbearance and generous forgiveness.

Finally, and above all, my thanks go to my long-suffering but uncomplaining darling wife whose role throughout has been encourager, consultant, proof reader and loving critic.

John Smith

Preface

We live at a time when the preservation of financial legacies is threatened by punitive taxation. It is therefore prudent to take steps to ensure that the size of the shovel the Chancellor of the Exchequer digs into an estate is as small as legally possible. But what can be done to preserve for the family the legacy of happy memories? Hilarious incidents, scary moments and even that rare pearl of wisdom, shared at a meal table, may be forgotten next week, to say nothing of next year. The only remedy is to write it all down.

That is why I have written this book. It is for the benefit of my children, their children and perhaps even *their* children. I hope they will enjoy reading about my life as much as I have enjoyed living it! As we get older we reflect on the legacy we will leave those we love. Blessed is the one who will leave a legacy of happy memories. This I have tried to do to the best of my ability and memory! Events of the past have been resurrected and hopefully have not suffered too great a distortion in the process.

While recording the events of my life, I have been reminded repeatedly of the guiding hand of God. This should not be surprising, for He Himself promised to guide us. The Authorised Version of Psalm 32:8 puts it beautifully: 'I will instruct thee and teach thee in the way which thou shalt go; I will guide thee with mine eye.' This is a very sensitive guidance. God guides with His *eye*. Many have been the times when, on the verge of committing some social solecism, I have caught my wife's eye. It has been very effective guidance! But to catch the eye you need to look in the face! There's the rub. If we don't seek His face, we don't catch the look, and we may miss out on some of the wonderful plans that God has for our lives.

Looking back over the years, the most distinctive thread in my life has been the love of God, shown pre-eminently in the amazing facts of the life, death and resurrection of Jesus, so that we could have life. But God's love has also been shown in His choice of Valerie to be a loving partner in my life. We have enjoyed nearly fifty-five years together, and each succeeding year has brought its particular blessings. That doesn't mean that there have not been times of pain and sadness. Our broken engagement was traumatic. The miscarriages and our stillborn babies brought sharp pain, disappointment and distress, but never mistrust.

In his splendid book, My Utmost for His Highest, Oswald Chambers makes the profound observation, 'There can be no progress in the Christian life until we face the fact that life is more tragic than orderly.' To argue the contrary is nothing less than sophistry. It is an indisputable fact, that in the world tragic things take place for which there are no easy answers; but that doesn't mean that God doesn't care, nor does it mean that there is no purpose. Lines from Tennyson's In Memoriam resonate with this:

Life is not as idle ore, but iron dug from central gloom,
And heated hot with burning fears and dipped in baths
of hissing tears,
And battered with the shocks of doom to shape and use.

We have not always been able to see purpose in some of the shocks that have touched our lives, but while we may not have discovered deliverance *from* all those difficulties, we have known deliverance *in* the midst of them. Deliverance *in* is no less a deliverance than deliverance *from,* and it is all for a purpose. We are not His puppets on a string, but He has woven threads of destiny for us. My hope is that some of the lessons I have learned, and tried to record in these pages, will encourage you to look for those threads of destiny in your life. In Jeremiah 29:11, God says: 'I know the plans I have for you… plans to give you hope and a future.' May God bless you as you seek to walk in those plans? You couldn't have a better future!

John Smith
October 2009

Part One
"A BOY!"
(1929-47)

Chapter 1
That 'dear little boy'

"It's a boy," said the midwife.

"A boy!" exclaimed my mother, "Oh dear, we so wanted a little girl."

It was 4th March 1929.

Happily, my mother didn't share her disappointment with me until much later when it didn't matter. Looking back on my life I'm glad I was a boy. Had I been a girl I suspect my life might have been a little less adventurous! In the event I share my birthday with a fellow adventurer, Henry the Navigator, the son of King John I of Portugal. No doubt you will recall that it was Henry who, in 1424, explored the coast of Africa!

Sharing his birthday with Henry and me is the composer and violin virtuoso Vivaldi of The Four Seasons fame. The three of us share our birthday with Giovanni Schiaparelli, the Italian astronomer. Now let me tell you something that might come in handy for those who find themselves on 'Who wants to be a millionaire'. It was Giovanni who discovered the asteroid Hesperia and also plotted the Canals on Mars. It would be appreciated if the source of that information was remembered when the million pounds is banked.

Returning to 4th March 1929, King George V was on the throne and Stanley Baldwin in 10, Downing Street. Over in the United States of America, Calvin Coolidge was President in the morning but by the evening Herbert Hoover had moved into the White House, a move he may have regretted for it was in 1929 that the New York Stock Exchange crashed and the World Depression started.

In 1929 the average weekly wage was £4 and a loaf of bread cost a penny farthing. The fact that the average price of a house was only

£600 was not of the slightest interest to me. Underweight and sickly, staying alive was my complete preoccupation. When I came along my mother already had two sons on her hands, Fred, who was eighteen months old, and Bill, who was eight. I should perhaps explain that Bill was my half-brother. My mother, who was christened Norah Evelyn Davies, was well acquainted with my father long before she met Bill's dad. Both my mother and father were very accomplished ballroom dancers; in fact they met at a fancy dress ball to which my father went as Geronimo, the Red Indian Chief and my mother went as 'Cook'. They took the first and the second prize; to be exact, they took joint first prize. After the award they did a demonstration dance together. It was that dance that led to my arrival on 4th March 1929; but that was not until ten years had passed.

Dad as Geronimo
The Red Indian Chief

Mum as Cook

Despite being greatly attracted to my father, my mother refused to marry him, opting for a less dazzling but more reliable spouse in the person of Herbert Hughes, the local postmaster. In due course Bill arrived making an idyllic family. Five years later tragedy struck. Herbert Hughes was killed when his horse reared up, throwing him to the ground where his head fatally struck a rock.

My mother was a very attractive lady and over the next twelve months had many suitors, one of whom was her one-time ballroom partner. My father was born in Norwich and christened Sydney Samuel Smith. Leaving school he helped his father in the family bakery business in Norwich. In 1914 World War I started and, adventurous to the core, my father volunteered for the army, joining the 7th Dragoon Guards.

Dad in the 7th Dragoon Guards in 1914

After the war the family bakery went out of business and, with unemployment widespread, my father got a job as a footman. Being a personable young man, he was soon in great demand and by the time my mother became a widow he was under butler at Burleigh House, the Marquis of Exeter's palatial home in Casterton near Stamford in Lincolnshire. That senior position would have commanded a salary adequate enough to support a family so Dad was an eligible bachelor and it was not long before Mrs Hughes became Mrs Smith.

Shortly after the marriage my father was offered a post as butler to the fabulously wealthy Mr Champion. William Needham Longden Champion inherited a modest fortune from his father and in a very short time turned it into a large one! One of the uses to which he put his fortune was to build Riddlesworth Hall, an impressive mansion in Norfolk which incidentally had 365 windows, one of which features prominently in this narrative! But Mr Champion's real

Dad, when Under Butler for the Marquis of Exeter

5

Front entrance to Riddlesworth Hall

ambition was to use his wealth to attract to his daughter's side an eligible bachelor from the nobility. His daughter frustrated this objective by falling in love with a handsome infantry colonel. The resentful father refused to attend the wedding and promptly disinherited his daughter. Undeterred, the couple settled down in the colonel's ancestral home, Rockbeare Manor, in Devon. There they had a baby girl, Delia, who was to play a significant role in my future. Meanwhile Grandfather Champion decided to leave his entire fortune to Delia.

Before the sad episode of the estrangement of father and daughter, Mr Champion had as his butler a man rather like The Admirable Crichton. Mr Champion wished to house his butler in a style that reflected his own intended station in life. To this end he gave his butler carte blanche to have a house built to his own specifications and not to stint the cost. The result was a magnificent four bed-roomed house which he disingenuously called 'The Cottage'. With large rooms, bay windows and ornate plasterwork ceilings, it might well have been the creation of The Admirable Crichton himself! An extraordinarily large front room was in addition to a large but more comfortable sitting room. The front room even had a genuine marble Adam fireplace surmounted by a gigantic ornate mirror. We'll return to that mirror later.

The Admirable Crichton's Cottage

Unfortunately, six months after the house was completed, The Admirable Crichton died leaving Mr Champion without a butler. It so happened that the Marquis of Exeter was acquainted with Mr Champion and Dad was recommended to fill the vacant patent leather shoes. The couple, together with seven-year-old Billy, moved into this wholly desirable residence just three months before my brother Fred was born. A lusty, healthy, ginger-haired paragon, Fred caused his parents no anxieties. Those were to come after my arrival, for it was not long before I was crawling into every kind of mischief, including going up the chimney and bringing down an avalanche of soot into the living room.

My narrowest escape occurred when I was climbing an ornate garden structure surmounted by a heavy stone flower pot. I have no knowledge of the event but my mother told me that she heard this fearful crash and, rushing into the front garden, found the broken flower pot, a pile of soil and flowers but no sign of me! Perceiving a slight movement under the soil she frantically scrabbled around and found me; my ears, eyes, nose and mouth were full of compost and loam but apparently I was none the worse for my adventure.

Just after my first birthday my mother was diagnosed with advanced TB and was whisked off to hospital and subsequently to a sanatorium.

This hospitalisation was to last two years. Dad's sister, Aunt Ethel opened her home to my brothers Bill and Fred but my poor father was at his wits end to know what to do with me. He was discussing the problem in the local post office when a lady customer said, "I'll look after that dear little boy." She lived two or three miles away and had probably only seen that dear little boy once or twice at the most and clearly had never heard of his exploits. As far as Dad was concerned it was a matter of any port in a storm so the dear little boy was farmed out.

My foster parents were Mr and Mrs Dack. Mr Dack was a shepherd who also ran a small-holding. They had a teenage daughter named Olive who had waited in vain for a baby

Just after my first birthday

brother. With my arrival her dreams had come true and she lavished on me her devoted attention.

On the very first evening of my arrival there was a serious contretemps with an existing member of the family. I only vaguely remember it but it seems that I had perched myself on the edge of a low seat which was the exclusive preserve of Snowball, a huge white cat. Jumping on to the seat he sent me sprawling on the floor. By all accounts I picked myself up and to his and the family's astonishment promptly knocked him off the seat. Thereafter we shared the seat perfectly amicably and in fact became inseparable friends.

The Dacks had on their small-holding a surprising number of animals. There were goats, pigs, ducks, geese, turkeys, chickens, guinea fowl, rabbits, ferrets, guinea pigs and rats, the latter being uninvited squatters. Within a very short time, with the exception of the rats, I was on friendly terms with all of them including a particularly savage guard dog and a temperamental shire horse who weighed over a ton.

One evening I could not be found. They told me that the family looked everywhere but I wasn't in any of my usual haunts. They eventually concluded that I must have fallen down the deep well outside the back door. They were preparing to lower Mr Dack down the well to recover my body when I was located in the stable. Apparently I was fast asleep, curled up in the straw between two shaggy front hooves as big as dinner plates. A restive animal, the horse always remonstrated whenever anyone entered his stable. On this occasion he didn't move an inch but lowered his massive muzzle and gently nudged me. The gesture was completely lost on me for I remained fast asleep, which was probably just as well for otherwise I might well have been smothered by a nearly hysterical Olive.

On another occasion when I disappeared I was found asleep in the kennel of the guard dog that then refused to let anyone near the kennel. Apparently it was not until an hour or so later, when I awoke and crawled out of the kennel, that the dog allowed anyone near me. The problem was that he was infested with fleas and after an hour in his company so was I, so for a while I continued to be kept at arm's length.

Mr Dack was one of nature's gentlemen. He never raised his voice but it carried a quiet and effective authority. We loved each other. Many years later I learned that every evening he would sit me on his knee and sing me hymns and songs. He knew them off by heart for he was a captain in the Salvation Army. I often wonder whether my becoming a committed Christian later in life was in some measure due to this good man's early influence.

In due course my mother returned home and on the very same day I was collected. It was a time of great rejoicing for the Smiths but of heart break for the Dacks who had thought I was on permanent attachment. Not surprisingly it was trauma all round for, whereas my mother had waited two years for the reunion, 'that dear little boy' was yelling vociferously, "I want my Uncle and Auntie!" Later, when I could ride a bicycle and was allowed to venture out on my own, I would make periodic visits to them. I was always treated with great love and tenderness.

Chapter 2
My Boyhood

"John, it's your bed time," my mother would say.

"Why is it *my* bed time and not *Fred's*? We're the same age." Actually Fred was eighteen months older than me but there were times in the year when I would argue that he was only a year older, but it was never any use. "You need your sleep," Mum would say. It always seemed to be at the most interesting time in the evening that I had to go to bed.

I remember one evening when we were all listening to a scary ghost story on the radio that my mother said, "John, it's your bed time."

"Oh Mum, it's nearly the end of the story!"
"No, it's your bed time! Besides, these stories are not good for you. You have bad dreams and you need your sleep."
"How about Fred, doesn't he have bad dreams?"
"These stories don't frighten Fred, off you go to bed." Muttering under my breath I stormed up the stairs.

I was about to get into bed when suddenly I had a brilliant idea. Hauling the white sheet off the bed I ran down the stairs in my pyjamas and bare feet. We had a large reception hall through which you had to go to get to the stairs. In the corner of this hall we had a four foot tall flower pot in which we had a huge aspidistra. With the sheet draped over me I crouched behind this aspidistra and waited for Fred to come to bed. The hall was floored with tiles and, as it was the middle of winter, soon my teeth were chattering like castanets.

In those days we didn't have electricity or gas. Lighting was by oil lamps and candles so apart from rooms that were occupied the whole house was in darkness. With all the horror of the ghost story still fresh upon him, Fred came into the hall carrying a candle. Suddenly an eerie white form rose up from behind the aspidistra and, without a sound, Fred sank to the floor in a dead faint! The candle went out and there was complete darkness. I groped around cautiously thinking that Fred might be pretending and was about to inflict fearful retribution on me, but no, he was out for the count! Grabbing him by the feet I dragged him out of the hall through our lounge and into the kitchen.

"Mum, I think Fred must have tripped and fallen in the hall," I said. He came to after a few minutes and made such a complete recovery that before I eventually got into bed I had received a severe beating; but it was worth it. I never let him forget that he was afraid of ghosts.

* * * * *

One Christmas we were given a huge Meccano set. The solid wooden box measured about three feet by two feet and was six inches deep with beautifully made sections. Fred was mesmerised by it. By Christmas evening, while I was busily detaching the corks from the safety strings of my new double barrelled pop gun and taking pot shots at some of the ornaments in the house, Fred was constructing a fabulous fair ground. Later, with my pop gun confiscated, I lay on my tummy watching this fair ground grow before my very eyes. I was not allowed to touch anything until it was finished. I couldn't wait! After a while I could almost hear the organ playing the fair ground music as the roundabouts turned. It was without doubt a wonderful piece of construction. When Fred turned a wheel at the back everything started to move.

"Can we play with it now?" I asked eagerly.
"Not yet. That pulley is slipping and needs tightening."

There always seemed to be something that needed adjustment and by the time it was finished it was, "John, it's your bed time!" The next morning I rushed downstairs to play with this amazing toy only to find it in pieces and back in the box. I couldn't believe it.

"Why?" I asked.
"Oh. I've decided to make a suspension bridge," said Fred.
"*You* decided! I thought it was *our* Christmas present," I said indignantly.

"Well, *you* make something." But I could never get the little nuts to go on the tiny bolts without crossing the thread and, in any case, I was never going to make anything that actually worked. Much later I learned from Mum that the Meccano set was more mine than Fred's. It was all a matter of inheritance. When I was born there was some debate between Mum and Dad as to what names I should be given. Apparently they were so expecting a girl that they hadn't prepared for a boy! Dad suggested Basil.

"Basil," said Mum, "why on earth should we call him Basil?"

It seems Dad had a relative by the name of Basil and he, according to Dad, had a bob or two. Dad's notion was that if I was called Basil after this relative then, at some time in the future, I might come in for an inheritance. Tragically Basil died when he was in Quetta and all we got was the Meccano set and a toy railway steam engine. I have always thought that having the name of Basil was a heavy price to pay for such meagre dividends.

* * * * *

Dad had the facility of turning the most mundane task into an adventure. In fact everything we did with Dad was turned into a game. If we went to get pea sticks from the wood we would be Red Indians stalking an elk. Bringing the sticks home wasn't a cycle ride, it was a cavalry charge, and when at the height of the charge I came off my bike and badly cut my knee, I wasn't a hurt little boy, I was a wounded soldier who quickly had to get back on his horse before a counter attack caught up with him. I would arrive home proud of the gore and ignoring the pain insisting to an aghast mother that "... it was nothing."

Dad turned our palatial front room into a war zone with my brothers Bill and Fred against Dad and me. At each end of the long room a fortress was constructed from wooden bricks and a number of lead soldiers positioned in defence. Between the two opposing armies was the sea on which each side had a fleet of paper ships. Cannons were made using sawn up lengths of curtain rails for the barrels and roller ball bearings as shells. Powerful springs were fixed in the barrels to fire the shells. A Meccano frame with two wheels made the cannons look very realistic. At this time Bill was sixteen and had left school to start

13

an engineering apprenticeship so he made the gun barrels and the spring fixings. Fred, who was very clever at making things from Meccano, made the gun carriage frames. I was given the job of making the paper ships and repositioning the soldiers in the forts.

All of this preparation took a number of days and we were totally engrossed in the project. Eventually all was completed and we were ready for what was expected to be an epic battle. It turned out to be a dramatic one.

A Saturday afternoon was chosen for the event. Dad usually had afternoons free when a footman did duty up at The Hall. The whistle went at two-thirty precisely and each side started hurling cannon balls and abuse at each other. It was all very exciting. The idea was that the side which had no ships and no soldiers still standing had to admit defeat.

The battle was proceeding at a furious pace when I had the notion of a double charge. I put two roller ball bearings into my gun, pulled back the lever holding the powerful spring and let fly. Unfortunately I was not strong enough to hold the gun steady and instead of hitting the enemy fortress the shells hit the aforementioned ornate mirror over the Adam fire place. There was an ear splitting crash and the mirror came down in a myriad of tiny glass shards. Dad's reaction was to shout, "Keep on firing, we haven't won yet!"

The battle continued, but hearing the explosion, my mother came rushing into the room. "What on earth has happened?"
"Don't stand there, Mum. You'll get hit by a shell," said Dad.
"But the mirror!" gasped my mother.
"War casualty," replied Dad, as he fired another shell! Mum departed, eyes raised to the ceiling in resignation.

Their side won but it was a great battle. When it was all over we swept up the debris. Dad told Mr Champion what had happened and to Mum's relief he was told to get a replacement mirror, so it was a happy ending to what had been a really exciting day.

At that time every boy had a clock-work Hornby Railway engine which made its rather tame way round a track. A completely new dimension was added with the advent of the steam engine that came with the Meccano set. We put trestle tables up in the front room and laid out an impressive track complete with signals, points, junctions, tunnels and level crossings. On a given Saturday afternoon we were to have an inaugural run from London to Edinburgh.

The little steam engine had been beautifully crafted with a water tank, a furnace and genuine pistons. The furnace was a strip heater fuelled with methylated spirits. Soon we had sufficient steam up for the wheels to turn and the pistons to go in and out with a strangely satisfying and realistic "Shhhuff, chuff, shhhuff, chuff." We put the train on the track and linked it up with a tender, some carriages and a guard's van. Majestically it made its sedate way round the track, dutifully responding to point switches and signals. We fetched my mother who approved of a scene that, for once, seemed to pose no obvious danger.

"If we put a bigger wick in that furnace," said Dad, when Mum had gone, "it'll go much faster." Fred and Bill set to work taking the wick out of one of our oil lamps and inserting it into the furnace holder. When lit, it made a splendid flame and soon the little engine was spitting steam out of its safety valve.

"Let's call her Spitting Annie," I suggested and thereafter that's what she was called. Placed back on the track it shot off at a tremendous speed, the carriages swaying from side to side. When the train reached the first bend it left the track completely, plunging off the table and taking the tender, the carriages and the guard's van with it.

"Those carriages are too light," said Dad. "It needs some heavy trucks to pull." So we temporarily removed the furnace, unhitched the carriages and guard's van and linked to the engine some open goods-wagons which we loaded with heavy lumps of coal from the coal scuttle.

When we replaced the furnace the little engine started to splutter steam from its pistons as well as the safety valve! Back on the track the wheels began to spin exactly like a real engine leaving a station. My head was level with the top of the trestle tables from which view point the engine looked very realistic indeed as it sped round pulling along half a dozen or so coal wagons. Once it got going the problem was how to stop it! With steam whooshing out in all directions and the boiler tank being scolding hot, Spitting Annie was quite formidable!

Fred solved the problem by donning some thick gloves, fielding her as she came steaming round a corner and deftly removing the furnace. Spitting Annie certainly lent excitement to our train set.

* * * * *

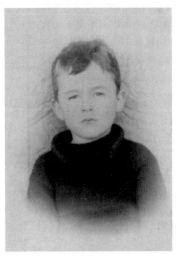

About eight years old

One day, when I was about eight and Fred ten, he took me on one side and whispered that he had formed a secret society. It was called TGRS. "What does that mean?" I asked.

"It's The Gang of Revenging Spies," he announced solemnly. I thought it was splendid.

"Who are we revenging?" I asked.

"Can't tell you that until you're a member," said Fred, a bit evasively.

"How do I join?" I asked eagerly.

"You must swear loyalty and unswerving obedience to your leader," said Fred.

"I swear," I promised recklessly, "what do we do now?"

"I'll show you our headquarters," announced Fred importantly.

"Who else is a member?" I asked.

"Just you and me at the moment, but when they next come we'll let in cousins Kenneth and Ronnie. But we'll be the ones who founded it." I briefly wondered how it got 'losted' but I didn't say anything. After all, I had only just joined.

That afternoon we went up to The Hall. Telling me not to talk and walking quietly, Fred furtively led the way round a cobbled yard. In fact there was no one about and even if there had been,

The cobbled yard with the door leading to the TGRS HQ

they wouldn't have given a second thought to seeing Fred or me, because we were regarded up at The Hall as part of the furniture. Sliding through a stable door we surreptitiously entered a long stable room containing stalls. These would have been used to stable visitors' horses. In the far corner of the stable a fixed wall ladder reached up to the ceiling where there was a small trap-door. It was all very exciting.

Beyond the trap-door an amazing sight met my eyes. We were in a spacious hay loft, although long since devoid of any hay. To my wondering eyes it looked like an Aladdin's Cave with silk drapes, beautiful cushions, carpets on the floor and all kinds of treasure. In reality the flooring was probably only bits of carpets and the drapes were old curtains, but I was looking at these things through founder member rose tinted spectacles.

"Where did you get all this?" was my amazed question.
"Oh, I cadged it from Clara," said Fred.
"Cadged from Clara!" I gasped with undisguised admiration. Miss Clara Thraxton was the housekeeper and the one person at The Hall of whom I was absolutely terrified. Even Dad treated her with great caution and, Walter, one of the footmen went in constant fear and dread of offending her. My own tenuous relationship with her had suffered a severe deterioration ever since I scored a bull's eye on a tender part of her anatomy with my pop gun.

"Of course," said Fred, "I didn't tell her what it was for. It was all going to be thrown out anyway. She probably thinks we needed them at home." I wondered what Mum would have made of that but again I kept quiet. A leader who was not afraid of Clara deserved unquestioning loyalty.

Clara was tall, thin and rigidly prim and proper. She was always severely dressed in black which seemed to highlight her extraordinary appearance. Her face was etched with purple lines round peculiar blue blotches, the whole being surmounted by a long sharp nose that was positively crimson. No wonder she terrified me.

One of the chamber-maids was a very pretty girl called Alice who, to Walter's disgust, was always encased in a stiff, long, white uniform. It was Walter's ambition to see Alice out of her uniform but she resisted all Walter's advances. On a certain Monday in February Walter happened to come across Clara's allocation of bath days for the staff. Alice's day for a bath was the coming Friday.

By Friday Walter had discovered the bath time and the bathroom. Walking back to The Hall from an hour's fishing, he was idly working out which of the many dozen windows facing him was the female staff bathroom when, suddenly he stopped, rooted to the ground. If he was right, then not only was the window next to a down pipe but it was a clear glass window instead of being frosted. Being high up on the top floor would have accounted for this.

Some of Riddlesworth Hall's many windows

Frustration with Alice led Walter to think of a daring undertaking. At the witching hour he would climb up the pipe and at last see what was under that stiff white uniform! The frosty night, the treacherously slippery pipe and the height to which he had to climb, all made the undertaking a perilous one. Nevertheless, faint heart never won fair lady so there was to be no turning back and up he went.

Eventually, after many nerve racking moments, he had reached the window.

The Top Floor Bathroom window next to the down pipe

18

Real frost had by now put a crystal film over the entire pane but although indistinct, there sure enough in the bath was a naked lady *and she was about to get out of the bath!* Taking out his handkerchief he huffed on it and carefully started to wipe away a small circle of frost. Unfortunately, as he gingerly worked at it, about a square foot of ice fell away. Even more unfortunately, it attracted the attention of the bather. Walter could now see clearly into the bathroom; too clearly, for the face he was gazing at in stupefied horror was not that of Alice, but of Clara! Ordinarily purple, it was now mottled and suffused with seething rage.

Walter was badly shaken. For a full minute he stood on his perilous perch completely paralysed, looking at Clara who, now wrapped in a bath towel, glared back at him. It says a great deal for Walter's nerves that he made a safe descent down the slippery drain pipe, for with every descending step he knew that on the morrow he was in for the high jump. He was not mistaken. Clara was awaiting Dad's arrival and he was left in no doubt that this was not a matter for his jurisdiction. This had to go to Mr Champion himself.

So it was that at breakfast The Old Man learned of the daring-do of one of his footmen. In due course, Walter was conducted by Dad to Mr Champion's study. The Old Man stood looking at him in silence for an unnerving three minutes. Then while Dad looked on, trying to keep a straight face, Mr Champion said, "Walter, I thought you were a man of sound judgment. That you should risk life and limb to gaze upon Clara in the bath shows how wrong I can be. Clearly, you should leave this establishment in disgrace and without a reference. A better punishment will be for you to remain here, the recipient of the vituperation that Clara's malice will undoubtedly mete out to you." By all accounts she meted it out liberally.

The day after my admission to the ranks of The Gang of Revenging Spies I again asked Fred who we were revenging and who we were spying on. "Never mind that just now," replied Fred, "I'm going to show you our secret escape route out of headquarters." I was pleased about that because the ladder was causing me a lot of anxiety, especially the going down bit. I thought I'd probably prefer the secret route to the ladder.

TGRS Escape Route

Up in our elevated HQ Fred showed me a door. In fact this was the door through which the stable hands would have brought up the bales of hay. The hay was hoisted up to the loft by a chain on a little crane that could be swung out through the door. Fred explained that in an emergency, we could open the door, swing out the crane, let out the chain and swarm down the chain to the road below. I noted that the door overlooked the graveyard of the nearby church and thought they wouldn't have to take me far if I ever had to use our secret escape route! Unadventurously the little crane and chain has now been replaced by a prosaic metal fire escape ladder. I never did discover the object of revenge nor on whom we had to spy! Mum had made us each an impressive black hood with 'TGRS' on the front beneath which, appropriately enough, was a luminous question mark!

* * * * *

To our great astonishment one day we looked out of the window and saw an elephant walking past the house. We raced out hardly believing our eyes. It really was an elephant. Riding on it was a gorgeously dressed mahout complete with turban. Behind the elephant paraded a small group of dancers and, upon our rushing up to them, they gave us an invitation to a circus. It was to be held in the village of Garboldisham three days hence.

Never before had anything so sensational come into our lives. The circus was to perform on the Thursday and Friday evenings. My mother promised to take us on the Friday. Garboldisham was five miles from Riddlesworth, a longer bike ride than I had ever undertaken. Giving ourselves plenty of time for mishaps, Mum, Bill, Fred and I set out. The road from our house to the nearest village was a private road maintained by an estate workman who filled potholes with broken flint stones. Bicycle punctures were common and to our great dismay, having gone about a mile, Bill found that his bike had a puncture. Immediately Mum declared that she wasn't keen on circuses and Bill could ride her bike; she would wheel Bill's bike home. Half heartedly we tried to dissuade her but she was adamant and so we again set off and in due course arrived at the circus.

We were early and able to get seats near the ringside. The Ring Master, resplendent in red coat, white breeches, shiny black boots, top hat and enormous whip introduced all the acts which were amazing. There were performing dogs, acrobats, trapeze artists, clowns and magnificent horses. In between the acts the clowns did wonderful tricks. Two clowns then brought into the ring a couple of chairs while a scantily dressed lady entered. She rested her head on one chair and put her feet on the other. The Ring Master then invited anyone under twelve to come into the ring to perform a tap dance on the lady's tummy. Being nine I qualified and was the first to leap from my seat and up to the ring. After asking me various questions I was invited to climb onto the lady's tummy. This proved more difficult than it looked because she was quite wobbly and there was nothing respectable that I could hold!

The Ring Master then asked me to do a tap dance on the lady's tummy. This I was able to do, the wobbly tummy inadvertently making it quite sensational! After performing a shaky bow, I was lifted down by the Ring Master who told the audience that he was going to offer me a permanent job with his circus. I was given a smacking kiss by the lady who then led me back to my seat amid tumultuous cheers from the audience. All the way home I was sustained by the prospect of a wildly successful career in a circus! When we told Mum what had happened she declared that the only reason she was sorry not to have been there was that she missed my tap-dancing! Sadly my career in the circus never materialised!

* * * * *

It's an amazing thing that no one in our family ever got shot. We had all manner of shot guns including a double-barrelled twelve-bore which had an extremely delicate hair trigger. We also had an old service rifle which had been modified to take shotgun cartridges. Early one morning, Dad shot three partridges with one shot from that formidable weapon. Actually they were on the lawn all drinking from a bowl Mum had put out to soak during the night. The bowl was shattered to pieces... but the partridges were delicious!

I loved going out with Dad on shooting expeditions. One day in December I heard Dad saying that he was going out very early the next morning. Asked why, he said that he was going to get the Christmas Goose. "Can I go with you?"
"Of course."
"Do you think he should?" asked my mother. "It will be dark and very cold."
"He'll come to no harm." So at about 6:00 the next morning I had an early call and soon Dad and I were making our way down to a spinney beside the river. There had been a keen frost and it was perishingly cold. Two game keepers had been up even earlier and they were making their way along the banks of the river from opposite ends planning to get to the place where the geese spent the night just as dawn broke. As Dad and I crouched on the edge of the spinney a great cacophony arose on the river bank and with much honking the geese took to the air. They were flying away from us and gaining height rapidly but at the last moment they banked and came back straight towards us but now very much higher. As the geese passed over, Dad fired and a goose tumbled out of the sky. We had our Christmas Goose.

At breakfast Mum asked, "Who's going to pluck that goose?"
"John, of course," said Dad. "He helped to get it, it's only right that he should have the privilege of plucking it. It's best to do it straight away while it's still warm." I felt very important! Half an hour later I was in the wash room plucking the goose. I couldn't see across the room for down. There were clouds of it and I could understand why geese were able to swim around in freezing cold water. It took about six months to rid the wash room of all the down and during that time it appeared on every article of clothing we wore. Mum was a splendid cook and our Christmas Goose was delectable.

* * * * *

As I got older I found it more fun going out on my own and soon I knew every hole and corner within a couple of miles of our home.

Down in a reed bed one day I came across a duck's nest with twelve eggs. I was wearing a brown tweed coat with a large hole in one pocket. Carefully I inserted the eggs through the hole in my pocket and down to where the lining met the fabric of the coat. With my hands in my pockets and with arms held out, in the manner of a cormorant drying its wings, I made my way home.

Duck eggs are delicious but these were full of baby ducklings about to hatch. We usually had a broody hen and normally we considered them a pest but this time one came in handy and soon she had twelve lively little ducklings to look after. Wild ducks are the very dickens to rear. From the moment they are hatched they can run at amazing speeds. They are also very vulnerable, particularly from rats of which we had a fair share. If we were to rear these ducklings it was obvious that they needed to be completely encased, top, bottom and sides in escape-proof and rat-proof netting. It had to be large enough to give at least the appearance of freedom. Then they needed feeding. I caught tiny fish in jam jars in order to appease the appetites of these voracious little creatures.

Day after day, week after week and month after month, I spent hours on those ducks, and then, when they were fully grown and ready for the dinner table, I simply hadn't the heart to eat any of the delectable dishes my mother prepared. It seemed like cannibalism! The rest of the family hugely enjoyed the meals while I disconsolately went into the garden and mourned the loss of my little family.

Chapter 3
The Smiths of Norwich

Dad had one brother, George, and two sisters, Ethel and Bessie, all of whom lived in Norwich. Each one was an extraordinary character.

Ethel was the oldest, then Dad, then Bessie and last was George. Uncle George had married a very pretty girl called May and Aunt Ethel had married a chap by the name of Dick Warner. Periodically the whole family would come to Riddlesworth for a day's outing. Invariably it would be a sensation. A curious thing about the Smiths in Norwich was that they all seemed to have pots of money while none of them, with the exception of Uncle George, seemed to do any work. Uncle George was the general manager of a boot and shoe factory.

Aunt Ethel was a very handsome and sophisticated lady who always dressed very fashionably. Whenever she visited us her hair

Dad, Aunt Ethel and Aunt Bessie

would be a startlingly different colour. At one visit it would be jet black, by the next it would be platinum blonde, at the next it would be bright ginger. On one occasion, just before a projected visit to Riddlesworth, she had asked her hairdresser to give her hair a nice lavender tint. "That will give them something to talk about at Riddlesworth," she had said to the hairdresser. There was never a shortage of things to talk about when Aunt Ethel came but the hairdresser overdid it with the tint for, when the towel was taken off her head, Aunt Ethel's hair was a bright purple! At first the hairdresser thought Ethel was having an apoplectic fit; in fact she had burst into laughter.

"Don't worry," she said to the distraught hairdresser, "it'll rinse out." But it didn't rinse out. They tried every kind of shampoo and detergent but the hair remained obstinately purple. In desperation the girl tried the blonde treatment and, horror of horrors, Ethel's hair ended up a blotchy green! She took one look and said firmly, "There's nothing for it; you'll have to take it all off and I'll have a wig."

When she arrived at Riddlesworth a few days later, to everyone's unstinted admiration, her hair was a beautiful auburn and magnificently coiffured. In the afternoon we all had tea on the lawn. In the middle of the lawn was a plum tree. Carrying a tray of cakes, Aunt Ethel was passing under the plum tree when a twig deftly lifted her wig from her close shaven head. To everyone's relief she let out a shriek of laughter. Placing the tray on the floor she retrieved the wig and deliberately set it on her head back to front.

The family of which we saw the most was that of Uncle George and Auntie May. They had two boys, Kenneth and Ronnie. Kenneth was nine months older than me. He was tall, strong and very good looking. Girls swooned at the very sight of him! Ronnie was two years younger than me but a proper little tough guy and well able to hold his own in all the escapades in which we were embroiled during their holiday visits.

The plum tree – still fruiting after 82 years

When Uncle George and Dad got together there was usually a riot of fun and laughter, particularly at meal times. We had a large dining room table which seated us all comfortably. I suspect that both Mum and Auntie May would have preferred a smaller table so that the boys could have had their meals in another room! Both Dad and Uncle George were great story tellers and, while Auntie May and Mum were in constant dread of what would come next, we boys hung on every word.

Nearly every story would be the cause of a remonstrating, "Sydney!" from Mum, or "George!" from Auntie May. Sometimes the most innocuous comment would bring about a quiet word of reproof. One lunch time we were having a game pie. Standing at the head of the table Dad addressed Auntie May with, "Now ma'am, what will you have, back, belly or bum?"
"Sydney!" said Mum.

Uncle George

On another occasion when we were having a celebratory meal, Auntie May had real cause to blush and her *"George!"* was probably justified. I rather suspect that Uncle George was a trifle tipsy for the conversation got round to wind, a subject Dad would never have raised. We boys glanced at each other and tried to look solemn. It's a curious thing that lavatorial humour is always excruciatingly funny to small boys. Uncle George made the observation that wind was highly inflammable! Auntie May made a valiant attempt to change the subject. I think she knew what might be coming but we were not to be deprived of what promised to be a good story.

"What makes you say that, Uncle George?" asked Fred with assumed innocence. Auntie May gave him a fierce look.
"Well, as a matter of fact I have seen proof of it," started Uncle George. "I was at a dinner a few weeks ago, when this subject came up and a chap insisted that wind was inflammable. One man at the table said he didn't believe it, whereupon the first chap said he'd prove it.

So there and then he pushed aside the things near him on the table, took off his trousers, climbed on the table and positioned himself appropriately for the demonstration. He then told the man seated next to him to stand by with a lighted match. With a cry of 'Stand back,' he let fly and a sheet of flame shot down the table." We boys gave a great shout of delighted laughter. This was entertainment of no mean order! Then we saw Auntie May's face and we knew that poor Uncle George was in deep trouble.

Later, I came across my mother chuckling to herself. "What are you laughing at?" I asked.
"I must confess, I'm laughing at that dreadful story your Uncle George told at the table. But my goodness, Aunt May has given him what for." We thought it was worth it.

Chapter 4
War Declared

Sadly, these special times were to come to an end. Just after 11:00 on the morning of Sunday 3rd September 1939 my mother called my brother and me into the sitting room where we had a radio. The Nation had been told by the BBC to stand by for an important announcement. Then the Prime Minister, Mr Neville Chamberlain came on the air to tell the country that we were at war with Nazi Germany. It was a truly historic occasion of such significance that I will give his Message to the Nation.

I am speaking to you from the Cabinet Room at 10 Downing Street. This morning the British Ambassador in Berlin handed the German Government an official note stating that unless we heard from them by 11:00, that they were prepared at once to withdraw their troops from Poland, a state of war would exist between us. I have to tell you now that no such undertaking has been received, and consequently this country is at war with Germany.

You can imagine what a bitter blow it is to me that all my long struggle to win peace has failed. Yet I cannot believe that there is anything more or anything different that I could have done or that would have been more successful.

Up to the very last it would have been quite possible to arrange a peaceful and honourable settlement between Germany and Poland, but Hitler would not have it. He had evidently made up his mind to attack Poland whatever happened, and although he now says he put forward reasonable proposals which were rejected by the Poles, that is not a true statement. The proposals were never shown to the

Poles nor to us, and although they were announced in the German broadcast on Thursday night, Hitler did not wait to hear comment on them, but ordered his troops to cross the Polish frontier next morning.

His action shows convincingly that there is no chance of expecting that this man will ever give up his practice of using force to gain his will, and he can only be stopped by force. We and France are to-day, in fulfilment of our obligations, going to the aid of Poland, so bravely resisting this wicked and unprovoked attack on her people. We have a clear conscience; we have done all that any country could do to establish peace. The situation, in which no word given by Germany's ruler could be trusted and no people or country could feel safe, has become intolerable. Now we have resolved to finish it, I know you will all play your part with calmness and courage.

When I have finished speaking certain detailed announcements will be made on behalf of the Government. Give these your closest attention. The Government have made plans under which it will be possible to carry on the work of the nation in the days of stress and strain which may be ahead of us. These plans need your help. You may be taking your part in the fighting Services or as a volunteer in one of the branches of civil defence. If so, you will report for duty in accordance with the instructions you have received.

You may be engaged in work essential to the prosecution of war, or for the maintenance of the life of the people in factories, in transport, in public utility concerns, or in the supply of other necessaries of life. If so it is of vital importance that you should carry on with your job.

Now may God bless you all, and may He defend the right. For it is evil things that we shall be fighting. We shall be against brute force, bad faith, injustice, oppression and persecution. Against them I am certain that Right will prevail.

When he had finished my mother looked at us and said, "Well, that's that! We're at war again." I was ten years old.

Initially, the war didn't have much of an impact on me. Our war effort was to help Dad build a huge air raid shelter amongst the trees adjoining the house. It was a splendid affair, completely below ground level, six feet deep, eight feet long and four feet wide. It had an entrance and an exit, both of which were gas proof. The roof was reinforced with iron hurdles and corrugated iron sheeting on which was piled two feet of soil. One side of the shelter was lined with shelves on which Mum stored enough provisions to last a veritable siege.

Site of our air raid shelter among the trees

Taking our cue from the Prime Minister that right would prevail, we cleaned the guns and placed what cartridges we had nearby. If Adolf Hitler came we'd give him what for! In fact, throughout the six years of the war, with one notable exception, no enemy came anywhere near us. This was a cause of great disappointment to me; however the war brought never-to-be-forgotten experiences which even included my flying a B17 bomber – but I am jumping ahead.

* * * * *

The declaration of war brought about the Evacuation. Because of the fear of large scale bombing, parents of children living in large cities were encouraged by the Government to consider evacuating their children into the countryside. Arrangements were made for folk living in the country to take in the refugees and larger establishments were earmarked as clearing houses. Riddlesworth Hall, being very large and in the heart of the Norfolk countryside, was considered ideal for this purpose.

Coincidental with this development, but completely unrelated, was the sudden death of Mr Champion. Having said it was unrelated, the likelihood is that if The Old Man had survived until our particular refugees arrived, he wouldn't have lasted long! They were a gang of little thugs! After Mr Champion's death my father continued to be responsible for the running of The Hall. It was then that Evacuation became government policy and Riddlesworth Hall selected as a clearing centre. Dad was 50 years old and during the time the evacuees were billeted on him he aged perceptibly.

Riddlesworth Village School

Another establishment that experienced trauma was Riddlesworth Village School. This was housed in a tiny one-roomed building located only about 200 yards from our house. The school was centrally positioned to serve three villages, Riddlesworth, Knettishall and Gasthorpe. In fact it was a good mile from any of them and three miles from the homes of some of the children. There were two teachers, one for the infants from ages five to eight and one for the seniors who were aged from nine to fourteen, the school leaving age.

The school was comfortably full with about twelve infants and twenty seniors. That was before the Evacuation! Suddenly there descended on this well ordered establishment a veritable gang of about twenty street-wise youngsters. The poor teachers didn't know what had hit them. Gradually the evacuees were billeted with families in the village.

When I was eleven years old I was about to leave home one morning to go to school when I saw a little girl standing by the gate. "Can I come in to your garden? I want to see the pretty butterfly." She had been following a butterfly for some time and then it had flown over the hedge into our garden. She was a refugee. Aged about seven she looked very like a pretty butterfly herself.

"Let's look together," I said and brought her into the garden.
"Oh, what a pretty garden," she said. There were a number of butterflies around and we spent a few minutes watching them.
"Come back tomorrow," I said, "you can spend more time then, but now we must go, or we'll be late for school." Hand in hand we walked to school while she vivaciously chatted away telling me about her life in London.

Tragically, that little girl never came back to our garden. On her way home from school that afternoon she was murdered. From time to time Fred and I would create hideouts in woods and copses. They were part of a fantasy world in which we lived. They were furnished with bits of carpet and perhaps a small chair. The little girl had been dragged into one of our hideouts and brutally murdered.

A Chief Superintendent from Scotland Yard headed the investigation and within a week he had found the murderer, a Polish soldier stationed about three miles away. Of course there was a trial, initially at the magistrate's court in neighbouring East Harling where the man was remanded for trial at The Old Bailey. I was summoned as a witness, much to my delight and my mother's horror. A day was set for the trial and I, escorted by our headmistress, Miss Barbara Samples, travelled to London. I'd never been farther afield than Norwich, so despite the circumstances this trip to London was very special. Having got to The Old Bailey we discovered that the trial had been postponed for a day.

"So, what shall we do?" asked Miss Samples.
"How about going to the zoo?" I suggested. That's exactly what we did, but on the way we had a most scrumptious meal in a posh restaurant, all paid for by His Majesty's Government.

We were back in The Old Bailey again the next day. The jury found the accused guilty and the judge decreed that he should be detained indefinitely at Broadmoor. It transpired that under the Nazi Occupation of Poland the man's entire family had been killed. He vowed that he would escape to England in order to help fight the Nazis, but clearly his mind had become unhinged.

Later, when I was about thirteen, a couple of girl refugees were billeted on the Dacks. They were real bobby dazzlers and it was not long before I fell madly in love with both of them! In a rash moment I offered to take them to the cinema. The bus ride was always an adventure in itself. The bus made the journey to Thetford once a week on a Saturday. It was a Bedford and had hard wooden slatted seats. Occasionally it would break down and everyone would have to get out and push to get it started again! Despite these failings the bus was looked upon with universal favour. A trip to Thetford was considered a highlight. As the fare was threepence, it was a highlight not often enjoyed by us.

I had cycled three miles to the Dacks in order to walk with the girls the two miles to the bus stop. They paid their own fare but in the cinema I bought each of them an ice cream. On our return in the evening I escorted them the two miles back to the Dacks. It was at this point that I committed a tactical error. I suggested that cycling six miles and walking four deserved a kiss of thanks. Their response was immediate and in unison: "Get lost." Cycling the three miles home I swore that I was finished with girls for ever! The film we had seen was The Wicked Lady starring Margaret Lockwood. I considered the Wicked Lady had nothing on those two refugees!

* * * * *

The months went by and although we were supposed to be at war, to us in the heart of the Norfolk countryside nothing seemed to be happening. In fact a great deal was going on. Terrible destruction was being dished out by the German Luftwaffe as they carried out bombing raids. There was nothing worth bombing in the countryside so the bombers focussed their attention on the cities, particularly London. The capital was over 100 miles away from where we were on the borders of Norfolk and Suffolk and we saw nothing of the bombers. This was not the case for those living in Norwich and the coastal town of Felixstowe situated at the bottom of Suffolk.

Although there was nothing in Norwich or Felixstowe that was worth bombing the problem for these towns was that many German bombers, prevented by the RAF from dropping their bombs over London, found themselves heading back with a full load of bombs. Rather than take them home they dropped them on the towns that were most in line with their return route. That was Norwich or Felixstowe.

One morning in Norwich the air raid siren went and everyone headed for the shelters, including Uncle George. Half way there he remembered that he had left his pipe in his office and, telling a colleague he would only be a minute, he went back to get it. Moments later the factory received a direct hit and he was killed instantly.

Our whole family was devastated, but the effect on Dad was immediate and drastic. Officially Dad's age precluded him from enlisting but despite this he eventually persuaded the authorities to take him. As an experienced ex-soldier from World War I, he insisted that he was of more use to the nation in the army than playing at soldiers in the Home Guard. The recruiting colonel was impressed and recommended Dad's enlistment into the Military Police. Dad was overjoyed about being accepted but doubtful about the Military Police. He had wanted to be where there was plenty of action. He was to see action enough, but that was in the future. Within four months he was promoted to sergeant and subsequently to warrant officer. Eighteen months later, on 6th June 1944, he was on the Normandy beaches throughout the long hours of D Day directing the tanks and troops of the Third Canadian Division. The Allied casualties were severe but Dad was a born survivor.

Meanwhile, back in England the German Luftwaffe jettisoning their bombs over Felixstowe involved us as a direct consequence. Those German high flyers had little knowledge that they were dropping their bombs on some of England's high flyers! These were the pupils at the elite Felixstowe College for Girls. This school has some very high flyers among its Old Girls, one of whom was Princess Diana, but when she was at school in 1973 Felixstowe College for Girls had relocated to Riddlesworth Hall and was called Riddlesworth Hall School. Back in 1942 the Board of the school was desperate to find a location that was safer than Felixstowe and heard that Riddlesworth Hall was vacant. It was ideal for the purpose and within four months the school had moved in as tenants. Fred and I were no longer able to

The tiled passageways Fred and I scrubbed for sixpence

stroll around the house and grounds as if we owned it! On the contrary, the nearest we got to strolling around was on our way from the kitchen to the passageways which, for sixpence on a Saturday morning, we were now scrubbing! We struck up some friendly relationships, but officially boys were strictly taboo.

With Dad in the army the family finances took a significant tumble so when the headmistress of the college asked if Mum could occasionally put up visiting parents for a weekend, Mum jumped at the opportunity. It is funny how little incidents remain in our memories and others, probably of greater significance, are forgotten. I recall a couple who were staying with us one weekend. The husband had left his shoes outside his bedroom door and in the morning I saw them. I thought this rather a cheek but felt the prestige of the house was at stake and decided to give them a polish and return them to the bedroom door. When Mum was serving breakfast the man commented on the fact that someone had tried to clean his shoes. I had spent a lot of time on those shoes and shown them to Mum who had said she could almost see her face in them.

"Were they not done to your satisfaction?" asked Mum rather stonily. She was always very defensive of her boys.
"No. They were not done properly. The insteps were not polished."

The insteps are that part of the underneath between the raised heel and where the sole touches the ground. "*Insteps* not polished. I've never heard of such a thing," says Mum.

"It's important to polish the insteps," was the reply. "This deficiency would be very evident when I am kneeling for communion at the altar rails."

Mum nearly blew a fuse. "I am quite sure that the good Lord is more interested in your *kindness* than the shininess of the *underneath of your shoes*," Mum said with uncharacteristic asperity.

A concerned headmistress spoke to Mum about the incident and hoped that Mum was not offended. Mum said that if the man had been foolish enough to have spoken about it then he was too foolish for her to give him another thought. We learned that the man was in the Diplomatic Service! The incident had a beneficial effect though. In her indignation Mum doubled her charge rates! She still had more requests for accommodation than she could cope with.

* * * * *

We didn't see a great deal of Dad but when we did it was always dramatic. One day Fred and I arrived home from school to find a tank parked outside! Well actually it was a Bren Gun Carrier, which is a kind of mini tank. Dad had a friend in the Tank Corps near Thetford and had persuaded him to drive him home in it. He thought we would enjoy driving a tank. He was right. We had a wonderful time careering all over the park!

On another occasion when he was home for a night Dad offered to give the Home Guard a demonstration on the use of the Sten gun. The Sten is a small mass-produced automatic machine gun, ideal in house-to-house fighting. I suspected that it would be highly entertaining and I asked Dad if I could go with him. He readily agreed. Nothing pleased Dad more than having an audience, especially a member of the family! Together we went to the meeting which was to be held in the little school. Dad was resplendent in his uniform and medal ribbons. I was very proud of him. He started by explaining how the gun worked. He told a number of stories and got a lot of laughs. He then said he would give a demonstration of how the gun should and should not be used. I waited with heightened anticipation.

He got them all to imagine that they were a group of German soldiers; he then went out of the classroom into the hall and closed the door. After a moment there came a timid knock and a small voice asking if there were any enemy soldiers in the room! Slowly he opened the door and poked his head round in a furtive and scared manner. He was very funny. He then went out again. After a short delay there was a tremendous crash as the door came off its hinges and flew across the room, instantly followed by Dad shouting "Tat, tat, tat, tat, tat." Half his audience leapt to their feet in alarm. It really was terrifying. I was expecting something of the kind but even so I nearly jumped out of my skin! Afterwards, Dad turned to one of the Home Guard who was the estate carpenter and said, "Ned, could you fix that door by tomorrow morning?"

"Leave it to me, Syd," said Ned with a grin.

On the way home I said, "That was a dramatic entrance you made."

"To be honest, I only meant to kick the door open," said Dad. Then he added with a grin, "It certainly made the point that you can't mess about."

"I'll say! You scared me to death."

Chapter 5
Thetford Grammar School

For a number of years, in fact ever since I was a small child, Delia, Mr Champion's granddaughter would call at the house to see if I was available to go for a walk with her. She would have been in her mid-twenties when I was about ten. Apparently she found my company entertaining. Mum was in constant dread of what family secrets I might share with her but on one of our walks I shared my disappointment that I had failed to obtain a scholarship for the grammar school. On our return from the walk Delia wanted a chat with Mum.

"I am determined that John shall go to the grammar school," she said.
"I'm afraid we've just heard that he's failed to get a scholarship," Mum replied.
"I know that, but I want to pay the fees for him to go. Would you mind?"

Mind! Mum thought she was a veritable angel from heaven. So my future education was going to be at East Anglia's most famous school. Founded in 900 AD Thetford Grammar School had a reputation for sound scholarship. I was destined to be one of its unique students, but alas, not one of its adornments.

The school was nearly eight miles from home which involved a round cycle journey of sixteen miles a day. Short for my age in any case, it was discovered that by the end of my first term I was actually an inch shorter! The headmaster's report said: "He appears to be settling down nicely."

Things didn't settle down at all nicely during the second term. The rot started in the woodwork room. The class was divided into teams of four, each assigned the task of making an oak stool. It didn't take long before my three team mates discovered that I was no carpenter and decreed that I should confine my activities to sweeping up and pretending to look busy. The woodwork master was a small Highland Scot with a most pronounced accent and the name of Fraser. His sparse ginger hair was plastered down with brilliantine and a thin ginger moustache adhered perilously to his upper lip giving him a sinister appearance. Much of Mr Fraser's time during lessons was spent standing over an evil smelling glue pot which bubbled and burped over a Bunsen Burner. It is highly likely that our Mr Fraser was one of the original glue sniffers.

Clearly this didn't occupy the whole of his attention for during the stool making programme, which took up a number of lessons, he must have observed a curious lack of constructive activity on my part for during one lesson he stood behind our group in what was an unmistakably threatening manner. One of the team thrust a piece of wood into my hands and told me to cut it to the length where it was clearly marked.

The piece of wood was intended to be one of the four legs, which in itself showed Mr Fraser to be a tyrant. Any understanding master would have instructed us to make a three-legged stool when the lengths didn't need to be so precise! Delighted to have a real job for a change, I set to with a great deal more enthusiasm than skill.

I had only been going a few seconds when I was interrupted by Mr Fraser's sinister voice. "Wa dya think ya doon boy?"
"I'm cutting this stool leg to length, sir."
"An hoo many times ha ya bin told to cut to the west wood side?"

To knowledgeable carpenters it is of course standard practice to cut a piece of wood, if anything, a little longer than is needed. If it is a shade too long you can always trim it back in a number of ways but if you cut it too short you've wasted the wood and have to start again – hence the term 'cutting to the waste wood side'. I hadn't caught on to the logic of this nor had I realised how misleading was the Scottish accent! I replied: "I was cutting it as you told us, sir."

"An hoo do ye mek that oot?" By this time all work had stopped and the whole class was listening to this interchange with more than passing interest.

Thetford Grammar School Library
Note the Weather Vane!

"Well sir, you told us always to cut to the westward side. So very carefully I lined the wood up according to the weather vane on the library there and I am cutting to the westward side, as you said." To my complete and genuine surprise and to Mr Fraser's great anger, the whole class erupted in a shout of laughter to be instantly followed by a deathly and fearful silence. Mr Fraser's wrath was the greater because, understandably, I wore a genuinely innocent look. I think I must have been the only one in the room who was unaware of the cause of Mr Fraser's evident fury.

Through thin lips he hissed, "For blatant insolence, boy, ye'll have an appointment with the headmaster tomorr-r-row morr-r-ning after assembly."

As news of the event spread throughout the school I was completely bemused to find myself acclaimed a hero, not only by my classmates but by seniors as well who revealed a covert admiration for this wholly unexpected display of sheer valour. Wiser heads foresaw dire consequences! In fact circumstances were to conspire to make those consequences worse than had been foreseen.

That evening a senior class, of which my brother Fred was a member, had been in the gym and had been left by the PT instructor to lock the building for the night. The shower room adjoined the gym and in an act of premeditated vandalism they plugged all the drains and left the showers running. By morning water was everywhere but especially all over the beautiful parquet flooring of the gym. The caretaker had done his best to clear up but the damage had been done.

At assembly the headmaster was in a towering rage. He stormed up and down the platform threatening to thrash every member of the delinquent class. Knowing I was in for a hiding anyway, I was earnestly praying that the Head would carry out this threat. He was a very big man but my hope was that by thrashing over twenty real delinquents a great deal of that formidable strength would be drained by the time he came to me! The hope was short lived and I had to face the Head's pent up fury alone. In growing horror I watched him divest himself of his jacket and waistcoat and roll up his sleeves to reveal mighty biceps of which even Samson himself would not have been ashamed.

Determined to keep a stiff upper lip throughout the ordeal, I was very nearly overset by the evident sympathy and support I received on all sides. Arriving at length to my appointed classroom I was greeted with a round of applause by the class. The teacher was Mr Tromans, the deputy head and he quickly restored the class to order but again nearly broke down my defences by kindly inviting me to, "Remain standing – if that will be more comfortable!"

The cycle ride home that evening and for the next week was carried out standing on the pedals. In the privacy of my bedroom Fred, who unsurprisingly, was very sympathetic, carried out an assessment of the injuries. He was able to announce solemnly at school the next morning that the blisters were at least half an inch high.

* * * * *

Perhaps my first real conscious act of heroism occurred at the end of my first year. Thetford Grammar School had a proud history of academic achievement going back over 1,000 years. In this hot house of learning I achieved what might well have been a first. In the examination results I came last in every subject, 26th out of 26 in *everything.* You've got to be very good at being bad to be as bad as that! But the heroism lay in the fact that I took my school report home!

When I was there Thetford Grammar School had a student body of 240 divided into four houses, which meant that each house had about 60 students. The ages ranged from eight to eighteen so at any age level anyone with a modicum of aptitude could find himself in a house team of some kind. It so happened that I had some skill as a fast bowler. My house was Reed's and in my second year at school we won the School House Cricket Cup. As a result of this, although I was still a junior, I was selected to play for the school against other schools in the area. One of our fixtures was against King Edward's Grammar School in Norwich. King Edward's had consistently beaten Thetford at cricket, so enormous significance was attached to this fixture. It had an added significance for me because my cousin Kenneth went to King Edward's and he was always crowing about how much better than Thetford was their cricket team.

The match was on a Saturday in Norwich and the team was to catch the 9:15 train from Thetford. It will be recalled that I lived eight miles from Thetford and normally cycled to school. On this particular Saturday morning I had arranged to have a lift in a farm lorry that took churns of milk to the station.

Owing to some hold-up at the farm the lorry was late picking me up and, although the driver drove furiously, we arrived at the station just in time to see the train pulling out and my team mates waving from the windows. There was nothing for it but to hitch a lift. Outside the station was a post office engineering van, the dark green box-like vehicle that at that time was everywhere but now is a museum piece.

As I walked past the van the driver started his engine. "Are you going anywhere near the Norwich Road?" I asked.
"Where do you want to get to?"
"Well I really want to get to Norwich but anywhere on the Norwich Road will do." "You're in luck, son. We're going to Norwich ourselves. Hop in." Not only did they take me to Norwich, they actually dropped me off at the gates of the school and to the astonishment of the team I was there to welcome them when they arrived.

Norwich won the toss and opted to bat first. I was to bowl the first over. With the very first delivery the ball clipped the bat and struck the wicket; out, played on. One wicket for no runs was a good start. The second ball was a wide; too wide for the wicket keeper to stop and the ball headed for the boundary. Four runs! One for four. Not so good. The third ball took the middle stump clean out of the ground. Two for four! The fourth ball was a bad length and it was lofted towards the boundary, but one of our team made a simply spectacular catch. Confident of a six the batsmen hadn't even run a single! Three wickets for four runs! Norwich was devastated but nothing untoward happened in the rest of the over. No more wickets and no more runs.

Our second bowler was a spin genius and in his over two more wickets fell and no runs were scored. Five wickets for four runs... and those had really been my wide! The remaining five wickets fell in just three more overs with only twelve runs added to the score. Ten wickets for sixteen runs! We went in to bat and scored twenty runs for no wickets in just 25 minutes. The whole match had taken just over an hour. We were heroes! At assembly on the Monday morning the Head heaped lavish praise on the team. All was forgiven. No longer did I dream of the Head and Mr Fraser being boiled in a massive glue pot!

Chapter 6
The United States Army Air Force

From Lowestoft to Diss, Norfolk is separated from Suffolk by the River Waveney. From Diss to beyond Thetford they are separated by the Waveney's tributary, the Little Ouse. Passing within a few hundred yards of our front door, this was the river that featured so prominently in many of my boyhood adventures. It was in the Little Ouse when I was about nine years old that I caught a two pound pike using rough string as a line, a piece of stick as a float, a primitive eel hook and a worm as bait. I had dropped the line between the planks of a bridge and was fishing for gudgeon in the hope of using one as live bait for a pike.

Looking between the planks I noticed that the float was under the water's surface. Thinking it was snagged on the bottom, I pulled in the string and set off a colossal thrashing in the water. I had a pike on the end of the line. A pike is an extremely powerful fish, which is why it is called the Freshwater Shark. Happily the string was exceptionally stout so I was able to fasten it to the plank without fear of it breaking.

Dropping into the water, I went under the bridge and untied the string. I then made my way up the river, the still thrashing pike in tow. About 50 yards upstream there was a shallow drinking area for cattle and I was able to drag the pike onto the bank. It was the biggest fish I had ever caught. Later I was to catch a much bigger pike with some very exciting consequences, but meanwhile I carried my catch home and Mum cooked it for tea.

The much bigger pike was caught when I was fourteen and led to the most amazing experiences of my young life. I was using a spinner and as soon as the pike struck I knew I had a real monster on the end of the line. This time I had proper fishing tackle but the breaking strength of the line was no more than three pounds. Desperately I let

45

out the line until the fish was at least 100 yards away. At one point the pike leapt clean out of the water and came down with a great splash.

A man on the river bank had been watching me but when the fish made that great leap he came running up to me. "Do you think you can land it?" he asked.

"No," I shouted, "can you?"

"I'll have a go if you like." Thankfully I handed over the rod and for half an hour I watched a real fisherman at work. Eventually he had it out of the water. It weighed six pounds and I was very glad of the help to land it.

The man introduced himself as Captain Mark O'Brien of the United States Army Air Force. A new airfield had been constructed no more than a mile and a half from our house. It was the base for about 100 B17 bombers. Capt O'Brien was one of the pilots. I took him home for tea and Mum made a great fuss of him, talking with him about his favourite subject, his wife and two children.

Fred and I were in the Air Training Cadets, which pleased Capt O'Brien but he was shocked to discover that we had not done any flying with the RAF. "You must get in some flying time," he said.

"I wish," I thought, but after tea he proposed taking me up to the aerodrome and introducing me to his colonel.

"This is my friend, John. Wa'd'ya know, he's been in the Air Cadets for six months and has never flown in all that time."

"Well, I reckon you can fix that, O'Brien."

"I sure can, sir," replied Captain O'Brien. Then turning to me he said, "Come on John, let me show you over my plane."

The Flying Fortress

Cockpit of the Flying Fortress

So I was introduced to The Flying Fortress. It was huge and I was shown everything. I sat in all the gun turrets in turn. Then I sat in the pilot's seat while Capt O'Brien explained some of the dials, the huge throttle handles for the four engines, the pedals for the ailerons and the joystick which was like half a steering wheel. The tour took an hour and a half and I really believe Capt O'Brien enjoyed it as much as I did. We then went to the parachute room where I was fitted out with a parachute and shown the lockers. "Every time you go out on a trip take your 'chute from this locker. It's your locker. See, I've put your name right here." I was speechless. "Every time... It's your locker... " In a state of sheer bliss I was driven home in a jeep.

The main flight path of the planes was directly over our house. Watching them fly over, it seemed amazing that such huge things could ever get off the ground particularly with a full bomb-load. In fact the take-off was imperceptible as I was to discover.

A few days after my introduction to the colonel a jeep arrived for me and my ever-anxious mother saw me off. Up at the 'drome I collected my 'chute and was driven round the perimeter to one of the bays. Capt O'Brien was already in the cockpit and he gave me a welcoming wave. As I walked to the ladder under the huge fuselage the grinning ground crew lined up and gave me a salute. I solemnly saluted back, American style, which delighted them.

Up in the plane the navigator invited me to follow him. Threading our way past the two side gun turrets and across the narrow gangway over the empty bomb bays, we worked our way forward to the cockpit. There I was introduced to the co-pilot, a young lieutenant who only looked about eighteen. "We're in the middle of a routine check," Capt O'Brien informed me. "We don't want to find something is wrong when we're 8,000 feet up!" The very thought of being 8,000 feet up gave me a distinct feeling of unreality! The check completed, one by one the engines started with an initial bang and a cloud of smoke. It was quite alarming at first.

I was given a set of headphones and heard the control tower calling Capt O'Brien. "OK Cap'n, you're free to go. Give our greetings to the Limey Kid." Hey, that was me. Here I was, fourteen years old, actually inside the cockpit of a Flying Fortress which was about to take off. It was so exciting!

The plane taxied to the end of the runway; there was a slight pause and then, with a great roar, it started forward, rapidly gathering speed. Suddenly I realised that we were already about a 100 feet in the air. I hadn't noticed the moment of take-off. Within seconds the cows in the fields were like toy farmyard animals and houses looked as if they belonged to a Monopoly board. Four hours passed very quickly and soon there was a definite diminishing in the roar of the engines. The navigator asked me to go back to the cockpit and told me to stand behind the two pilots. "We'll be landing in a few minutes," said Capt O'Brien, "I thought you'd like to be up here to see what we do." A dull clunk was the landing gear coming down.

Trees grew larger and cows more life-like. Soon things were flashing by at a great rate. A very slight bump and we were down and taxiing back to our apron. A jeep took us back to the parachute room where I handed over my parachute. "Enjoy the trip, John?" the man asked.
"How'd he know my name?" I whispered to Capt O'Brien.
"Know your name! Why you're now the station's mascot! Everybody knows your name."
"Will they put my 'chute in my locker for me?"
"Of course, but first they check it out and rewrap it. They'll do that every time for you. C'mon! Let's go get some chow." Dinner in the

officers' mess was something else! There was a huge plateful of turkey and vegetables with a liberal helping of peanut butter. This was a far cry from our normal rationing diet.

The Battle of the Atlantic was being fought against German submarines which exacted a fearful toll on merchant shipping. The result was stringent rationing. Each person had a ration book which controlled the purchase of most foods. Some of the rations were minute. For example, the weekly ration of butter, tea and cheese was 2oz! You were allowed one egg a week. The weekly ration of meat was to the value of one shilling and two pence, which is 6p in today's money, though not today's value. One pound of jam was allowed every two months. Rationing was not strictly applied to milk when it was collected direct from a farm as we did, but ordinarily it was half a pint a day. Although rationing was severe it didn't affect us living in the country as much as it affected those living in the towns. We had a large flock of chickens supplying both eggs and meat and we were surrounded by rabbits all the year round. From October to March we were able to shoot pheasants, partridges, ducks and the occasional goose.

My adoption as mascot by the Americans meant the introduction of unheard of luxuries. Every time I visited them, which was as frequently as possible, I would come away loaded with provisions that were totally absent from the shops. There would be huge tins of boned and rolled turkey, hams, jams, cheeses, chocolates, biscuits, peanut butter, to say nothing of exotic foods of which we had never even heard.

Some of this Mum was able to share with folk in the nearby village but a great deal of it I would take to school and sell. Soon I had a reputation at school that any shopkeeper would envy. I was neither restricted by quantities nor price! Hopeless at maths in the classroom, I could calculate like lightning when doing business.

Meanwhile I was really getting in some flying hours! During the period of the war I clocked up 308 hours in Flying Fortresses. Because I was in the cadets I had been given a Flight Log Book. It unfolded twice and had five pages of lines on which flights could be logged with spaces for the pilot's signature. Prior to meeting Capt O'Brien the only entry in my pristine log book was where I had written my name and details. Soon that log book was filled with all the flights I had been on. To the somewhat envious officer running our cadet group I explained what was happening and he gave me a second log book. By the end of the war I had two full log books and a third practically full. I still keep them as souvenirs! Unbelievably, eight of those 308 hours were actually flying the planes myself – safely up at about 8,000 feet admittedly – but nevertheless *flying, in the pilot's seat!*

Whenever I went with Mark O'Brien he would give me landing lessons. Of course this wasn't landing at ground level but it was nevertheless very exciting. We would pretend that 5,000 feet was ground level and make simulated landings on clouds! I would be in the pilot's seat and Capt O'Brien would be my co-pilot! It was so unreal that frequently I felt like pinching myself to make sure I wasn't dreaming.

As our imaginary landing strip drew closer I'd reduce our air speed. Still losing height I'd approach the edge of the cloud until we were a foot or so above the 'ground level'. I would then ease forward the four throttles slightly, reducing air speed still further. Then, when we reached the correct speed for landing, I'd gently pull back the stick. When at ground level the plane, with insufficient power to respond to a climb, would gently sink on to the runway in a perfect landing! The big difference with us was of course that there was no ground on which to gently sink and the plane would drop like a stone! This was the moment to pull back the throttles, push the stick forward and then gently pull the plane out of the dive. It was tremendous fun for me but not much fun for the crew! The intercom would crackle: "O'Brien! Are you letting that lousy Limey Kid fly this plane again? If so I'm bailing out!" But when we landed they'd be saying things like, "Hey, kid, you're not bad. They'll be sending you on missions if you don't watch out!" It cannot be imagined how I felt.

The Slow Timing flights were often used by the station personnel to go to a holiday destination in far distant parts of the country. At times we would have five or six holiday makers on board all hitching a lift. Thus it was that I had splendid views of cities as far north as Edinburgh and south as Plymouth. However we kept clear of London and the East Anglia coastline because of the possibility of meeting enemy fighters. On these flights all the guns were removed for checking and overhaul. On at least one flight it would have been good to have had the guns on board.

Most of the flights I went on were during the day but Capt O'Brien suggested I might like to go on a night flight with him. My mother protested that I would be home very late but the captain assured her he'd bring me home in his jeep as soon as we had landed. Little did we know what was about to overtake us.

We took off at about six in the evening just as it was getting dark. As we waited on the perimeter suddenly the runway lights came on and the headphones crackled. "OK O'Brien, you're clear to go. Have a good time, Limey Kid."

Soon we were rising into the black night. Passing through the cloud base we came into a wonderful starlit world. It was fascinating and the four hours quickly passed. At about 10:00 pm the throttles were eased forward and I watched Capt O'Brien going through the exact routines that I had been learning 5,000 feet up.

With the landing gear down, we were a few hundred yards from the runway, which was brilliantly lit with the rows of landing lights, when suddenly all the lights went out and the control tower came on the air, "Control Tower to O.B.410; Control Tower to O.B.410. *Abort landing, repeat, abort landing.*" Captain O'Brien pulled back the throttles and the engines roared. "Control Tower to O.B.410. Turn 90 degrees, *now*. Watch your height." With maximum thrust from the engines this amazing machine did a sharp bank, the tip of the right wing seeming to skim the ground. In reality we were probably 100 feet or so above the ground, but, perched behind the pilot, to me the ground looked mighty close.

Just as the plane banked a firework display opened up on the far side of the airfield. Enemy planes were attacking the aerodrome and anti-aircraft and heavy machine guns were firing back. The tracer bullets made a very pretty picture but the show was not to entertain, this was the real thing! "Control Tower to O.B.410. Well done O'Brien, now get the hell out of here. We've got unwelcome visitors. Is the Limey Kid OK?" The Limey Kid was very OK. His only regret was that we didn't have guns on board!

After cruising over the Cambridgeshire area for a couple of hours we were told to make our way back to the airfield. Approaching the runway, again the lights came on and we landed safely.

When we reached our apron there appeared to be an abnormally large number of people around. As we climbed down the ladder the Station Commander came up, shook O'Brien's hand and said, "Well done and thank you." Then with a grin he said, "It wasn't you we were worried about. It was your passenger! How'd he cope?"
"Our Limey Kid. Don't worry about him. He loved every minute of it!"

So I did; which is a great deal more than could be said for my poor mother. Her bedroom window faced the airfield and just as she was getting into bed she saw the tracer bullets flashing across the sky and heard the bangs from the anti aircraft guns and the rattle of the heavy machine guns. I was taken home straight away by Capt O'Brien. "This is the last time you're going to that airfield," was her greeting.
"*Mum*!" I said.
O'Brien whispered in my ear, "Don't argue. Just give her a big hug and get off to bed."

The next morning Mum said, "That O'Brien could charm the birds out of the trees. Make sure you only fly with him when you go on these jaunts; and for goodness sake take care on the road to school."

Until Capt O'Brien told me what he'd said, I thought that was an odd thing for Mum to say. "Ma'am," he'd said, "believe me, he's safer up in the air with me than he is riding his bike every day on these dangerous roads." I thought that was a high risk strategy and I might end up having to walk to school, but it worked and my flying and trading activities continued unabated.

However there was a sombre side to these events. A trip for me meant that earlier the plane would have been badly damaged. When an engine had been repaired or replaced it had to be tested with a four-hour non-operational flight called a "Slow Time Run." Whenever I arrived at the aerodrome I would go to the control tower where I would be told when the next Slow Time Run was due for take-off. The officer in charge would contact the pilot and ask if he would take me on the flight. None of the pilots ever refused to take me. I would then be taken in a jeep to the apron and the waiting plane. It all worked with a smoothness that to me was nothing less than miraculous!

Of course it wasn't just engines that were shot up. Often we would stand in our garden watching the squadrons come in from a raid. The damage to some of the planes would be obvious. There would be great holes in the wings or the fuselage and propellers would be stopped. Once we saw a plane coming in very low over the house at an awkward angle. Three of the four propellers were not turning. A few seconds later there was an explosion as the plane crashed and a great mushroom of smoke rose into the air. Later we learned there were no survivors. Even when a plane landed safely it might contain members of the crew who had been killed or seriously injured. Particularly vulnerable were the rear gunners. Some of those killed were young men who, 24 hours earlier, had been having a family tea with us in our house. Some were like sons to Mum and as we learned of the casualties among our friends, we shed many tears. War is a dreadful business.

Chapter 7
A New Job for Dad

It was some time since we had heard anything of Dad. Later we were to learn of the preparations for D Day and the secrecy that surrounded that gigantic operation. Dad had been in the thick of it! Surprise is often the essence of success and certainly secrecy was of paramount importance when it came to the Allied invasion of Europe. Whatever resistance was met, it was anticipated that there would be enormous casualties. Would Dad's legendary luck hold out?

Dad had certainly been lucky in the 1914-18 War and, while he seldom spoke about them, he had some hair-raising escapes. Part of a cavalry brigade, on one occasion Dad had been involved in penetration reconnaissance and was on his way back to the rear for a rest. They had to find somewhere to sleep for the night, so leaving the troop of a dozen mounted men on the road, he trotted off to a farm about 200 yards away to ask permission to use a large barn. While he was talking to the farmer a colossal explosion threw both him and the farmer to the ground. Picking themselves up they saw a huge shell crater exactly where the troop had been. Of the men and the horses there was not a trace. Dad was the sole survivor.

Dad was in the catastrophic Battle of the Somme from the very beginning to the end. It started on 1st July 1916 and continued right through to November. Whole cavalry regiments, including Dad's, were dismounted and put in the trenches where they were to experience a horror that was to last for five months without respite. On that first day of July 1916, Dad, together with 200,000 other British soldiers, was in a trench facing the enemy. At 7:30 on that sultry summer morning, the platoon commander's whistle went summoning Dad to leave the trench and brave the cratered waste of No Man's Land. Within minutes he discovered that the Allied barrage of shells had failed to cut the barbed wire entanglements. There was no way through and no way back because of the press of line-after-line behind. The enemy machine guns opened up and with bullets whistling about his ears, Dad dived into a shell hole. About twenty others dived on top of him!

There they remained for the rest of the day, intermittently firing at German machine gunners. This little group in their shell hole were obviously a nuisance, for by the evening enemy shells were beginning to fall perilously near. Thinking it an unhealthy place to spend a night they all wormed their way out of the hole. Hardly had the last of the group left the hole when a shell landed right in the middle of it, exploded and showered the escapees with mud. They kept on crawling until they found another shell hole. This was to be home for the whole of the next day. That night they left their shelter and crawled about a mile back to the trenches they had left 48 hours earlier. All along the 90-mile front the Allied army had made no progress whatsoever yet they were paying a fearful price. On the first day alone the British suffered over 50,000 casualties. Yet the offensive continued, with the inevitable and useless slaughter of about 10,000 a day.

On and on went the offensive, through the 2nd of July and the 3rd, and the 4th. Still it continued, week after week through August, September and October and into November. An infantry colonel at the time, Winston Churchill wrote from the trenches... *the open country towards which we are struggling by inches is utterly devoid of military significance. There is no question of breaking the line, or letting loose the cavalry in the open country behind, or of inducing a general withdrawal of the German armies in the West.* It was fortuitous for our country that Colonel Winston Churchill survived.

The sheer bestiality of such deadlocked trench fighting is unimaginable; blood, filth, rats, thirst, mud, slime, the fear of death, the fear of gas, bombs and shells... these things should have sickened for ever those who were involved in warfare; yet here was my father, 28 years later, on D Day back in Normandy, standing in the middle of a sandy beach near Courseulles, bullets whistling past his ears while he calmly directed troops whose immediate ambition was to get off the beach as quickly as possible! It is almost unbelievable, but this was something for which he had volunteered! He may have been a survivor but, looking back, sometimes I wondered if he was completely sane!

* * * * *

Following D Day, came the Battle for the Beachhead. Dad was with the Third Canadians as they closed in on Caen. This was to prove one of the toughest battles of the invasion but eventually Caen fell. Afterwards, the Ninth Canadian Brigade, of which Dad was a part, was withdrawn for a rest. On his way in to Caen Dad had noticed a very attractive farmstead and thought: "That'll make a nice place to recuperate." He was responsible for finding a suitable billet for his men so he led them back to the farm. This time he didn't leave them on the road while he made enquiries! In fact they found the place empty.

Having settled everyone in, Dad got them together and said: "This is a Normandy farm. Hidden in here somewhere we will find calvados, stacks of it!" They looked everywhere without success. "Right! Move the furniture!" Beneath a huge dresser they found a trap-door leading down to a cellar where there were hundreds of bottles of calvados! They had a great party. Dad claims that the next morning when he eventually woke up, his right eye focussed on a fly on the ceiling while his left eye independently roved round the room!

About a month later, while being driven in a jeep near the front line outside Falaise, the driver went over a land-mine hidden in the road. The jeep, Dad, the driver and an escort were blown clean over a nearby hedge. The jeep was totally destroyed, the two men with Dad were killed outright but all Dad suffered was a sprained finger.

Later he was picked up by an armoured car and taken to a field hospital but almost immediately discharged. Protesting that it wasn't necessary, he was nevertheless given a few days' rest-leave behind the lines. There a happy reunion took place when Dad discovered that my brother Bill was part of a nearby tank repair unit. They had a great time together, particularly as Dad still had some bottles of calvados left!

With the fall of Caen the bridgehead was secure. Tens of thousands of Allied troops were daily pouring into Normandy and, by the middle of July, 30 Allied divisions were ashore. Half were American and half

My brother Bill in the Army in 1943

British and Canadian. An important event then occurred. On July 17th Field Marshal Rommel was severely wounded. His car was attacked by RAF low-flying fighters and he was carried to hospital in what was thought a dying condition. He made a wonderful recovery but a little later he was to meet his death on Hitler's orders.

It was at this time that Berlin rang Field Marshal von Rundstedt asking what was to be done. The Field Marshal was in overall command of the Western Front. His curt reply was, "Make peace you fools!" He was promptly replaced by General von Kluge, a general who had won distinction in Russia. But the end was in sight. At 2:41 am on 7th May 1945 an instrument of total and unconditional surrender was signed by Lieutenant-General Bedell Smith and General Jodl. All hostilities ceased at midnight on 8th May.

The formal ratification by the German High Command took place in Berlin in the early hours of 9th May. Air Chief Marshal Tedder signed on behalf of General Eisenhower, Marshal Zhukov for the Russians and Field Marshal Kietel for Germany. The war was over. There had been fearful casualties but both Dad and Bill had survived.

* * * * *

Trailing about a quarter of an hour behind Fred on our return home from a Boy Scouts' meeting one evening in June, I was surprised to see Fred hurrying back to meet me. "Guess who's at home?"
A wave of hope took hold of me. "Not Dad!"
"*Yes!*" Together we raced back. Half an hour earlier, on entering the house, Fred had heard Dad's laugh. Thinking I might not come straight home, he went back to meet me with the news. Dad was home.

Despite the estrangement from her father, Mr Champion's daughter, Mrs Follet, was enormously grateful to Dad for the tireless way he had looked after her father, particularly in the latter stages of his terminal cancer. Thus it was that when Dad returned from the war she wanted to do her best to help him find an appointment that suited both his abilities and experience. The moment was opportune because it occurred at exactly the time when a friend had expressed to her the need for a butler.

The friend was Sir John Ramsden who had succeeded to his father's Baronetcy. The Ramsden family owned huge estates and properties. Amongst these was Bulstrode House in Beaconsfield, now the HQ of the World Wide Evangelisation Crusade. The Ramsdens also had a large house in Sunninghill, another in Gerrards Cross and a property in London. Most impressively, they also owned two castles. One was Muncaster Castle in Cumbria and the other, the family's principal seat, Ardverikie in Scotland. Both of these castles were to have a significant impact on my life.

At the very moment that Dad was looking for an employer just like Sir John Ramsden, here was Sir John looking for a man just like Dad. That is serendipity. Incidentally the word serendipity has an interesting origin. At the age of 22, Horace Walpole, the famous author and youngest son of Robert Walpole, the statesman, in the company of Gray the poet, made a tour of France and Italy. While on this tour he came across a Persian fairy story, 'The Three Princes of Serendip'. The story is about a ruler who sent his three sons out on exploratory expeditions. In turn they came back with the story of their adventures, a characteristic of which was the way circumstances accidentally combined to bring about a happy outcome. It was this that led to Walpole coining the word serendipity.

* * * * *

After the horrors of the war, it was a very happy outcome for Dad to be offered the appointment as Sir John Ramsden's butler, an appointment which he accepted with alacrity and which resulted in us all moving from Riddlesworth to Gerrards Cross in Buckinghamshire and to the house reserved for Sir John's butler. It was a curious house, nothing like the size of the one we had just left but with two stair-cases rising from separate halls. The largest room was a sort of sitting room leading from a narrow kitchen cum scullery. The front door, which looked like a massive church door, was set back in a large tiled porch and led into a small hall with a room on each side. Straight ahead was a steep flight of stairs with a tiny landing at the top leading to a bedroom on each side. You could go through the bedroom on the right to another large bedroom which in turn led into a WC. An exit from this closet led down the other flight of stairs.

All the windows faced south and down an amazingly long garden. At the bottom of the garden was what was called either The Lake or The Pond, depending on which side of the water you lived. Those to the left of us looked down manicured lawns to an ornamental lake, while those to the right looked out of their kitchen windows and diminutive back gardens onto a pond! We were sandwiched between the hoi polloi on the right and the filthy rich on the left. Effortlessly I was to move from one to the other with a sangfroid that would have pleased the absent chief of TGRS!

Chapter 8
Royal Grammar School

Royal Grammar School, High Wycombe

The Royal Grammar School, High Wycombe, was huge. Whereas I had been used to fewer than 250 fellow students now I had more than 1,500! It was very different. The headmaster was different too. In my spare time I was reading Charles Dickens' books. One afternoon, after lunch break, I was sitting on a flight of stairs in one of the many buildings, completely engrossed in Dombey and Son. Suddenly I had the feeling I was being watched. Looking up I realised that, in contrast to the normal crowds of boys rushing to and fro, there wasn't a soul in sight. Looking round I saw Mr Tucker, the headmaster sitting on the stairs about five steps up.

"You enjoying reading Dombey and Son, Smith?" he asked. I had only been in the school a few weeks and hitherto had never met him to speak to, but he knew my name. "What do you like about Dickens?" Enthusiastically I shared my thoughts with him. After asking a few more questions he said, "Have you any idea of the time?" I hadn't, but realised I should have been in a class. "Who are you supposed to be with?"

"Er, Mr Hollingsworth, sir."

"Well, Smith, run along to your class. Give Mr Hollingsworth my apologies and explain that I have been detaining you." What a man. What a headmaster.

Mr E.R. Tucker

I had occasion seven years later again to appreciate Mr Tucker. That was when I had to visit him to confess a shocking transgression. I should make the point that I am not proud of what I did.

As is the normal custom, students sitting Certificate Examinations at the end of the school term had to sit Mock Exams. If there wasn't a chance of you passing a particular examination you were withdrawn from that subject so that you could concentrate your efforts on those where you had a better chance of success. I sat my 'Mocks' with catastrophic results.

My three years' trading at Thetford had earned me a fabulous amount of money but academically I had learned very little. At the end of my first few weeks at RGS I was detained by a French Master. "Smith, how many years have you been studying French?"

"Three, sir."

"Smith, I have to tell you, that in my long experience, and I am an old man, you are unique."

"Thank you, sir!" I said.

"It wasn't a compliment! Never," he went on, "never in all those years have I met anyone as ignorant as you!"

Going through the Mock results in alphabetical order, the Form Master skipped my name. As we all filed out he called me over. "Smith," he said, "in all my time I have never seen anything like your results." I had a growing feeling that I was not about to be congratulated. "I'm afraid there is no point in you continuing at school. Not only have you failed in *everything* but you have failed *abysmally* in everything. How is this possible? You're not exactly stupid!"

Clearly I had been stupid. Now was not the time for excuses so I told him everything about my last three years. I told him about my trading and my flying; then I promised him if he let me stay I would work as he had never seen anyone work before. He looked keenly at me for about three full minutes. Then he said, "I'll have a word with the Head." Whatever that word was it was very effective for I was to be allowed to sit *nine* subjects: English Language, English Literature, French, History, Art, General Science I, General Science II, Maths and Geography. On my way home that evening I realised I had been given another chance and thus I embarked on a process of relentless, non-stop study that was to last two months.

As I applied myself to my studies I began to realise how huge were the gaps in my knowledge. My daily train journeys to and from school were coaching lessons from the school swots who were astonished at my ignorance. Arriving home I would get out my books before tea then immediately after tea I'd be back at my studies and I'd stick at them until 2:00 or 3:00 in the morning. Frequently my mother would call down, "John, go to bed." Patiently I would explain that I had calculated how many hours a day I had to work if I was to have the remotest chance of success. Studying for eighteen hours a day I covered four years' work in two months.

Just before the examinations I had made some good progress in many of the subjects but I realised that my Achilles Heel was History and French. The period of history on which we were being examined was from Napoleon to Hitler. I simply did not know enough of the detail but I guessed that one of the questions would be on the unification of Germany under Bismarck and another would be on the unification of Italy under Cavour. There would be a slant to the questions but I was sure that the process of unification would be required in any event.

At the time that I took the examination the answer sheets for most of the subjects were all blank except for the Stationery Office seal. When the examinations started, I slipped half a dozen sheets of the official paper from my desk up inside my pullover, transferring them to my satchel after leaving the examination room. That night, leaving a three or four inch space at the top for an introduction related to the questions, I wrote up, first the unification of Germany on one lot of papers and of Italy on another. The text was accompanied by simple but very accurate charts and maps.

On the day of the History exam I took these papers with me in my satchel, putting them under my pullover before going in to the exam room. After an appropriate passage of time, during which I feigned great industry, I slid the papers from under my pullover on to my desk. The questions suited the written answers perfectly.

French was a different problem. We had a boy on the train who was a linguist and could speak perfect French. I related an incident to him and asked him to translate it into French for me and then rehearse me in it until I was word perfect. It was all about an elderly gentleman who was taking his dog for a walk and got entangled in the lead. It was a simple story but that was what I needed. On the day of my French viva I went in to the examiner who was a lady. She asked me how I was. That was easy, I could answer that! Then she asked me if I'd had a good morning! Quite naturally I was able to launch into my little narrative of a scene I had seen that morning on my way to school! I told the story with a great deal of laughter and demonstration. Soon the examiner was laughing with me. At the end of my story I was thinking, "Now what do I do?" but, with an approving smile, she told me I was a natural linguist and sent me off! The other examinations did not seem to be too bad but then I had to wait for the results. The one subject, apart from History, where I really thought I had done well was Art. I had drawn a cracking bowl of fruit!

The day dawned when a little buff envelope was put through the door. This was a moment of truth. I opened it and the first thing I saw was: "Art – Fail." The bowl really had cracked! I couldn't believe it. I thought I'd get at least a credit. If I had failed Art, how badly had I done in the others? I dared hardly look but it had to be faced: English Language – Credit; English Literature – Credit; French – Credit; Maths – Credit; General Science I – Credit; General Science II – Credit; Geography – Credit; History – Credit. Eight credits and only one fail. I was geared up for the results to be completely the other way round! I had gained a London Matriculation Exemption.

Two years later when I was in the Army in Malaya, I became a committed Christian. It wasn't long before the Lord put His finger on my History examination. I felt even more ashamed. "Lord," I said, "I promise that when I get back to England, I'll go to see the Head." One of the first things I did on arriving in England four years later was to make an appointment with the headmaster of the Royal Grammar School. It was still Mr Tucker.

Seated in his study he said, "Are you still reading Dickens?" What a memory! Nearly 3,000 students had passed through his hands in those intervening years but he had remembered that little incident on the stairs. Briefly I described to him what I had done. Then I told him how I had become a Christian and how the Lord had spoken so clearly about my making a full confession. As Mr Tucker sat looking at me in silence I fully expected my entire Certificate to be withdrawn. Eventually he said, "John, in all my years of teaching I have never heard anything as fantastic as this."

"Well, Mr Tucker, I'm bound to tell you I am thoroughly ashamed of myself."

"I don't mean the way you passed your history examination, though that indeed was reprehensible; I'm talking about your conversion and how that has influenced you."

"But my Certificate. Should that not be cancelled?"

"I am really grateful that you've shared this story with me. I'll remember it for as long as I live. But as for cancelling your certificate, I believe the Lord would want you to keep it. I suspect you'll make good use of it." He stood up and held out his hand. "Thank you for coming to see me."

Chapter 9
Valerie Hignett

When we moved into the house in Gerrards Cross in 1945, one of our ornamental lake neighbours was the managing director of the Hoover Company. His name was Mr Bunn. He looked exactly like the baker in our card game of Happy Families! He had a daughter called Pat who was a captivating little flirt. It was not long before she numbered me among her conquests although I am bound to say that I was completely unaware of my good fortune! Pat Bunn went to Ellerslie, a toffee nosed boarding school in the Malvern Hills in Worcestershire.

Groups of from six to twelve girls were allocated their own sitting room where they were supposed to learn gracious living. Pat Bunn wasn't into gracious living, being totally absorbed in the all important business of life, romance. Bored with polite conversation one evening, Pat said, "Let's play boyfriends."
"Boyfriends! We haven't any boyfriends," was one rejoinder.
"That doesn't matter, you can all have one of mine. You can have Brian... you can have Christopher... you can have John... "

Valerie Hignett

"John? John who?" was the suspicious response.
"Oh, John Smith."
"I don't believe you have all these boyfriends. You *certainly* haven't a boyfriend called John Smith."
"Well I *have!*"

The challenge came from Valerie Hignett, a stickler for the truth and nothing but the truth. "Pat, I'm sorry, but I don't believe you."

"Alright, come home with me for the Easter holidays and I'll introduce you to him."

Thinking she was calling Pat's bluff, Valerie Hignett said, "Thank you, I will."

"Let me introduce my boyfriend, John Smith!"

At the beginning of the Easter holidays Pat had gone to London to meet Valerie off the train and to accompany her on the Green Line, London to Oxford bus. Acting on instructions received from Pat, a group of us were waiting at the bus stop outside The Bull Hotel. As they stepped off the bus Pat, with a mischievous smile, said to Valerie, "Let me introduce my boyfriend, John Smith!" Thus it was that I met the individual who was to become the most important person in my life.

"Is your name really John Smith?" she asked, as she held out her hand. I took the hand but was unable to say anything. It was as if I had received an electric shock. I was looking into a perfectly lovely face totally devoid of guile.

"You see," said Pat, "he's real!" In fact, I was feeling less real than I had ever felt in all my life. I was eighteen years old when Cupid let loose his arrow, which, as it turned out, was to be the only one he had to aim at me! Valerie stayed with Pat for two weeks and I visited them as often as propriety allowed. We went cycling to Bourne End, swimming in Beaconsfield, walking in Bulstrode Park and, on one inauspicious occasion, we went to the Gerrards Cross cinema. The film was Blithe Spirit. I was trying to summon up the courage to hold the hand of the blithe spirit sitting next to me when suddenly she had a massive nose bleed.

"I'm very sorry about this but I'm afraid I shall have to go out," she said to me. With great alacrity I offered to go out with her, but for once, Pat's romantic nature failed to assert itself and she came too. It was probably just as well. Romance is not particularly aided by heavy nose bleeds!

The holiday came to an end and I was determined to go to London to see my blithe spirit safely on to the train. Unfortunately about six others decided to do the same. Waiting under the clock on Paddington station's number one platform, I was rehearsing a speech of lifelong commitment when, without warning the guard blew his whistle and waved his little green flag. In a great bustle Valerie got on the train just as it started to move. Leaning out of the window, she waved a tiny embroidered handkerchief at us and she was gone.

I had discovered that Valerie's birthday was just ten days after leaving us. By then she would be back at boarding school. I decided to send some flowers. We had some splendid Lilies of the Valley in the garden and a quantity of these were carefully picked and laid in a well moistened box lined with tissue paper. I had occasion now and then during the two weeks that she was with us to give Valerie a note. This was written in my usual purple ink. Knowing that she would recognise the ink if not the writing, I placed a card in the box which read simply 'With love!' and posted the box to her at her school.

A couple of weeks later I received a fairly guarded note of thanks. It wasn't until very much later, that I learned what had happened when the flowers arrived. Being a very strict seminary, all parcels and correspondence passed under the scrutiny of the headmistress, Miss Sayle. When my box arrived, it was duly opened but the identity of the sender was obscure. Valerie was summoned to the office and asked for the name of this unknown admirer. "Oh, those flowers are from my mother," lied Valerie glibly. Clearly she was not as devoid of guile as her appearance had made out!

Meanwhile, back at school, I was taking those ill-fated mock exams. I was about to be given the devastating news that, owing to my scholastic ineptitude, I was to be thrown out of school. These were serious times and I came down to earth with a bump. As has been narrated, I was given a second chance and I intended to grasp it.

During the May and June of 1947 I threw myself into such an intensive programme of study that it precluded everything else, even romance. That would have to wait!

Part Two
A PALESTINE POLICEMAN
(1947-48)

Chapter 10
Palestine's Problems

It was now my turn to do National Service. Normally there was a choice of the Army, the Navy or the Air Force but, just prior to my National Service falling due, the Government added another option: The Palestine Police Force. The British in Palestine were having a very thin time. Their problems went back to 1917, although in a very real sense the problem goes back to the time of Abraham and his two sons, Isaac and Ishmael! Because I became personally involved in the problems of Palestine, it might be helpful if I give some background to the situation facing me when I arrived in the October of 1947.

On 2nd November 1917, Arthur James Balfour, the British Foreign Secretary, wrote to Lord Rothschild. The Rothschilds were considered by many Jews to be the most influential of all Jewish families; they were certainly one of the wealthiest. Their influence in America was considered to be very important to the British Government. Arthur Balfour's letter became known as the Balfour Declaration and it led the Jewish people in Britain and America into believing that Great Britain would support the creation of a Jewish state in Palestine, though there had to be safeguards for the rights of non-Jewish communities.

This communication was accepted by the Jewish people as Great Britain's support for a Jewish homeland. However, from a Palestinian Arab point of view, the same area had been promised to them for siding with the Allies in World War I and fighting against the Turks, who were on the side of the Germans.

When Palestine was given to Britain to govern by a League of Nation's mandate at the end of World War I, both the Jews and the Arabs believed that they had been betrayed, as both believed that they had been promised the same piece of land. After 1918, politics in the

73

Middle East was to become a lot more complicated as many Jews took the Balfour Declaration as read and emigrated to Palestine. The Arabs there saw the increasing number of Jews moving to the region as a threat to their way of life and problems quickly multiplied.

In June 1922 the League of Nations passed the Palestine Mandate. This was an explicit document regarding Britain's responsibilities and powers of administration in Palestine including 'securing the establishment of the Jewish national home' and 'safeguarding the civil and religious rights of all the inhabitants of Palestine'. The document defining Britain's obligations as mandate power copied the text of the Balfour Declaration concerning the establishment of a Jewish homeland. It read as follows:

> *His Majesty's Government view with favour the establishment in Palestine of a national home for the Jewish people, and will use their best endeavours to facilitate the achievement of this object, it being clearly understood that nothing shall be done which may prejudice the civil and religious rights of existing non-Jewish communities in Palestine, or the rights and political status enjoyed by Jews in any other country.*

Jewish immigration into Palestine met little opposition from the Palestinian Arabs until the early 20th Century. However, as anti Semitism grew in Europe during the late 19th and early 20th Centuries, Jewish immigration to Palestine began to increase markedly, creating much Arab resentment. The British Government then placed limitations on Jewish immigration into Palestine. These quotas were controversial, particularly in the latter years of British rule. Both Arabs and Jews disliked the policy, each side for its own reasons.

Beginning in 1936, several Jewish groups, such as the Irgun and the Stern Gang, conducted their own campaigns of violence against British and Arab targets. This prompted the British Government to label both as terrorist organizations. Between 1936 and 1939 the mandate experienced an upsurge in militant Arab nationalism. The revolt was triggered by increased Jewish immigration, primarily Jews who had been ejected by the Nazi regime in Germany, as well as rising anti-

Semitism throughout Europe. The revolt was led or co-opted by the Grand Mufti of Jerusalem. The Arabs felt they were being marginalised in their own country. In addition to non-violent strikes, they resorted to violence. Irgun replied with its own campaign, with marketplace bombings and other violent acts that killed hundreds. Eventually, the uprising was put down by the British using severe measures. The Mufti fled to Germany in late 1941.

As in most of the Arab world, there was no unanimity amongst the Palestinian Arabs as to their position in WWII. Many signed up for the British Army, but others saw an Axis victory as a likely outcome and a way of wresting Palestine back from the Zionists and the British. Some of the leadership went further, especially the Grand Mufti, who formally declared jihad against the Allied Powers.

Arabs were only marginally higher than Jews in Nazi racial theory, but the Nazis encouraged Arab support as much as possible as a counter to British hegemony throughout the Arab world. Nevertheless the British recruited about 6,000 Palestinian Arabs and about 26,000 Jews for the armed forces.

Following the war 250,000 Jewish refugees were stranded in displaced persons' camps in Europe. Despite the pressure of world opinion, in particular the repeated requests of US President Harry S Truman, the British refused to lift the ban on immigration and admit displaced persons to Palestine. The Jewish underground forces then united and carried out several attacks against the British.

In 1946, the Irgun blew up the King David Hotel in Jerusalem, the headquarters of the British administration, killing 92 people. Seeing that the situation was quickly spiralling out of hand, the British announced their desire to terminate their mandate and to withdraw by May 1948. This was the political situation facing the British in 1947, but on the ground the security situation was worsening daily and the British badly needed reinforcements.

Chapter 11
£20 a Month & All found!

Advertisements had been appearing in the British press: 'Join the Palestine Police Force – £20 a month – and all found'. To most candidates for National Service, £20 was a great deal of money in those days, although I am bound to say that in my trading days, £20 would have been considered a most indifferent month! Even so, the alternative was distinctly unattractive for, if I joined any of the services, my pay would have been 28 shillings (£1.40) a week which amounted to the princely sum of £6 a month. This did not appeal to me at all!

My mother was horrified at the idea of me going to Palestine. The papers were full of the atrocities committed by terrorists, but soldiers were the recipients of these atrocities even more than the police. If I joined the army I would in all probability be sent to Palestine anyway. There were other considerations. As a soldier I would travel on a troopship, sleep in a hammock and queue up in a canteen for meals. As a police cadet I would travel by passenger liner, have a cabin, eat in a dining room with waiter service and enjoy the status of a civilian. Quite apart from all that, when I arrived in Palestine I would spend two months studying law and police procedures, as compared with being a target of the Irgun. True, that was to come later, but for the moment there really was no contest. The £20 a month was distinctly better than service pay, but this was not a deciding issue. As a result of my trading, I had put into National Savings Certificates the equivalent of no fewer than six years' police pay. I felt like a proper plutocrat!

I was anxious to forestall the Army recruiting sergeant so, even before leaving school, I had applied to join the Palestine Police Force. Together with 22 others I arrived for examinations and selection at The Crown Agents for the Colonies at Millbank in London. The

77

process lasted all day and gradually our numbers diminished, with some failing the medical and fitness test and others failing a written composition or a maths test. Some fell at a test called 'Initiative'. At the end of the day only two of us survived and together we signed a contract of employment with the Crown Agents.

"Join the Palestine Police - £20 a month and all found."

The other successful applicant was a delightful chap called Anthony Michael Stapleton-Cotton. Back in 1809, his ancestor, General Stapleton-Cotton, commanded Wellington's cavalry in the Peninsular War with such distinction that he was awarded a peerage and became Lord Combermere. It was claimed that in 1815 the full dress uniform of General, Lord Combermere cost £500. Today, that is the equivalent of just over £20,000!

Anthony's uncle was Lord Combermere, but Anthony confided in me that the reason he was hoping to join the Palestine Police was so that he could send money home to help out the family finances, which depended on the sale of apples from the orchard. Owing to frosts in the May of 1947, the crop was virtually non existent and, if he wasn't able to help out, the entire family would be hard pressed until the next harvest!

Our port of embarkation was Liverpool and, when I climbed the gangway of the ship en route for Port Said, Anthony was there to greet me, a broad grin on his face. It transpired that we were sharing a cabin. We spent a great deal of our first day on board looking at the Royal Liver Building. On each of the two towers are the mythical Liver Birds, a cross between an eagle and a cormorant, the bird of good luck to sailors. The symbol of Liverpool, they are made of copper and are 18-feet tall with a total wingspan of 24-feet. Local legend has it that if they fly away, Liverpool will cease to exist. The clocks on the Liver Building are colossal. They measure 25-feet in diameter and are bigger than the clocks in London's Big Ben. Driven electrically, they were built to give mariners the correct local time and are said to be accurate to within 30 seconds in the year. Up on deck we watched the hands go round the clock and at times thought they had stopped! We were keen to get away. Within a few months we would have been content to watch them for a week.

* * * * *

The voyage to Egypt was comparatively uneventful but very instructive. Learning that we were in the Palestine Police, a fellow passenger insisted on teaching Anthony and me unarmed combat. He was an expert, and although we ended each day with multiple bruises, the lessons served to increase our self confidence. We were badly in need of this, for day by day we were hearing from those returning from home leave, the appalling situation into which we had dropped ourselves.

Two members of the police force on board had been kidnapped a year earlier by terrorists who had given them a very rough time before intending to execute them. Happily a police rescue bid was successfully carried out in the nick of time and the terrorists were captured. The experiences of the two men had been so bad that they were sent home on recuperation leave. Now they were on their way back to Palestine and neither of them was looking forward to it. In just two more years they would qualify for a good pension but that didn't alleviate their apprehension which they tried to overcome by topping up the alcohol in their bloodstream throughout the day.

They very nearly didn't make it back to Palestine. En route the ship stopped at Valetta Harbour in Malta. The gangway was lowered to a launch to take passengers ashore. The two policemen were among the first party to go but, climbing unsteadily down the gangway, one of them stumbled and fell. His companion grabbed him by the collar but in turn was pulled off the steps and both fell about 50 feet into the sea. Two of the crew in the launch promptly dived in after them. One was easily rescued but the other struggled so madly that his would-be rescuer was in danger of going under as well. When they came to the surface, the seaman, who was a burly character, gave the policeman such a colossal blow to the jaw that it knocked him out. He was then towed unceremoniously back to the gangway where four other seaman fished him out and carried him up to the sick room.

It seemed the ship's doctor decided his patient needed drying out in more ways than one for we didn't see him again until a few hours before docking in Port Said. By then he was looking very spruce in his summer police uniform. On his chest he carried two rows of medal ribbons!

Apparently the Inspector General of the Palestine Police Force was not depending entirely on Stapleton-Cotton and me to restore peace in Palestine, our departure from Egypt not being scheduled for a further two days. During this time we were free to do some sight seeing. We saw The Citadel Al-Qalaa, the fortress built by Salah ad-Din in the 12th Century; then there was the Step Pyramid of Djoser, part of a huge archaeological site which includes underground Persian tombs. Perhaps the most ancient site is St. Mercurius Church which was built in the 6th Century AD and still has its original foundations.

But it was the people who fascinated me. I had lived a very circumscribed existence up to this time. The only foreign people I had seen were in a circus! Now I was in the middle of Egypt's most multi-racial city.

We went everywhere, enjoying everything we saw and did. It wasn't until the morning of our departure, when we shared our experiences that we learned of the dangers lurking on every street. Perhaps our manifest ignorance and consequent friendliness disarmed any with evil intent or perhaps, at the look of us, they had concluded we weren't worth robbing! Little did they know that, with £20 a month and all found, we were men of affluence.

Chapter 12
Police Training and Haifa

Jenin Police Training School

We left Cairo before dawn and 350 miles later we were approaching the Palestine Police Training School just outside Jenin 50 miles north of Jerusalem and overlooking the plain of Armageddon. We hoped we were not going to be involved in the epic battle of the "end time"! The twelve foot high iron fencing with rolls and rolls of barbed wire on both sides, together with twenty foot high, sandbagged guard points, made the place look like Stalag Luft I Prisoner of War camp in Germany.

There were twelve of us on our course which was to last two months. The worsening terrorist situation virtually made ordinary police activity redundant. The subtle differences between petty larceny, theft and robbery became less relevant when the event occasioning these

Jenin overlooked the Plain of Armageddon

crimes was a colossal explosion that brought down two or three buildings in one blast. More and more police activities were military operations so it was not surprising that our curriculum at the School focussed more on Weapon Training and less on British Mandate Law.

At first we didn't appreciate what a reprieve this was, but after a few lectures on law we were glad of the focus on survival. Britain exported its legal system to the Commonwealth countries during the British Empire days. In the case of Palestine, when the British assumed the mandate from the then League of Nations, the whole of the land had been governed under what was known as Ottoman Law. The British then attempted to apply the system of English jurisprudence, albeit amended to some extent by the existing Ottoman Law. As the immigration of Jewish people gathered pace there was a demand for various amendments to the law to accommodate the hereditary principles and practice of the Jewish faith.

At various international legal conferences the law in Palestine underwent further changes, making the study of it a nightmare. I very quickly lost interest, thinking the whole thing was academic at the time and would be redundant in a few months anyway. In the meanwhile I would major on survival. Priority was given to the use of hand guns. Our first session on weapon training was with the little .38

revolver. Out of six shots at a silhouette of a man I scored three body hits and two limb hits. "Not bad!" said the sergeant instructor. "Not bad at all." He used to be in the Coldstream Guards and at our first lesson he told us that by the time he had finished with us we would be more afraid of him than of any terrorist we were likely to meet. At the time we believed him. At the slightest deviation from the strict procedures that he laid down he would scarify us. Later we would gladly have made a swap.

The little .38 revolver

After the .38 we moved to the much larger Colt .45, the weapon seen by viewers of Wild West films. The Colt .45 is a huge hand gun that I could barely hold. Taking up my position I aimed and pressed the trigger. There was a colossal bang and the gun nearly leapt out of my hand. I had not only missed the target I'd missed the background screen as well. "Not good," said the sergeant. "Not good at all." Out of six shots I only hit the target once and that was in the foot. "You're well on your way to the morgue," was the comment. The rest of the class were to keep me company.

Gradually we got better and then moved on to the Bren gun. This is a serious automatic weapon with 25 rounds to a magazine. Although a very heavy gun, it is mounted at the front on two legs that fold back under the barrel. Our first lesson on the Bren gun was how to clear a stoppage. The sergeant instructor would give the various sequences: "Take up position," whereupon three cadets would hurl themselves down behind their guns, keeping as low a profile as possible. "Load." This was the order to grab a magazine and fix it to the gun. "Commence firing." There was no live ammunition, so each gunner would shout out a simulated: "ta, ta, ta... " making sure he only let off three or four ta, ta, ta's at a single burst. "Gun jams," would roar the instructor, "mag off, clear stoppage, mag on, continue firing," all of which had to be done in less than ten seconds. The guns 'jammed' very frequently which made the Bren gun appear to be a peculiarly vulnerable weapon. At the end of a Procedures lesson on Powers of Arrest, I was chatting with the instructor about our exciting time with the Bren gun and asked him why it jammed so often.

"The Bren is a splendid gun; the jamming is caused by a bullet being wrongly put into the magazine."
"In what way?" I asked.
"Why are you asking?"
"I was just curious."

So he explained: "Each bullet has a slightly proud rim at the percussion end. It is this rim that the forward movement of the gun's bolt catches and pushes the cartridge into the breach. When the cartridges are loaded into the magazine each rim has to be in front of the rim beneath. If it is behind, the gun will try to push both cartridges forward at the same time and the gun will jam. The problem is that it is very easy to push a cartridge behind the one beneath, especially if you're in a hurry." Then he added, "Don't forget that. One day it may save your life." It was to be a significant comment.

We all passed our 'law exams' and, against the dire predictions of our instructor, we all also passed our weapons' tests. Ordinarily, at the end of a course a new recruit could apply for attachment to a specialist branch of the force. If he liked camels there was the possibility of the Desert Border Patrol; if he was a horseman there was the Mounted Police. The dramatically worsening security situation meant that neither of these options was open to us and all of our intake was

posted to the town of Haifa. There the police were desperately trying to keep the peace between the Arab and Jewish factions while fending off increasingly violent attacks against the police themselves.

Desert Border Control

My time in Palestine was closely associated with the ill fated town of Haifa. On the very day that I arrived in Palestine the Irgun terrorists attacked the Haifa Police Headquarters. A 40 gallon drum packed with high explosives was fixed to the centre of the axle and rear wheels assembly of a three ton lorry. It was then mounted and secured to a huge launching chute that had been built on a truck. The chute enabled the bomb to be launched over the security perimeter fence of the Police HQ. The resulting explosion was devastating. Ten people were killed, including three British Constables, and over 50 people were injured, some critically.

Mounted Police

Kingsway
Haifa Main Street in 1946

Haifa Police HQ before
and after the explosion

This was the high risk town in which I would be spending the rest of my service in the Palestine Police Force, but it wasn't just the towns where the police were threatened. In rural areas danger was always lurking on the roads. Someone had the enchanting notion of removing roadside white painted stones and replacing them with up-turned four gallon tins filled with explosives powerful enough to blast an armoured car off the road.

As our contingent of twelve newly graduated British Constables moved out of the Training School our transport from Jenin to Haifa was an open truck. It can be imagined with what intensity we viewed the sides of the road, but with the adventurous attitude of youth we were looking forward to an exciting time in Haifa. This is the city at the foot of Mount Carmel on which the amazing prophet Elijah overcame 450 of his enemies. He was an inspiring example to those of us who wanted to become heroes.

It was a short lived ambition. We learned very quickly that survival was not merely a subject on the Training School curriculum; it was a daily necessity. I was eighteen years old and had experienced a totally sheltered upbringing. Now I was the colleague of army veterans who had known the terrors of combat. Some had been prisoners of war. One would have thought that such fearful experiences would have engendered a highly developed sense of self preservation, yet frequently these veterans would slip off to bars to drink themselves into a state of oblivion. Increasingly, the police were a target of the terrorists yet the threat of abduction, torture and murder seemed to have no effect on the behaviour of some of my colleagues.

Our armoured cars patrolled the city, but along the station perimeter there were four other armoured cars. These were not mobile; in fact they didn't even have wheels. Manning one of these positions fell due about once every ten days with six-hour shifts covering the 24 hours. The first time I was on one of these duties it was a midnight to 6:00 am shift. Although we had been given a thorough briefing I really had no idea what to expect and was completely unprepared for the fierce gunfire between Arab and Jewish factions. During a particularly prolonged and noisy exchange of gunfire the door to my armoured car was wrenched open and our brusque station sergeant clambered in. "Hotting up tonight. Are you scared?"

"To death." I replied.

"Good," he said, "that's the way to stay alive." With that he opened the door and was gone!

That same night I detected a number of shadowy figures approaching the armoured car in two columns. Swivelling the mounted Bren gun in their direction, I yelled the mandatory, *"Halt... who goes there?"*

After a short pause the groups continued to move forward, so I completed the rest of the warning: *"Halt, who goes there. Halt or I fire."* They didn't halt so I fired! I remembered the training of short bursts in rapid succession. With the first magazine empty, it took me about five seconds to change magazines and let fly another couple of bursts. There was a cry and then silence. I waited but nothing happened. The next half an hour was pretty tense. Gradually my racing pulse returned to normal. It was very scary, but I was glad that I had unloaded and recharged those magazines.

At four in the morning I heard an unusual noise: clack, clack. Then a few seconds later: clack, clack. So it continued, getting slighter louder each time. Suddenly there was a bang on the door of the armoured car and I nearly had a coronary!

With revolver drawn I waited as the door slowly opened. Outside was a diminutive Arab standing next to what looked like an old barrel organ. "Coffee, your honour?" With that he poured out a tiny cup of Turkish coffee and handed it to me. It was the most delicious drink I had ever tasted!

The second time I was on this duty there had been another vigorous gun battle. At about four in the morning, above the din of gunfire and explosions, I again heard the clack, clack and then clack, clack. An overwhelming feeling of relief swept over me. I had survived the night. Again the coffee was like nectar! Ever since, I have been very partial to Turkish coffee, but never have I tasted anything as delicious as the coffee made by that street vendor.

* * * * *

One day the station sergeant sent for me, "The DS wants you to go with him to Jerusalem." The DS was the District Superintendent whose rank would be more or less equivalent to a Chief Superintendent in the Metropolitan Police.

"Why me? It's my afternoon off."

"Don't ask me; he must want his head testing asking for you! Go and get ready and take a couple of Sten guns from the armoury." Ten minutes later we were humming along the Haifa to Jerusalem road in a Humber Super Snipe car.

There were some nasty bends on this road and I was expecting an ambush at every corner, but with my Sten gun at the ready, I was determined to act out my role of body guard, so any conversation was desultory to say the least.

"For goodness sake," said the DS, "put that damn gun down; you're scaring the daylights out of me!"

I looked at him reproachfully. "I'm here to protect you," I said.

"If you carry on, you're much more likely to kill me. Don't worry about an ambush. This car is armoured." I later discovered that it was nothing of the kind but his comment resulted in us chatting away in a more relaxed fashion. We weren't in Jerusalem above an hour before we were on our way home again. Back at my Haifa Police Station the DS said with a smile, "Thank you for protecting me. I appreciated your vigilance."

Haifa area was one of the favourite spots for illegal Jewish immigrants to land. There were long stretches of the coastline that were ideal for beaching small boats and as the date for the withdrawal of the British mandate in May drew near, the scale of illegal immigration grew. Despite large numbers of the military assigned to help, the police were overwhelmed. Many of the immigrants had escaped the Nazi holocaust. They had made their way to ports such as Marseilles and there they had paid extortionate fees to the owners of dangerously unsafe vessels to take them to The Promised Land.

As these ships approached the coast of Palestine, many of them were intercepted by the Royal Navy and the would-be immigrants found themselves back in prison camps, this time in Cyprus, and their jailers were the British. It was no wonder that the police and the military were unpopular and Haganah, the Irgun and the Stern Gang increasingly active, but Britain was responsible under the terms of the mandate to limit immigration to 1,500 a month. Maintaining law and order in Haifa was an unenviable job.

Just before my leaving Haifa, the terrorists detonated a bomb near our Police Station. It went off in the early hours of the morning. I had not had any sleep for 48 hours and had not got to bed until about four that morning, with the result that I slept right through both the explosion and the ensuing pandemonium.

When I turned over I was awakened by the sound of falling glass. My bed was covered with pieces of glass and bits of ceiling plaster. Sitting up in bed I was dazzled by the sun which was streaming into my room with a strange brilliance. I could now see why the room was so light. Not only had the blinds gone, but there weren't any windows. Even though the explosion had blown in the windows of my room I had not been awakened by the noise. I pulled on some shoes and in my pyjamas made my way gingerly across the bedroom floor to the landing. There was not a soul to be seen and there was an eerie silence. Slowly I made my way down the stairs to the entrance hall and some steps leading down to a courtyard at the back. As I started down the steps there was a shout, "There's Smithy!" A crowd was gathered in the courtyard and out of this group a figure ran towards me. It was the station sergeant.

This hitherto fierce fellow ran up to me and, throwing his arms round me said, "Where've you been, boy?" He then lifted my arm and examined my hand. Unnoticed by me, my hand was bleeding profusely.

Giving me an enamel mug, the station sergeant half filled it with an amber liquid. "Here boy, get that down you." It was neat whisky. I was put in a chair while my hand was bandaged. Folk milled around looking at me as if I had come back from the dead. Someone had gone into my room but, seeing the room and bed covered with plaster and glass shards, assumed there was no one there.

From then on I was excused all duties. "I'm not sending you out again my boy," said the station sergeant, "I'm putting you down as wounded."
"Sarj, it's only a scratch," I said.

"You're wounded," he said fiercely, "and don't call me sarj, you cheeky beggar," or words to that effect! Then he said, "You're to stay here in this compound. Do you hear me?" He was his old fierce self again, but I was amazed and quite touched by his concern for me.

A few days later a convoy of trucks, escorted by armoured cars, took a number of us down to the harbour where we boarded the ship that was to take us home to the UK. That afternoon we cast off and slowly pulled away from the jetty. We had gone no more than a few hundred yards when there was a muffled explosion and a mushroom of smoke appeared over the houses. The terrorists were giving us a good send off! I wasn't sorry to say good bye to Haifa.

Haifa town and harbour

Chapter 13
Home

On the second day of our voyage home I was talking to a chief petty officer in the early afternoon. "We're headin' into a terrific storm. Force ten's forecast. It's goin' to get rough and this tub rolls somethin' chronic."

I remembered reading somewhere that the best way to handle a storm is in a hammock in the hold. Almost jokingly, I said to the petty officer, "You haven't got a hammock and a spare space in the luggage hold have you?"

"You a seaman?" he asked. I wasn't in my uniform.

"No, I'm a policeman."

"Palestine Police?"

"Yes."

"You come along 'a me." We went down a deck and from a locker he pulled out some canvass and a few lengths of rope. "Let's see if we can fix you up," he said, and led me down three more decks to the hold where our baggage was held.

Threading his way to the very centre, he proceeded to tie a rope round a solid- looking pillar. He then attached the canvass, which I could now see was a huge hammock. Another length of rope was tied to the other end of the hammock and in turn tied to a second pillar.

"Now you listen to what I'm goin' to tell you," he said. "You find yourself a real good book. Don't wait until it gets rough. You come back 'ere as soon as you can and get into this 'ere 'ammock. I'll get three blankets and put 'em in 'ere for you. Put two in the bottom of the 'ammock and just have the one on top, right?"

"Right," I said.

"Good, now you listen. I'm goin' to put a couple of packets of biscuits in 'ere, a couple of apples and some bottled water. That'll last you till the storm's over. Now, when it gets rough, and you'll know that soon enough, 'cos it'll look as if this 'old has gone mad, you keep your eyes on your book. I've put the 'ead 'ere next to this light on the pillar so's you can see clear. Right?"

"Right, thank you!"

"No need to thank me. Glad to do it for a Palestine Policeman after what you lot 've 'bin through." I felt a proper fraud, for in all conscience, I'd had a wonderful time.

"Now then," he continued, "you go up to the readin' room and you get yourself that book. If you should need it, there's a toilet just through the door at the top of that gangway. Now then, if you should start to feel queer, you start tuckin' in to them biscuits and 'ave a drink of water, but keep your eyes off the 'old. Don't look at anythin' 'cept that book, right?"

"Right," I said.

"Now mind, when you've got that book, you stay 'ere 'til the storm's over, right?"

"Right!"

Then with, "'Ave a good sleep," he was gone.

I forget what book I chose, but I remember there wasn't much of a choice. On the way back I noticed there was a howling gale outside; the rain was lashing down and it was getting very much colder. I was glad to find the blankets. Under the blankets there was a large bottle of water and two huge packets of biscuits. They were enough to last the voyage, never mind the storm.

I had just got settled down between the blankets and opened my book when the ship gave a series of shudders. I was surprised to see the hold moving gently from side to side while the hammock was quite still. Mustn't look, I reminded myself.

Half an hour later I noticed an intermittent but regular swish... swish. Intrigued I looked around. The baggage was moving, perhaps three or four inches, first one way then back again. It was the luggage that was making the swishing noise.

I then looked up and could hardly believe my eyes. In relation to the hammock, which was perfectly still, the hold appeared to be swinging from side to side through about 60 degrees; 30 degrees one way then through 60 degrees to 30 the other way. Mesmerised, I watched for a couple of minutes and immediately began to feel distinctly unwell. Quickly I opened my store of biscuits, grabbed one and frantically started chewing. Resolutely I kept my eyes on my book until I couldn't keep them open any more and fell into a dreamless sleep.

I must have slept for about eighteen hours for it was 8:00 in the morning when I woke up. The swishing noise had stopped and the oscillations were down to about fifteen degrees. Dressed and feeling quite perky, I went on deck. It was strewn with near corpses! Picking my way to the galley I chose a huge breakfast of fried eggs, sausages, bacon, mushrooms and fried bread. The galley man looked at me with undisguised admiration. "You're the first one to want a cooked breakfast this morning," he said. "In fact there are only four others who have asked for any breakfast at all." I wasn't surprised. Without that hammock I think I would have died.

As I was having breakfast the petty officer came to the table carrying a huge mug of steaming coffee. "'Ave a good night?"
"A brilliant night thanks to you."
"My pleasure," he said. "The worst's over. It'll be plain sailin' from now on 'til we get to the Bay. If it's bad I'll watch out for you. Leave the 'ammock and blankets. I'll put 'em away, but you'd better 'ang on to them biscuits. They may come in 'andy." I hoped they wouldn't but I appreciated the thought.

In a surprisingly short time we were approaching Liverpool. It was still there, as the Liver Birds, perched majestically on their building, attested. All disembarkation procedures had been completed on board ship. I was one of the first off the ship and, grabbing a taxi, I headed for the station. A train was leaving for King's Cross in just fifteen minutes, so within half an hour of leaving the ship I was on my way home. I am bound to confess that over the preceding six months there were moments when I thought I would never see home again, but as I stood outside the church-like front door of our house and raised the knocker, I realised at last that I really was home.

It was tea time. As we were having tea, my mother said, "Have you heard the dreadful news about the terrorists?" I had been hearing dreadful news about terrorists for six months. It wouldn't be all that

93

dreadful; but it was. Terrorists in Malaya had assassinated the Hon John Ramsden, son and heir of Sir John. Little did I know that in a very short time I would be standing on the very staircase where John Ramsden had stood when he was murdered, or that my job would be to help find his murderers.

A week later I had a letter from my employers, the Crown Agents for the Colonies, regretting that they had to terminate my employment. As this constituted a breach of contract they would pay me compensation. In addition I would receive, in one lump sum, my salary for the period from when I left Haifa to the day I arrived in the UK plus 56 days' leave pay. A cheque was enclosed for £196. It was not a fortune but it was exactly £50 more than the entire amount I would have earned in two whole years had I been in the Army. Besides, the Government was actually paying me £196 for knocking eighteen months off my National Service!

In contrast to the way the civilian population in Palestine treated the Palestine Police Force, in the UK they were treated as heroes. On 20th July 1948, two months after the stand-down of the Force, there was an impressive ceremony at Buckingham Palace where His Majesty King George VI inspected a Stand-Down Detachment of the British section prior to taking the salute at a march past. His Majesty addressed the contingent with the following comments:

> *I am happy to have this opportunity of inspecting a detachment of the British section of the Palestine Police Force and presenting medals to members of the Force in recognition of their gallantry and meritorious service. I am glad to be able to mark the respect which we in this country feel for the manner in which you have done your duty in Palestine.*

> *The conflict between Arab and Jew made it necessary that there should be in the British section of the Palestine Police an impartial force to maintain law and order and to assist in carrying out the heavy task laid upon us by the Mandate. This has meant that the British police have had to face calumny and provocation as well as murderous attack. I have admired the forbearance and courage with which you have met the difficulties and dangers of service in Palestine. Many of your*

*20th July 1948. HM King George VI inspecting the Stand-Down
Detachment of the Palestine Police at Buckingham Palace*

*British Constable Lawrence McDonald of the Mounted Division of the
Palestine Police leading the Parade down the Mall*

comrades have given their lives and many others have been injured in that service; their sacrifice will not be forgotten.

Your task in the Palestine Police is now completed and you can look back on a job well done. You will soon be turning to employment elsewhere, and, wherever your future may lie, I wish you every success.

Following the address there was the March Past and a Final Parade down The Mall led by British Constable Lawrence McDonald of The Mounted Division riding Fairway, the horse frequently ridden by HM The Queen at The Trooping of the Colour.

Chapter 14
Israel

The storm that struck our ship in the Mediterranean, described in the previous chapter, was nothing compared with the violent storm that was to strike the tiny fledgling State of Israel. My colleagues and I had left Palestine at a historic moment. On 14th May 1948 I was safe at home listening on the radio to the accounts of the momentous events going on in the country I had just left.

Just six months earlier, on 29th November 1947 while I was still being trained at the Jenin Police Training School, the UN proposed that the land of Palestine be partitioned into Arab and Jewish states. The resolution was accepted by the Jews but rejected by the Arabs. The British mandate was due to end at midnight on 14th May 1948, when Palestine would be on its own. The Jews knew that their hour had come.

The odds against them were overwhelming. The Arab nations stood poised to drive them into the Mediterranean Sea should they take the step of declaring their nationhood. The highly respected American, General Marshall, had advised the Jews to delay the announcement until they had built up their military strength. In response to this, David Ben-Gurion, who became Israel's first Prime Minister, had said,

> *Here then was the counsel and military appreciation of our situation by a friend who was one of the world's outstanding soldiers. On the face of it, such advice could not be dismissed lightly. Yet it could not deflect us from our chosen course for General Marshall could not know what we knew, what we felt in our very bones: that this was our historic hour. If we did not live up to it, through fear or weakness of spirit, it might be generations or even centuries before our people were given another such opportunity.*

Egypt, Syria, Iraq, Transjordan and Lebanon would sweep into the nation from all fronts. The Arab armies were well equipped with the latest British and French fighters and bombers, tanks, heavy artillery, bombs and ammunition. The Jewish State was a sorry contrast. Israel at that time had no regular army but some semi-autonomous paramilitary groups; each having their own command and agenda. They had no tanks, no military planes, no artillery and only 10,000 rifles. But they had a will to survive, and they were resolved to proceed with their declaration.

About 3,600 Jewish and non-Jewish men and women, volunteers from nearly 30 different countries, battle-hardened and experienced from World War II, responded to a call for help. They came secretly into the country and were assigned to their units in the newly formed IDF, Israel Defence Forces. These volunteers were called the Machal.

Meanwhile Israel scoured the world for military equipment left over from World War II, and had it secretly shipped to their country. They bought desperately needed military planes and other equipment and much needed supplies from some willing sellers, and were charged highly for them. All these were ferried or flown into Israel in clandestine operations, during which many of the crews lost their lives or were captured by hostile governments in the process.

So it was that while Egyptian fighter-bombers flew overhead at 4:00 pm on 14th May 1948, in Tel Aviv at an Art Museum, in a simple, solemn, emotional ceremony that began with the singing of Hatikvah, the national anthem, the state of Israel was proclaimed by its first Prime Minister, David Ben-Gurion.

But there was little time for celebration in a city already blacked out to protect it from the Arab invasion everyone expected. The Israeli Defence Force fought courageously for about a month when, on 11th June, the United Nations called a truce. Fighting then broke out again on 9th July, but by January 1949 the Arabs had had enough and called for a cease-fire.

The Jews had managed to arm themselves and with the help and the expertise of the volunteers, many of them from their home Air Forces and Navies, they fought and won the war and the Arabs finally withdrew. The War of Independence was over. It was Israel's costliest but the most decisive of their wars. Thousands of Israeli and Arab soldiers died, and approximately 600,000 Palestinians fled their homes, thus creating a refugee problem that continues to trouble the region to this day.

Looking back now on that astonishing victory, won by poorly armed amateurs fighting professionally trained soldiers armed to the teeth, reminds me of another victory won by an equally weak Israel against a formidable foe. In the same way that Israel had just faced overwhelming odds, so, about 3,000 years before, the Israel of that time also faced overwhelming odds. It is one of my favourite Bible stories.

We find it in Judges Chapter 4. It's intriguing and exciting – a veritable Star Wars event. By way of introduction it is significant to say that in Chapter 11 of the New Testament Letter to the Hebrews, the writer gives a list of God's faith heroes. One of them is a man named Barak.

In Judges 4 we find that, instead of being a shining example to the rest of the nations, God's people are an utter disgrace. They are actually behaving worse than some of their benighted pagan neighbours. God sent warning after warning but all to no avail; so eventually, in order to bring them to their senses, He allowed His people to be invaded by the sadistic king of Canaan. King Jabin had a huge and terrifying army, which included a sort of panzer division of 900 iron chariots. For twenty years King Jabin made the lives of God's people a misery. Then in their anguish they called out to Him to rescue them, and God intervened. Enter Barak, or rather, enter Deborah.

In those days the Israelites appointed a wise and godly person to adjudicate over their affairs. They were called Judges. In Barak's day the Judge was a woman called Deborah who seemed to have a hotline straight to God. She was the first to appreciate that God was about to show up on behalf of His people. God gave to Deborah a message for our man Barak, so Deborah sent for him.

Now Barak lived in the north of Israel and Deborah was way down towards the south. There was a total curfew at night and execution awaited anyone caught away from their home area. Using goat paths, Barak makes the perilous journey south through the mountains to

Deborah. Good for Barak! So far so good; but that journey is hardly worth a portrait in the Gallery of Faith.

Deborah has a crazy message for Barak: "The God of Israel has commanded you, go, take 10,000 men and gather at Mount Tabor and I will draw to you Jabin's army with Sisera and his chariots and his multitudes." Barak knew all about Jabin's army, his chariots and his multitudes. He knew that it was a huge, highly trained army that was armed to the teeth. He also knew that the Israelites were completely untrained and had no weapons whatsoever. What Barak wanted to hear was that Jabin's army would be drawn *away* from him, not *to* him! So he bluntly told Deborah that if she was so convinced that they were going to have a great victory then she had better go with him. If she wouldn't go, he wasn't budging. So much for faith!

Deborah's not best-pleased with Barak, but she agrees to go with him, and Barak sets about gathering 10,000 men on the top of Mount Tabor. There, every morning, they have a grandstand view of General Sisera parading his 900 iron chariots and his multitudes of foot soldiers down on the plain of Jezreel. Morning after morning Barak would look down on the plain and there was the army just like the day before, and so it went on, day after day, until, suddenly one morning, without any warning, Deborah shouts to Barak: "Up Barak, *today* is the day that the Lord is delivering Sisera into your hand."

Now I'm bound to admit that if I had been in Barak's sandals, I would have wanted to know what made today different from any other day. Every day the sun had been shining from a cloudless sky and there it was today. The Jezreel plain was the same today as yesterday. The little River Kishon was little more than a dry bed, just the same as yesterday. So I would have asked: "So what's special about today?" But not Barak. To his eternal credit, Barak started off down the mountain, and his 10,000 farm workers, armed only with wooden staves, followed him to face a terrifying army on the plain of Jezreel.

Listen to how the Book of Judges tells us what happened next. I'm quoting from Judges Chapter 4: "The Lord confused Sisera, all his chariot drivers and all his army, and Barak pursued after the chariots and all the army of Sisera fell by the sword; not a man was left."

But the Israelites didn't have swords. So the scoffers have a field day saying, "Well, it's only a story. Of course it didn't really happen. It's obvious. An untrained bunch of farm workers couldn't possibly defeat so utterly such a large and highly trained army." But this isn't a fairy tale. It's the Word of God. So let's look a little closer.

Immediately after this stunning victory Deborah writes a song. In this song, which is in Chapter 5 of Judges, she mentions the trials the people were suffering, the curfews, travellers having to take the byways, the fact that they were defenceless with no weapons and so on. But the key to the victory is in verses 4 and 21. This is what she wrote: "The Earth trembled, and the very heavens dropped; yes the clouds dropped water... and the River Kishon became a torrent... an onrushing torrent." What does the cynic say to that?

"OK, so there was a thunderstorm. OK it was a *big* thunderstorm. Yes the little River Kishon would have overflowed its banks right in front of those heavy iron chariots. Yes, the chariots and horses would have got bogged down and the nimble hillbillies could have swarmed over the sides of the chariots, bopped the soldiers on the head with their staves, pinched their swords and finished them off. But that's not such a big deal. It's really quite straight forward once you know that there was a thunderstorm. Mind you, I'll admit that it was a lucky thing for Barak, that the thunderstorm arrived just in the nick of time."

But *was* it luck? If we look at Deborah's song again we find an intriguing little comment, and this is the delightful surprise. It's in verse 20: "From the heavens the stars fought. From their courses the stars fought against Sisera."... and in the very next verse... "The torrent Kishon swept the foes away..." Stars! One almost wonders if Obi Wan Canubi would appear at Barak's side! But stars! How could the stars have fought against Sisera? What have stars got to do with the little River Kishon becoming a torrent? Deborah probably didn't know much about stars, but God, who inspired her to write her song, does know about stars. He put them in the sky in the first place.

In certain climatic conditions there is a phenomenon described by meteorologists as electric storms. These are a kind of super thunderstorm. In Palestine I experienced one of these storms. Dense black clouds appeared, seemingly out of nowhere, and in a matter of ten minutes the whole of the sky from horizon to horizon was a heaving lurid purple mass out of which came lightning and colossal crashes of thunder. Then the rain came - like a solid wall of water.

What causes these crashing super jobs? Meteorologists now know why they happen. It is when the tail of a stream of cosmic dust stretching down from the sky reaches the earth. But where does cosmic dust come from? They are caused, would you believe, by stars! You are looking at a night sky and suddenly a star shoots across like a firework leaving a little streak of light. What we may have seen last night, happened millions and millions of years ago. It takes millions of light years for that little streak of light, travelling at 197,000 miles a second, to reach Earth.

Three thousand two hundred years ago, there was an electric storm over the Jezreel Plain, right under the hooves of Sisera's horses and the wheels of his iron chariots. Millions of light years earlier God looked down the corridors of time and exploded a star, just for Barak! During the millions of years that followed, God guided the cosmic dust from that exploded star. He brought it across millions of miles through the universe, eventually bringing it into the Earth's atmosphere and over Palestine bang on cue, for Barak!

At that precise moment God alerted Deborah and she, in obedience to God, sprang into action. "*Today* Barak. *Today's* the day," she cried and Barak, bless him, immediately set off, down Mount Tabor, to a victory planned by God millions of years earlier. No wonder God inspired the writer of the New Testament book of Hebrews to put Barak into the Hall of Faith Heroes in chapter eleven.

The hymn writer said: "God moves in a mysterious way, His wonders to perform." We have no problem believing that. Our problem is believing that, 'God moves in a mysterious way, His wonders to perform *for us*'! We don't think that we are important enough to God to justify Him performing a wonder on our behalf. We are, after all, just ordinary folk. Well, Barak was ordinary; refreshingly ordinary. But look what God did for him! To the very end of his life Barak would never again be the same. Whatever life or death situations faced Barak after that day on the plain of Jezreel, he would *know* that he could commit his life and his eternal soul into the hands of a loving God who was prepared to go to immense lengths on his behalf.

For Barak, God sacrificed a star. For *us* God sacrificed His Son. God has millions of stars. He only has one Son. *That's* how much God loves us, cares about us and wants to be involved in our everyday lives. That's the message of Barak and why it's one of my favourite Bible stories.

Part Three
A 'CLOAK AND DAGGER MERCHANT' (1948-53)

Chapter 15
Profitable Employment

Shortly after my return from Palestine, I received a very official looking letter notifying me that I had been granted 56 days' leave. I didn't appreciate the significance of this letter until later, for my contract of employment had been terminated and I'd had a cheque for £196 to prove it. When in Palestine I had the notion of writing a book about the conflict in that land. With so much money in the bank I reckoned on using some of the coming months to write the book. I was in for a rude awakening.

World War II had been over for three years, but the nation was experiencing severe austerity. Rationing was still in force; indeed in 1948 it was more severe than it had been in 1945. It was vital for the economy of the country that every able-bodied person was profitably employed. The problem for the Government was that, with the war over, the general public thought they deserved a rest. In reality the country was facing a crisis nearly as great as the 1940 threat of invasion. In those days every man, woman and child knew of the threat and responded in whatever way they could. In 1948 the crisis was not a military but an economic one, although few people were really aware of it.

Herbert Morrison, the Home Secretary, had the responsibility of tackling what he described as the National Economic Illiteracy. He tackled it with enormous vigour and colossal expenditure. By the end of 1947 four out every five bill-board posters in the country were Government sponsored and they pointed an accusing finger at the wilfully unemployed.

An Act of Parliament was passed, the essence of which was to empower the Government forcibly to draft into profitable employment those considered by the courts as currently unprofitably employed. The profitability of course related to the National Economy rather than profitability to the individual. Passed into law in 1947 it was called the Redeployment of Labour Act, quickly to become known as The Spivs and Drones Act.

It got this name during the debate in the House of Commons, during which a Labour member expressed his contempt for "... the idle rich, the 'Spivs' and 'Drones', who sit on boards as so-called directors, collecting fat fees but never doing a stroke of what an honest man would call work." Even Emmanuel Shinwell, the highly respected veteran Labour MP, declared during the debate that as far as he was concerned, there would be no seats on any board for which he was responsible, offered to 'Spivs' or 'Drones'. The Tories, at whom these comments were directed, responded furiously, but they were the minority party and helpless. To the delight of the Government all of this was given great prominence in the daily press.

The popular concept of Spiv underwent a dramatic change. No longer was it the padded shouldered, swift-looking man in the loud suit and black and white patent leather shoes. The cartoonists had a field day with prosperous directors shaking hands with shady-looking customers and calling each other brothers. The Government's propaganda was very successful and there arose a general feeling of resentment towards anyone who appeared to be unprofitably employed. It was into this category that I innocently stepped in May 1948. But first I had the immunity of 56 days' leave.

* * * * *

During my six months in Palestine I had maintained a tenuous link with Pat Bunn's school friend, Valerie Hignett. After one particularly traumatic patrol I arrived back at the station to find an air-letter from her assuring me that she prayed for my safety every day. I was grateful for her prayers.

I wrote to Valerie advising her of my return to England and awaiting my arrival was a letter inviting me to visit her at her parents' home in Birmingham during her half-term holiday. This was now just a week ahead. "If you are going to visit Valerie's parents," said my mother, "you had better get yourself some presentable clothes. The best place is Harrods in London. Go to Harrods. Put yourself in their hands and you will get the best service and the best clothes."

I planned to go to Harrods on my way to Birmingham. The morning of my departure my mother said, "I've just seen a wonderful sale being held by Gamages in London. They're selling excellent suits for just £3.12.6. Go there first." That is exactly what I did.

In the men's department there was a long queue of men interested in those 'excellent suits'. I joined the queue. I could see the suits hanging on a rack and one by one they were going to the folk in front of me. Eventually there were just three suits left with six people in front of me. I nearly turned away but noticed that four of the men were tall and large. The suits looked a bit too small for them so I stayed. There was only one that appealed to me; it was a brown herring bone tweed suit and it was exactly what I wanted.

The customer at the head of the queue took a blue suit leaving just two. The next four customers were indeed too big and one by one they left with nothing. Now only one man was ahead of me. Which of the two remaining suits would he take? He tried on the brown suit. It looked a treat on him but he shook his head and left without making a purchase at all, which pleased the man behind me! I now had a choice. I went for the brown and tried it on. It was a perfect fit. I paid my £3.12.6 and left feeling very pleased with myself.

Off I went to Harrods. This was a very different establishment. In the men's department I asked for the department manager who turned out to be a most helpful individual. "I want a very good all purpose suit," I said. He immediately took me to a rack of pin-striped grey suits, selected one my size and I tried it on. It was a perfect fit. It cost £24.15.4. I bought it without a second thought and only afterwards realised that I had just given more than a whole month's pay for a suit.

"Now I want a really good pair of black shoes," I said, so I was handed over to another department manager. The shoes I bought cost six guineas. That was a great deal of money in 1948 but they were extremely good shoes, leather lined and beautifully crafted. Sixty years later I still wear those shoes. They certainly don't owe me anything.

* * * * *

Sartorially equipped, I made my way to Birmingham. Valerie's father was a metallurgist, a chemist and a physicist. He was the director of the development laboratory of the Henry Wiggins manufacturing company. Valerie's mother, in partnership with another couple, had bought Berrow Court, a hotel in Birmingham. This was the home to which I made my way. It was very impressive.

I arrived at about six in the evening and just in time for a bath before dinner. I was still in the bath when Valerie knocked on the door to tell me everyone was going in for dinner and would I hurry up! I leapt out of the bath, hurriedly dried myself, scrambled into my new Gamages herring bone brown suit and dashed downstairs to the dining room.

After dinner Valerie, her mother and I were sitting in deck chairs on the extensive lawns while Valerie's father was mowing with a huge Atco lawn mower. I offered to help. Taking off my Gamages jacket I took over the job of mowing. The lawn was very large and the first swathe was away from the seated group. On turning to come back on the opposite cut I noticed that the family were in positive whoops of uncontrolled laughter. "What's the joke?" I asked.

In reply Valerie took me by the arm and led me to a large window which showed our reflection in the glass. "Turn round and look," she said. There stitched to the seat of my trousers was a huge red sign, 'SALE. Bargain on offer'.

At the end of the week Valerie returned to school. Any romantic notions I cherished would obviously have to go into storage. I returned to Gerrards Cross with the intention of getting down to writing my book. I had barely started when I had a letter from the Department of Employment wanting to know in what profitable employment I was proposing to be engaged. I replied that I was intending to write a book that would lift the flagging morale of the nation. I had a stern reply in which I was told that the nation was in crisis and the strenuous effort of everyone was needed to alleviate the situation. I replied that I would dutifully apply myself most strenuously to writing my book.

Back came, not a letter, but a summons to attend at court. I thought this was a splendid platform from which to air my views on a number of issues. I barely escaped arrest for Contempt of Court and was left in no doubt that if within two weeks I was unable to give evidence of profitable employment I would be drafted into the steel industry in Sheffield. I went home considerably subdued. I spent only a few moments considering the steel industry as a career and then decided to join the army. As I only had two weeks I immediately made enquiries about the nearest recruiting office. It was High Wycombe, home of the Royal Grammar School.

About a month before leaving Haifa I had gone on a shopping spree and bought myself an outfit, which at the time I thought was rather striking. The jacket was a light rust colour and had exaggeratedly padded shoulders. The trousers were a light fawn. To go with a chocolate coloured shirt I bought a chocolate and yellow striped bow tie. To complete this wonderful ensemble I bought a pair of tan shoes with very thick cream coloured crepe soles. My colleagues called the shoes 'brothel creepers'!

In a moment of mental aberration I donned this fancy dress and set out for the army recruiting office in High Wycombe. I had already gripped the door knob when I paused. What was I doing outside an army recruiting office? For the last six months I had been congratulating myself on having successfully avoided the army. In Palestine, while on joint operations with army personnel, I had heard first hand of the horrors of army training establishments and the indignities and hardships suffered by recruits. Active service would almost by definition be where the action was and I had seen first hand the brutal murder of young soldiers.

Now, here was I, about to volunteer for this kind of life. I had almost voluntarily entered the portals of the very establishment from which I had hitherto considered myself fortunate to have escaped. I took my hand off the door knob and turned away, looking blankly at my reflection in the plate glass window.

As I looked, in my imagination the reflected image seemed to change. My loud jacket and pale fawn trousers seemed to be replaced with dark blue overalls. My fancy shoes became heavy, steel-capped workers' boots and on my head was a yellow protection helmet. My clean scrubbed face and hands looked engrained with soot and metal dust. In my imagination I was in an iron foundry in Sheffield and I shuddered. At that moment the door to the recruiting office opened and a sergeant stepped out, closed the door behind him and was about to cross the street when he noticed me standing looking in at the window.

"Thinking of joining? There're worse jobs, believe me. I've been in the army for 22 years and I don't regret any of 'em. Good luck."
"Well I'm here," I thought, "I might as well see what they have to offer." But what did I want to do in the army? I definitely didn't want the infantry. I looked at the posters and cardboard cut-outs on display in the window. One was of a soldier in a chef's hat; I'd be washing the dishes. There was the Military Police directing traffic; in Palestine I had been a real policeman, surely I could do better than this.

I thought of my eight credits in the School Certificate, which gave me a first year's exemption in the matriculation. But I had to work for those. In the process I had learned something about the correlation between motivation and effective study. On the way to High Wycombe the bus had passed through Beaconsfield where, on the side of the road, I had seen a large sign: 'Wilton Park – Home of the Army Education Corps'. That's the one for me. I'll join the Army Education Corps, and with that I entered the Army Recruiting Office. It was a moment of destiny.

* * * * *

No pleasant looking sergeant was there to welcome me. Instead a fierce looking colonel sat behind a desk. A florid frowning countenance was hiding behind an enormous white walrus moustache, in contrast to which his grizzled hair was cut very short. He was in full service uniform complete with highly polished Sam Brown belt. On his chest he carried a row of medal ribbons. Round his neck was a black ribbon at the end of which was a monocle.

When I entered he looked up from his desk. As his gaze took in my bizarre raiment, his hand reached for his monocle which he screwed into place. As I came to a stop in front of him he stood up and through his monocle examined me closely from my uncut hair to my brothel creepers. Belatedly I realised that if I had wanted to impress the military I should have donned my sober grey pin-striped suit, my six guinea black shoes, a white shirt, my Old School Tie and had a hair

112

cut. I felt angry with myself for this lack of judgment, an anger exacerbated by this close and frankly discourteous inspection. Assuming a nonchalance I was far from feeling, I said, "I am interested in a career in the Education Corps."

"Have you got a degree, boy?" he asked.

I decided to ignore the 'boy'. "Not yet," I said.

"You need a good degree to get into the Education Corps. What's wrong with the infantry?" I could have told him why I thought the infantry was wrong for me but I didn't reply.

"The Household Cavalry, then?" and he added under his breath, "They'll soon sort you out."

Clearly I looked as if I needed 'sorting out' but I said, "I beg your pardon. What was that you said?"

He didn't reply but returned to his desk on which was a list of all the Army Regiments and Corps. Although the list was upside down for me, I could see, at the very bottom, 'Intelligence Corps'. "Put me down for the Intelligence Corps," I said.

"You see yourself as a 'Cloak and Dagger Merchant', do you?" he said, looking pointedly at my fancy footwear. Dismissively he added, "Intelligence Corps personnel are transferred from other regiments."

Fearing I might get hi-jacked into the cavalry I decided to stick to my guns. "Let me try for the Intelligence Corps and we'll see what happens."

Resuming his seat he said, "I can tell you now what will happen. You'll be refused."

"Well, I'd like to try, anyway."

He took a deep breath, "I'm not prepared to recommend you."

"Well, don't let it worry you. I didn't come in for your recommendation. I'll do it my way. Good day." Outside, my nonchalance deserted me and through gritted teeth I said to myself, "I'll show that puffed-up bag of wind!"

It didn't take long to find the address of the Headquarters of Army Western Command and I wrote to the Recruiting Officer. I couldn't send a photograph of me in my sober pin-striped grey suit but I did spend a lot of time on the letter. I said that I had been in the Palestine Police Force, was interested in counter intelligence and I would appreciate their evaluation on whether I might be of any use to the Intelligence Corps.

Almost by return I had a most courteous reply inviting me to an interview at Command HQ in Hounslow and sending me a voucher for a return train fare. This was more like it. On the appointed day I attended the most extraordinary employment interview imaginable. I was shown into a waiting room where there was a chap reading the newspaper. On seeing me he said, "Seen the paper this morning?" In fact, while waiting for the train, I did get a newspaper and had read the leading article with interest. The headline news was about a republican body that had been deeply critical of the Royal Family. I had a very high regard for both King George VI and Queen Elizabeth. In next to no time we were deep into a discussion about the advantages of a monarchy and the weaknesses of a Republican State.

After a while the man left the room and a young woman came in carrying a crying toddler. After a couple of minutes she said she didn't know what to do because she had to make an urgent telephone call but couldn't because of the child. Not knowing whether it was a boy or girl, I said, "Leave it with me."

"Oh thank you. By the way, he's a boy," and she promptly thrust the yelling infant into my arms. I put him on the floor, got down on my hands and knees and, placing coins on the floor in front of him, started to use them like tiddly-wink counters. When the mother came back into the room the little boy was crowing and laughing away quite happily. "Thank you very much. That was really kind of you, especially as you are here for an interview yourself," and out she went.

"How did she know that?" I thought.

A very superior looking chap then came into the room. Abruptly he asked where he could find 'The Colonel.' When I entered the building I had noticed an enquiry desk in the foyer. I was about to suggest he should enquire there, when it occurred to me to go myself and at the same time find out when I was due for my interview. "You sit down while I find out for you," I said.
He looked at me narrowly but didn't say anything other than, "Thank you, that's very civil of you." Out I went.

"Can you tell me where the colonel's office is?" I asked the ATS sergeant at the desk.

She gave a quick smile and then said very rapidly, "First corridor on the right, second corridor on the left, up the stairs in front of you then first right and then second left. The colonel's office is the third door on the right." I was about to ask her to repeat it and then thought better of it.

"Thank you," I replied. Back in the room I said, "I've found out where the colonel's office is but you'd do best to ask at the desk."

"Where is it?" he said.

"Well, if I've got it right, it's down the corridor immediately opposite this room, then take the second corridor on the left. Go up the stairs in front of you then take the first right and then the second left. The colonel's office is the third door on the right."

"He hides himself away very effectively doesn't he?" he said.

"Wouldn't you if you were a colonel?" I said, laughing. "I would."

"Humph," he said and off he went.

I was about to go back to the ATS sergeant, having forgotten to ask about my interview, when a captain in the Intelligence Corps came in.

"Mr Smith, can I check on some of the details you gave us?"

"I thought you'd forgotten me," I said.

"Good heavens, no. Now, you did well at school I see. Eight credits – very good. Studying comes easily then?" I kept quiet. I didn't think this was the moment for either frankness or confessions!

"Palestine Police Force. Mm, well Mr Smith, I'm pleased to tell you that you have done well in your interviews."

"My interviews? I think you're mixing me up with another candidate. I haven't had an interview."

"Ah but you have. All those people you've been meeting this morning have been your interviewers, including my wife with my small son. By the way, how did you manage to stop him crying?" He didn't wait for an answer but said, "Come and meet the boss."

Away we went, down the corridor immediately opposite, along the second corridor on the left, up the stairs in front of us, then first right and second left to the third door on the right! The captain went straight in without knocking and I followed. Inside it was very plush. Sitting in one of the three easy chairs was the very superior person who wanted to find 'The Colonel'. He came forward with a smile, shook my hand and said, "I hope you decide to join us. We think you'll do very well."

The spectre of Sheffield's steel industry was rapidly fading. "From what I've seen I think I've already decided to join you," I said. "What happens next?"

"Well that's a good question. To be honest, I'm not quite sure. Normally new entrants go to an infantry regiment for basic drill and weapon training but as you were in the Palestine Police I'm going to recommend you be excused that painful experience and go straight to The School of Military Intelligence in Sussex. If you are certain about joining us, we can go through all the formalities here and give you a travel warrant and a start date. What do you say?"

"Splendid! Let's do that."

Two hours later I had completed half a dozen forms, had a medical examination, sworn loyalty to the King and was on my way home. I had a new job. Half way home I realised that I had no idea how much I would be paid. I hadn't bothered to ask and they hadn't told me. It didn't seem to matter, either to my interviewers or to me. I laughed out loud. What with trading at school and compensation from the Crown Agents, the King's Shilling wasn't an issue. I was virtually financially independent. It was a good feeling. Then I had a delicious thought: "Eat your heart out, Colonel Blimp!"

Chapter 16
The School of Military Intelligence

Tucked away just outside the delightful little Sussex village of Maresfield, the School of Military Intelligence was to be my home for the coming months. They were months of challenge and enormous fun. Maresfield is located about twenty miles north of Brighton and ten miles East of Haywards Heath. I was to become very well acquainted with the whole area.

On entering the gates of the School, the first person I met was the Commandant. Tall and handsome, he looked a highly intelligent individual, which was just as well for otherwise he might have been taken for a veritable scarecrow. He was in 'uniform', or what passed as his uniform, for the only article of clothing that was recognisably military was his battledress blouse. He wore an Australian bush hat, baggy brown corduroy trousers and brown suede shoes. However, on his battledress he had two rows of medal ribbons. I was to discover that he was greatly liked and hugely respected by everyone at the School.

When I arrived he was chatting to a couple of young soldiers in overalls, something that I was hardly ever out of in the months ahead. He nodded to them. They saluted smartly and went off. "Well, sir, what can we do for you?" was his greeting.
"I'm to be one of your students, sir," I said.
"Good. What's your name?"
"Smith, sir. John Smith."
"Good name for this outfit, eh? Land you in trouble in some quarters I fear. Ah yes! Palestine Police Force weren't you? They're expecting you up at the office, but check in here at the Guard Room first." Then he lowered his voice and added, "Take care how you speak to the wee

mon. He's our Provost. He's a sergeant but you call him 'Provo' and stand to attention. He'll like that."

The Guard Room was a hut with a small table in one corner. Sitting at the table was 'the wee mon'. He was dressed in a most extraordinary uniform. I later discovered he was from a Scottish Highland Regiment noted for its strict discipline. He wore a battledress blouse below which was a colourful kilt. In one of his thick knitted stockings there was thrust a sinister looking dagger. On his head he had a khaki 'tam-o'-shanter', attached to which was a bright red feather.

Smartly I marched into the Guard Room, halted and remained stiffly to attention. "New recruit reporting for duty, Provo. My name is Smith, Smith J.B." I didn't want to land myself in trouble from this quarter.
"Ye need no stand t'attention fa mee, laddie. A'm noo an officer."
"Sorry, I'm new to the army."
"Have ye noo bin to a Trrainin Camp?"
"I'm afraid not."
"An hoo does that come aboot?"
"I've come straight from the Palestine Police Force." He thawed visibly.
"An wherrre aboots in Palestine wererrr ye?"
"Haifa."
"Ah was in Jerrrusalem and thaat was bad enough. But Haifa! Ye must have a charrrrmed life laddie. Compared with that, this is a kinder garrrten. It's a gude place reet enough. Therrre all a nice lot o' laddies here. Aye. I volunteered for this job an' a'm tellin' ye, they'll no get me back in the Regiment."
"Why is that?"
"'Cos it's murrrder, thas' why. For the noo get yer sen up t' office. It's strreet ahead on the rrreet. See ye."

I collected various papers, instructions and directions from the office and then, pulling a little trolley, I went from one place to another collecting my bedding, clothing and a bewildering array of equipment. The Quartermaster's Department spent a great deal of time and effort finding clothes that fitted well. I was very impressed. I learned later that they didn't have to do it very often because most of the students came from other army units and were already fully equipped.

My last port of call was a barrack room containing sixteen beds, all but one neatly made up. There was only one occupant at the time and as soon as I entered with my trolley, he came over, introduced himself as Geoff Coney and promptly started to make up my bed for me. He was a qualified lawyer from the Isle of Man and was doing his National Service. He had arrived a week earlier from an infantry training centre. "What was it like?" I asked.

"Murder! In comparison, this is Paradise." He told me that I was the last of the intake to arrive at the School.

In twos and threes others came in and introduced themselves. "What infantry camp were you at?" one asked.

"I wasn't at a camp at all. I've come from the Palestine Police."

Immediately there was a clamour of voices. "Palestine Police, that's great! We've already got two of you guys in here, I'll go and find them." With that the speaker rushed off, returning a little later with two huge companions.

Each came up and shook my hand. "Welcome copper!" one said while the other smilingly looked on. Later I learned that both of them had been on five year contracts. Unfortunately, the withdrawal of the mandate coincided with the end of their service commitment so they didn't receive any compensation. They reckoned still being alive was compensation enough. So now we were three. My two colleagues had already created a very good impression at the School and, without my doing anything, it spread like a mantle over me as well.

* * * * *

The emphasis of my intake was training for work in Europe but particularly focussing on Berlin. Of course the Berlin Wall had not been built; that went up in 1961. After the war, the city of Berlin had been divided into four sectors: American, British, French and Soviet sectors. While there was no wall separating the Russians from the rest there was a great deal of barbed wire, nearly 100 miles of it in fact. Despite intensive Russian manning of their border there was a significant amount of migration from the Russian sector and an understandable keenness on the part of the others to gain information from these escapees. But the traffic was not entirely one way and it was this counter infiltration that presented opportunities for 'useful observation'. At the School of Military Intelligence every imaginable

119

situation was being simulated and acted out, even to being captured and subjected to Third Degree Questioning.

As a nineteen year old I found it all great fun, even though very physical at times. On one occasion I was talking with a suspected KGB agent. A trestle table was between us. Unexpectedly he pulled out a pistol! I had been sitting with my right ankle resting on my left knee. As I put my hands up, I lashed out at the table with my right foot, sending the table crashing into the agent's midriff knocking him backwards. As he went back his chair toppled over and he hit his head with a sickening thud against a large iron heating stove. I was about to make my escape when it occurred to me that he was lying very still! Expecting a trap, I approached warily but, just like Fred at Riddlesworth, he was out cold. I called to an Exercise Referee who took one look at my adversary and rushed out to call for the ambulance. We had our own ambulance at the School and, indeed, we had our own hospital, so the KGB agent was quickly receiving expert attention.

Another exciting part of our training was learning how to handle a motorcycle in rough terrain. There was a large area of heath land near the School and after a number of basic lessons we were taught how to go cross-country with maximum speed and minimum injury. At the best of times it was scary but when we came to be tested there had been a heavy frost and the roads, paths and tracks were treacherous. While our instructor was delighted we were horrified. Not one of us escaped a crash and although we were extensively bruised no bones had been broken. At the end of the day we returned to the School feeling that we had all failed miserably, a view encouraged by the instructor who had been scathing. At breakfast the next day one member came running up with the news that not only had we all passed but we had each passed "despite severe adverse conditions."

* * * * *

Our training was to end with a passing out parade which was now only a few days away. Unfortunately we had not excelled at drill and the instructor responsible put us on a course of intensive training. Observing an unusually disastrous drill period the colonel approached and said, "I hope you do better on the day. We've got a colonel from a Highland Regiment taking the salute."

The passing out parade was an unmitigated catastrophe. It began with our right marker going sick in the night. Despite our pleas to delay his admittance until the afternoon, he was bundled off to hospital by the MO. The right marker is key to a successful parade. Everything centres on him. Chosen because he was tall, our man had been specially coached for the role. Now he was in hospital! The next tallest man in the group was an extremely handsome young man whose father, before the war, was a Czechoslovakian prince and a member of that country's diplomatic service. In the diminishing minutes available he was given a crash course in right marking but we could all see that problems were looming ahead.

By ten o'clock a little platform of upturned empty wine boxes had been constructed on the car park which was to pass muster as our parade ground. The dais was just big enough for one man. Our band was a wind-up gramophone with a large trumpet attached, in much the same fashion as is seen on His Master's Voice records. From the early hours we had been polishing buttons and boots and pressing our uniforms.

Our colonel had already given us the once over and appeared content with our appearance. He himself looked exceedingly smart in his service uniform. His great height of six feet four made him positively awesome. It was not long before a staff car approached. As the door opened and the occupant got out there was an audible gasp from every one of us, quickly silenced by a warning cough from the captain leading our parade. Our visitor was a diminutive five feet tall but it was his uniform that startled us. He was wearing a kilt, a cut-away dress jacket, stockings complete with dirk and Boy Scout like red tabs to the garters. In his lap was an enormous sporran dangling from which were numerous little animal tails. On his head was a peculiar looking blue bonnet flying a bright red hackle.

As this apparition crossed our car park we went through the movements of a General Salute and then the Open Order ready for our inspection. It all went miraculously well and our quaint looking visitor was conducted by our solemn colonel past the rows of men, on whose faces their lurked unmistakable amusement. Our colonel tried to look fierce but it didn't come naturally to him, unlike his companion whose face, as he progressed down the ranks, grew grimmer with every step. The inspection over, the two went over to the little pile of boxes which had been covered with a red blanket and the VIP climbed up. It didn't look at all safe! Even when standing on the boxes he only came up to our colonel's shoulders... and he was standing on the ground!

We were brought back to marching order.

"Parade. Leeeeft TURN."
"ONE, two three, ONE", we said under our breath. First class. Who needs to go to the infantry to learn drill?
"PARADE, BY THE LEFT... QUICK MARCH." This order was the signal for the man operating the gramophone to lower the needle on to the record. The quick march tune of the Intelligence Corps is The Rose and Laurel, but the previous day the man in charge of the music had broken the only record he had, so he had substituted 'Colonel Bogey', the tune to which soldiers sing some rather ribald words! He had been told to listen for the order "Quick March" and place the needle where the music started instantly. He heard the order but the sound delay meant we were half a beat out of step with the music which, coming from behind the garages, sounded muffled. Barely in step, we moved off the car park.

Worse was to follow. Our route took us behind the garages back onto the car park and thus up to the platform of empty wine boxes for the March Past. By the time we rounded the garages we had got ourselves together and were merrily bowling along perfectly in step with Colonel Bogey. "Da da, te da da da da da; da da, te, da da da da da," we were humming happily to ourselves.

At this point I must pause to explain a thing or two about a March Past where the participants have rifles. It is not a thing to be undertaken by the inexperienced. This is especially the case when it comes to the part to be played by the right marker. In our case, it will be remembered, our stand-in right marker had no experience whatsoever. The officer leading the parade gives the order, "Eyes Right." He smartly turns his head to the right and gives a salute.

122

Everybody else *except* the right marker, also turns his head smartly to the right and at the same time brings his right hand across to slap the butt of his rifle. The parade then marches past the officer taking the salute. On the command "Eyes Front," everyone jerks his head to the front, except, of course, the right marker, who hadn't turned his head in the first place but kept looking straight ahead. At the same time the officer smartly drops his saluting arm, which resumes the swing while behind him each soldier, with equal smartness, brings his right hand back from his rifle and continues marching.

So, that is how a March Past should be done. It was a great pity that our new right marker didn't know how it should be done! We approached the dais, all perfectly in step and the march going well.

"PARADE... EEEEEEYES RIGHT." I was on the very last row of three and I could see everything that happened. The officer duly turned his head and saluted. Everyone else, INCLUDING the right marker, turned his head and banged his rifle butt. The right marker should not have turned his head nor should he have struck his rifle butt; instead he should have continued swinging his right arm as before. Belatedly, he remembered this but, seeing the captain in front of him salute, he did the same! The man immediately behind, seeing him salute must have thought, 'Oh my! I should have saluted,' so he transferred his hand from the rifle butt to a salute. This triggered an amazing mixture of rifle butt salutes, ordinary salutes and then back to butt salutes. From the rear it looked as if we were giving our visiting colonel a friendly wave. We, in the last two rows, who'd had a grandstand view of this entertainment, could contain our mirth no longer and marched past the dais with broad grins on our faces.

It was obvious that our colonel himself was hard pressed to keep a straight face. The visiting colonel's face was a picture. Purple with rage, he started jumping up and down on his little dais. Not constructed for this kind of treatment it collapsed under him! Meanwhile our captain, blissfully unaware of the chaos behind him, gave the "Eyes Front." In the moment before switching my fascinated gaze from our visiting colonel to the front, I saw him try to break his cane across his knee. He was completely beside himself.

As we disappeared behind the garage, the record ran out of music. This was the last straw and, while the captain marched on alone we simply fell about in helpless laughter. Our merriment was short lived, for round the corner strutted our VIP, his face like thunder. In a high pitched voice and trembling with rage, he vowed that if it was the last thing he did he would teach "... you intellectual imbeciles how to DRILL." This he promptly set about attempting to do! With a drill sergeant's voice and language to match, he put us through a quarter of an hour's drill. It was a complete pantomime but after fifteen minutes we'd had enough. The word went round, "When we are heading for the garages, completely ignore the orders."

"Squad, about turn," shouted the colonel. He had reduced our status from a parade to that of a mere 'squad'! To a man we all marched on. "ABOUT TURN," he screamed, but it was too late and we were all milling around up against the garage doors in splendid confusion! Lining us all up again, the little colonel tried to remonstrate. Although Prince Rudolf could speak half a dozen European languages his English was significantly less than perfect!

Completely undaunted, he broke ranks, walked up to the colonel and with an exaggerated foreign accent said, "Excuse pliz. I not understood vot it vos you say. Explain pliz." Talking on parade is definitely not allowed, leaving ranks to do so is unpardonable. With an oath, our VIP stalked off the car park, got into his car and was driven off. He was supposed to have had lunch with the colonel but he left without saying a word.

Seeing him leave, our colonel, who hadn't moved from his position beside the collapsed dais, now came slowly up to us. "You lot are a perfect disgrace!" he said. There was a very long silence, then: "However, I'm bound to admit that, never in all my life, have I had a more entertaining morning. Parade, dismiss."

Our postings were to be listed the next day but in the afternoon I was summoned to the colonel's office. "Well," I thought, "I wasn't the ringleader of that fiasco this morning. Why me?" But the meeting was nothing to do with the parade. The colonel didn't mention it.

"Ah, Smith, I know you have worked hard and I've got good reports of you, but I'm afraid I have some disappointing news for you. You're not to go to Europe after all."

'Please, not a Scottish Highland Regiment,' I prayed.

"You're wanted in Malaya. The terrorist situation is worsening and your experience in Palestine will be invaluable to our people out there where they are working in conjunction with the local police. It will be a four-and-a-half year tour of duty so I am recommending that you have an extra two weeks' leave on top of your two weeks' graduation leave." He stood up, shook my hand and said, "Good luck. Don't do anything foolish out there, like getting yourself killed!"

"I'll do my best, sir, and... thank you. You've taught me a great deal." I saluted and left.

I hadn't told anyone that I knew about my posting and the next day I went with the others to see the Orders for the Day posted next to the Adjutant's office. Two of the group were going to MI5. Prince Rudolf had a star beside his name. We learned later that he was going to MI6, the Secret Intelligence Service. I was posted to Operational Services, Taiping, Malaya. All the rest were posted to Europe. I was not in the least disappointed about not going to Europe. My colleagues were going to be cold in Germany and colder still if any of them had the misfortune to end up in Siberia! I had liked the summer heat in Palestine and would be glad to leave the British winter behind. On the day of embarkation the temperature had dropped to five degrees below freezing. I had read that the average temperature in Malaya is about 80°F. I was very glad to be on my way. Behind the scenes Threads of Destiny were being woven.

Chapter 17
The Far East

Certainly I was glad to be on my way, but what was this country like in which I would be spending the next four-and-a-half years? I had discovered some things about the country but not a lot. As far as my work was likely to be concerned there appeared to be a formidable number of languages spoken including several Chinese dialects. There was a significant number of Indians in the population but most of them spoke Tamil, apparently a very difficult language to learn. A redeeming feature was that English was widely spoken.

I was looking forward to the warm climate; I petrify when it gets cold. Except in the highlands, Malaya was hot and humid throughout the year. Apparently there were two monsoons a year, the northeast monsoon between November and March and the southwest monsoon from May to September. I was to discover that during the monsoon season rain was totally predictable and very heavy. March and October were the only non-monsoon months in the year.

The early history of Malaya is obscure. At the end of the 18th and beginning of the 19th Century the British, for trade and political reasons, moved into the area and took control, first of Penang, then Singapore and Malacca. To work the tin mines they imported Chinese and Indian labourers who then became involved in territorial disputes with the native Malays. The British, therefore, worked indirectly through the hereditary Malay rulers, the sultans, so that in the ensuing peace and order their trading interests would be protected.

Restoring peace and order was still on the agenda of the British in 1949 which was why I, together with many hundreds of other soldiers, was on the high seas. We had only been at sea a couple of days when I was asked to report to the Bursar's office. There I was introduced by a major to an Intelligence Corps sergeant and two sergeants from the Education Corps. Confirming my low opinion of Colonel Blimp, I discovered that neither of the Education Corps fellows had degrees.

We were asked to lay on an education programme for the entire voyage. I offered to organise a series of quizzes. In the event they proved very popular. On Quiz Days there was a general hush as the answers to the previous quiz were read out followed by the new questions. Shortly after the quizzes had started I met one of the ship's officers at a gangway. "You the chap doing the ship's quizzes? They're very good. Even the captain's doing them."

After the second quiz an immaculately dressed soldier came up to me saying, "Do you want any help with the quiz programme?" His name was Bill Deane, a trooper in a hussar regiment.

"Thank you. It would be greatly appreciated." He was an encyclopaedia of knowledge and had a delightful sense of humour. One of his questions was: 'Who wrote Grey's Elegy?' We heard of some amazing answers to that one, including Winston Churchill and William Shakespeare!

On the first Sunday morning Bill appeared at my cabin with, "John! Church!"

"Church? Why?"

"It's Sunday dear boy. It's Sunday. Come on bustle about. It'll do you good." So off we went to the church service held in the ship's canteen. As soon as we found a seat Bill disappeared. "Well he's got a cheek, dragging me off to church while he goes gallivanting!"

The service started but there was no sign of Bill, but as getting out meant pushing past a number of worshippers, I stayed where I was. The service was taken by the chaplain; the ship's captain read one of the lessons and a brigadier, the Senior British Officer, read the other. The preacher was the chaplain. I didn't think the sermon was very good. There then followed communion. To my complete astonishment when a white robed figure came to me with a plate full of wafers I found myself looking into the face of Bill Deane! I was so surprised that I forgot to eat the wafer and was sharply reminded to do so by the chaplain who was standing waiting to serve the wine.

128

After the service I caught up with Bill. "How come you were helping the chaplain?"

"Oh! I'm often asked to do that sort of thing!" I didn't think that was a very adequate answer but I let it go. Thereafter Bill saw to it that I went to church every Sunday. He was always enthusiastic about the sermons. To me they seemed completely irrelevant to our situation. Of those on board that ship some might not be making the return journey. I genuinely thought that I could have preached a more meaningful sermon!

One Sunday Bill said, "Cracking sermon, wasn't it?"

"No, it wasn't."

"Wasn't?"

"No."

"Why not?"

I had to stop and think. Why did I think it wasn't a good sermon? "Well," I said, "a good sermon shouldn't leave me thinking, 'That was a cracking good sermon'; rather it should leave me asking: 'How can I be saved?' "

Bill gave me a very peculiar stare. "Saved?"

"Isn't that what it's all supposed to be about?" He changed the subject.

Gradually the ports slipped by: Gibraltar, Malta, Port Said, Aden. It was now much warmer and we had changed into tropical kit. Aden was followed by the long haul to Colombo in Ceylon as it was then called. It was in Colombo that I had my first ride in a rickshaw. Tourists pay thousands of pounds to do what we were doing and see what we were seeing. In the Indian Ocean we saw a huge pod of whales and every day the flying fish were a fascinating sight but we were getting a little sick of the ship by the time we arrived at Singapore.

At the dockside there were a number of people with small cardboard placards announcing who they were meeting. Eventually I found my name on a list with half a dozen others. When we were all together we piled into an open truck and set off for the railway station. From where we were dropped it was quite a walk to the station but first we had to go to an armoury.

"Name?"

"Smith. Smith J.B."

"Intelligence Corps?"

"Yes."

"Here y'are mate," he said, giving me a heavy Lee Enfield rifle. "There's only five rounds in the mag so use 'em sparingly." I had no pressing desire to use them at all, but I said nothing and turned to go. "Hang on, mate. You'll need a tin hat."

I was getting a trifle overloaded. I had a heavy kit bag, a suitcase, a rifle and a tin hat. "Where can I find a porter?" I asked him.

He turned to his fellow armourers saying, "Little Lord Fauntleroy 'ere wants a porter! Anybody seen a porter." There was a short burst of laughter. Then to me, "Listen mate, don't give nuffin to nobody, see. 'Specially that rifle. Keep an eye on everyfin. Stuff walks around 'ere."

With a sigh of resignation I picked up all my belongings and trudged to the station. Happily the train was waiting and, having stowed away all my gear, I sat facing it to make sure none of it walked.

After a few minutes a sergeant came down the corridor stopping at each compartment. "On your own mate?"

"Yes Sergeant."

"Listen, if the train is attacked, stay on the train. If you get left behind you'll have had it."

"Thanks."

Goodness me. Out of the frying pan into the fire! I lifted my rifle and tin hat down from the luggage rack where I had stowed them with all my gear. I took out the five rounds and carefully put them back into the magazine, each rim in front of the one beneath. With only five shots I couldn't afford any stoppages. I was still the only one in the compartment and thought I would have welcomed some company, of the right sort.

The train was due to leave at midday and, surprisingly, on the stroke of twelve, the whistle went and the train slowly moved out of the station. Singapore is an island and soon we were crossing the causeway linking the island to the mainland of Malaya. We were making very good time when suddenly we came to an abrupt halt. There was a great deal of shouting and about 30 swarthy-skinned soldiers dashed past my compartment heading for the front of the train. As well as a rifle, each had a wicked- looking curved knife in his belt. They were Ghurkhas. Thank goodness for that, I thought.

I put down the window next to me and sat with my loaded rifle on my knee and my tin hat wobbling uncomfortably on my head. After a while I took it off. About half an hour later all the Ghurkhas returned laughing and joking. I stopped an officer, "What was the problem?" "Cows on the line." In five minutes we moved off again.

Gradually the train made its way up the peninsular, through Kluang and on to the capital, Kuala Lumpur. It was a through train and its stay in KL was brief. We were soon off again, this time on the long haul to Ipoh and then Taiping.

Chapter 18
Taiping

As the train pulled into Taiping station I saw a tall sergeant holding up a board: 'John Smith'. It was reassuring to see that I was expected. We drove in a jeep through the little town of Taiping and turned into a most salubrious area of large colonial-type houses and bungalows. The road was called Swettenham Road. At number 12 we turned into a long sweeping drive and stopped under an enormous porch. A most spacious bungalow was at the top of a number of long steps, down which

12 Swettenham Road, Taiping

three sergeants came to help with my gear. This was a vast improvement on Singapore station.

The Taiping garrison was the main service centre for most of the military operations in the north of Malaya. Here a military hospital received the many soldiers wounded in the constant battle against the communist terrorists. A Brigadier was the officer in charge of the garrison and he lived in a bungalow right next to us at number 10 Swettenham Road. Just up the road on the same side as us lived Justice Garton, the local judge. In an entirely acceptable way, I was to come to know Justice Garton very well indeed; in fact, he came to my 21st birthday party. This was very much to the annoyance of my new boss who was a captain from the same highland regiment as that ridiculous visiting colonel. Extraordinarily, the sergeant major responsible for discipline at 12 Swettenham Road was also from that very same regiment. It seemed that the Provost at Maresfield wasn't the only one getting away from it.

I hadn't been in the place above five minutes before a sergeant took me on one side and said, "You're from the Palestine Police aren't you?"

"Yes Sergeant."

"Forget the sergeant stuff with me. Just listen. You haven't been to an infantry barracks for basic training, have you?"

"No, I haven't. When I joined the colonel..."

"Yes. I know. It's all in your records, here. It looks as if you did very well at Maresfield. Well done, but the captain here and the sergeant major have concluded that your training has been skimped. They intend to make your life hell here. Normally you'd be promoted to acting sergeant straight away, like us, but they intend keeping you as a private until they think you know what it is to be a proper soldier. Don't let them get you down and you'll come through all right."

"However bad it is," I thought, "it can't be worse than the steel industry."

* * * * *

At the end of my first day I had to prepare for our mess dinner in honour of my arrival. It was to be a memorable one. The captain didn't mess with us, or, to be more explicit, perhaps I should say he didn't have his meals with us! According to strict army protocol, privates should not mess with senior NCOs and Warrant Officers. Under normal circumstances every new arrival to the bungalow was immediately promoted to sergeant. The fact that I was the only exception lends significance to the dilemma I encountered during that first dinner.

An extraordinary amount of liquor of all kinds was consumed before the meal. To all events by the time we sat down to dinner I believe I was the only one who was reasonably sober. I discovered we had a large staff attending to our needs. One of these was a delightful Chinese cook. I happened to meet him earlier and had quite a chat with him and he left me with the impression that he was both dignified and competent. Gastronomically at least, we were in good hands.

Halfway through the meal, my friend who earlier had taken me on one side with sundry warnings, declared in a loud voice, "This food is terrible." This was surprising as I had thought it was delicious.

"Get the cook," was the peremptory command to one of the waiters. The cook was duly brought in, looking remarkably relaxed.

"This food is dreadful," said the sergeant.

"Velly solly, sir," was the cheerful response.

"Sorry! Sorry is not good enough. What should we do with him?"

"Hang him," was a reply.

"Good idea. Yes. We'll hang the cook." Immediately one of the sergeants went out and came back with a length of rope in which he expertly tied a noose. The other end of the rope was thrown over a beam immediately over the table and a chair put on the table. Up to then I had thought all this was in jest, but suddenly I realised they could all be drunk as wheelbarrows.

"On the chair, cook. For serving below standard food we sentence you to death. Do you have anything to say in mitigation?" As he climbed onto the chair the cook shook his head. He looked remarkably sanguine for someone who was about to be hanged. "All in agreement put up their hands." I kept mine down.

"Our newest member doesn't agree with the sentence," said the sergeant major.

"The food is delicious," I said. "As the dinner is in my honour, may I plea for clemency?"

"There's no pardon for this crime," said the sergeant. "Cook, by a majority verdict you are sentenced to death!" The rope was put round the cook's neck and was pulled taut and secured.

"He won't have to fall far for it to break his neck," I thought. I nearly called out, "Take care," but refrained.

"On the count of three, pull the chair from under him. One. Two. *Three*," and, to my horror, the chair was pulled away. I really didn't think they would do it, but in case they did I was ready. In a flash I was out of my chair and on to the table. Glasses, bottles, plates and food flew in all directions! Rushing to the cook I threw my arms round him and lifted him up. He was very little. Taking the noose from round his neck I helped him off the table.

"Cook," I said, "this group will thank me tomorrow when you provide another meal as good as the one you have prepared in my honour. I want to thank you very much for your kindness. Now my friend, if I were you I'd go while the going is good." With that I walked with him to the door and then resumed my place at the table and, as nonchalantly as possible, continued my meal which happily had not ended up on the floor. There was a short pause and then a round of applause. I looked up questioningly.

"Well done!" said the sergeant. "Don't worry about the cook. He's used to it. We do this with every new arrival! I think we can say you have passed the test with flying colours." Everybody clapped again, including the sergeant major. Thus ended my first day in Malaya.

In fact the whole event was less dramatic than it appeared. The cook was never in danger for the rope hadn't tightened. Unnoticed by me, on the count of "*Three*" he had grasped the rope above his head and taken the strain out of the fall.

* * * * *

The next day I was put in the charge of a delightful Intelligence Corps sergeant who was doing his National Service. He had a thorough grasp of the political scenario in Malaya and attempted to explain it to me. For those who find these things interesting, I will comment on the situation, not only because it is relevant to why I was in Malaya in 1949, but because it has a contemporary application to the quagmire in which the British found themselves in Iraq in 2007. When I arrived in Malaya in 1949, terrorist attacks were as few as 100 a month, but the number of attacks steadily increased and by mid-1950 the attacks were averaging 400 a month.

This is when, had the Brits operated in our current media and political environment, columnists would have witheringly declared that all was lost, and calls from across the political spectrum would have gone up for us to quit. With a patience born of fighting many small wars in dusty parts of the world, the British simply set about fixing what they had done wrong.

Most fundamentally, they realised that counter-insurgency depends on winning a political battle for hearts and minds, a phrase incidentally that originated in the Malayan fight against terrorism. Military operations were conducted on a smaller scale; the jungle dwelling population was secured from guerrilla influence; a Malayan army was built, with Chinese involvement; elections were organised and independence promised. Slowly, the air went out of the insurgency, but it took a further seven years, the worst of which were from 1949 to 1953, precisely the time that I was there.

But it might be helpful to go back a few years to understand what The Emergency was all about. The basic problem lay in European domination. This led to the most fateful event in Malay history, the Anglo-Dutch treaty of 1824. This treaty drew a frontier between British Malaya and the Netherlands East Indies, which became Indonesia. This arbitrary division of the Malay world has proved permanent.

European domination also led to the mass immigration of Chinese and Indian workers to meet the needs of the colonial economy created by the British in the Malay Peninsula and North Borneo. The Chinese and Indians posed a profound threat to the Malays, dominating economic life and the professions, and at one time threatening to make the Malays a minority in their own country.

British power in East Asia was fatally wounded by the Japanese occupation of the region in 1942-45. The Japanese occupation unleashed the forces of colonial nationalism in Malaya as elsewhere. But Malay nationalism triggered a reaction from the Chinese, who feared Malay and Islamic domination and turned in large numbers to the Malayan Communist Party.

It took a tough military response from the British, and concessions by both the Malay and Chinese political leaderships, to end the communist insurgency and bring about the establishment of an independent, multi-racial Federation of Malaya in 1957 but it was a hard road.

* * * * *

As well as briefing me on the political scene, my colleague introduced me to Malaya's newspapers. I was shown how to extract anything that was likely to throw any light on the political leanings of anyone who was anybody. As some of the papers were openly hostile to the British, every day brought a spate of cuttings.

"What happens to these cuttings?"

"They go to the captain."

"What does he do with them?"

"I dunno', I think they get thrown away." I'd only been there five minutes and already I was feeling like looking for another job in the organisation. I was given one that very afternoon.

After the midday meal the sergeant major called me into his office. "Smith, tomorrow morning at 6:00, I want to see you in FSMO outside the front of the building."

"Yes, sir." I replied. He looked surprised. "Anything else, sir?"

"No! That's all."

I went out and whispered to one of the older sergeants, "What's FSMO?"

He was obviously astonished at my question. "Why?"

"The sergeant major has told me I have to parade outside the building at 6:00 tomorrow in FSMO."

"What did you say?"

"I said, 'Yes, sir.' "

"Good for you, young'un. Leave this with me." A short while later he left in a jeep.

FSMO is short for Field Service Marching Order. This is the mass of webbing straps and little satchels used during the war when soldiers went into battle. It was hardly ever used after the war and was not a standard issue in Malaya. That afternoon my colleague visited all his Quarter Master friends in the garrison and together they raked up the full kit. He then got a group of soldiers scrubbing the webbing, polishing the brasses and squaring the pouches with stiff cardboard fillings to make it look smart.

When it was assembled, which incidentally was a notorious nightmare, he brought it all back and put it in my room. He then sought me out with the words, "I see you've got one of those old fashioned FSMO kits in your room. Quite an Old Soldier aren't you! Now remember this and somehow repeat it tomorrow morning: *'Always be prepared to go into battle, for you never know what's round the corner.'* Have you got that? Good." With that he winked and went off.

Back in my room I examined my gift. It was an amazing assembly of harness and pouches. I spent the rest of the day and all evening putting a gloss on my boots and pressing my uniform. I got an early morning call from the cook and by six o'clock I was out in front of the building looking like a new pin and wearing my newly acquired FSMO. The sergeant major came out also dressed as if for a parade. He spent a good ten minutes examining me and all the equipment.

"This your FSMO, Smith?"

"Yes, sir," I truthfully replied. "Well turned out, Smith. I'm surprised. How much time did you spend on this sort of thing when you were in the Palestine Police?"

"They were sticklers for it. But it was worth all the effort. The fact is, sir, *we always need to be prepared to go into battle, for we never know what's round the corner.*"

"Do you know, Smith, that's *exactly* what I'm always telling these fellows here. The problem with them is, they've never been in a battle. Were you ever in a battle?"

"The whole thing was a battle, sir. A never-ending one."

"Were you ever wounded?"

"Yes, I was, sir." But I didn't show him the miniscule scar on my hand! "Lost some blood but they patched me up."

"To be honest, Smith, I've misjudged the Palestine Police. They're better than I thought. But now you listen to me. Let me give you a word of advice. You watch out for the captain. He's a proper bastard. He's a stickler for this kind of discipline. This parade was his idea, so you watch your step."

"Thank you, sir." I don't know how I kept a straight face. "Discipline doesn't worry me, sir. I'm used to discipline. Wouldn't be alive today otherwise."

"That's true of me too, Smith, true of me, too. Now listen. I was told to give you some drill this morning but I don't think I will. What do you think?"

"It's entirely up to you, sir. I'm willing, but it wouldn't do to wake the Brigadier at this hour would it?"

"Do you know, I hadn't thought of that. Well, off you go then... I mean, dismiss."

I went up the steps and turned into the office where I found my friend by the window. He had heard every word of this bizarre exchange and was nearly choking with laughter. "Well done. But you watch your step, young'un. You be *very* careful." I intended to be, but some months later I realised I wasn't careful enough.

Chapter 19
Church Again

Towards the evening of the Sunday of my first week in Taiping, three of my new colleagues were standing in the foyer. "Going out?" I asked. "Yes."

"May I come with you?"

"Of course." So, just as I was, wearing an open-necked shirt and slacks, I set off with them. Instead of turning left to go into the town they turned right.

"Where are we going?" I asked.

"Church," one replied.

Abruptly I halted. "Church?"

"Why not? It's Sunday!"

"I had enough church on the ship. I had to go every Sunday."

"Well, why break the habit? Come on, we must set the natives a good example!" So I went with them to church. Here was another turning point in my life, but at the time it was heavily disguised.

The Anglican Church was only 300-400 yards away from our bungalow and was surprisingly full. Most of the congregation were Indians but there were a few Chinese and a dozen or so Brits. We sat at the back. The priest was a small Indian cleric who rattled through evensong at a great rate. Outside the church after the service we encountered a fair haired, dapper little man of about 25, dressed in an immaculate white suit. As we came out he said in an Oxbridge accent, "Would you fellers like to come home for a spot of dinner?"

"Rather," I said, but the others shook their heads. Thinking they were shaking their heads at me and that I might be creating a security risk, I tried to back pedal. "Well come to think of it, no. I'm not properly dressed for dinner, no tie and no jacket."

Rolf Hjorth and Jean Thomson

"No problem," said one, "you can have mine." So there wasn't a prohibition after all and dutifully I put on my borrowed robes. With a pleasant nod to my companions the dapper little man led the way across the road to an exceedingly smart car.

"My name is Hjorth, Rolf Hjorth, spelt H, J, O, R, T, H. What's yours?"

"Er Smith, John Smith."

"I'll remember that!" he said. His voice had a foreign edge to it. "Where do you come from?"

"Denmark, originally, but I've lived in England most of my life. Ah! Here we are."

We had turned into the drive of a very large house. As the car stopped a couple came out, welcoming smiles on their faces.

"What, only one, Rolf?"

Rolf turned to me and said, "Let me introduce you to our hosts for the evening! Hugh and Jean, John." I shook hands with the couple who were about 35. Then, turning to Rolf I said, "You mean to say this isn't your house?"

"Oh no, I live in Penang."

Hugh and Jean Thomson

"Don't worry," said Jean, "he does this every time he comes to stay with us."

Hugh broke in with, "We were expecting three or four of you, but we're delighted you could come." They spoke with soft Scottish accents and immediately I felt as if I had known them all my life.

"Come in and sit down, dinner is waiting," said Jean, so I went in and sat down to what was the first of a great many delicious curried dinners in their house.

* * * * *

During the meal I learned a little more about our hosts. Hugh Thomson was a naval architect working for a tin mining company, designing dredges that floated on the little lakes created by the dredging. He was obviously a very clever engineer. He had been in Malaya since 1938 and was due to return home on furlough when the Japanese over-ran the country and he was made a prisoner of war.

Later, Rolf told me that Hugh had volunteered to help the Japanese repair the road and rail bridges that the retreating British army had destroyed. What the Japanese didn't know, and fortunately for Hugh, never found out, was that he built specific weaknesses into the designs with the result that there were some spectacular collapses. At the end of the war when Hugh returned home he weighed a mere five-and-a-half stone. There to meet him at Glasgow Central Station was Jean Rennie. Engaged to Hugh, she had expected to be married in 1942. The wedding was postponed until 1945. They both returned to Malaya in 1946.

A State Registered Nurse, Jean helped as a volunteer at the British Medical Hospital in the Garrison just outside Taiping. Through Jean I gained a pretty accurate picture of the casualties our forces were suffering at the hands of the terrorists. It was sobering.

After dinner we went upstairs to a spacious lounge. At the bottom of the stairs Hugh had removed his shoes. I didn't follow suit for I rather suspected that I was wearing my bachelor socks, those you could put on from either end! As Rolf kept his shoes on I didn't feel obliged to reveal my suspect knitwear. I forget what we talked about, but I know I felt completely at home.

At about half past nine Hugh said, "We must get you home. We'll have a reading before you go." With that he went out of the room and came back with an enormous black Bible from which he read one of the Psalms. His Scottish brogue lent the reading a peculiarly attractive quality.

When he had finished he closed the Bible and said, "Let us pray," whereupon, he, Jean and Rolf got down on their knees. I followed suit. He must have prayed for about five minutes but it was praying such as I had never heard before. Certainly it didn't come out of the Book of Common Prayer. Amongst other things he prayed that I would be kept safe, but as the safest place was in the arms of Jesus, he prayed that I would very quickly find my way there. All the time he was praying I had one eye on the group in order to see what was happening. Nothing did and after the prayer everyone said "Amen", with my "Amen" half a beat behind the others. We then all got into Rolf's car and I was driven home.

My most earnest prayer that evening was that my new colleagues would see me arrive in the posh car, but no one was around. We all said good night and the car moved off down the drive. As it reached the road, the uniformed figure of the sergeant major turned into the drive. He stopped, came smartly to attention and saluted as the car passed him! How I wished he had arrived two minutes earlier so that I could have returned that salute!

* * * * *

One morning during the following week, while I was busy with the newspapers and a pair of scissors, a sergeant came to me and said, "You've got a visitor."

It was Hugh. "I thought I'd drop in to find out if you're free next Sunday evening for dinner." Free! I had nothing to do on any evening! "Fine, we'll pick you up here at about six." Promptly at six on Sunday, another posh car drew up at the bungalow and picked me up. "We're going to church first, if that's OK." But the car had turned left to go into the town.
"I thought the church was the other way," I said.
"Oh, no, we're going to the Gospel Hall."
"What denomination is that?"
"We don't place a lot of emphasis on denominations but the Hall is run by missionaries." I wasn't fussed; whatever it was like it couldn't be worse than last Sunday and I was looking forward to another curried dinner! At the end of the High Street we turned into a large compound. On the left there were two attractive looking bungalows and opposite them was a chapel into which an extraordinarily large number of people were making their way.

In a few moments we were part of a congregation consisting mainly of Chinese. The Hall measured about 50' x 80'. At the end opposite the door there was a small platform on which stood a lectern. On the wall behind, in large letters were the words: JESUS SAVES. To the left of the platform was a small pedal organ behind which Hugh took his seat. A tall white man came up to me and Jean introduced him as Mr Oliver. He mounted the platform and the service began with a hymn I had never heard before: 'Will your anchor hold in the storms of life', which took me back to the force ten storm in the Mediterranean and I thought: "You need to know the Chief Petty Officer!"

The sermon was a straight gospel message: God loved us so much that He sent Jesus into the world to live and die for us; salvation was not of works but came from trusting in what Jesus had done; God could do no more; it was now up to us to respond. If we refused this way of salvation there was no other. If we left this world unsaved and, regrettably, ended up in hell, we'd only have ourselves to blame.

Over dinner Jean said, "What did you think of the sermon?"
"I'm not sure. I'm still thinking about it," but deep down I was disturbed. Was there a hell? Is that really where I was going? The more I thought about it the less I liked Mr Oliver and his sermon. I smiled wryly to myself when I thought about my comment to Bill: "A good sermon should not leave me saying, 'That was a cracking sermon,' it should leave me asking, 'How can I be saved?' The fact was, I didn't want to be saved. I decided I wouldn't go back to Taiping Gospel Hall.

* * * * *

On the Wednesday of the following week I was working on my newspapers when I had a tap on my shoulder. Standing behind me was a smiling Bill Deane. "Bill! What on earth are you doing here? Don't tell me the Hussars have come to Taiping."
"*They* haven't but *I* have!" said Bill. "I've got a transfer to the Intelligence Corps."
"What! How did you manage that?"
"Ha! Ha! You see it's not what you know but who you know. The first thing I did when I caught up with the Regiment was to see the Adjutant who made some enquiries at Command HQ. Between you and me things are hotting up and they badly want to increase the number of you guys around; so there and then HQ approved my transfer. I asked if I could come here to Taiping and that was agreed too. So, here I am, no longer Trooper Deane, Fifth Hussars, but

Private Deane, Intelligence Corps. They told me I'd be promoted to sergeant as soon as I arrived. Can't be bad, can it? I've written to tell my Dad. He'll be pleased."

"You won't get promoted to sergeant if you tell the captain you know me," I said.

"Why? What have you done?"

"That's the problem. Haven't done anything, except mess about with these wretched newspapers. Because I haven't been to an infantry battalion the CO here doesn't think I'm a proper soldier. It's an ambition of his to turn me into one."

"I'll put a word in for you, dear boy!"

"You'll do no such thing. He's an ex-ranker and doesn't know your language. I'm not absolutely sure that as a Cavalry Man you're completely fireproof yourself. You'll be seeing him tomorrow morning so spend the rest of the day polishing your boots and pressing that terrible uniform you're wearing. Stand stiffly to attention and say 'sir' very loudly after each sentence."

"Crumbs, it's like that is it?"

"Worse. Much worse. But above all, try not to speak in that posh accent of yours."

"Accent? I haven't got an accent."

"Oh no! Just shout everything you say. That'll disguise it and he'll think you're a bone head which will please him no end. He thinks there are too many clever clogs around him already."

"I think I'm going back to the Hussars."

"It's too late. Serves you right for having pretentious ideas above your station! If you do get promoted don't try ordering me around or I'll get my friend the cook to poison your dinner. Which reminds me... " and I told him about my first dinner.

When I later asked if we were hanging the cook that night I was told that, as most of the food had ended up on the floor on my first night, the tradition had been dropped. In contrast Bill was welcomed in a most decorous way and had responded in a very military fashion, which pleased the sergeant major but made the rest look down their noses. He'll do all right, I thought.

* * * * *

On the following six or seven Sundays Hugh and Jean called at the bungalow with an invitation to go to church, and every time I declined. Whatever else they displayed they certainly showed a remarkable perseverance. Later I learned that every day they prayed for me. Bill was delighted to learn that the Anglican Church was just round the corner; but he couldn't get me to go.

At this time I had decided to buy a car. It cost the equivalent of £300 sterling. Foolishly I signed a hire purchase contract and either I was misled or I misunderstood the Chinese car dealer but hidden in the small print was a savage interest charge compounded weekly. That was the first and last time I ever failed to study the small print. It would take some weeks for me to get the money from home, by which time the interest would have accumulated at an alarming rate. Somehow I had to find the money and find it immediately.

In desperation I thought of Hugh, and one morning I went to his office and explained the position. He got out his cheque book and wrote a cheque for M$3,000.

"Pay me when you get the money from home," was all he said. Three weeks later the banker's draft arrived from the UK and I took it straight to Hugh.

"Pick you up on Sunday?" he said. How could I say no? So it was that the following Sunday I was back in the same seat in the Gospel Hall. This time the preacher was a Doctor Samuels, an Indian and one of Malaya's most eminent physicians. After the service we were chatting together.

Suddenly he said to me: "John, let me ask you a question. Do you know Jesus personally?"

Did I know Jesus personally? Well, of course I knew *about* Jesus, but did I know Him *personally*? I had to confess that I didn't. "Well" said the doctor, "He lived and died and rose from the dead so that you *could* know Him personally. Why else do you think you are here?" Then he said: "Don't take my word for this. Get a Bible and find out for yourself." I told him I'd tried reading the Bible once and got stuck in Leviticus and that I couldn't make head nor tail of it. "Well," he said, "I suggest you read John's gospel; you won't get stuck in that. Faith comes through the Word of God, so persevere at reading it."

Then he said: "If you don't mind I'd like to pray for you." I couldn't remember anyone offering to pray for me before, but I didn't think it would do me any harm, so right there and then he started to pray.

I had closed my eyes and expected a short prayer but he kept on praying. After a couple of minutes I decided to take a peek at him. He had his eyes tightly closed, but as he prayed, tears rolled down his cheeks. I'd never heard praying like it before, in fact apart from Hugh's prayer about three months earlier, I'd never heard much praying of any kind except at church parades. This was something very different. By the time he'd finished I was nearly crying myself! When we were being drilled by the police sergeant in Palestine, he once declared that I made him weep; but I don't think he shed many tears. What I'd seen here were real tears.

I promised Doctor Samuels that I would get a New Testament and I'd read it; and so I did. Every day I read it. Initially I read it because I had promised I would; but soon I found myself reading whole chunks of it, and the more I read, the more fascinated I became with Jesus of Nazareth. The problem was, the longer I had this little New Testament the more difficult it became to read. It was the monsoon season and I was for ever getting drenched to the skin. Practically every day I'd get soaked by a tropical downpour.

When it didn't rain I'd be soaked with sweat, so the pages of my little New Testament got stuck together and I'd have to pry them apart and the leaves got torn; but I persevered. Late one evening I was again reading John's Gospel. I'd got to chapter three where Jesus was approached by a clever fellow called Nicodemus. He was a ruler in Jerusalem and Jesus says to him, "You must be born again."

I'd heard about born again Christians but I hadn't a clue what it meant. I was thinking, "Born again? What does that mean? How can you be born again?" I read on and discovered that Nicodemus asked exactly the same question. At least I was in good company and asking the right questions! Then I read something that was astounding. It was verse sixteen of chapter three. I've since learned that most Christians know John 3:16 off by heart, but to me it came like a bolt from the blue. In the Authorised Version, which I was reading, it goes like this: 'For God so loved the world, that He gave His only begotten Son, that whosoever believeth in Him should not perish, but have everlasting life.'

It was that 'should not perish' bit that caught my attention, probably because the way things were, perishing seemed to be a strong likelihood. 'Shall not perish... ' Who shall not perish? I read back: 'Whosoever'. The word stood out as if in neon lights. Whosoever! *I* was a Whosoever!

What happened next is difficult to explain, but it was something like those outline drawings that have portraits concealed in them. At first nothing makes sense; then suddenly the picture emerges. It was a bit like that. One minute I couldn't see anything then suddenly it all became clear. I used to make fun of folk who had 'seen the light' but that's just how it was. Quite suddenly the issue was crystal clear. It wasn't a matter of how many celestial brownie points I could chalk up to offset all the black marks. The real issue was what was I doing about Jesus Christ, the Son of God, who had lived and died for me?

Then I remembered the words of Doctor Samuels: "Jesus lived and died and rose from the dead so that you could know Him personally! Why else do you think you are here?" The enormity of my attitude to Jesus hit me with overwhelming force. This Creator God had become a baby, born in a stable; He'd lived a life of rejection at the end of which He was nailed to a cross and died a death of unutterable agony – *for me!* Then He rose from the dead so that I could know Him personally and love Him in return; and what had been my response? Instead of welcoming Him I was busy keeping Him at arm's length.

With tears streaming down my face I knelt by my bedside and asked Jesus to forgive me and come into my life. An extraordinary peace and joy seemed to flood my entire being. There was nothing dramatic about it, just, "I'm really, really sorry, Lord. Please forgive me. Thank you for dying for me. Thank you for loving me. Please come into my life and help me to love you." There were no flashing lights, no appearance of angels, no heavenly voices; but in that little room in Malaya, 8,000 miles from home, a miracle had happened. I believed! Faith had come... by the Word of God, and I experienced the amazing joy of sins forgiven and peace with God. All those things of which I used to make fun happened to me that night. I had 'seen the light'. I was 'born again'!

It was all so amazing and wonderful that, although it was late at night, I had to tell someone. Bill! Bill Deane! He'd be delighted. I rushed off to Bill's room.

He was fast asleep. He won't mind. "Bill! Bill! Wake up!"
"What's the problem?" Suddenly he was wide awake.
"No problem. Quite the contrary. Bill. I've become a Christian."
"Christian? My dear boy, what on earth are you talking about? A Christian! You've *always* been a Christian."
"Well, I wasn't, but I am tonight. Bill, I've been born again!"
Bill looked at me as if I was something the cat had brought in. "Born again! Don't be absurd."
"Well, never mind that now. Bill, there's so much I want to know and you can tell me. How do I read the Bible and how do I pray?"
"Read the bi...? Pray...?" Suddenly Bill was looking very worried. "Listen to me dear boy. You've been overdoing things. Go to bed. You'll feel better in the morning."

In the morning I was worse, at least in Bill's opinion. This was the most wonderful thing that had ever happened to me. Everybody needed to know that Jesus was an amazing Saviour. There and then I started writing to everyone whose address I had with me. Over the next week I must have posted over 50 letters. I got two replies. One was from my horrified mother who earnestly warned me to 'have nothing more to do with those missionaries who, if you're not careful, will drive you into an asylum with religious mania!'

My mother was to become very anti evangelical Christianity, refusing to discuss it with anyone. During the Billy Graham Crusades in the seventies my mother said, "You're not going to tell me Billy Graham isn't making a fortune out of these crusades." Much, much later, she was amazingly and wonderfully saved, to the complete astonishment of my father. But that comes later in this narrative.

The only other reply I received from all my letters was an air-letter from Valerie Hignett, the school friend of Pat Bunn. It read: 'Dear John, I'm so glad that you've become a real Christian. Ever since I have known you I have been praying for you'. I was to discover that she had prayed for me for over four years. From that moment we corresponded regularly. She became more than a pen pal she was a prayer partner. During the next four years that I was in Malaya, I'd tell her about friends and colleagues, she would pray for them and they received Christ into their lives. It was a very exciting partnership.

* * * * *

Meanwhile I was making some discoveries. At breakfast the sergeant major was his usual obnoxious self but I found I was reacting totally differently. I found that all my suppressed resentment had vanished. It no longer seemed important that I was still a private when I should have been promoted to sergeant. My press cuttings job was no longer a menial task. Somebody had to do it. As I looked at the sergeant major I felt a genuine compassion for the man. He was so defensive and so vulnerable. I thought that he could be so very different if only he knew that God really loved him. Here was a man whom Jesus loved despite the fact that he used the name of Jesus as a swear word with nearly every comment he made.

It didn't take long for the news to spread that "John's seen the light!" As soon as the sergeant major heard he sought me out. His comments were highly uncomplimentary but not once did I feel negatively towards him. On the contrary I felt a genuine love for the man. It was a truly extraordinary experience.

The CO was even more scathing. "You can forget all that nonsense. I don't want any religious humbug around me. So don't you forget it."

That very day Bill was promoted to sergeant. It was the captain who broke the news to me. I was genuinely delighted for Bill. "That's very good news!" I said. "His Dad will be thrilled." The CO was looking at me with a baffled expression on his face. "Oh," I said, "you're wondering how I feel about it. Don't let it worry you. You'll make me a sergeant when you think I deserve it."
Instantly his face was like thunder. "Don't let it worry me! How dare you?"
I was surprised at this reaction. "No offence was intended, sir." Later he was to become deeply offended but that had an unexpectedly satisfactory outcome.

Another discovery was to find that Bill was not in the least interested in either reading the Bible or praying with me. When I tried to talk about the Lord he would switch off completely. "Don't let all this go to your head, dear boy. That sort of thing is alright for Sundays. You can't want to bring Jesus into everything you do. It simply won't do, you know." But that was exactly what I did want! Over the next few days I came to the shocking conclusion that, not only did Bill not know Jesus personally, he actually wasn't interested in knowing Him. This astonished me. I was to discover that many regular church-goers were just that – church-goers. It accounted for the many miserable faces in church!

On the following Sunday I went to the Gospel Hall and was overwhelmed with bear hugs from the men and kisses from the ladies. That was an unexpected bonus! I learned that an amazing number of people had been praying for me everyday for weeks. I was experiencing genuine Christian love and I was bowled over by it.

One of the most salutary discoveries I made was in connection with reading the Bible. I enjoyed reading it. It was fascinating. I loved reading about the life of Jesus. It was all so new. This euphoria lasted a whole week and then I came down to earth with a bump. I was about to learn that the Christian life was one of obedience to this Word I was enjoying so much.

Ardverikie Castle in Scotland

Muncaster Castle in Cumbria

It will be remembered that my father was butler to Sir John Ramsden who had huge properties including a couple of castles, Ardverikie Castle in Scotland and Muncaster Castle in Cumbria. Muncaster Castle was impressive but Ardverikie looked as if it came straight out of a Hans Anderson fairy tale. It is recognizable from its starring role in the BBC drama, "Monarch of the Glen".

During my month's leave before sailing for Singapore Dad had arranged for me to have an extended holiday at Muncaster Castle. He was in Scotland with The Family at Ardverikie, but he had organised things with the head game keeper at Muncaster for me to have a gun and a supply of cartridges. I had complete freedom to go anywhere on the estate and even had a footman to act as a loader! I shot an impressive number of pheasants, some of which I posted home for Mum.

That stay in Muncaster Castle must have sown the seeds of a big deception, for when I first met Hugh and Jean and they had asked me what my father did, I thought they would be more impressed if, instead of telling them that Dad was a butler in these castles, he actually owned them! Despite being shown photographs of both castles neither Hugh nor Jean appeared to be in the least impressed at my lineage! However the word got around that John Smith was part of the landed gentry. When the subject arose I didn't deny it and soon it was no longer a topic of conversation.

Seven days after my conversion I was reading John's gospel when I read 'The truth will set you free...' The words seemed to stand out in neon lights and suddenly, before my eyes, as if superimposed on top of the printing, were pictures of Sir John's castles! I could almost hear the Lord speaking to me, "What about those lies?"

"They're not interested in those castles now. They'll have forgotten them." But God hadn't forgotten. Every time I opened my Bible to read it, there were these castles, sometimes one, sometimes the other and sometimes both at the same time, as clear as if they were photographs.

Resolutely I tried to put them out of my mind but a lot of things happened. I found I couldn't pray. I no longer enjoyed reading the Bible. I stopped telling colleagues about Jesus. Initially I couldn't make out how this change had come about, but then I realised it was all because I was refusing to be obedient and confess to the lies about the castles.

After four days I could stand it no longer. I did a complete round of the folk to whom I had spoken. "There is something I have to tell you. My father doesn't own those castles. He's only a butler in them." "Castles, what castles?" and I had to explain the details. It was a humbling experience but it was also liberating. That wonderful joy returned. The Bible was as fresh as ever and now I had even more for which to thank God. I learned that if a thing is important enough for God to put his finger on it, then it's important enough for us to attend to it without delay.

That was probably the most important lesson I have ever learned in my Christian life. It's a lesson I am still learning! Growth in the Christian life is not related to how many years we have been a Christian. It is related to frequency of obedience to God. In fact we could almost say that a unit of Christian growth is an act of obedience.

* * * * *

Another test was in the pipeline. About three months after my conversion, I learned that there was to be a baptism in the Gospel Hall. This was new to me. I read accounts in the Acts of the Apostles of folk being baptised and, despite having been christened as a baby and then confirmed, I thought that perhaps I should be done again! I discovered that post conversion believer's baptism by immersion was the norm in most non conformist churches and also in some Anglican churches. I asked to join the preparation classes.

The classes were taken by Mr Oliver, who I found to be a splendid Bible teacher. He and his wife had been missionaries in Japan when the Japanese bombed the US Naval Base at Pearl Harbor on that terrible 7th December 1941 "... a day" in the words of President Roosevelt "... that will for ever live in infamy." One of the consequences was that the Olivers were made prisoners of war in Japan and severely suffered from deprivation and malnutrition. Despite this, during the four years that I knew them they never expressed anything but compassion and sorrow over the Japanese. They were a salutary example to me of love and forgiveness.

Under Mr Oliver's tuition I discovered that baptism was a great deal more significant than I had supposed. Just as Jesus died, was buried and then rose from the dead so we in baptism die to our old selves, we are buried with Christ and then we are raised again in newness of life. The Apostle Paul seemed to make it all so clear and I was glad I had decided to be 'done'!

The day came for my baptism. It was to be part of the evening service. The lectern and the platform had been removed to reveal a gigantic bath called a baptistry. Despite the hot weather the water looked perishingly cold. I thought how fortunate I was to be baptised in Malaya and not in Germany, or England for that matter.

Prior to their baptism, candidates give a testimony. This is a brief account of the circumstances leading to conversion. I simply said I had been encouraged to read the Bible and then explained what had happened when I was reading John 3:16. My actual conversion I likened to stumbling around in a dark room when suddenly the light was switched on. After my testimony I was baptised. The water was even colder than it looked but I had been obedient. It was another milestone in my Christian life.

Chapter 20
Penang

I was now attending the Gospel Hall regularly and one of the preachers was Mr Justice Garton the local judge in the High Court. We had been introduced and he had invited me to his home to have dinner with him and his wife. In fact they were near neighbours at 20 Swettenham Road. It had been a delightful evening and their small son of three and I had got on very well. They were planning to spend the weekend up Maxwell Hill, the local retreat for the very senior army and police officers, and folk such as Judge Garton. I was asked if I would care to join them. "I would be delighted."

The CO was not delighted. It was necessary to get his permission so I went in to see him and requested leave for the weekend.

"Leave? Where is there to go around here?"
"I was thinking of Maxwell Hill, sir."
He goggled back at me. "Max... Maxwell... Maxwell Hill! Don't be absurd!"

Taiping from Maxwell Hill

"Well, I've been invited to go, sir."

"You've been invited! Who by?"

"Mr Justice Garton."

"Justice Garton! The High Court Judge? Are you trying to be funny?"

"No sir! They have indeed invited me to spend the weekend with them in Court Bungalow."

"How did you get this invitation?"

"They suggested it at dinner last night."

"*Dinner!* With Justice Garton and his wife? What were you doing there?"

"Having dinner, sir."

He stood up so violently that his chair toppled over. Eyes blazing out of a purpling face, he said, "Don't you dare be cheeky with me, Private Smith, or you'll regret it."

"I had no intention at all of being cheeky, sir. You asked me what I was doing and I told you we were having dinner. I had been invited to go for dinner with them and that's why I was there."

He stood very close, his face no further than four inches from mine, remaining there for some time. Suddenly I felt an overwhelming compassion for this poor inadequate man.

"Well you're not getting permission from me to go up Maxwell Hill, only colonels and above get accommodation up there. Request refused." He picked up his chair and sat down.

"Would you mind giving Mrs Garton a ring, sir, and explain that I can't go. She'll be disappointed though. I think she thought I would be good company for their little son, David. Would you mind? Frankly, I wouldn't know what to say?"

He glared at me for about three minutes. "Well, if you want to be a baby sitter, that's up to you. You wouldn't get *me* doing it. Get out of my office."

The incident nearly had dire consequences for it was not long before the sergeant major approached me saying, "The CO has decided to get you transferred to The King's Own Yorkshire Light Infantry. They're up on the Thailand border. Just thought I'd warn you. He says you're a liability in the Intelligence Corps."

I was about to protest when I remembered a verse I had read that morning in my Bible: "Commit your way unto the Lord and He will direct your path." I kept quiet. Later the sergeant major came to me and said, "You don't need to worry about that transfer. Some of your own people have told the CO that he hasn't got the authority to transfer you so it looks as if you'll be staying here for a while yet." It looked as if my paths were indeed being directed. It was a comforting thought.

* * * * *

As far as the Intelligence Corps was concerned the most sought-after appointment in the whole of the north of Malaya was in Penang. The sergeant in charge of the Penang office was Jim Brennan, the most senior sergeant in our section and a veteran soldier. Periodically there would be a meeting of all our personnel operating in North Malaya. A short while after the latest fracas with the CO there was one of these meetings. When it was over Jim went in to see the CO. There ensued a colossal row with a great deal of shouting on the part of the CO. The racket could be heard all over the building. We all wondered what on earth was afoot. We were to find out as soon as Jim emerged.

"Pack up all your gear," he said to me tersely.

"What?

"Go and pack. Pack up all your stuff. You're coming with me to Penang. Don't stand there gaping. I'm leaving in fifteen minutes, don't keep me waiting." I was outside the building in less than ten minutes, waiting for him!

The sergeant major came out to me. "So! You're going to the Pearl of the Orient are you?"

"Am I?" I said.

"You're going to Penang laddie; it's called the Pearl of the Orient." Then he looked at me and said, "You're getting out of here just in time. The CO's been breathing murder ever since you went for the weekend up Maxwell Hill."

At that moment Jim came up in a jeep. The sergeant major helped put my gear into the jeep and I climbed in. As we left I saw the CO glaring at me out of the window of his office.

"You're well out of this little lot, son," said Jim Brennan as we turned out of the drive. "That's why I thought it would be a good idea to ask for you to come as my assistant in Penang."

"What was all the shouting about?"

"You! When I asked for you, he said, 'Over my dead body.' I told him that might be arranged! Anyway, I said I wasn't leaving without you. He only understands shouting. But I'll tell you this, lad, he doesn't like you one little bit."

"Well, I really believe I could have won him round if I had stayed."

"I doubt it," he said, "anyway, Penang, here we come."

"Sergeant Brennan, how often does the CO come to Penang?" I asked. He looked across at me with a wide grin and said, "He never leaves Taiping. And don't call me sergeant. I'm Jim to you."

It didn't seem long before we were approaching Butterworth, the mainland town from which a ferry crossed the four miles to George Town, Penang's principal town. We were able to get straight on to the ferry and within a very few minutes we were underway for this Paradise Island which was to be my base for the next four years.

Above:
My office in
Penang!

Above:
My interpreter
Mustapha

Right:
Interpreter and
bodyguard Jack

160

We drove off the ferry and through the town keeping to the coastal road. About half-a-mile out of the town the jeep pulled into the long sweeping drive of an impressive-looking mansion. The building overlooked the sea and a long sandy beach. We stopped outside two massive double doors that led to a huge mosaic-covered floor. At the top of a wide staircase a notice read 'Army Intelligence'. Entering a large room we were greeted by Mustapha, a Malay and Jack, a Eurasian. By far the best interpreters in the whole section, they were fluent in five languages. This was a great relief because I was still struggling with Malay. Of even more relief was the fact that Jack was an unarmed combat expert! They welcomed us with warm smiles and we shook hands all round. We all knew one another having met in Taiping.

"Unpack and bring me all your jackets," said Jim.
"What do you want them for?" I asked.
"I'm taking them to the tailors to get your stripes sewn on. As far as I am concerned you're a sergeant." I was back in about ten minutes. "I'll get your Palestine Medal ribbon sewn on too." Mustapha and Jack looked impressed.

I liked my new boss. He was an experienced intelligence operator and knew every official in the town who might be helpful. He also knew some distinctly shady characters that were even more helpful! He immediately set about introducing me to this information network. Our territory stretched from south of Butterworth right up to the Malayan border with Thailand. It was along this border that many of the terrorists operated. The problem was finding out precisely where they were.

* * * * *

In nearly every letter I was receiving from home I was being asked if I had been able to visit the Ramsden's rubber estate? Now that I was in Penang I was able to do this for the estate was only 30-40 miles away. I was able to combine the visit with some other work that I could do so early one morning I set off. Crossing to the mainland by an early ferry I was soon on my way, not on my usual route to the mountain and jungle area but to the cultivated rubber plantations.

These are kept free of undergrowth and consequently shunned by both terrorists and dangerous animals. Soon I was driving through mile after mile of countryside given over exclusively to rubber estates. One of the largest of these was Sir John's plantation. With thousands of acres and hundreds of thousands of rubber trees it was huge. It even had its own golf course. The estate employed several hundred rubber tappers and was managed by a Scot named Mr Bruce. It was he who showed me round the estate.

A large mansion standing about a mile from the road was truly on a grand scale. Mr Bruce took me all over the house. There on one of the double staircases, was a deep scar where the bullet killing John Ramsden had lodged. The police concluded that it was a politically motivated killing, one of many carried out by terrorists all over Malaya in the late forties in the hope of forcing the British to leave.

I spent all day with Mr Bruce and found the business of rubber production fascinating. Mr Bruce didn't say anything to me at the time, but he asked a lot of questions about my training and how I would go about leaving the army if ever I wanted to do so. Apparently he wrote to Sir John saying that he thought he had found a successor as manager of the estate in the son of Smith, the butler. On my next visit to the estate I was indeed offered the job of assistant manager with the likelihood of becoming manager within three years when Mr Bruce expected to retire.

The rubber tapper is very often at the bottom of the social scale. Many are women, illiteracy is high and the pay is low. Child care and education is rudimentary at best. Living conditions are quite primitive. I saw these at very close quarters because the Indian boy who looked after me in Penang had parents working on a rubber estate. This Indian lad was wonderfully saved and on occasions I took him to visit his parents on the rubber estate. In comparison, Mr Bruce's estate was vastly better in the provision made for the workers but even there, it was all very primitive.

I had a delicious meal with Mr Bruce and left him later in the evening after promising that I would come back as soon as opportunity allowed. It struck me that, despite having a house full of servants, his was a very lonely existence.

In stark contrast my days were crammed with meeting a wide variety of people. Jim Brennan kept me very busy and under his tuition every day was an education. However I quickly discovered that my highly intelligent and competent boss had a problem. He was an alcoholic. He had experienced a number of very narrow escapes in the north of our territory and going into the jungle so scared him that he couldn't go until he was anaesthetised against the fear. When I confided to him that I was a total abstainer, he turned and gave me a huge bear hug. "You stay off it lad. That way we might both survive."

A few months after my visit to the rubber estate Jim started having delirium tremens, an acute form of alcoholism. He had terrifying visions of snakes and alligators. Jack and Mustapha were seriously worried about him and persuaded him to report sick. He was immediately admitted to hospital and two weeks later he was on a ship bound for the UK.

Almost immediately after my arrival at the Penang office I had been given the job of writing the weekly security report. I put a great deal of effort into writing those reports both in regard to the content and the wording of them. They were sent to Taiping where they were collated by our Chinese Chief Clerk and sent to GHQ. It seems they created something of a stir for the unexpected but pleasing result was that I was officially promoted to sergeant and, when Jim was sent home, I was put in charge of the prestigious and coveted Penang office. I never did know the full story of this sudden elevation but apparently during this time everyone in our Taiping office was keeping his head down while the CO stalked around looking for victims. Meanwhile I was advised by the Chief Clerk to stay away from Taiping. I should have heeded his advice.

Writing the weekly Security Report

Chapter 21
Arrested

Our main concern was collecting reliable intelligence from as many quarters as possible. Understandably the average citizen was reluctant to give information in case it led to reprisals. It was a matter of winning people's trust and confidence. Quite unintentionally I acquired a huge number of contacts who trusted me. As a result of my involvement in the Taiping Gospel Hall I was invited to speak at other churches and soon I was visiting churches as far south as Kuala Lumpur and north up to Alor Star. This put me in touch with a vast network of people who were perfectly willing to share with me any information that they thought helpful to the security forces. It also involved me in a great deal of travelling. At every opportunity I passed information on to my colleagues but it was my personal involvement with informers that was the secret of getting information.

It was when I was contacting someone with hot information that I found myself in Taiping and literally bumped into our sergeant major. I found it more helpful and indeed safer to dress in the garb of a typical tin mining worker than being in uniform. On this occasion I was looking more than usually disreputable in tattered shorts and shirt, wearing sandals and unshaven. The last thing I looked like was a member of the security forces. All the sergeant major's military instincts were offended by my disreputable appearance.

"What are you doing dressed like that? Why aren't you in uniform?"
"Never mind that just now I'll explain later but I urgently need to see someone here in Taiping. I won't be long and I'll be up at HQ shortly to put you in the picture."
"You're coming to HQ *now*. I'm placing you under arrest for being absent from your place of duty."

"I *am* on duty, very much so. We are on to a group of terrorist sympathisers right here in Taiping."

A flexible mind was not one of the sergeant major's strengths. "*We?* This is nothing to do with me. I don't know anything about terrorist sympathisers."

I was growing impatient. "If you had bothered to read my reports you *would* have known about them. But let's not waste time, I'll go and get the information we need and then I'll... "

"You're not going anywhere. You're under arrest and are coming back with me." I could see it was no use arguing. I'd explain it all to the CO and then go to my contact. A short delay wouldn't matter; so off we went. As we walked up the drive of our HQ the CO came out on the steps.

"I've placed Smith under arrest for being improperly dressed and being absent from his place of duty, sir."

"I *was* on duty until this bandit fouled things up!" I said indignantly.

But the CO's mind ran along lines similar to the sergeant major. "Look at you!" he said, "Sandals on bare feet; disreputable shorts and shirt; you haven't even shaved. Call yourself a soldier!"

"I was trying *not* to look like a soldier. You see... "

"Trying! You don't have to try. You never have looked like a soldier. Take him away sergeant major. Get him a uniform. Be in my office in half-an-hour, clean shaven."

Half-an-hour later I was in his office being given short shrift. "For being absent without leave you are stripped to the rank of private and are hereby sentenced to fourteen days detention. March him out sergeant major."

"Prisoner. About turn," shouted the sergeant major in my ear.

I didn't move. "Let me explain what I was doing?"

"March him out, sergeant major!" screamed the CO.

"Sir! I'm afraid I can't accept this. It's completely wrong. I wish to appeal."

"Appeal rejected," said the CO.

"Prisoner, about turn, quick march," shouted the sergeant major.

"I'm not deaf sergeant major," I murmured and slowly walked out of the office, while he shouted in double quick time, "Left right, left right, left right, left right... halt! Prisoner, *halt!*" I had walked on into our lounge and there I sat down. The sergeant major followed me.

"Sergeant major, even you must agree, this is all wrong. No defence. Not even allowed to say anything. A fourteen day prison sentence for doing my job is completely absurd. I cannot accept the sentence. As the CO has rejected my request for an appeal I'm going to ask for a Court Martial."

In a low voice he said, "Listen, son, don't make life difficult for me. I'm only doing what I'm told. He's been waiting for this opportunity for weeks and you gave it to him on a plate. Why *were* you dressed like that?" This obsession with dress amazed me when our job was to catch the terrorists who were constantly murdering our troops.

"I've already told you. It was early this morning when I was given this tip off. I would have got nowhere dressed as an army sergeant." I was suddenly very weary. I had been weary for weeks and it was catching up on me. "What's the use of explaining? You're not in the least bit interested in what we're doing and the CO's just as bad. He hasn't even asked what I was doing, or who I was going to see. What happens now?"

"Nothing, you've got fourteen days' detention. That really means prison, but as we don't have one you'll just stay here for fourteen days under house arrest. I'm supposed to lock you in your room, but I won't do that."

"What about my work in Penang?"

"That's nothing to do with me."

"Well it should be. In case you didn't know, it's what we're here for!"

"Don't be cheeky. You're a private now you know."

Just then Hugh Thomson walked in. "What's going on?" Apparently our Chinese Chief Clerk had rung him at his office and asked him to come down to see me. 'He needs a friend right now,' the Chief Clerk had said. With the sergeant major standing next to me I told Hugh what had happened.

Hugh had a short fuse and he exploded. Turning on the sergeant major he said savagely, "You and that precious CO of yours are a disgrace to the British Army. John, you have no choice. You must appeal."

"He's already done that," said the sergeant major. "It's been turned down."

"By whom?"

"His Commanding Officer."

Hugh snorted, "Commanding Officer indeed! You must appeal for a Court Martial through the Brigadier."

Owing to a dramatic sequence of events that occurred just a few weeks earlier, the Brigadier and I were involved in an incident in which not only were both our lives saved, but also the life of Sir Oliver Lyttleton, the then Secretary of State for the Colonies. He had been due to land at a Penang airfield and I was responsible for security. That morning I had been admiring a very powerful motor-cycle owned by a clerk who worked in our building and he suggested I borrowed the machine for the day. It was to be a most providential gesture.

While we were waiting for the plane to come in, the Brigadier, who was standing next to me said, "I must go to the toilet. I don't want to be taken short!" and off he went. He had no sooner entered the nearby building when Sir Oliver's Dakota appeared. Wanting to make the most of a fairly short landing area, the pilot was flying very low and unfortunately hit the raised bank of a rice field. Crashing through the earth bank the plane hit the ground just on the edge of the airfield. Slewing round on its fuselage it lost a wing and came to a stop. I rushed into the building where the Brigadier had gone and hammered on the toilet door, yelling, "The plane has crashed, you'd better hurry."

The Brigadier came out in a lamentable state of undress! As we ran I told him I had a motor-bike just outside and, rather than wait for his staff car, we'd do better to use the motor-bike. In no time at all the powerful motor-bike was taking us across the airfield at top speed, the Brigadier doing up buttons as we sped along!

We were the first to reach the plane, which was spilling fuel all over the place. As we approached, Sir Oliver staggered out of the door of the plane and stepped into this aviation fuel. As he stood there, with shaking hands he took out a cigarette case and a lighter. By now we were only a few feet away from him so we were able to relieve him of the cigarette lighter before he sent us all to Kingdom Come. About a minute later the fire truck and an ambulance arrived. Sir Oliver was not injured but he was very badly shaken. The ambulance took him back to the airfield buildings and I took the Brigadier back on the motor-bike.

When he got off the motor-bike he turned to me and said, "I think this speedy bike of yours saved both our lives, to say nothing of the life of our visitor. But I think we should keep that little incident with the cigarette lighter to ourselves. Do you agree?"

"I certainly do," I said.

The Brigadier was clearly relieved. "Good man," he said, and with that he grasped my hand and gave it a hearty shake. This was the Brigadier to whom I would be making my appeal!

"I'd like to be at that Court Martial," said Hugh to the sergeant major, and then to me he said, "In the meanwhile you need a good lawyer. I'm going to see Mr Justice Garton."

"Oh lor', that's tore it," said the sergeant major and quickly went in to the CO's office.

"There's nothing Maurice Garton can do," said Hugh, "this is a military matter but it may scare them into seeing sense! I'm off now. By the way, Jean and I are going to Fraser's Hill next week for a fortnight. Tell that silly CO that you want 14 days leave and come with us."

Fraser's Hill! That was where the High Commissioner went for *his* holidays! It was even more exclusive than Maxwell Hill.

The sergeant major and the CO were together for over half-an-hour. When he came out the sergeant major said, "Would you step into the CO's office?" Then in my ear he whispered, "I think we're in something of a mess."

"I hear you intend to appeal to the Brigadier," said the CO.

"Look sir. The fact is I *was* doing my job, as you very well know. But I don't want to make a fuss. I am sure this can be settled satisfactorily."

"How?" he asked.

"Just put the clock back a few hours. There's nothing I *need* to report. I'll see if my informer will go to the police and then I'll go back to Penang and carry on as if nothing had happened."

"The problem is we can't do that," said the CO with a genuinely worried look.

"Why not?" I asked.

"I've already entered your sentence in your Service Book and reduced you to private."

"That was a trifle hasty, wasn't it?" was my tactless rejoinder.

The CO nearly floored me with, "Yes, I'm afraid it was," but clearly he was thinking that he was the one in a pickle and not me.

"Well sir, it shouldn't be difficult to get a new Service Book. Copy everything in from the old one, sign it as a true copy and get the sergeant major here to witness your signature. You can then 'lose' the old one. I'll be happy with that providing you put in all the nice things they said about me in Maresfield, and you leave out all the nasty things you've said!" He was too preoccupied to notice the dig.

"Can we do that sergeant major?"

"Can't see why not, sir. I know someone who can get the new..."

I interrupted. "I don't think I should be in on this conversation."

"Er, indeed not and er, *Sergeant* Smith, er, thank you." I was astonished. Now was the moment for extra leave!

"Sir, I've been working very hard during the past few months and I'd appreciate a few days off, fourteen days actually."

"Of course. Very understandable. Where do you want to go?"

"I was thinking of Fraser's Hill, sir."

He gave a nasty laugh. He thought I was joking. "Of course! Fraser's Hill! The very place! Fraser's Hill! Where else?"

I went out and the sergeant major said, "You're not really going to Fraser's Hill are you?"

"Yes, I am, but don't let on. He thinks I was joking. Let's not spoil the joke."

Before I left for Penang the sergeant major said to me, "That was a good idea about the Service Book, but the CO is worried that you might still report the whole thing to GHQ."

"He needn't worry, I've already forgotten about it."

"That's what I told him, but I can tell you this, he's really scared. He's just said to me, 'Make sure he leaves for Penang and stays there.' In fact he said he doesn't want to see you here again."

His wish was fulfilled to the letter. A new Service Book arrived in our despatch satchel from Taiping. Everything was as before. There was no mention of the detention or demotion. A week later I went down to Taiping and stayed with Hugh and Jean overnight before setting out with them for Fraser's Hill. We'd been there about a week, when, one morning, Hugh, who had been reading the newspaper, suddenly said, "Touch not the Lord's anointed."

Golf with Hugh Thomson at Fraser's Hill

"What's that, dear?" asked Jean.

"Touch not the Lord's anointed. John's CO is dead!"

Sure enough, there in the paper was a photograph of the CO. Apparently he had run his jeep off the road and crashed down a hillside. He was pronounced dead when the search party found him.

"I'm afraid it'll be that sergeant major's turn next," said Hugh.

Three months later the sergeant major was arrested for embezzling the mess funds. One of the sergeants had suspected fraud and called in the Special Investigation Branch. The sergeant major was tried, found guilty, reduced to the rank of private and given four years' detention. I was still very naïve as a Christian but Hugh's comment worried me. I resolved that I was going to be very careful and not provoke anyone into being horrible to me.

When I heard about the sergeant major I felt really sorry for him. I was particularly sorry that I hadn't had the courage to tell him about the love of God. "Too late," I thought, but, when I was returning home from Malaya, there he was, a prisoner under escort on board. It wasn't too late after all.

* * * * *

Compared with the lot of many servicemen in Malaya, when I moved to Penang my situation was practically idyllic. The fact that I was left to set my own priorities and chose how and where to work meant that I learned a great deal about self discipline and personal organisation. This experience was to be crucially important when later I left the army. Parallel with this was the wonderful provision of friendship with Dr William Lees.

I met Bill Lees in Taiping in 1949 when he was a visiting preacher at the Taiping Gospel Hall. Although on the staff of the Penang General Hospital, Bill was actually doing his National Service. Because he had qualified as a medical doctor the Government had given him the option of a commission in the Royal Army Medical Corps or two years with the Colonial Medical Service. In the army those who were really sick when overseas would be sent home. Bill wanted to treat the really sick so he joined the Colonial Medical Service. He was employed by the Crown Agents for the Colonies who, curiously, at the time of Bill's appointment in 1948, were also employing me when I was in Palestine.

The meeting with Bill in Taiping was a thread of destiny for me. We had no idea how closely our futures were to be linked. There in Taiping Bill delivered a deeply challenging message on the need for missionaries to be church planters and disciple makers. That message made a profound impact on me. I had read the words Jesus spoke to His disciples immediately before returning to the Father, "Go into all the world and make disciples." The problem was how to set about doing it. I didn't know it at the time but, having delivered the challenge, this same Bill Lees was to show me how to meet it.

As soon as I was transferred to Penang I made contact with Bill and very quickly he became my mentor, a role he was to fill to the present day, for much later he came to Reading and has been here ever since. Back there in Malaya he would set me a book of the Bible to study and in addition he would lend me a Christian book to read. Sometimes it would be a book on doctrine, sometimes on mission. Whatever the book, I knew that I would be quizzed on it when we next met. All this training, very demanding at the time, was to be critical for my work in the future, a future in which Bill was inextricably involved.

Bill demonstrated what he taught. When we went on the ferry to the mainland together he would give me four bundles of leaflets to give out to the passengers. "You take that side and I'll do this. Here you are, Malay, Chinese, Tamil and English." Then Bill would pray that God would bless the little booklets, while I, under my breath, was praying we wouldn't get thrown overboard!

When Bill was due for some local leave he decided to go to Fraser's Hill and asked me if I would care to accompany him. We drove to Fraser's Hill in Central Malaya in Bill's black Austin A40. I remember it well, for it was very nearly the death of me. Bill had arranged for us to be joined in Fraser's Hill by Gordon Blair, a New Zealander who was an Army Scripture Reader. Bill had asked me to go down to pick Gordon up from the rail station. This was about fifteen miles away at the bottom of a perilous road that wound its way, not only round hairpin bends with precipitous drops of about 1,000 feet, but through areas known to be used by the terrorists.

It was on this same road that the High Commissioner for Malaya, Sir Henry Guerney was murdered so I was not inclined to dilly dally. The brakes on the Austin were inclined to be a trifle spongy and there was a fractional delay in the braking effect. Approaching a bend rather too fast I braked and because of the fractional delay, braked harder, too hard, for the car went into a skid stopping *very* near the edge of a precipitous drop. At that point I didn't appreciate just how near I was to the edge. I opened the door to get out and, looking down, saw the jungle roof about 1,000 feet below! The car could not have been nearer the edge. Very slowly I slid across to the passenger side and got out. The near side front wheel was resting against a rock!

During that holiday at Fraser's Hill Gordon told us about some amazing things that God was doing amongst a Bornean tribal people called the Lun Bawang. As will be seen from Part Six of this narrative, strong threads of destiny were being woven that would affect both Bill and me.

Chapter 22
Farewell to Malaya

Soon we had a new CO. He could not have been in greater contrast to his predecessor. An army Cambridge graduate, he originally intended working in the Ciphers and Signals wing of the Intelligence Corps but he quickly decided he would be bored to tears with ciphers and volunteered to attend a course at Maresfield. With the death of our CO the opportunity arose for him to come to us and he jumped at it. He was a very impressive man, never missing and never forgetting a thing. He had an amazing memory. He had the facility of being able to glance at papers on a desk and have instant and accurate recall of the contents of everything he had seen. He was very sharp but with all that ability he was also utterly charming and kind. It was my constant joy to work with him.

Soon after his arrival in Taiping, he paid us a visit in Penang. When he walked into our office we all had the strong feeling that here was a friend. As he moved round chatting with Jack, Mustapha and me he showed a genuine interest in us. I was astonished to hear Jack sharing some of his background with this newcomer. Jack was very reserved and resentful about his time of imprisonment and torture at the hands of the Japanese, but within ten minutes he was laughing and sharing some of those experiences with a complete stranger. Somehow it was cathartic for Jack and from then on he was visibly different.

The new CO wanted to know everything we were doing. As he went through all our case files, carefully updated by Mustapha, he looked at the three of us with obvious approval. Soon he was asking some very penetrating questions, but Jack or Mustapha had the answers. After a couple of hours of this, to my dismay, Jack stood up, went to the CO and clapped him on the shoulder. "Welcome," he said, "I think you're going to do all right!"

The CO burst into a shout of laughter. "From all that I have heard, coming from you, that is a great commendation. Now let's get down to some serious business. Who's free tonight?"

We all said we were free. We weren't going to miss anything, but I thought he wasn't wasting any time before getting down to some serious business. "Where's the best restaurant in town?" Then to Jack, "Book a table for four. Say seven o'clock. Could you pick me up at the P&O Hotel at a quarter to seven?"

We had a delicious meal and a most entertaining evening. Our new CO was very good company. After dropping him back at the P&O, Mustapha and Jack took me home. When they dropped me off Jack got out of the car and came round to me. Very solemnly he said, "Boss". He'd never called me that before. "You deserve this fellow. You'll do alright together."

"We all will," I said. Apparently we were the only ones in the Section who had developed a working relationship with the police and the CO wanted to meet them all. Very quickly he had them eating out of his hand. It was an education to watch him at work and two days passed very quickly.

Before he left he said to me, "I'd be grateful if you'd come down to Taiping and introduce me to some of your friends there." I went the following week and had great pleasure introducing him to Hugh and Jean, Maurice Garton and a number of Chinese and Indian friends. We went for a meal at the Thomsons' where the CO learned there was to be a Sunday School party held in the Garton's garden the following Saturday afternoon. He asked if he could go. Not only did he go but he had his photograph taken with about 100 small Chinese and Indian children. The photograph appeared in the local paper on the Monday morning. Over the photograph a caption read: "SECURITY CHIEF GOES TO SUNDAY SCHOOL." I had returned to Penang but he sent me the cutting from the paper with a note: "That's me in the middle!" All the others were tiny children! He became a regular visitor to Hugh and Jean and when I went to Taiping we often all had a meal together there. They thought he was a star.

* * * * *

Meanwhile we had a job to do and it was proving increasingly difficult. Our work involved making contact with friendly villagers who would keep us up to date on the movement of terrorists who came into the villages to demand food. The terrorists were not popular in the villages, nevertheless there was always the possibility of one member of a village being prepared to betray us and then the boot would have been on the other foot and we would have been the hunted ones.

The work was extremely frustrating, for having got the location of a band of terrorists, we would inform the infantry who would go in after them. The problem with the jungle is that it is very easy to hide in it, especially if it has been your home for ten years or more, as was the case with most of the terrorists in Malaya. It was also difficult for our heavily armed infantry soldiers to move quietly in the jungle. Even moving quietly was not good enough. The need was to move silently.

Despite the many sorties carried out the infantry patrols would find that the terrorists had simply melted away into the dense parts of the jungle, a procedure I myself had found life saving. While chatting to a friendly village head man, someone might rush up, arms waving wildly. Grabbed by the arm I would be hustled out of the village and along unseen paths to a dense part of the jungle and left there to sweat it out for an hour or two or, sometimes, for an entire day!

It was while I was sweating it out in a particularly dense patch of jungle one day that I had a heart-stopping scare. Hearing a vague noise behind me I turned and there, staring at me through the dense undergrowth, was a huge tiger! At the scent of man a tiger will turn away. It is only man-eating tigers who will venture anywhere near a human being. Here was one no more than ten feet way! I was carrying a tiny revolver which would not have stopped the tiger. So I did nothing. The tiger also did nothing. There we were, simply looking at each other! It only took me a few seconds to realise that the tiger was not as scary as it looked. A hunter had shot it and tied it on his bicycle with its head resting on the handlebars. It was while the hunter was making his way back to his village that he stumbled on me in my hideout!

On another occasion when I had a brush with a tiger it was very much alive. I had been deposited in a hut about a mile away from a village. I was to spend the night there because it was considered safer than in the village. There was a simple canvass slatted bed in one corner. As I looked at the roof I thought the corrugated iron sheets didn't overlap very well and if it rained I'd get soaked, so I moved the bed. I was just going to sleep when there was a tremendous crash and the whole roof sagged. At first I thought a tree had fallen on the hut, but whatever was up there was moving. The roof sagged ominously as the weight shifted. Then I saw four long claws appear between two of the corrugated iron sheets. As I gazed in horror the end of the sheet started to lift.

It looked as if I was about to be served up for dinner unless I did something pretty quickly. But what could be done? Running would be useless. In desperation I picked up the bed, placed all four legs against one corrugated wall and, yelling at the top of my voice, ran the legs of the bed against the corrugations the whole length of one wall. The noise was terrific. The roof nearly gave way altogether as the tiger leapt off. I had no return visit but, I have to confess, I didn't sleep very well that night!

As the months went by I became aware of a change in the attitude of many villagers who had hitherto been helpful. By acting as informants they were running enormous risks and they were expecting the military to protect them. This of course was impossible. The sober truth was that if we didn't show fairly quickly that we were getting on top of the problem then we'd lose whatever support we were getting. Mustapha, Jack and I spent many hours discussing the problem, so it was not surprising that during one of the CO's visits to us we should raise what was a preoccupation of ours. We spent most of the day discussing virtually nothing else, looking at the problem from every angle. The fact was the terrorists were winning. We had to have a different strategy. We had to think outside the box.

By the time the CO left he had some new ideas. It so happened that a little while later he had to attend a high powered conference in Kuala Lumpur convened by General Sir Gerald Templar, the new High Commissioner for Malaya. I don't know whether it was our CO's suggestion but shortly after that conference there was a complete change of policy.

Huge floodlit encampments were built in the jungle and heavily armed watch towers guarded the perimeter. These new villages were well equipped with running water and large vegetable allotments. The jungle dwellers were then encouraged to live *inside* the perimeters where they would be safe from marauding terrorists. Very quickly the word got round and soon nearly all the jungle dwellers were isolated from the terrorists. Deprived of food from the villages, the terrorists had to grow their own. To do this they had to clear the jungle and plant out their own allotments, but these were clearly visible to observers in reconnaissance planes. The area would then be surrounded and the terrorists captured. Within three years of adopting the strategy the militants in the jungle had been defeated. This happened after I had left Malaya but it is a nice thought that perhaps our little strategy meeting in Penang might well have sown the seeds of the policy that brought success out of failure.

* * * * *

One day when I was on a jungle path I came across two savage-looking characters with boar tusks in the top of their ears and gigantic bangles dangling from their earlobes. Each carried a wicked-looking three foot knife in one hand. I was with Mustapha who, with commendable aplomb, asked the men who they were. They replied in Malay that they were employed by the Army as trackers. "Ask them where they come from," I said.

"Sarawak," was the reply. They were Dyaks. Here was the authentic head hunting Wild Man from Borneo! Later I was to learn the reason for the tradition of head hunting. Nearly all the Bornean tribal people used to be animists. They worship spirits who are everywhere. The people believed that the spirits had the power of life and death and of health and sickness. Head hunting arose from the notion that a man could not handle temptation and disease in his own strength, but if he could acquire the additional strength of someone else, then he would be a two-man-power and therefore more able to resist the afflictions of life.

Clearly it would be unethical to chop off the head of a near neighbour! A much better idea is to attack an enemy tribe and gain heads that way. So off they would go and come back with heads they'd chopped off. As soon as they had set the head ceremonially over the door of their home, all the spirit strength of the decapitated man would enter his executioner who would now be a two-man-power. The more heads chopped off the stronger the man-power! Much later, when I was in Borneo, I came across a man who was a 37 man-power man; he had chopped off the heads of 36 men! He had been a man of some significance in his village. When I met him he had heard the Good News of the Gospel, had turned from animism to Christ, delivered from the fear of spirits and was a most delightful Christian.

The philosophy of head hunting has something of a biblical parallel. In chapters 7 & 8 of the Apostle Paul's letter to the Romans, he makes the point that on our own, not one of us, in our own strength, is capable of resisting temptation and doing what we know is right. On the contrary, despite our best intentions, we find within us a strong tendency to do the very things we know to be wrong. In other words, left to itself, human nature will 'swerve to rot'. In answer to the question as to who can help us out of this dilemma, Paul explains how receiving Christ gives us the needed strength. It's not our strength at all but the power of God that gives victory over sin and temptation. His power is given to us in the Person of God the Holy Spirit. What an amazing discovery it must have been for that 37 man-power Bornean to discover that his deliverance did not lie in the death of his 36 victims but in the death and resurrection of Jesus!

* * * * *

Seeing those two Dyaks made me think that Borneo needed a missionary or two. Perhaps I should be thinking about how I could best prepare myself for the task. Teaching certainly seemed to be nearer mission work than the job I was doing. Increasingly I was becoming convinced that I should transfer to the Education Corps. I decided to discuss the matter with the CO. He asked a lot of searching questions after which he agreed that I should explore the possibilities by seeking a preliminary interview with the Education Department in Singapore.

We concluded that the first step should be for him to write to the Education Department on my behalf. This he did and in due course I received an invitation to attend for an interview. The train journey to Singapore passed without incident and at 10:00 on a Tuesday morning I reported for my interview.

When I entered the interview room I was astonished to find myself confronted by an impressive row of senior officers seated behind three trestle tables. The previous day had seen the arrival in Singapore of Colonel Bedall on a visit from the UK. As Director Designate of Army Education he was to be promoted to brigadier on his return. Hearing that there was an interview board, most unusually, he had asked if he could chair it. He then invited the colonel and major who had travelled with him to sit on the board. The board normally consisted of the head of the Far East Education Department, a full colonel, his deputy, who was a lieutenant colonel and a major. So when I walked in I was faced by two full colonels, two lieutenant colonels and two majors.

Colonel Bedall was a large man with a long head from which hung two enormous ears giving him an appearance of Fred Basset! Pointing to a solitary chair positioned directly in front of him he invited me to take a seat. Feeling curiously at ease in the presence of all this brass I sat down. "So you want to transfer to the Corps, do you?" he said. It's characteristic of the British Army that every Corps member calls his own Corps "*The* Corps."
"Well, sir, hitherto I have always considered myself a member of *The* Corps, but if I should transfer to the Education Corps, no doubt I shall be equally proud to call that *The* Corps."
I saw one of the majors bristle but Colonel Bedall smiled and replied, "Well said, sergeant. So… you want to be an educationist do you? Why are you thinking of a transfer?"
"Well, sir, I've enjoyed my work in the Intelligence Corps. It has been rewarding and worthwhile but I suspect I will find it even more rewarding in the Education Corps. I've been in the army long enough to appreciate that the modern soldier needs more than courage; he needs character. This is not something that comes from ingrained repetitive training, nor is it something that can be pinned on like a medal. I believe it is a spiritual thing that comes from within him.

That is where true character comes from and that's what our soldiers need." There was a long silence.

"Where does this spiritual character come from?" asked Colonel Bedall.
"Well it doesn't come from the occasional church parade and perfunctory prayers. It comes from a personal experience of God."As one, two of the colonels and one of the majors shifted in their chairs looking shocked and disapproving.
"Do *you* have that personal experience of God?" asked Colonel Bedall.
"Yes, I do." I replied.
"How did it come about?" he asked. One of the majors started to say something and Colonel Bedall looked at him enquiringly. Whatever the major was about to say he turned it into a cough! Starting with the dinner at Hugh and Jean's I shared with this group how I had become a Christian.
"So you believe this experience will help our soldiers?" asked Colonel Bedall.
"It's not so much a matter of ordinary soldiers being helped as of it being absolutely vital for *all* ranks." As I said this I looked at the major who'd coughed! "What's more it is equally vital for everyone of us when we eventually leave the forces and face civilian life. That's our responsibility as well." Unconsciously I was speaking as if I was already in the Education Corps.

At this Colonel Bedall turned to his fellow board members. "I don't think it's necessary for Sergeant Smith to retire from the room. It is manifestly obvious that this is the kind of man we need in the Corps. He's hit the nail right on the head. Anyone disagree? No! Good!" Then he turned to me and said, "I will recommend this transfer myself and send it to your CO."

He hardly waited for any response either from his colleagues or from me but stood up and held out his hand. "I hope you decide to join us and if you do, welcome to *The* Corps." It was a classic demonstration of how not to chair an interview panel. The whole thing had lasted no more than twenty minutes and the three colonels and two majors had only contributed one smothered cough between them!

I had been back in Penang about a week when I had a letter from the CO. Sure enough Colonel Bedall himself had written a letter recommending my transfer and approving my attending a course at the Army School of Education in Beaconsfield. This was confirmation to me that I was doing the right thing. It was to transpire that Colonel Bedall's personal recommendation was critically significant. Here was another Thread of Destiny.

* * * * *

The morning I received the letter from my CO I went down with dengue fever and was rushed off to hospital. The fever is transmitted through a bite from an infected mosquito and, as the incubation period is about a week, the likelihood is that I was bitten while on my way back to Penang from Singapore. The distressing thing about dengue fever is that it ebbs and flows, with very high temperatures for a few days and then a temporary remission only to flare up again. After a week in hospital I was beginning to feel very fragile.

It was during the second week that I had a strong conviction that I should pray for Bill Deane. He was still in Taiping. Realising how indifferent he was to any personal relationship with the Lord I had now been praying for him for what seemed ages. Suddenly, there in that hospital ward, I had this great compulsion to pray more earnestly for him. With nothing else to do I set about the task and prayed almost continuously for two days and frequently into the night as well. In the middle of the second night, I got out of bed and knelt to pray. As I did so it was just as if the Lord had tapped me on the shoulder and said, "You can stop praying; Bill is going to be saved."

It was so real that I stood up and started dancing around the ward! A nursing sister came up to me and whispered fiercely, "What do you think you are doing? You're ill! You should be in bed." I was so excited I nearly threw my arms round her to give her a big hug, but she was a captain in the Queen Alexandra's Royal Army Nursing Corps, and I thought she might not appreciate it! So I quietly went back to bed and lay there and hugged myself instead.

The next day Hugh and Jean walked into the ward. Word had got back to them that I was dangerously ill and they were expecting to see an invalid. Instead I was bubbling over with excitement. I had introduced Bill to them and they knew him well. As soon as they were in range I called out, "Bill is going to be saved!" Their looks of concern deepened. Clearly they thought the fever had got the better of me and I was delirious! "Last night the Lord told me that Bill is going to be saved!" I said.

"Take it easy, son," said Hugh.

"I'm telling you. Bill is going to be saved," and I told them how the Lord had told me to pray and then said I could stop.

I was so animated about it that a nurse came in and said to Hugh and Jean, "I think you should leave him now. He really is very ill you know."

"I can see that," said Jean. As a nurse she should have known better.

"No, I'm fine," I protested. Then, as the nurse held my wrist to take my pulse, I said to Hugh and Jean, "Look, you pray. The Lord's told me, He'll tell you too!" The nurse looked first at Hugh then, significantly at the door. Hugh very briefly prayed for me and they left.

"That couple really cared for you didn't they?" said the nurse. I didn't much like the past tense! Three days later I had a letter from Jean:

Dear John, An amazing thing happened last night. We'd gone to bed when there was a great hammering on the door. We opened it and there was Bill Deane. His first words were, 'What have I got to do to be saved? For three days now I have known for certain that I am not saved. I really want to know Jesus as Saviour but I don't know what to do.' Well, we sat down and just explained how all we have to do is ask Jesus to forgive us and then accept Him as Saviour. There and then he got down on his knees and prayed... and what a prayer. We were all in tears but such happy tears. We took him back to Swettenham Road a transformed person. It was wonderful to see. So you see the Lord really had spoken to you. How wonderful that He should have told you in advance what He was going to do.

I let out a great "Halleluiah," which brought the nurse to me.

"Is the pain really bad?" she asked.

"No, I'm fine, but I've just heard that a friend of mine has been healed," I said.

"Was it serious?" she asked.

"Very, it was terminal!"

"How wonderful," she replied.

* * * * *

It took two months for me to recover fully from the dengue fever. During that time I became convinced that indeed I should transfer to the Education Corps and the wheels were set in motion. I was sent an excellent chap to be my successor. He fitted well into the team and within a few weeks I was free to leave. It was hard saying goodbye to the many friends I had made over four years, but I knew I was doing the right thing.

There was one person I had promised some time back to visit but pressure of work had precluded it. It was Mr Bruce, Sir John's estate manager, so I decided to go and see him. He was delighted to see me. It struck me when we met that his greeting was excessively enthusiastic. All was soon made clear. He had heard from Sir John and had been given carte blanche to try to get me out of the army on to his estate.

Of course I was flattered at the offer, but I had to explain the way I thought the Lord was leading me. I might well be back in the Far East but as a missionary. He tried to persuade me that there were opportunities galore for missionary work on his estate and, what was more, I would be paid handsomely for doing it.

The immediate salary was mind boggling but the prospects, as he saw them, even more so. I spent a long time with him and shared the whole of my testimony of salvation. He was desperately disappointed that I couldn't be persuaded to join him. He was a good, honest, likable man. He would make a splendid boss, but not for me. I discussed with him the future of Malaya and the inevitability of government going to Malays, and when that happened the future of expatriates would be numbered. His best course was to find a really capable Indian whom he could trust and make him his assistant. In fact, within just five years all rubber plantations in foreign ownership were nationalised. Sir John's estate was one of the first and Mr Bruce was on his way home permanently.

After leaving Penang, my first stop was at Taiping where I spent a week mainly having lunches and dinners. One of the dinners was laid on by all my colleagues who had travelled from all over North Malaya. As I looked around I realised how blessed I had been to have them as friends. Best of all, a number of them now knew and loved the Lord.

I look back on those years in Malaya with unspeakable gratitude to the Lord, first of all for saving me and then for keeping me safe. Throughout the whole of northern Malaya I had friends from every walk of life and nationality, from a High Court Judge, to a number of 'Orang Asli', the aborigines of the Malayan jungle. Many friends had come to know Jesus as their personal Saviour. For my own part, starting from scratch, I had been given a grounding in the Christian faith by my mentors, Hugh and Jean, Maurice Garton and Mr Oliver in Taiping, and Bill in Penang. These were the lasting rewards with which I left Malaya.

* * * * *

The train journey to Singapore was uneventful, evading both terrorists and mosquitoes. As I climbed the gangway to board the homeward-bound ship, I was happy to say goodbye to both. On the second day of the journey home I was walking round the top deck for exercise when I saw in front of me two red-capped military policemen. Between them there was a man who was obviously a prisoner. About twenty paces ahead of me they all turned round to retrace their steps. The prisoner was my old sergeant major from Taiping. Not knowing the protocol affecting police escorts I stood on one side and the three walked past. I went straight round to the office of the Senior British Officer and asked if I might be allowed to visit the prisoner. He gave me a note to give the Military Police and thus I was able to make good my omission of not sharing the good news of God's love with the ex-sergeant major.

He was astounded that I should want to talk to him at all, let alone visit him, but soon he was pouring his heart out. His world was the army and suddenly it had fallen apart. In the army, mess accounts are considered sacred and fiddling your own mess members is an unforgivable crime. With that on his record his career was finished.

Over the following days I visited him regularly and was able to point out, amongst other things, that there were other records far more important than his military one. The difference with the records kept by God was that the slate could be wiped clean of everything that was wrong.

Curiously, what really registered with him was not only that complete forgiveness was available for those who trusted in Jesus, but God chooses to "remember our sins no more". It wasn't that He would merely forget them; He positively chooses not to remember them. The truth of that thought made a profound impression on the ex-sergeant major.

I was only allowed a short time with him on each visit but I was able to give him my Bible and some daily reading notes and pray with him. His gratitude was very touching but as far as I know he never made an open commitment to Christ. He and his escort were the first off the ship at Southampton but as I saw him getting into a military police truck, at least I had the satisfaction of being assured that he knew God loved him.

There was a vehicle at the Southampton dock waiting to take me to Maresfield which was only two hours away. Soon we were driving through the entrance and past the Guard Room. I couldn't see the provost and we didn't stop. We went up the road, past the garages and the infamous car park. There were no courses on and most of the staff were on leave. Everywhere was quiet and empty.

Suddenly I realised I didn't belong any more. The Intelligence Corps was no longer *The* Corps. I had transferred my allegiance. I only stayed one day at Maresfield before collecting my transfer documents. As I left the School of Military Intelligence I felt a deep sense of gratitude for all that I had been taught and the many experiences I had been through, but I would be glad to get home.

PART FOUR
An 'Educationist'
(1953-56)

Chapter 23
The Army School of Education

My mother was overjoyed to see me home safe and sound and not suffering unduly from religious mania! She had been through an anxious and lonely five years. Her three sons were abroad. After leaving the army Bill had emigrated to Canada. Fred had been in the RAF in Cyprus. When demobbed he went to Faraday House Engineering College in London where he got a good degree but then promptly emigrated to Australia. There he landed a top job, met Betty, a lovely Australian girl, and has since become a father and grandfather of a wholly delightful family. Meanwhile Mum's "baby" had spent, for her, a nerve-wracking time, firstly in Palestine and then in Malaya. She wholeheartedly agreed with my transfer to the Education Corps. "That's a very good idea. It'll be much safer!"

One of my first tasks on arriving home was to visit Mr Tucker, my old headmaster at the Royal Grammar School. I wasn't looking forward to it but the happy outcome, recorded in Chapter 9 of this narrative, was a huge relief. I had passed the army recruiting office on my

My brother Fred in the RAF

Fred and Betty in Australia

way up to the school and had hardly given it a second glance. I was obviously feeling lighter hearted on the way back for I thumbed my nose at it as I went past in the bus!

Another task awaiting me was to claim some baggage I had sent home by freighter. This consisted of a huge rosewood chest. It was beautifully carved and lined with camphor wood. I had bought it in Penang just before my departure and arranged with the shop owner that I would leave it with him until I had filled it with such goods as were in short supply in the UK. As this was just about everything it didn't take long to fill. Virtually nothing in the UK could be bought without the all important coupons: clothes and china were particularly difficult to get so I bought a complete eight-piece dinner and tea service, two other tea sets, silk clothing of all kinds and an assortment of oriental vases and ornaments. All of these things were dutiable on their arrival in the UK but even so they were very good value for money. The chest itself would also be dutiable but I thought, if the worst came to the worst, I could sell the chest to pay the duty.

Awaiting my arrival at home was a letter from Her Majesty's Customs and Excise. Actually the headed paper said, His Majesty but Elizabeth had only just acceded to the throne and they hadn't changed the paper. No matter, I still had to report to Tilbury Docks to claim my baggage. Meanwhile there was an accompanying form on which I had to disclose any dutiable goods.

I completed the form as best I could but added a note to the effect that I rather suspected all the contents of the chest would be dutiable. In due course I arrived at Tilbury Docks and was passed from one customs officer to the next, each of whom had taken one look at the papers and said, "Come with me," only to be handed over to another officer who had one more gold ring on his coat sleeve and a bit more scrambled egg on the peak of his cap.

Eventually I was ushered into the rather posh office of a man dressed like the Admiral of the Fleet. I noticed that his cap, which was hanging from a hat stand, had a double row of little golden oak leaves on the peak. Wordlessly he pointed to a chair in front of his desk while seeming to be completely engrossed in whatever was on his desk.

Without looking up he said, "How did you obtain all this contraband?"

"I bought it," I replied.

"Where?"

"Most of it from one shop, 'Oriental Craft', in Farquhar Street, Penang in Malaya."

"What were you doing in Penang?"

"I was in the army."

"How long were you there?"

"Four-and-a-half years."

"How much did all this stuff cost?"

I had made a list of all the 'stuff' with the cost of each item. I had been tempted to knock a percentage off one or two of the items but when I remembered the hard bargaining in the shop I thought they were pretty good value and had put the full amount down. I gave the Admiral the list which he closely studied for a few minutes then said, "Have you any idea what the duty will be on all this?"

I smiled as I said, "I have no idea, but if Her Majesty's Customs and Excise want to extract more from me in duty than I have already paid, in blood, toil, tears and sweat in the jungles of Malaya, then they'll have to sell that chest in order to get it."

Unsmilingly he said, "Have you declared everything that's in the chest?"

"It was crated up and despatched by the shop, which was why I bought the stuff there; but as far as I can remember that's everything."

"You're sure of that?"

"As far as I can remember, that's everything," I repeated.

"Alright, come with me." He was certainly no conversationalist.

He led the way to an enormous warehouse. At the far end a group of three men were chatting together. As we approached I recognised my crate. It was empty and beside it was the rosewood chest which was also empty. Strewn around an area of about 50 square yards were the contents.

"All this your stuff?" asked the 'Admiral'.

"I'm afraid it is." However I couldn't see anything that wasn't on the list.

"Pack it all up," he said to the waiting men. Then turning to me the Admiral said, "Mr Smith, if you had lied to me, I would have charged the maximum duty on everything in that chest of yours. It would have come to a pretty penny I can tell you. However, I'm pleased to tell you there'll be no duty. Thank you for being honest. It's saved us a lot of time and you a lot of money." We shook hands and he left.

One of the men said to me, "I've never known him do that before. Good for you young man." The chest was put back in the crate, repacked and the crate sealed. "You should get this within three or four days," one of them said. With that I returned home ready to face a completely new sphere of life as an 'Educationist'.

* * * * *

The Army School of Education is set in Wilton Park on the London side of the outskirts of Beaconsfield on the A40. It was a ten minute bus ride from our home in Gerrards Cross. When I reported to the reception office I was taken to the major in charge of new intakes.

As soon as I mentioned my name, he said, "Ah! Sergeant Smith, Intelligence Corps. I'm afraid there's been an unfortunate mistake. Your transfer to the Education Corps is out of the question."
"Why?"
"Well, I'll tell you, and a right mess they've made of it. The trouble is they don't think of the army as a whole. They think the world revolves around their Corps or their Regiment. I'm sorry Sergeant but it won't do. You see the army has spent a lot of money on your training and by the look of your reports you are a valuable asset to the army, but not, *not* in the Education Corps. Frankly, you will do much better in the Intelligence Corps. I've got to be open with you; there is no chance of you getting a commission in the Education Corps unless you get a good degree. I'm sorry to tell you that. It's a very great pity you weren't told all this at the time of your interview. The whole thing is ridiculous. Where were you interviewed?"
"Singapore."
"That accounts for it. These overseas interviews are always botched. I'm really sorry about this but I'm afraid I'll have to send you back to Maresfield. By the way, who interviewed you in Singapore?"
"Brigadier Bedall."

"*Brigadier Bedall? The Director of Education?* Nonsense, the Brigadier's in Eltham Palace, our HQ. Are you trying to pull my leg?"

"Of course not. It really was Brigadier Bedall who interviewed me."

"Come, come Sergeant! Whatever makes you think *he* interviewed you? The Brigadier would never conduct an interview himself!"

"He did me! Mind you it was nearly six months ago and he was a full colonel then. The board he chaired also had on it Colonel Watson, Lt Colonel Jeffries, Lt Colonel Andrews, Major Sinclair and Major Stevens." I didn't add, 'But none of them said a word'!

"The *Brigadier himself* recommended your transfer! Why?"

"Well, modesty makes me a little reluctant to say," I began, not in the least reluctant! "What he actually said was, 'It's obvious that this is the kind of man we badly need in the Corps' or something like that. What made him say such a thing I have no idea!" The major gave me a long stare, looked at the papers again and, shaking his head, murmured to himself, "Brigadier Bedall. *Brigadier Bedall.*" I waited.

Then, "Well Sergeant, if you *want* to transfer to the Education Corps and if *Brigadier Bedall* recommended it, it's got to be right, hasn't it?" and he gave me a grin. "Welcome to the Education Corps."

"*The* Corps," I responded!

* * * * *

The Army School of Education was not as exciting as Maresfield but I learned a great deal about the principles and practice of teaching, communication and public speaking. I also had some practical experience of the latter because on the administrative staff was a Lance Corporal who was a committed Christian and much in demand by local churches as a visiting preacher. He asked if I would care to do the same and so on most Sundays I would go to one of the chapels in the area to be their visiting preacher.

One of the war-time responsibilities of the Education Corps would be to produce frontline newspapers so this featured prominently in our training. Part of this training included a course actually held in Fleet Street. This was very well organised with visits to different newspaper publishing houses. There we would meet the editor and reporters who gave us a great deal of their time. Particularly relevant were those reporters who had been with the forces during World War II.

It wasn't just Fleet Street that was instructive. The journey there was extremely educational! We went by train to Marylebone Station where we got the tube to Fleet Street. The trains were always crowded so we would be strap hanging which brought us face to face with the advertisements in the trains. I can remember some of them to this day. A number advertised wool and one went:

> Before Queen Ann Boleyn was sacked,
> She'd got her suit case ready packed
> And labelled it in letters large,
> To the Bloody Tower, per Royal Barge.
> Her friends admired her savoir faire,
> Until they missed their underwear
> For Ann, you see, was no-one's fool;
> There is no substitute for wool!

Another was:

> Fair Venus emerged from the spray,
> And no more work was done that day.
> The Elders came, they turned bright pink,
> They coughed and said, "We think,
> Some well placed wool would do no harm,
> Indeed it might enhance your charm.
> Besides you'll find the evenings cool;
> There is no substitute for wool"!

One of the advertisements was for beer:
> When Theodore discovered that,
> Burglars had been and robbed his flat
> Stolen his wife's new coat of mink,
> And even stopped to have a drink
> He said, "I'm most put out my dear,
> They might have left my Barclay's beer!"

Chapter 24
The Outward Bound Mountain School

While we were on the course at Wilton Park we had a visit from the Warden of The Outward Bound Mountain School in Eskdale, Cumberland. He had received permission from the War Department to give a lecture at the Education School and ask for volunteers for temporary secondment to the Mountain School staff. I volunteered.

The very same major who was dubious about my joining the Education Corps was part of the interview board, in my view, significantly reducing my chances of a satisfactory outcome. They weren't getting much out of their investment in me anyway and secondment to the Mountain School would reduce their margins still further. During the interview I told the warden that I knew nothing about mountaineering but I had climbed a lot of hills in Malaya. To my surprise I was accepted and within a couple of weeks I was heading north to Whitehaven station in Cumberland. There, a bearded man, who looked as if he had just spent four weeks on Everest, was waiting to take me in his ramshackle car to The Outward Bound Mountain School.

Outward Bound was the innovation of a German educationist, Kurt Hahn who founded Gordonstoun School where Prince Phillip was a founder student in 1934. The first Outward Bound School was opened in Aberdovey, Wales in 1941 and it grew out of Hahn's work in the development of the Gordonstoun School and what is now known as the Duke of Edinburgh's Award.

Outward Bound's founding mission was to give young seamen the ability to survive harsh conditions at sea by teaching confidence and tenacity. Captain JF 'Freddy' Fuller took over the leadership of the Aberdovey School in 1942 and served the Outward Bound movement as senior warden until 1971. Fuller had been seconded from the Blue

Funnel Line following the wartime experience of surviving two successive torpedo attacks and commanding an open lifeboat in the Atlantic Ocean for 35 days without losing a single member of the crew. The name Outward Bound derives from a nautical expression that refers to the moment a ship leaves the pier. This is signified by Outward Bound's use of the nautical flag, the Blue Peter.

From the beginning community service was an integral part of the programme, especially in the areas of sea and mountain rescues. The Outward Bound maxim was 'to develop a righteous person who is an active citizen, vigilant and has a sense of duty to his fellow men and to God.' Industrialists and schools were invited to send junior apprentices and students to the Outward Bound Schools where they could learn that their potential was so much greater than their present achievements had indicated. Today Outward Bound has 40 schools all over the world and serves over 200,000 students each year.

The Outward Bound Mountain School, founded in 1950, had been going for four years when I was seconded to the staff. It was located in a magnificent country house, Gatehouse in Eskdale in Cumbria. Built in 1896 as a secluded retreat, Gatehouse gave immediate access to some of the best walking and climbing in the country.

Gatehouse in Eskdale, Cumbria
Home of The Outward Bound Mountain School

Back in November 1953 the course consisted of about 50 lads between the ages of sixteen to eighteen. They were divided into four teams named after the explorers Scott, Mallory, Shackleton and Wilson. Each of the teams had a personal instructor. The course set out to teach the basics of map reading and elementary rock climbing but, above all else, comradeship and mutual help in the face of trial and difficulty. My team had more scope than the others when it came to trials and difficulties!

On the evening that I arrived six of us on the staff sat down for dinner. I had eaten nothing all day and I was ravenous but even so I was unable to eat all of the vast quantity of food piled on my plate. In contrast, not only did my fellow diners eat every scrap but they sent their plates back for more. After dinner we went for coffee into a large lounge with oak panelling reaching up to the very high ceiling. While we were pouring out our coffee, one of the instructors who had been looking at the panelling said, "That'll make quite a challenging climb" and while we all watched he proceeded to climb the panelled wall. I could see very little of what might be described as hand or footholds but up he went until he reached the top and, after pretending to view the scenery, climbed down again. One or two others started to do the same. Having had problems with trees as a youngster there was no way in which I could climb a blank wall, so I sat down on a brickwork stool that was an integral part of a large fireplace. Seated on the stool opposite was a very small man reading the New English Version of the Bible. He looked up as I sat down and he nodded to me.

"Is that a good book you're reading?" I asked.
"Very good," he replied. "Do you know it?"
"Not only do I know the book, I know the Author!" I replied.

He was delighted. It transpired that he was the chief instructor, and after discussing it with the warden it was arranged that we would have an enquiry clinic in the evenings for the lads to ask questions about those issues that were bothering them. About half of the student body came the first night but thereafter the numbers grew until we had 100% attendance. A significant number made a personal commitment to Jesus Christ.

In the second week Sir John Hunt, the leader of the 1953 Everest Expedition came to the School. He made a point of ensuring that he spoke to every member on the course, chatting about the Expedition but all the time finding out the interests of the lads and encouraging them to persevere. Here was the very personification of perseverance and he made a profound impression on everyone to whom he spoke. He was an amazing person and had a great memory for names and faces. About fifteen years later I was on the underground escalator at Trafalgar Square Station, now Charing Cross, when I saw a tall man ahead of me. Although I could only see the back of his head I recognised the grizzled ginger hair. Coming up behind him I said, "This is easier than Everest, isn't it." He turned and his face broke into a smile. "John Smith! Outward Bound Mountain School," he exclaimed without a pause. I was very impressed. Together we walked across Trafalgar Square chatting about the Outward Bound Movement.

Every morning before breakfast at Eskdale I went with all the lads for a cross- country run. It was always perishingly cold. Threading its way around rhododendron bushes the route went past a tarn which was usually covered by a thin film of ice. On the last day of the course I was running round as usual when, just where the path ran close to the tarn, I was pounced on by a group of lads lying in ambush among some rhododendrons, picked up bodily and thrown into the lake. The water was paralyzingly cold and I am not a strong swimmer, which lent an element of drama to the occasion. However I was helped out by the same hands that had thrown me in.

Wondering what I had done to deserve this treatment I continued my soggy and shivering way round the rest of the run only to be received by a welcoming committee with blankets, hot water bottles and hot chocolate. It seems I had been nominated by the lads as star of the staff and had thus received my dubious reward. Afterwards I learned that I had been nominated because of the exciting exploits Shackleton team had experienced. These were partly due to my ignorance of map reading and my total inexperience of even elementary rock climbing.

On one occasion, having become hopelessly lost, we came to a gorge with precipitous sides. We decided to climb down using ropes. This was fine until I had to come down without a rope! On my way down

Shackleton Team, Outward Bound Mountain School

I was aware of white faces looking up at me accompanied by a deathly hush from the team waiting at the bottom. When at last I arrived a great cheer went up. Then one of them took me by the arm and pointed to a large sign at the foot of the climb which read, 'DANGER. Climbers with little experience should not attempt this climb. An easier climb will be found 300 yards further up the gully.' We had all climbed down it! From then on they all considered themselves experienced climbers. I was thankful to conclude the course with no injuries, let alone fatalities on my hands.

I arrived back at Wilton Park in time for our onward postings. It is sad to record that there was no passing out parade. In a most prosaic fashion our postings went up on the board and thus we learned our destinies. My posting was to an Army Apprentices School at a place called Arborfield near the town of Reading.

Chapter 25
The Arborfield Army Apprentices School

The Army Apprentices Schools are training establishments for future Warrant Officers and senior Non-Commissioned Officers. Lads of fifteen or sixteen, who want a career in the army, are admitted straight from school. The training lasts three years and consists of an intensive programme in technical training, educational subjects and military training. The level of achievement at the end of the course was an important factor for promotion when the graduates joined the army proper.

There was thus a very strong motivation for maximum effort. The results of this motivation were dramatic compared with results achieved even in the new comprehensive schools. Lads would come from schools where O-Level achievements were relatively low. Despite the demands of time and effort devoted to their technical and military training, 85% of the lads at the apprentices schools would gain at least one O-Level. The difference was due neither to superior student ability nor to better teaching, but entirely due to motivation.

Failure to achieve a satisfactory result at the end of each year resulted in a transfer to an infantry regiment with attendant slower promotion. What is more, there was never any problem with discipline. A recalcitrant student could be marched off to the guard room one day, up before his CO the next and be sentenced to a week's duty cleaning toilets. He could even be transferred out of the school. It was a paradise for teachers. My role was teaching English and a hugely rewarding task it became.

It was at this time that I had the most devastating experience of my entire life. When I arrived home from Malaya I had a letter from Valerie Hignett, my prayer partner now of four years standing. The reader will recall that Valerie had been praying for me ever since we had met. Struck speechless by her when she was fourteen, I was completely bowled over now that she was twenty. I fell deeply and permanently in love. Three months later, at two o'clock in the morning of Christmas Day, having just returned from the midnight service, we got engaged. I was living in the wonderful world of a perfect romance. I was to descend with a catastrophic crash.

One day, shortly after my arrival at the Apprentices School, I was praying and the Lord drew my attention to a significant omission. He reminded me that I had not consulted Him in connection with the engagement to Valerie. I was very frank about it, confessing that I hadn't done so in case He should disapprove. I was left in no doubt that He *did* disapprove and I *had* to do something about it. I tried every kind of argument: "Lord, what is there to disapprove of? Lord, this will be nothing less than breach of promise. Lord, nobody, but *nobody* is going to understand this. Lord, if I say *You* have said 'No' then *You* will get the blame and where will *Your* reputation be then? Lord, Valerie's parents will think I've found someone else and they'll think I am not only being unfaithful but dishonest about it! Lord, just think how *Valerie* is going to feel. Lord, don't You care? Lord, I'm really sorry but it's out of the question! Alright, then, I just refuse to do it. I'm sorry, Lord, but it's Your reputation as well as mine, and that's final."

Two weeks later I was still trying to work out how to break this news to Valerie when she came to Reading to attend a conference. So it was, on a cloudless Sunday afternoon that I joined her and shared with her what I believed the Lord was saying to us.

In the back of my mind was the thought that the Lord might have said something similar to Valerie. That would still have been awful but at least it would have been a little easier for her. But no, it seemed the Lord had said nothing to Valerie and so it came as a sudden and devastating shock. It was completely and comprehensively ghastly for both of us, but incomprehensible to Valerie.

Was it possible that I had got it wrong? In a situation as important as this, surely the Lord would speak to both of us. We agreed that we would try to be as open minded about it as was humanly possible and ask the Lord to confirm His will to both of us and at the same time to give us some insight as to why.

We arranged to meet again two weeks later when I would travel up to Birmingham. In the meanwhile I went with her to Reading station. From her seat on the train, out of a white, tear-stained face, Valerie looked at me uncomprehendingly through the dirty window. As the train pulled out of the station, I stumbled to a station bench and sat full of despair and rebellion.

Of course it was unfair to blame God. It was I who had brought this on us by my refusal to seek the Lord's mind and plan in the first place. Deep down I knew it only too well, which didn't make me feel any better. There had to be a reason, and indeed there was a very good reason, but at the time all was blank and bleak.

* * * * *

It is perhaps pertinent to ask why God seems to act in a way which to us sometimes appears almost capricious. The truth is that we are called to walk by *faith*. We are called to a life of *trust*, but we much prefer to walk by *sight*. We want God to put up signposts that clearly say 'This Way'. That doesn't require faith and trust and God knows that if He made a habit of putting up signposts, in a very short time we would be turning them into crutches and leaning on them rather than on Him.

I don't know how long I remained on that station bench but gradually a kind of equilibrium returned. I'd had first-hand experience of the love and kindness of God. I *knew* He was not capricious. I *knew* Him to be a kind and loving Father who only wanted the best for His children. I *knew* that the bottom line was that I *could* trust Him. The really difficult thing was that I had to leave Valerie to struggle through the darkness on her own.

I was hoping that, at best, it would turn out to be a ghastly mistake on my part. At second best, God might speak some kind of confirming word to Valerie. It was not to be. The two weeks passed during which the hope of a mistake on my part evaporated. On the other hand I had no idea whatsoever why we had to take this course. It was all beyond understanding. I was not looking forward to my visit to Birmingham. Whatever I said was going to sound specious in the extreme.

The visit to Valerie's parents was not a happy one. There were funereal looks all round. It would have been much easier for me to have been able to say that my love for Valerie had gone and as a result we should not be married. The agony was that I was as deeply in love with her as ever. It is a tribute to Valerie's lovely mother that she was civil to me. She did it for Valerie's sake. When I left three days later it was all as incomprehensible as when I arrived. We were two people deeply in love separating completely and irretrievably for no apparent reason.

Hindsight is of course a great gift. Looking back later we were able to see the glorious truth that God *does* work everything out for the good of those who love Him and He *does* have a magnificent plan for each of us. At the time it was heavily disguised but as the weeks and months passed it became clear what God was doing.

On the Monday it was back to work. That same evening I had an opportunity of sharing the gospel with one of the Junior Division lads. His name was David Platt. To my surprise he asked how he could become a Christian and there and then invited the Lord into his life. I had said to him that no matter how daunting the prospect, before getting into bed that night he had to kneel down by his bedside to pray so that everyone in his barrack room would know that he had become a Christian.

"They'll murder me," he said, "there're 26 others in my room."
"No, they won't murder you, there's a law against murder in this country!"

The next evening he told me what happened. He had been kneeling beside his bed and when he opened his eyes, standing in front of him was his neighbour whose bed was across the room from his. "What were you doing?" asked the neighbour.
"Praying," said David cautiously.
"Are you a Christian?" he was asked.
"Yes, I am."
"How long have you been a Christian?"
"Only one day!" David replied. "Are you a Christian?"

"Yes."

"How long have you been a Christian?"

"Oh years."

"*Years!* Then why haven't you been kneeling by your bed as you should?"

The next day these two got together and agreed they would pray for the lad whose bed was next to David's. At lunch time that same day this lad came to sit next to them in the dining room and they spoke to him about Jesus. He had lots of questions but ended asking how he too could be saved. Together these youngsters led their friend to trust in Jesus for salvation. When I caught up with this trio, they were busy making a list of the college desperadoes.

"What are you doing?" I asked.

"We're asking God to give us the names of people to pray for so that they'll get saved," one said.

"Ah, but it doesn't always happen like that," I said. But they were very enthusiastic about their list, adding a name here and sometimes crossing one off there. I was thrilled with what had already happened, but my fervent prayer during the following week was not that those on the list would be saved, but rather that the faith of these young Christians would not be shaken when things didn't happen as they were expecting!

I was dumbfounded when a week later the little gathering had increased from three to fourteen, eleven of whom were among the twelve on the list! "It was you who told us to pray," they said, "why are you so surprised?" They were right, but my expectations, unlike theirs, were minimal.

What followed was truly amazing. Everywhere and at all hours there would be little groups clustered around one lad here another there, in practically every barrack block. A Gideon New Testament in one hand and a gospel tract in the other, they were enthusiastically, if not always accurately, proclaiming the gospel. Over 150 lads were saved. I was continually amazed, unlike those young Christians. They were praying and expected things to happen.

They were truly disconcerted that weeks had passed and the twelfth man on their list was still unsaved. By this time we were hiring double-decker buses to take them all to Greyfriars Church in Reading. One Sunday evening, I was in the leading bus as it pulled out from the school gates. About 200 yards up the road was a bus stop where a local bus was waiting. Running to catch the bus was one of our senior boys. As he neared the bus stop the bus pulled away. I went to the front of our bus and asked our driver if he would stop to pick the lad up. It was Lance Corporal Bull, the Twelfth Man on the prayer list!

John Bull was not a pleasant lad. He was tall and forbidding even when in a good mood. In a bad mood he looked positively menacing. "Coo. You going to church, Bull?" someone asked.
"Church," he snarled, "you won't get me in church," but when I sat down in Greyfriars Church, who should be sitting next to me, but Lance Corporal Bull. The minister was the Rev John Page and he preached a simple gospel message.

When he finished I got a dig in the ribs from John's elbow. "I want to 'ave a word wiv 'im," he said. After the service I introduced him to John Page and they went off for a chat. The church laid on tea and cakes especially for us after the service and we were all together when John Page came into the room with Lance Corporal Bull.

"I'm sure you will all be interested to hear what your friend John has to say," said the Rev Page.
There was instant silence broken by a voice quite near me saying, "He ain't no friend of mine!"

John Bull stood looking round at all the faces staring at him. You could have heard a pin drop. "I know what's bin 'appenin'. You lot've bin prayin' for me. I know that 'cos I ain't bin able to eat; I ain't bin able to sleep an' tha's all bec'os you lot've bin a prayin'. Well, you can stop all this prayin' 'cos tonight I've joined you lot." There was complete silence for a few moments then a great chorus of hoorays, and everyone clapped.

One of the original three musketeers came up to me and said, "Our twelfth man!"
"I know," I said "it's amazing!"
"What's amazing about it? We prayed for him!" The trio had been expecting John's conversion for weeks.

* * * * *

I was on a very steep learning curve. Every day more lads would be coming to know the Lord. On Sundays I would send teams of young Christians out to little congregations in the villages around the school. They came back with stories of people being saved in churches where this hadn't happened for years.

I still meet folk who vividly remember "that apprentices school team visiting us in our church. They knew the whole of the New Testament off by heart." They didn't of course, but what they did know they used to good effect, or rather the Holy Spirit used. Every night there would be a stream of lads wanting to see me about something they couldn't understand, or how to answer this, that or the other question that had been raised. Life was very busy and gradually it dawned on me that I had the equivalent of a small church on my hands and had I still been engaged to Valerie in Birmingham I could not have been at the school every weekend and available to meet these needs. It helped, but the pain was still there. Meanwhile the Christian Fellowship flourished. Lives were transformed. The atmosphere of the entire school was undergoing a change. One day I was talking with the commandant, Colonel McGee, who said that he was beginning to see that the most important thing in life was to be born again. Senior members of staff, seeing the dramatic change in the attitude of many of the apprentices, themselves became born again Christians.

During a holiday period, about eighteen months later, I was attending a youth conference at Hildenborough Hall in Kent. Late one night I was praying when the Lord spoke to me, "You can marry Valerie now." It wasn't an audible voice, just a strong conviction. Even so I thought I was imagining things, but insistently and increasingly the conviction grew. At last I was convinced that it was the Lord, but my reaction surprised me.

"So *now* you tell me. She's probably married with a family on the way." I know I was being petty but, fortunately God is gracious and understanding. After a while I was able to think with fewer emotional overtones. What should I do next? I needed to find out where Valerie's affections lay. I didn't want to create a problem for her so I had the notion of writing to Valerie's brother Bernard and suggesting that we met to discuss things confidentially. But if I wrote from Reading the family would see the post mark and the cat would be out of the bag.

Best man at the wedding of Bernard, my brother-in-law

So I wrote to Bernard but put his letter in a separate envelope addressed to the Post Master in Birmingham. In that envelope there was a request that the letter be posted in Birmingham. I explained why in the hope that the Birmingham Post Master might be pleased to help a potential romance! When Bernard got the letter he was discretion personified and no suspicions were aroused. I was greatly indebted to this splendid man who was shortly to become my brother-in-law. In some measure I was able to repay the debt I owed by being best man at his wedding. After emigrating to the USA he later suffered frightful injuries in a skiing accident and sadly has been severely disabled ever since. Back there in 1954 he ensured that the letter with the Birmingham post mark went unnoticed by the family.

In due course we arranged to meet. The venue was Stratford on Avon, more or less the halfway point between us. Not only was Valerie unattached but she was still mourning the broken engagement. Bernard went home and put his mother in the picture. She shared the news with Valerie the same day. The result of all this was that I had a lovely letter from Valerie. Not long afterwards, in December 1954, we got re-engaged and fixed 23rd July 1955 as the wedding day.

Gerry and Barbara Muldowney

During the next eight months I was very busy and for that reason Valerie visited Reading as often as possible. One of the civilian lecturers in the Department of Electronics was Gerry Muldowney. He was a committed Christian and became one of the main stays in the school Christian Fellowship. He lived in Reading with his wife Barbara and small son Jeremy. When Valerie came to Reading she stayed with Gerry and Barbara.

210

There are people in this world to whom outrageous things happen but they are able to speak about them in such a way that makes it sound excruciatingly funny. Gerry and Barbara are such people. I committed a proper faux pas with them which caused considerable amusement. Frequently Valerie and I would have Sunday lunch with them. The first time we sat down for a meal I said, "This dinner service is a very fine imitation Wedgwood, isn't it!" Gerry and Barbara went into fits of laughter. The very fine imitation was the real thing and a family heirloom!

Gerry was building a boat in their dining room so two of us had to sit on the side of the boat when we had a meal. It seemed a most natural thing to do with Gerry and Barbara. When the boat was finished it was too big to go through the patio doors and these had to be taken off their hinges. Gerry and Barbara were very good to us in every conceivable way and are still very close friends. When I left the school Gerry continued to run the Christian Fellowship and did so for many years.

Chapter 26
Married, At Last!

The day before the wedding I travelled to Birmingham where great preparations were being made. The reception was to be in the garden of Valerie's parents. A huge marquee had been erected and was being furnished with silk drapes, chandeliers, tables and chairs. Valerie's brother Bernard was to be my best man so he, his father and I went into town to be fitted out by Moss Bros. Meanwhile Valerie was putting the finishing touches to her wedding dress which she had made herself. Valerie and her bridesmaids were most anxious that I didn't catch a glimpse of my bride before the ceremony. They certainly didn't want to be seen during the morning of the wedding because they all had so-called mud-packs on their faces.

Valerie's father was commissioned to keep me occupied in the garden but not to let me get too dirty. Above all else he was not to let me wander anywhere in the vicinity of Valerie. In his efficient way he managed to do this with the result that I didn't see Valerie until she came down the aisle on his arm. As the organist at St John's Church, Harbourne played the Wedding March and I turned and looked at my radiantly happy bride, the previous three years conspired to make it an almost overwhelming moment. We said, "I will" with great emphasis and sat, holding each other's hands, as Bill Leatham, the minister preached a short sermon. Neither of us have the remotest idea what it was he said.

There were about 60 guests at the reception during which Valerie's father gave a very witty speech. Bernard caused a great deal of amusement because he had broken his glasses just before leaving for the church and, as he is practically blind without them, when it came to reading the telegrams he was ad-libbing and guessing most of the

My radiantly happy bride!
From left to right: Bridesmaid Irene Bowman; Chief Usher, John (Ginger Rawcliffe);
My Mother; The Happy Couple; Valerie's Mother and Father; Best Man,
Bernard Hignett (Valerie's Brother); Bridesmaid Julie Douglas, now Julie Lees

time. It was very entertaining for everyone except him. However he wasn't so blind that he couldn't sabotage my going-away suitcase.

Mr Hignett had kindly loaned us his expensive car to take on our honeymoon. It was a green Jowett Javelin and a delightful car to drive, which was just as well for we were going to Scotland. Our first night was spent at Rowton Hall, about five miles south east of Chester and just off the A41. Rowton Hall was an 18th Century mansion, once owned by Mr Hignett's great, great, great, grandfather, John Hignett. The month before our wedding, builders had just completed turning it into a first class hotel.

We had decided not to divulge that we were on our honeymoon, determining not to leave a trace of confetti anywhere. When I unpacked my case and shook out my dressing gown a shower of confetti floated into every corner of the room. Although we collected every last piece we would have done better to leave it for the sly look that the receptionist gave us when we booked in as 'Mr and Mrs John Smith' said eloquently, "Oh yeah!" However we were fully authenticated the next morning for when I opened my wallet to pay the bill I showered the receptionist with more confetti!

Our next stop was planned to be a campsite in the Lake District. There were no motorways in those days and the rather tortuous journey took us longer than expected. Dusk was rapidly approaching when we passed through Kendal and we hadn't seen one campsite. Suddenly, on the side of the road and stretching away for hundreds of yards was beautiful parkland with noble-looking trees and a large lake. An open gate led into this promising area which we thought would make a splendid place for camping, and so it was. In the growing darkness we pitched our tent, pumped up our new Lilo, had a bite to eat and went to bed. The Lilo had a puncture! Worse still, we had no repair kit! So the second night of our honeymoon was spent sleeping on the rather hard surface of Mother Earth.

In the morning we decided we'd go to a hotel for breakfast, packed up the tent, took a lingering look at the magnificent view and set off across our parkland for the road. The gate, which had stood so invitingly open the previous evening, was now forbiddingly closed and locked with a huge padlock. We looked at this barrier in dismay and were wondering what to do next when a farmer came along the road driving a tractor and trailer. We must have looked the part of travellers in distress for the huge man on the tractor stopped and looked at us.

"Warra yew doon thar?" he asked.

"Camping," I said, "but when we arrived last night this gate was open."

Silently he pointed to a large notice a little way up the road. It was about four feet square and the printing was in large red capitals.

PRIVATE

NO ADMITTANCE

THIS LAND IS A

WATER CATCHMENT AREA

NO HIKING

NO WALKING

NO CAMPING

By Order of the Cumbria County Council

"It was getting dark when we arrived last night," I said, "and I'm afraid we didn't see that notice. The gate was wide open when we arrived," then I added, rather unnecessarily, "but now it's closed." Then I said, "You see, we're actually on our ... ouch!" Valerie had trodden rather heavily on my toe! "Well, what I mean is, we're on our way to Scotland and we really need to get out. Do you know who holds the key?"

The man climbed down from the tractor and stood looking, first at the gate, then at us, then back at the gate. Then without a word he moved to the middle of the gate grasped it with huge hands and lifted it bodily, clean off its hinges at the one end, and swung the gate round on the large chain and padlock. With a jerk of his head he indicated that we should drive through, which we did, not without some sense of relief to say nothing of release. Our Samson then swung the gate back and lowered it onto its massive hinges. With that he nodded and climbed back onto his tractor. We had got out of the car and walked back to him, thanking him profusely. He just lifted one hand while with the other he started his tractor and, with a nod of his head, drove off. He was not the most loquacious man I have ever met but I reckon he was the strongest and strength was needed just then. We were glad of his help for we had a very long way to go.

* * * * *

Our route took us through Penrith, Carlisle, Edinburgh, Perth and Kingussie. Our Honeymoon Hotel was the Loch Laggan. Quite small and exclusive it suited us perfectly. That year Scotland had the sunniest summer on record. Every day the sun shone brilliantly. The only problem was that it created an acute water shortage in our hotel so baths were restricted. We thought it would be fun to bathe in the loch which was only 100 yards away. Valerie dived in, swam a discreet distance from the road, took off her bathing costume and there had what she claimed to be a super bath. Intending to keep her company, after all we were married, I followed suit and dived in. I nearly had a heart attack. The water was freezing cold and in about three seconds I had clambered out and stood shivering on the shore of the loch watching Valerie splashing away to her heart's content and calling out that the water was "lovely!"

On the other side of the loch from the hotel was Ardverikie, Sir John Ramsden's principal residence. The Family were not there at the time of our visit but Dad had left word that we would be calling and had given instructions for me to be loaned a rod and some fly fishing tackle. In due course we picked up this tackle but were told that Dad had thought we would have our own preference of flies. Not having the remotest idea about flies let alone preferences we decided to go to Inverness and there consult a fishing tackle dealer.

"I would like a fly, please," I said.
"What kind do you want?"
"The kind trout like to eat!"

Meanwhile he was producing tray after tray of the most beautifully made little flies I had ever seen. Any one of them must have been irresistible to a trout. "That looks a very tempting fly," I said pointing to a lovely orange and red one.

"Goodness me, no! Not this time of the year. So much depends on the surface temperature, whether it's sunny or overcast, morning or afternoon and the..."

I stopped him with, "Could you select a general all-purpose fly for moderate surface temperatures and midday fishing?"

He seemed disappointed at this clearly Philistine approach to the noble sport but after poring over a couple of trays, he produced a miniscule fly that looked more like a mosquito.

"How do I tie this on?" I asked.

"I'll put it on a lead and you can attach that to your line," he said helpfully. The mosquito cost the earth – well, anyway, quite a lot, for such a little thing. I determined there and then that if a fish swallowed it I would have to cut it out, because I wasn't going to buy another. Fishermen must spend a small fortune on tackle if they needed a different fly for every situation.

Equipped with our fly on a lead the next morning I set out determined to pit my angling skills against the wiles of the Scottish trout. I was certain who would come off second best; I had never been fly fishing before. Valerie's interest was more tepid than avid, but she came with me as I made my way to a private loch on the Ardverikie estate. As I looked at the little mosquito hanging dejectedly on the end of its lead it looked a good deal less appetising than when I saw it under the florescent lights in the shop.

"I'm not sure how you do this casting business," I said to Valerie. "Stand back; I don't want you to be bitten by this mosquito!" With that I swished the line backward and forward a couple of times and then allowed the fly to settle on the surface. Instantly there was a mighty splash and a tug that nearly pulled the rod out of my unsuspecting hands. I'd caught one! I really had caught a trout! It wasn't huge but it was certainly edible. Retrieving the hook and taking a firm grip on the rod, I made a second cast. Nothing happened. I cast again. No sooner had the fly touched the surface of the water than a fish tried to make off with my little mosquito. By the time I had landed fourteen I really thought I had a natural aptitude for a sport that was supposed to be notoriously difficult. It is much more likely that the trout in that loch were ravenously hungry and would have eaten anything, even the little orange and red fly!

"I've got another," I shouted. There was no reply. Come to think of it I hadn't seen Valerie for... how long was it? I looked at my watch.

Horrors! It was well past lunch time and Valerie was nowhere to be seen. Gathering up my harvest of fish I set off back to the hotel. The dead fish gave me a warmer look than the one I received from Valerie! The chef was very grateful for this sudden addition to the menu and the other guests were extremely complimentary but it took until tea time before normal communication had been resumed. I didn't touch a fly rod again for nearly 30 years!

* * * * *

We had decided to camp on the way home but we forgot to repair the Lilo! Instead we thought we'd stay at a posh hotel for at least one more night. Very early in the morning we set out on the return journey but ended up driving at one stretch all the way back to Birmingham. We were welcomed with open arms, not least by Valerie's father who was delighted to see that his car was still in one piece!

After two lovely days with Valerie's parents we started on what we thought would be the last leg of our honeymoon. As we approached Oxford it occurred to me that we hadn't stopped for our night at a posh hotel. At that very moment we were in Woodstock and just passing The Bear Hotel, so we pulled in there, had a most delectable dinner of roast duck and green peas and spent the night in their honeymoon suite complete with four poster bed.

That dinner was in a fiendish conspiracy with another identical dinner we had at the same hotel a year later. Those two dinners between them hatched a plot to put me in dire trouble. On the second visit Valerie was expecting Christopher and was suffering from occasional sickness. Remembering how excellent was their duck and green peas Valerie had the same, only to lose it all in a most violent fashion. Many years later we were entertaining some rather austere ladies to lunch when the subject of Blenheim Palace arose, which in turn led to me mentioning the excellence of The Bear at Woodstock.

"It has a really splendid restaurant." Then, turning to Valerie, I said, "Do you remember, darling, you had duck and green peas. You were expecting Christopher when we were on our way home from our honeymoon."

An arctic voice from the other end of the table said, "We were *not* on our honeymoon when I was expecting Christopher!"

After a full English breakfast at The Bear, we continued on our way to our new home. In keeping with tradition I carried Valerie over the threshold. A removal van arrived the same day from Birmingham with a complete bedroom suite of furniture that had been in Valerie's room plus a host of stuff given by Valerie's parents. In addition we had a mountain of wedding presents amongst which were twelve dessert sets. Happily we also had some cash presents and we were able to buy a second-hand lounge suite of two easy chairs and a large settee. The whole lot cost five pounds.

Chapter 27
Our First Home

Early in 1955 we decided to buy a house. Buying a house is a significant event but this being our very first home made it doubly special. By now we were fairly convinced that we would become missionaries and our idea was to buy a house and make it available to the War Department as officers' quarters. That way the rent would pay the mortgage during the time we were overseas.

The problem with that arrangement was that the house had to be reasonably large and therefore more expensive. Mortgage lenders would advance up to two-and-a-half times income but I was only on £500 a year which meant a maximum mortgage of £1,250. The price of houses suitable as officers' quarters would be nearer £3,000.

I was discussing this with our Chief Clerk at school one day when he said, "No problem. When it comes to you giving your income send the papers to me."
"You can't give a false figure," I said.
"As if I would do such a thing," he replied, "but you need to include such things as Married Allowance, Housing Allowance and all the other allowances. The important thing is to put down as large a deposit as possible. The larger the deposit the more you can borrow. Your job is to find the right house." We also needed to find the 10% deposit but in a wonderful way Valerie's mother came to the rescue by giving us £400. That was equal to nearly a year of my pay and was amazingly generous.

Finding the right house proved quite difficult because Valerie was in Birmingham but eventually we decided to buy a rather up-market new house that was due to be built that year and would be completed in June. When finished, 92 Redhatch Drive would have a large kitchen/dining room separated by a peninsular counter, an 18' x 15'

221

92 Redhatch Drive

lounge, three good-sized bedrooms, a bathroom and a separate toilet. A garage was attached. It was going to cost £3,225, more than double what we thought we could afford. However, thanks to my future mother-in-law and the Chief Clerk we were able to raise the necessary mortgage. The monthly payments were £4.3.4. The building work proceeded very satisfactorily and the house was completed by the middle of July. It was to be our home for sixteen years although during that time we found it necessary to extend it.

The home was fine; the problem was to be the garden. I had read Mr Shewell-Cooper's book on 'How to Make a Beautiful Garden' and discovered the essential first thing with a new garden is to double-dig the entire site. One of our wedding presents was a shiny new spade and thus equipped, early one morning I started on the process of turning our building site into a beautiful garden. After three hours of trying to excavate rubbish buried by the builder I was completely exhausted and my enthusiasm for gardening greatly diminished. I realised I was neither physically nor emotionally equipped to cope with this kind of gardening and decided to go to the Labour Exchange looking for a Mighty Man of Valour. They sent us Mr Definitely.

One morning there was a knock at the door. Opening it I found on the doorstep a creature looking exactly like the story book drawing of Puddleglum, the Marsh Wiggle in C.S. Lewis's book, The Silver Chair. He wore a conical hat over an extraordinarily thin face out of which peered two pale watery eyes. On his hands he wore a pair of dark blue mittens. Perhaps they used to be gloves but his rather grimy fingers now poked out of the ends. Whatever clothes he had on were completely concealed by a ragged garment that reached nearly down to the ground. From under this voluminous article of clothing an enormous pair of Wellington boots crouched. The owner seemed to be able to swivel round in these boots without them moving. They must have been size thirteen or fourteen and far too large for him for when he walked he slithered them along the ground, and when perforce he had to lift his feet, it looked as if he was screwing up his feet to stop the Wellingtons from falling off.

Having recovered from my surprise at seeing this apparition, I said, "Hello, can I help?"
"Definitely!" he responded.
"Definitely? How?"
"Garden, definitely," he said.
"Ah, you've come to dig my garden!"
"Definitely," he replied.

I asked him to come with me to the back of the house. He followed, slithering his Wellingtons under him. I pointed to my little excavations, "Now, you'll see I've started digging..."
"Definitely," he said.
"What?" I said.
"Oh! definitely, definitely," he said emphatically.
I decided to press on. "Well, I've started to dig this..."
"Definitely."
"... and you see I've hit a prob..."
"Definitely."
"The problem is this scaffolding pl..."
"Definitely."

I was definitely beginning to feel desperate, so I went into a different gear and without a pause rattled off: "Scaffold plank out... bottom of garden... dig trench... two foot deep... then dig out the top soil... loosen the bottom with a fork... dig the second trench on top first trench... dig third trench..."

At that rate I would very soon have arrived at the bottom of the garden but, having tried valiantly at every possible moment to interrupt with a "Deff..." he almost shouted "DEFINITELY."

Eventually, after innumerable interjections of 'Definitely', he took my spade and started to dig out a scaffolding plank that had been buried by the builder. It was out and taken to the bottom of the garden in next to no time. It would have taken me all day. I was impressed and left him to continue with the double digging.

Valerie had thought I had been exaggerating when I told her how often he had said 'Definitely' in the short chat I'd had with him, but it transpired that, during the day, every time she'd asked if he would like a cup of tea, he'd said, "Definitely, definitely."

It wasn't simply the repetitive nature of the response that was so extraordinary, it was the 'definiteness' of it! He would nod his head so vigorously that his hat wobbled and had to be steadied with his mittened hand.

I was driving down Redhatch Drive that evening on my way home from work, when I saw what at first looked like a gigantic crow flapping its huge wings in an erratic way as it made its way up the road keeping low to the ground. As I got nearer I could see it was our Mighty Man of Valour. I stopped the car. "Can you come tomorrow?" "Definitely, definitely," he said and continued on his erratic flight path up the road.

Valerie said that he had worked non-stop all day and certainly he had done an enormous amount of work. "There's something very unusual about him," Valerie said.
"You don't say!"
"No, but listen. I must have given him at least six cups of tea during the day but never once has he asked to use the toilet. He must be a fairy."
I thought I should change the subject. "Or an angel. He's got wings. He was flapping them on his way home just now. By the way, what's his name?"
"I don't know. We'll have to call him Mr Definitely!"

Mr Definitely came to us five days a week, every week for more than three months. Every day he worked non-stop. Every day he had nothing but six cups of tea and never once did he ask to use the toilet!

Mr Definitely was one of the hardest working men I have encountered, but another thing about him was that, rain or shine he never took off that long coat. Perhaps he didn't have anything else underneath... you never know with Marsh Wiggles!

* * * * *

Mr Shewell-Cooper's next instruction for the garden was to cover it with farmyard manure. I telephoned a farmer who agreed to deliver a wagon-load. He brought it the following day. It was an exceedingly inopportune moment for the delivery of manure! We were members of the Inter Varsity Fellowship, one of the activities of which was to provide hospitality to overseas students. We were expecting a rather special guest; he was the oldest son of the Maharaja of Jaipur. We were told his Indian name and titles but were asked to call him Patrick.

As I left home to go to the station to pick up Patrick on that Saturday morning, I looked in the driving mirror of the car and there, coming up Redhatch Drive, was a tractor pulling what looked like a ginger, fuzzy haystack, but because I was late I didn't give a great deal of thought to this phenomenon. I arrived at platform number five at the same time as the train from Oxford. The first person to descend from the train was an immaculately dressed young man of about twenty. He wore a dark blue suit, snow white shirt and a polka dot blue tie. His shoes sparkled with the brilliance of their shine.

"Patrick?"

"John Smith?" We shook hands. He looked as if he was dressed for a presentation at Buckingham Palace. Approaching our house in Redhatch Drive I saw that the ginger fuzzy haystack was now directly outside our front drive. As we got nearer we became aware of the appalling stink of the pig sty. Our noses had not lied. The fuzzy haystack was an enormous pile of pig manure! When placing the order for manure with the farmer, I had not specified the type preferred and the farmer had obviously thought this was an opportunity for getting rid of some unmarketable and definitely unwanted produce.

Closer inspection showed that the ginger hue and the fuzzy appearance came from the presence of about 1,000,000 ginger horseflies, 500,000 of which had settled on the noxious heap and the other 500,000 were looking for somewhere to land.

"What on earth are you going to do with that terrible stuff?" Valerie asked.

"You were right the first time. It's got to go on the earth."

"Well for goodness sake do it before we all go down with diphtheria or worse."

"I'll help," said Patrick.
"Not dressed like that you won't."
"Well, lend me some old clothes?"

Dressed very much in keeping with the task we set about carting this great heap to the back and spreading it over the garden. We took it in turns, alternately filling and wheeling to the bottom of the garden barrow loads of pig manure, while the other spread it and forked it in. We'd been going about an hour when Patrick, leaning on his reeking fork, burst out laughing. "What's the joke?" I asked.
"If only my father could see me!" he said, wiping his eyes.
"I'm glad he can't. He'd have me thrown to the tigers!"

By tea time we had spread it all over the garden and covered it with soil. Gradually the aroma of the pig sty departed together with the attendant ginger fuzz. I reckon the Maharaja of Jaipur would have found it difficult to believe that his son and heir had spent a whole day shovelling pig poo. In fact his son thought it was a great joke.

Before going to bed that night Patrick announced that he intended to give us a treat. "I will make the breakfast." The next morning, hearing activity in the kitchen I went down. Patrick was on his hands and knees trying to scrape on to a plate the remains of the third egg he had dropped on the floor. Yet another two had disappeared down the sink!

"What are you doing?" I asked.
"How do you break eggs?"
"Drop them on the floor! You're doing very well so far. What are you making?"
"An omelette, but I only have one egg left so I must take care."

We broke the egg into a cup. "Do you know how to make an omelette?"
"I've seen my servant make them, but I've never actually made one myself."
"You have a servant while a student at the university?"
"My father arranged it. My servant came with me from Jaipur." I left him to make Valerie's omelette. Ten minutes later there was a terrific smell of spices coming from the kitchen. Valerie hates spicy food but it was too late. A rather blackened omelette was covered with paprika, nutmeg, ground allspice and ground cinnamon.

"That looks terrific. Actually Valerie says she's not feeling very well and all she wants is a slice of toast. I'll have the omelette." It was awful but I ate it! Apart from his culinary skills Patrick was a delightful visitor.

PART FIVE
A Civilian
(1955...)

Chapter 28
An 'Ordinary' Job

As soon as we knew that Valerie was pregnant I looked around for a company with whom I could take out some life insurance. Soon I was overwhelmed with brochures, quotations and a mass of figures, most of which I didn't understand. Amongst all these papers was a prepaid card to the Sun Life Assurance Company of Canada. It was an advertisement for a plan that offered '£4,315 for you at 55.' All I wanted was life insurance but I sent off the card and three days later a Mr Harry Schofield arrived. He was a man of destiny.

Harry Schofield was able to recommend a policy that gave maximum protection for a minimum outlay. It was exactly what I needed and I signed the papers. He came back a week later with the policy and explained it to Valerie and me together.

Every time he said, 'Right?' Valerie responded with, 'Right'. I was glad about that because I could hardly understand a word of it. When he'd gone, I said to Valerie, "My goodness, I'm glad *you* understood all that, 'cos I didn't understand any of it."

"I thought *you* understood it," she said. That experience was to stand me in good stead in the future when I was a representative of this company. When going through a policy I would say, "Have I made that clear, or would you like me to go through that part again?" Nearly always clients wanted me to repeat it. When they knew exactly what the plan could do they were more likely to recommend me to their friends.

One morning at about a quarter to seven, three months after taking out this policy, Valerie and I were having breakfast. Those were the days before cholesterol when we had proper breakfasts: cereal with cream, bacon and eggs, buttered toast and marmalade and real coffee!

On this particular morning we were at the cereal stage and were talking about the future when Valerie said, "What would be your reaction if the Lord wanted you to be in an ordinary job?"

"What kind of ordinary job?"

"Well, I don't know, say something like that insurance man, Harry Schofield's job." My image of a life insurance man was of someone with bicycle clips collecting 2d per person per week. It didn't appeal at all but Valerie said, "Well that was only an example, but just supposing the Lord wanted you to have an ordinary job, what would be your reaction?"

I said, "I'm pretty sure He wants us to be missionaries, but let's pray about it."

I hope that doesn't sound pious because there was no piety about it. I put down my cereal spoon and prayed something like this: "Lord, we really only want to do what you want. Anything else is a waste of time, even being missionaries, but if you want me to do something else, such as a job like Harry Schofield's, would you show us so plainly that we can't miss it. Amen."

We then unconcernedly got on with breakfast but when we reached the toast and marmalade stage Valerie nearly choked. I looked up and she was pointing to the window. I leaned forward to see what she was pointing at and there walking up the drive was Harry Schofield! It was seven in the morning! I thought, "This can't be for real." The ringing door bell told me it was real enough.

I went to the door and Harry Schofield said, "Mr Smith, I'm sorry to be calling on you so early but I retire at the end of the week and I have promised my manager that I'll find a replacement for me before I go. I've got a shortlist of four and you're at the top of the list, but if you are interested you have to tell me today."

I held out my hand and said, "Mr Schofield, I'll take the job." He was so astonished he didn't take my outstretched hand but just stood looking at me. "Come in," I said, "and I'll tell you a story." So while Valerie made him a cup of coffee I told him what had happened over breakfast. He was stunned but not nearly as stunned as we were!

As soon as I arrived at the School that same morning I asked the office to find out what it would cost to buy myself out of the Army. The

Chief Clerk told me that having had two expensive training courses there appeared no chance of me being able to obtain a discharge by purchase but he would make enquiries.

In the afternoon, a highly amused Pay Sergeant came to see me and gleefully told me that all in all it would cost me about £2,000. Now this was nearly 55 years ago. Today's equivalent is approaching £100,000. The Pay Sergeant thought it a great joke. So did I.

Awaiting me when I got home was a letter from the Bank Manager complaining that our account was overdrawn... again, this time by £5.15.6, and would I take immediate steps to rectify the situation. I said to Valerie, "I'm looking forward to seeing his face when I ask him for £2,000!"

I made an appointment and soon found myself in the poshest office I'd ever seen. The Manager's name was Hargreaves; he was a tall, severe, cadaverous-looking man with piecing blue eyes that seemed to look right through me. I remember his words quite clearly, "Well, Mr Smith, I don't think this will take long. What can I do for you?"
I thought, "He thinks I'm here to ask for a £5 overdraft facility," but I said, "I'd like you to lend me £2,000... please." He burst out laughing, not a nasty laugh at all; he was genuinely amused.
Slowly the smile faded from his face and he said, "You're not serious, are you?"
"I'm afraid I am, perfectly serious. I need £2,000."
"What on earth for?"
"I want to buy myself out of the Army."
"To do what?"
"To sell Life Insurance."

He perked up at that. This was his sphere. "Oh that's interesting. What do you know about Life Insurance?"
"Nothing."
"Nothing! Have you been offered a job?"
"Yes, I have."
"Who's offered you the job?"
"The Sun Life Assurance Company of Canada."
He seemed quite surprised. "Have you indeed. What are they going to pay you?"

"Nothing, it's commission only. They won't pay me a salary."

He didn't actually say, "I'm not surprised," but he certainly looked it. What he said was: "Mr Smith, let me get this straight. Are you seriously proposing to pay £2,000 to come out of a secure and well paid job with a pension, in order to go into a complicated business about which you know nothing, working for a company who won't even pay you a salary? In heavens name... why?"

"Well, I realise it may seem absurd but the Lord has told me to do it."

"Lord? Lord who?"

"Not a peer of the realm. I mean God."

"GOD! *God* told you to do it?" I just nodded.

"So, you're on chatting terms with the Almighty are you? How long has this been going on?" He said it as if I had some dread disease.

"About six years."

"You've been chatting with God for *six* years! How did all this start?"

"It's quite a long story," I said.

"Oh, I've plenty of time." So I started at the beginning and told him everything right up to Harry Schofield walking up the drive. When I'd finished he sat looking at me and then he said, "So you think the arrival of Harry Schofield just then was a miracle?"

"Well I do, but not as big a miracle as you lending me £2,000!" I thought that was quite good and laughed. He didn't laugh. He just sat looking at me with his gimlet eyes.

Then he said, "Do you realise that Mr Schofield had already left home to visit you *before* you had prayed." I hadn't realised that but I was very impressed that he had. I didn't say anything but just sat thinking I'd be lucky to get out with a £5 overdraft facility let alone £2,000.

After about two minutes, which seemed like two hours, he said, "Alright Mr Smith, I'll lend you the money."

It all seemed absurd which made me wonder if he had really understood the situation. I said "I've got absolutely no security you know."

"Yes, I know that."

"We've got no equity in the house."

"I know that too," he said.

I was getting desperate. "Two thousand pounds is a terrible lot of money."

"Yes! It is a lot of money!"

Then I threw in what I thought was a clincher, "I won't be able to make any payments."

He seemed to be genuinely amused by that. I didn't think he had much to laugh at but he walked round his desk, put his hand on my shoulder and said, "John"... it was John now. "Don't worry about payments. Repay the loan when you're earning real money." Real money! *Five pounds fifteen shillings and sixpence* was real money to me! Then he absolutely floored me by saying, "You're going to need something to live on so I'll make an extra £1,000 available if you need it." An *extra* £1,000. £3,000 completely unsecured! Today that would be about £150,000. This was monopoly money! As if in a dream I saw him hold out his hand. "Good luck," he said. Then he added, "Somehow I don't think it will be luck." The interview was over.

The whole thing was like being with Alice in Wonderland. I couldn't decide whether it was good news or bad news! Together with our mortgage we would owe £6,000. In today's money that would be £300,000 – and me with no salary! I went home and told Valerie what had happened. We were both utterly astonished at the turn of events.

* * * * *

As we thought things over we realised that this really was God's doing. When I went to the School the next day I surprised both the Chief Clerk and the Pay Sergeant by announcing that I had decided to go ahead with the discharge by purchase. "Where will you get all that money?" When I told them about the interview with the Bank Manager they were astounded. "You say God is behind it. Even so I'd rather you than me," said the Chief Clerk, "but I'll get all the papers set up."

A week later I was with them both again. It was as if neither of them wanted to miss out on this drama. "I've had a good idea," said the Chief Clerk. "See where it says 'Requested date of discharge', put in 18th September. That's the day we start school again after the summer holidays, which start in a couple of weeks. That way you'll get paid for the eight weeks' holiday. It strikes me you're going to need every penny you can lay your hands on." Little did we know that his kind thought nearly back-fired.

I had been given a large quantity of sales material to read. One was a sales presentation called You'll Earn a Fortune. It was a beautifully made coloured folder with about twenty pages. The theme of the presentation was that every working person would earn in their lifetime a veritable fortune. There was a simple calculation based on the current salary for working out what that fortune was likely to be. Next came the proposition that part of the fortune ought to be kept for the future. There were some catchy phrases like, 'The difference between an old man and an elderly gentleman is *income.*' Incorporated in the presentation was a work sheet that enabled a tailor-made plan to be made for the individual showing the prospective retirement income, the amount available for the family if he died and the guaranteed cash values if the plan was surrendered. The attendant phrase was, 'Live, die or quit, you just can't lose.' I thought it was great and learned the whole presentation off by heart. I would sit in front of a mirror and sell myself policy after policy. I was totally convinced!

That part was not a problem; it was the mental arithmetic that floored me. I simply could not get my sums to come right. On the second day of my training course, my trainer, who was also my manager, said accusingly, "Have you sat our intelligence test?" I didn't think that was very kind! In fact I'd had no tests at all. Harry Schofield was a retired manager, so when he recommended me everybody assumed that he had done all the required selection procedures. The manager promptly sent me off to do the test.

I was put in a little room and given a paper on which were 75 questions, all of which had to be answered in 30 minutes. I had written my name on the paper and was trying to find a question I could answer, when the door opened and in walked a chap I thought must be the general manager. He wore a black coat with a dark blue velvet collar. Round his neck was an expensive-looking white silk scarf. Against a white shirt he sported a polka dot bow tie. He had on a black jacket and pin striped trousers. Over his black shoes in which you could see your face he wore some elegant light grey spats. In one hand he carried an ebony cane with a silver knob and in the other he

236

had a pair of dove-grey gloves. The whole appearance was slightly marred by a bowler hat worn at a rakish angle on the back of his head. I stood up.

"Sit down. Sit down. Are you the new boy?"

I nodded.

"You won't be any good!" he said.

I was well on the way to thinking I wasn't going to be given the chance to be any good. Slightly nettled, I said, "Why not?"

"You're too miserable!"

"Well, you'd be miserable if getting this job depended on you answering all these questions!"

"The point is, can you sell?"

"I can sell life insurance."

"How do you know?"

"Because the Lord told me so!"

"Lord? Lord who?"

Here we go again, I thought! "No! Not a peer of the realm. God told me!"

"*God* told you!"

"Yes!" I said defiantly, "*God* told me, *Himself!*"

"Well if God told you, why are you messing about with these tests?"

That's a good question I thought, but aloud I said, "The manager told me to do it."

"Have you told him that God said you can sell life insurance?"

"No."

"Why not?"

"I didn't think he would understand."

"But you think I do understand. Well, I'm not sure that I do, but you listen to me. You go in there to the Gaffa, you look him straight in the eye, and you tell him that you can't do his perishing test, but you *can* sell life insurance. If he asks how you know, you tell him. Right?"

I knocked at the manager's door and went in. He looked up and held out his hand for the test. I held on to it. "I can't do your test, sir," I said, editing my speech discreetly, "but I do know that I can sell life insurance." He gave me a piercing look and I looked straight back as if my life depended on it. We were like that for about a minute-and-a-half. Then I pushed the edge of the test sheet between his outstretched

237

finger and thumb. They closed on it and, without a word he dropped it into the waste paper basket. I gave a little nod, as if of approval, and backed towards the door. Feeling behind my back for the door knob I turned it, opened the door and let myself out.

The Toff was standing in the doorway of the little room where I had left him. "Well?"
"I told him what you told me to say."
"What did he say?"
"Nothing."
"What else did you say?"
"Nothing."
"Brilliant. That's the way to make a sale." He then turned to the office staff who were all at their desks looking at us. "You listen to me," he said. "You look after this young man." With that he put on his bowler hat and swinging his ebony cane, he walked out of the office.
"Who was that?" I asked.
"His name's Fred Taylor."
"Who's Fred Taylor?"
"Oh he's one of our representatives!"

He looked as if he had stepped out of a Gilbert and Sullivan opera!

* * * * *

Halfway through the course, apropos something I said, the manager said to me, "Are you one of these born again Christians?"
"Yes, I am," I replied.
"Don't tell me it was through the Plymouth Brethren?"
"As a matter of fact it was," I replied.
"God help me," he said.
"Well, He will if you ask Him. It's His speciality," I said. He glared at me. It wasn't exactly a propitious start, but over the ensuing years we became very good friends.

Towards the end of the course, while making myself a cup of tea, I made a cup for all the staff. In the afternoon, after a rather depressing training session, one of the staff members called out, "Don't worry, Mr Smith, if you fail the examination, we've all decided to offer you the job of tea boy!"

I thanked them but thought to myself, "Have I paid all that money in order to become a tea boy?"

To my astonishment, and to the astonishment of everyone else, I passed the examination. However, while I had been on my training course someone had really put the cat amongst the pigeons. It was Sir Anthony Eden, the Prime Minister.

Chapter 29
In Business as a Christian

Jubilant at successfully passing my examination I arrived home to find a letter awaiting me from the War Department. It was with great regret that they were unable to approve my discharge by purchase '... owing to the exigencies pertaining in Suez'. What had happened in the Middle East, later to be described as The Suez Crisis, is a complicated and rather messy business. As it had some impact on me it might be relevant if I tried to explain the gist of it.

The Suez Crisis was a war fought on Egyptian territory in 1956. The conflict pitted Egypt against Israel, the United Kingdom and France. The Suez Canal had been vital to Great Britain in maintaining control of India. For this reason it was considered important to keep the canal out of Egyptian control. The Anglo-Egyptian Treaty of 1936 gave the United Kingdom control over the canal. In 1951 Egypt repudiated this treaty and then in 1954, just when the United Kingdom had reluctantly agreed to pull out of Suez, President Nasser nationalised the Suez Canal Company, which operated the Suez Canal. By this stage, two-thirds of Europe's oil was being imported via the canal and Britain objected strongly.

The alliance between the United Kingdom, France, and Israel was largely one of convenience; the European nations had economic and trading interests in the Suez Canal, while Israel wanted to reopen the canal, closed for Israeli shipping by the Egyptians. The United Kingdom had not only foreseen the conflict, they had virtually engineered it. Sir Anthony Eden was the Prime Minister and, although the Government was divided over the issue and came in for severe criticism, he went ahead with plans to invade Egypt.

From July 1956 all releases from the armed forces were suspended. Israel invaded the Egyptian-controlled Gaza Strip and Sinai Peninsula and made rapid progress towards the Canal Zone. In accordance with a prior agreement, Britain and France offered to reoccupy the area and separate the warring armies. Nasser, whose nationalisation of the Suez Canal Company had been greeted with joy by the Egyptian public, refused the offer, which gave the European powers a pretext for a joint invasion to regain control of the canal and topple the Nasser regime. To support the invasion, large air forces had been deployed to Cyprus and Malta by the UK and France and many aircraft carriers were sent to the area. Eventually, pressure from the United States forced Britain, France, and Israel to withdraw and discharges from the armed forces by purchase were resumed.

* * * * *

At the beginning of the new term I faced an extraordinary situation. I had handed over all my teaching responsibilities and, as far as the School was concerned, I wasn't considered part of the staff. However I found plenty to do. Word got round that I was back at the School, having successfully completed a course about life insurance. I was inundated with enquiries. Initially I spent the mornings collecting queries and the afternoons going to the Sun Life office to get the answers and prepare application papers for appropriate plans. By the end of October I had sold a prodigious amount of life insurance.

I had no idea what the norm was in terms of number of applications and amounts sold, nor did I know that my first full month with the company was the month in the year when everyone pulled all the stops out and made special efforts. I was therefore amazed to discover that at the end of October I was the star of the branch, having sold more policies for a larger amount of life insurance than anyone else. For this inadvertent achievement I won a superb 'G Plan' bookcase and two very expensive tickets to a London Theatre.

The real pay-off however was that I had a significant number of new clients all willing to recommend me to their friends. It was a process that continued throughout all the time I was selling. I still found the calculations difficult but solved the problem by getting my clients to do their own sums! The important thing was that I was able to see how life insurance could be the answer to many problems. Later I was able to apply life insurance solutions to business problems. The office staff were amazed at all the business I did – but not as amazed as I was.

One of my new clients was a colleague in the Army Education Corps. His name was Barrie Machin. For over half a century our lives have been inextricably bound together in a number of ways. Barrie is an extraordinarily helpful individual. He positively looks for ways of being helpful to anyone who crosses his path. It was my great fortune to cross his path when I was leaving the Army. As soon as he learned that I was dramatically short of Army issue equipment he put the word round that I would be glad to receive any duplicate articles of equipment folk might have.

Barrie and Pat Machin

Soon my room looked like a Quarter Master's Store. The problem was that I had half-a-dozen of one item and none of another. I couldn't see myself saying to the Quarter Master, "I'll swap you four bayonet frogs for a right gaiter," unless of course he was addicted to the game of Monopoly. Thanks to Barrie Machin I was able to hand in a full inventory of equipment.

During the Suez Crisis, Barrie was one of the many who took out some life insurance. I recommended exactly the same kind of plan that Harry Schofield had recommended to me. "How are you enjoying your new job?" Barrie asked.

Apparently my reply stuck with him with unexpected results. "Barrie," I said, "I would *pay* what I earned in the Army to do this job. It's a fantastic job in every way." So impressed was he by my obvious enthusiasm, that when his service in the Army concluded, instead of going in for teaching, as he had intended, he applied to join the Sun Life of Canada. When excited, Barrie's voice goes up a number of decibels and as he was quite excited about joining the Sun Life, his interview with Geoffrey Hulbert, the Branch Manager, could be heard pretty well all round the building. At the time of Barrie's second visit to the manager I was out but arrived during the interview. A colleague said to me, "Guess who's in with Geoff?"

"I dunno. Who is it?

"Just listen." Barrie's laugh rang out at that moment!

I think Barrie had five interviews and by a process of attrition wore Geoff down to the point where self preservation dictated that he should take Barrie on! In due course he joined the company and became a very good salesman. He went on to become a unit manager, then assistant branch manager followed by branch manager and regional training manager. During the whole of that time we were close colleagues together.

* * * * *

Meanwhile, in those early days of 1957 and '58, more and more people came to me to buy life insurance. Soon I was earning an unbelievable amount of money and that enormous loan from the bank was very quickly paid off. We were very careful about how we treated this sudden wealth. We appreciated that none of it was really 'ours'. In fact we were coming to realise more and more that nothing we had was ours. In a sense we were only temporary stewards. We kept our rather dilapidated 1936 Ford which I'd bought for £100. We kept our stair carpet with holes in it. Most of our friends had carpets with holes in them so instead of buying expensive cars and new carpets we created a Charitable Trust for the benefit of missions. The simple fact is that it was a great deal more exciting! Immediately we made a big discovery: You can't put God in debt. As fast as you shovel it out – He shovels it in; but He has a bigger shovel!

In the middle of all this I was asked to become the UK Honorary Secretary of The Borneo Evangelical Mission. Because I was paid by commission and my time was my own, providing I was producing business at an acceptable level, I could take as much time off work as I liked. So half my time was now spent on mission business, and I was able to make visits to Borneo. The two jobs fitted together perfectly and in a wonderful way the Lord enabled me to do both of them well without one detracting from the other. Although only giving half my time to Sun Life work, consistently I led the branch in sales and on occasions led the whole country. I was continually astonished but of course none of it took God by surprise! He had planned it all from the beginning and organised the unmistakable call into both!

It gradually became clear that the Lord's purpose in my being in Sun Life wasn't just to enable me to be free to do the work for the BEM, although it is difficult to imagine a more suitable job. Nor was His purpose just to enable me to earn money, although wonderfully that was more than enough for me to cover all the expenses of running the BEM in the UK. In ways that were truly amazing, I was given all kinds of insights into the personal and domestic troubles of clients. Folk would say, "How could you possibly have known about that?" I would say that God had just revealed it to me because He was concerned for them and wanted to help. It was a very effective 'door-opener' into people's hearts. Invariably they were astonishingly forthcoming and open, leading to great opportunities of showing how they could know God personally. A 'life insurance' business interview might last an hour but when it led into 'eternal life insurance' I might be with clients for two or even three hours. They would be keeping me, not me keeping them, and, wonderfully, many of these times concluded with folk making a personal commitment to the Lord. It was all incredibly rewarding.

Some of the situations I encountered were positively bizarre, others a little scary. A client came in to see me one day and as he walked through the door I was *sure* the Lord said to me that this man needed a new suit, and that I should offer him a suit I had recently bought. It was the most expensive suit I had ever bought and I only got it because I was the main speaker at an insurance conference to be held in the Barbican in London. It seemed a bizarre idea to give the suit away and I put the notion down to indigestion! All the man wanted was a loan on his policy but insistently came the reminder that what he really needed was a new suit. "But Lord", I said, "I haven't even worn it! Not once!" No comment.

Eventually I said to the client, "Why do you need a suit?"
"Because I have to ... *how do you know I need a suit?*"
"I asked the question first. Why do you need a suit?"
"As a matter of fact, I've got to go to a family funeral at the end of the week and I ought to wear a suit, but I don't have one."
"Listen," I said, "do you believe God is interested in you?"

245

"I shouldn't think so for one moment," he replied.

"Well, let me tell you just how much He is interested in you. When you came in through the door just now, God not only told me that you needed a suit, but that I should give you one. We're the same size. I have a brand new suit that I haven't even worn. God wants you to have it."

To my astonishment he burst into tears. I didn't know what to say or do.

Then he said, "How can I get to know this God who is so interested in me?"

Paul tells us that it is the loving kindness of God that leads people to repentance. That man got more than a new suit; with eternal life he received a 'robe of righteousness'. How amazing that God has entrusted to us the job of sharing the Good News of salvation. Of course whenever anyone places a saving faith in Jesus, it is always a miracle. Our effectiveness is directly related to the extent that we are dependant on God. As far as my work was concerned, I had a huge advantage. From the first day of my training, I realised I was in a job that was way over my head. The intelligence test was proof of that! Ever afterwards, I always started the day with reminding God that it was He who had led me into the work, and asking Him to stay close or I'd be sunk.

When I came to read in the scriptures about the different gifts that God gives to help us, I assumed they were given to help us in the market place, rather than in church services. Obviously there is scope for the gifts given by the Holy Spirit to be used in the context of the church, but in some churches people treat them as spiritual toys and in others they are completely ignored. As far as I was concerned, these gifts were more for use from Monday to Saturday. Perhaps more than most, I realised that if I was to do the jobs into which God had called me, then I needed all the help I could get. Perhaps that was the reason I was always open to Him being on hand to help and why extraordinary things happened so frequently. Certainly many of my Sun Life clients became Christians but God had more in store.

I had been in the company a couple of years when in 1959 I was made a unit manager and asked to recruit my own team. The job of representative seemed tailor-made for Christians, so I recruited folk who were born again. The first member of the team was Sandy Penman, an accountant by profession with a thorough grasp of finance. He had an infectious laugh and a keen sense of humour. Most importantly he was interested in people. Unsurprisingly he was an immediate success and in many ways set a standard for others to try and follow. With two other new recruits, Roy Gould and David Turner, we were the smallest team in the country but we walked off with all kinds of awards and prizes.

The Smith Unit in 1963. We won the coveted McAllister Shield five years out of six. From left to right, back row: Kenneth Hearn, Arthur White, Ted Abbott, Jack Tribe. Front row: Sandy Penman, John Smith, Roy Gould

Gradually the team grew larger, initially with Arthur White, Kenneth Hearn, Ted Abbott, Jack Tribe and David Winter, followed later by many more, but in truth we were more than a business team; we were a fellowship with a real love for one another. As well as being a success, work was a joy. The great thing about it was that the company saw that it really was the Lord who was behind all this success. In fact the leaders of other teams often told me that it wasn't fair, because we had God in our team. Actually they were wrong. We were in His team!

Our regular business meetings always started with an extended Bible study and prayer. Members of our office staff in London would make up wonderful excuses for visiting us and would then ask if they could come to our 'special meetings and could they come early and attend the Christian bit as well.' Chapter three of John's gospel became a regular feature.

In 1971, I was told that our branch manager had decided to retire early and I was asked if I would succeed him as manager. I and my unit members were a large part of the branch and I knew all the others members of the branch very well. It was pleasing to know that they all would like to see me as their branch manager, but my existing contract of employment, gave me unlimited freedom to do the work required by the Borneo Evangelical Mission, and I was concerned that taking on the appointment of branch manager would curtail this freedom. When I shared this reservation with my boss, Jack Brindle, he insisted that I be at liberty to take as much time as was needed for the mission work. That too was very pleasing, but I had a further reservation.

The financial services world was becoming more and more complicated with every succeeding Budget, and the consequent enactment of Financial Services Bills. The branch manager is the one who has to apply the regulations, and to do that he needs to understand them! I therefore made the stipulation that if I was to become a branch manager I would need to have an assistant branch manager who was bright enough to understand all the regulations. Moreover I needed to be sure that I would be able to keep such an assistant in the future for as long as he wanted to stay with me. I made the point that if necessary I would supplement the salary paid to my assistant.

All of this was accepted and the job was offered to Barrie Machin, who not only knew all the multitude of regulations governing our business, but he was also an enthusiastic and competent trainer. Barrie Machin was delighted with the offer and became assistant branch manager. A year later Jack Brindle rang saying, "John, I know I promised..."
"You can't have him," I said.
"The situation is..."
"You promised," I said.
"I realise that, but we want Barrie to be assistant branch manager at Nottingham. Our plan for Barrie is that he becomes the manager of a new Leicester branch which we will split off from Nottingham."
"OK. But promise me I can choose his successor and you'll not ask for him unless he says he is open to a move."
"I promise!"

So Barrie went first to Nottingham and then to Leicester, where he was a great success as branch manager. His place in Reading was wonderfully filled by Arthur White, a delightful member of my old unit, a walking encyclopaedia of knowledge about our business and a veritable fount of wisdom. Before joining us as a representative Arthur was the manager of a company making and nationally distributing wooden pallets used for moving stores by fork lift trucks. Arthur was a totally committed Christian. He had a very quick wit and a delightful sense of humour. Quick witted people can easily say hurtful things but Arthur's essential kindness was an effective rein on his quick wit and never once did I hear him say

Arthur White

anything hurtful either to or about anyone. He had a lovely wife and three charming daughters. All the members of this family were a great blessing, not only to me and my family, but also to the whole branch. It would not be an exaggeration to say that Arthur helped keep me alive!

Over the following years the team grew and multiplied. The principal criterion for selection was a personal conviction that this was a calling from God. On occasions I felt the Lord prompting me to take on some who had never made a commitment to Christ and many of them subsequently came to know the Lord. Eventually the team grew to over 100 men and women whose job it was to discuss the personal affairs of the folk they met. When you've spent a couple of hours discussing a person's income, debts and investments, there's not much you can't talk about. Selling life assurance and sharing the gospel was a natural consequence of seeing both the practical and spiritual needs of people for whom you had a genuine concern. Large numbers of clients were saved and were introduced to local churches.

* * * * *

Just as selling had its interesting moments, so did interviews for the job of selling. I remember being in my office one day, when a lady was ushered in. She wanted to see me about becoming a representative. She was tall, immaculately and expensively dressed, and looked very formidable - a bit like the White Witch in The Lion, the Witch and the Wardrobe by C.S. Lewis! I had a routine that whenever anybody came in to see me I would just ask the Lord in a quick prayer: "Lord what is going on in this person's life?" Not always, but quite often, I would get some kind of insight. Some were very ordinary, others more dramatic. This turned out to be one of the more dramatic ones.

During the interview and quite out of the blue came an inner voice saying, "She's not telling the truth about her marriage." I needed to know whether she had a happy marriage. It had been a routine question, and she'd said that she and her husband were perfectly happily married. Now, seemingly, here was this rather formidable-looking female, not telling the truth about a rather ticklish subject. I came back to the question a little later, and again the inner voice said, "She's still not telling the truth!" So, about ten minutes later I *again* asked her about her marriage. This time she reacted really angrily.

"Look, Mr Smith, I came in to be interviewed for a job, not for an inquisition about my marriage. I have told you that I have a perfectly happy marriage, so now perhaps we can talk about the job!" Phew! I said something about it being very important, thanked her for her assurances and passed on, rather thankfully, to some other topic.

Meanwhile I was saying to the Lord: "A fine mess I got into there, Lord! Was that *you* speaking, or was it just my imagination?" It will be appreciated that all this was sort of 'Off Stage' while I was continuing with the interview. But then, again for no reason that I could see, this word came: "Ask her about her marriage."

Just in time I stopped myself saying out loud: "Absolutely *not*. I'm *not* mentioning her marriage again... It's my imagination... *Isn't* it, Lord?" Silence. "Lord?"... Silence. "Lord, I *can't* ask her about her marriage again. I've already asked her four times and the last time she nearly blew a fuse." Silence.

So, rather fatalistically, I interrupted whatever it was this woman was saying, and said in a voice that was intended to sound very brave: "Look, I must ask you *again* about your marriage." Her eyes opened wide and she went as white as a sheet. I held my breath and waited for the storm to burst. Then, after a long, long pause, she said, almost in a whisper: "*Who* told you?" and then again, this time rather fiercely: "*Who told* you that I'm leaving my husband? Even *he* doesn't know!"

I managed to say, in a casual voice, "I think you'd better tell me about it." Well, a tirade poured out. Husbands were the pits. Marriage was the pits. In her opinion there could be no such thing as a happy marriage. She was getting *really* worked up so I got out a Bible and we started a Bible study on Ephesians 5. That calmed her down a bit.

We hadn't got very far when she said, "But that's quite *impossible*. It's impossible for a person like *me,* to behave like *that*." So we looked at salvation through Christ and the promise of the Holy Spirit and His power to enable us to live a life as God had planned and as He enables. She was astounded. It was obvious that the Lord had touched her heart. I told her that God had sent her to see me, not about a job, but about her relationship with Him and her relationship with her husband. She was *very* impressed with *God*! She thought God was amazing. Well, He is, isn't He? She never did join our company, but I was able to put her in touch with some Christians in her home town.

In order to recruit born again Christians to the team, I ran an advertisement in the Christian Press. It read: *In business as a Christian or a Christian in business, either way we may have the job for you. Apply etc.* Incidentally, placing that advertisement in a paper in today's politically correct world, would probably lead to prosecution! That advertisement ran for a number of years and became well known. On being introduced to folk a common response was, "Oh, you're the 'In Business as a Christian' man are you." We certainly had a large number of responses to the advertisement giving rise to the need for very careful selection. Selling life insurance is a notoriously difficult job – in fact there was a music hall song that went: 'There's no-one got endurance, like the man who sells insurance'. The haemorrhage of failing new agents was the industry's greatest headache.

While being very alert to the guiding hand of God in this matter of selecting new members to the branch we also had an elaborate selection procedure which we had developed over the years. Basic to that procedure was a sense of calling and vocation which meant that the retention of new members was one of the best in the entire industry and certainly the best in our own company. Many of those who did leave us did so to become full time Christian workers either in the UK or overseas.

Not surprisingly the branch continued to grow in size. Whereas the average sized branch of our company was about 20, Reading Branch grew to become the leading branch in the country and then the leading branch in the entire worldwide organisation, a position we held every consecutive month until the branch was divided into three separate branches and became part of a region of which I was the regional manager.

It was when I was regional manager that a very significant event occurred in the life of Barrie Machin. The reader will recall that from being my assistant branch manager Barrie was promoted to become the branch manager of a new branch in Leicester. One of the leading representatives there was Ray Pearce, a delightful man who was a totally committed Christian. Barrie promoted Ray to become a unit manager and in a very short time Ray had brought into his team a number of new members, many of whom were also committed Christians. Barrie of course was delighted with this development, but behind the scenes more was going on than he knew. It wasn't just Jack Brindle who had plans for Barrie Machin; God had plans for him too!

Ray Pearce decided to have a regular prayer meeting in his office very early in the morning. This was attended by a large number of the branch as well as by Ray's unit members. As their branch manager was not a committed Christian, much of the praying was for Barrie! It wasn't long before Barrie wanted to know what went on at these prayer meetings so Ray invited him to join them. Barrie being there didn't inhibit the members from praying for him; in fact, they prayed all the more fervently and Barrie added a dutiful "Amen." In due course Barrie became the branch manger of Gloucester Branch and Ray became the branch manager at Leicester. The prayer meetings continued, as did the praying for Barrie.

When the opportunity arose for our region to have a regional training manager Barrie applied for the job and got it. He had a remarkable gift as a trainer and it was while he was in that role that a very significant event occurred. It happened on a journey we were taking together on the road to Oxford from Reading when we were going to a meeting of the region's branch managers. I was aware that a large number of people were regularly praying for Barrie, including his many friends in Leicester! Every contact with Barrie provided a potential opportunity of talking about the Lord, and while it was good to be alert to that, 'jumping the gun' could be totally counter-productive and something to be avoided.

Halfway to Oxford on this eventful day there was a serious traffic hold-up. While we were waiting for the traffic to clear Barrie said, "John, I'm a good father to my children; I'm a good husband to my wife; I'm a good neighbour; I don't know of any harm that I've done to anyone; I try to be a *good* person. What else can I do to be a Christian?" The question had come completely out of the blue.

As he was speaking I asked the Lord to give me the right words to say. It so happened that the previous day a couple of London's gangland, the Kray Twins, had been allowed out of prison to attend their father's funeral. Most of the newspapers had the Kray Twins on their front pages. As I prayed I felt the Lord saying, "Tell Barrie he's no better than the Kray Twins."
"Lord? Do you *really* want me to say *that*?" I should have known better than to ask.

"Barrie, in the eyes of *God*, you're no better than the Kray Twins."
Barrie laughed, looked at me, and said, "You're not *serious*. How can you say that?"
"Barrie, this is difficult for me to explain to you, but in God's eyes there are no shades of grey. We are either black or white. The Bible tells us that we are all black with sin. We may not like the word, but the fact is we are all in the same boat. Some are desperate fellows, like the Kray Twins; some, humanly speaking, are good, like you. But black is black. There are no shades of black. So it doesn't matter the *extent* to which we have done wrong, because we are not perfect we all need to ask God to take that black sin off us and replace it with His righteousness. We can't earn it; it's a gift. All we can do is admit our need for it and ask. Anyone who has not asked and received this gift of righteousness that God gives, is still black. Not a little bit black; not relatively black, but black. In *those* terms you are no better than the Kray Twins. In fact, they may well be in a better place than you, because at least they are more likely to realise that, before God, they are indeed black with sin. But so are all of us."

Barrie was completely silent. He didn't say another word all day. During our meeting a colleague said, "You OK Barrie?"
"Yup."
"You're not saying much."
"Nope."

Thus it was for the rest of the day, including the journey home.

When I dropped Barrie at his house, he said, "You didn't *really* mean what you said about the Kray Twins, did you?"
"I'm afraid I did, Barrie, every word of it."

He got out of the car and walked into the house without another word.

Sadly I drove off and said to the Lord, "There's a good friendship gone!"

The next day I was at another meeting in Oxford. This one was with a group of five unit managers, all of them Christians. I shared with them what had happened the previous day, and we spent some time together praying for Barrie. I had said to the receptionist at the hotel that I didn't want to take any telephone calls unless there was one from a Mr Barrie Machin. At three in the afternoon, the phone in the room rang.

"This is Barrie Machin!" I said to my colleagues, "He's been saved!"
I lifted the phone and at maximum decibel level a voice said, "Guess what?"
"You're saved!"
"*Yes!*"

On the phone that morning he had spoken to a Christian colleague in Leicester asking him how a person could be saved. He had then spent some time with a member of our staff in Reading, asking, "How can I get rid of my sin and receive God's righteousness?" That was an amazing question coming from a man who had thought he was 'good'!

Our colleague explained it was simply by asking. The result was that, there in the colleague's office, Barrie asked and received. It was as simple as that.

Pat, Barrie's wife, had become a Christian earlier. She had been at a meeting in our home and Valerie, who had been praying for her, said to the Lord that if an obvious opportunity presented itself she would speak to Pat. Just as she was leaving with all the others, she started to cough and asked Valerie for a glass of water. Ten minutes later she was tasting living water. She had asked the Lord into her life. Barrie and Pat have been our dear and close friends for over 50 years.

* * * * *

One day a senior manager in our company asked if he could spend a few days with us. He wanted to know the secret of the branch's success. "You see," he said, "if you don't mind me saying so, frankly you are all such ordinary people yet, in some ways, you are extraordinary." There was no disguising the fact that by any standards we were unusually successful. Before he left at the end of a week, during which he spent a great deal of time with a number of the members of our team, he said, "I know now what the difference is between your team and my team. Your team all love one another." Then he added, "I suppose it's all because they're Christians."

From time to time I would get a telephone call from other branch managers around the country asking me if I knew of any Christians in

Bulstrode House

their area whom they could recruit. Soon there were small groups of Christians in other branches of the company. Many of these would join with us when we met regularly at Bulstrode House, the Headquarters of the World Wide Evangelization Crusade in Beaconsfield. Jim Graham was the pastor at Gold Hill Baptist church in nearby Chalfont St Peter. He also joined us for our fellowship days and claimed these days were high spots for him. We looked on him as our Honorary Pastor. Nearly all the members of the team were heavily involved in their own churches, and their church members looked on them as missionaries and regularly prayed for them. A large number of the team were involved in different ways with various missionary societies.

One day I had a telephone call from the Religious Editor of the Guardian Newspaper. Afterwards he admitted that the reason for his call was that he thought he had heard of a group who were exploiting religion for business purposes and he was going to write a sensational exposure of what he thought was a scam. After a long telephone call he asked if he could come to see me, which he did. The result was an amazing article on the front page of The Guardian. It read 'Business with a Prayer' and it gave all the glory to God. It was quite something.

It is wonderfully true that the Lord has promised to guide us but it always involves stepping out in faith and sometimes the step is into the dark. The scenario I have unfolded was no exception. It all started with a step of faith into the dark, a step which at the time many described as lunatic. Not in my wildest dreams could I have imagined an outcome such as the one the Lord clearly had in mind when He got Harry Schofield to walk up our drive. Truly it was a high calling. But, no matter what the work, when the Lord calls, it is always a high calling.

Chapter 30
Our Children Arrive

I've spoken about the step of faith associated with our joining the Sun Life Assurance Company of Canada, but it is easier to cope with attendant risks, when you are *actively* involved. It is sometimes harder for those in a more *supportive* role. An illustration of this is the situation in which Valerie found herself. She was totally involved in the decision-making process that landed us in an extraordinarily vulnerable situation. We had a debt twelve times as large as the income I had just traded in for no guaranteed income whatsoever! On top of that, Valerie was eight months pregnant, which meant that she had to give up her well paid job as a physiotherapist.

Vulnerability doesn't come much sharper than that, yet during these successive crises, Valerie was not only an amazing support, but an enthusiastic partner. Suez crisis! Twelve times our income in debt and then no income at all! Having to give up your job when the income is most needed! A baby due in four weeks! It was just as well that she was as solid as a rock, for at times my own heart nearly failed me.

Yet the challenges I may have presented to Valerie, all pale into insignificance when compared with the one she gave me shortly after we were married.

"I think twelve is best," she had said.
"Twelve?" I responded, "twelve what?"
"Children," she said calmly.
"*Twelve*!" I squeaked. Then laughed, "You're joking, of course?"

But she *wasn't* joking. She'd been reading Galbraithe's book, 'Cheaper by the Dozen'. After our first, I had second thoughts about two, let alone twelve. One evening I arrived home and, just as I was putting my key in the door, it was opened by Pat, our neighbour from across

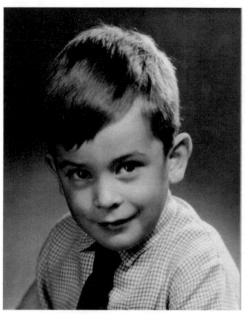
Christopher John

the road. As I stepped into the hall her friend Cora came out of the kitchen. They were both district nurses and, were not only two close friends, but they had both just become new clients of the Sun Life Assurance Company of Canada.

"Hello!" I said, "Have you come for supper?"

"No!" they replied together, smiling enigmatically.

"Well, it's lovely to see you, anyway. Er, why are you here?"

"Can't you guess?" said Cora.

"I have no idea," I said.

"Valerie's having a baby."

"Yes, I know! It's wonderful isn't it? Just another couple of weeks." I went into the kitchen to give Valerie a kiss. She was standing by the cooker making the supper.

"But she *is* having a baby!"

"Yes, so you told me! Actually, would you believe, I've known about it for some time!"

Valerie turned to me, "Hello, darling. They're right. I *am* having the baby."

"Yes, I know you're hav... What do you mean *having* it?"

"It's on its way!"

"On its way! Here? Now?"

"Yes!"

"Well for goodness sake, what are you doing down here, cooking supper? You should be in bed! What if you have it down here?"

"Don't panic. It'll be a little while yet."

In fact it was a further three hours. Pat and Cora went home, but I promised to let them know if it was a boy or girl. "I'll hang out a blue towel if it's a boy and a pink one if it's a girl. If it's neither we'll send it back!"

The midwife came and eventually, Valerie was persuaded to go to bed. Part of Valerie's job as a physiotherapist had been to give relaxation lessons to pregnant mums, and she certainly looked as if she knew what she was doing. It was a great pity there hadn't been relaxation lessons for expectant Dads. I was like a cat on hot bricks. Things were about to get much worse.

The baby was quite definitely on its way when the midwife said, "Gas?"

"Please," Valerie gasped.

"Gas?" I queried.

"It's only gas and air. It helps relaxation. Now where did I put it? Oh my goodness I've left it behind. Would you mind nipping up and getting it, as quickly as possible?"

The nurses' home was about two miles away. I was there in less than three minutes but then they couldn't find the gas cylinder. Five long minutes ticked by before they produced it. Three minutes later I thrust the equipment into the hands of the midwife. Valerie smiled at me, but there were little beads of perspiration on her forehead.

I was just going to explain why it had taken me so long when, "They've given you the wrong gas cylinder," said the midwife. "What we need is a *blue* cylinder with the number LD 234." I went down the stairs three at a time. A sudden cry from Valerie lent wings to my feet as I sprinted for the car and tore back to the home and beat a thunderous tattoo on the door. There was no reply. I was giving the door another onslaught when it was snatched open and I nearly fell into the hall.

"It was the wrong cyl... " I began and then saw that I was speaking to a man who was a total stranger. He was in his pyjamas and looking very cross.

"What do you think you're doing?" he demanded. It took me a moment to realise that I had knocked at the wrong door! All the houses in that road looked alike!

"I'm very sorry," I said, "but I've got the wrong cylinder." Despite the blank look on the poor man's face, I didn't stop to explain, but rushed to the house next door.

"Wrong cylinder!" I gasped to the nurse who opened the door. "Blue. LD 234, and please, hurry." The nurse ran off shouting at the top of her voice, "LD 234." At the back of the house I heard other voices calling, "LD 234." I wondered what LD stood for. Life or Death perhaps! Back came the nurse with two LD 234s.

"Thanks," I said, rushing back to the car. Engine racing, gears crashing and tyres squealing, I sped off. Back at the bedside the midwife had problems fitting the new cylinder to the system. She gave it to me and after some frantic fumbling it clicked into place.

"It won't be long now," said the midwife. It certainly wasn't long. In fifteen minutes it was all over.

Nothing in my domestically sheltered life had prepared me for what happened next. I was standing beside a dressing table when I heard a baby's cry. The midwife now had the baby in her hands. I could hardly believe my eyes. Horrors! The midwife's hands and the baby seemed covered in blood! The baby itself looked like a very badly skinned rabbit!

I used to feel faint if I saw a surgical operation on television *in black and white*. As I looked at the midwife's hands and the baby, the room started to go round and round and then up and down. I clutched the dressing table and hung on for dear life. The last thing the midwife wanted was a fainting father.

Through the swirling mist I heard the midwife say, "Isn't he a beautiful little boy?" He was decidedly little, but how on earth anyone could say he was beautiful was beyond me. At least I was now a father, but of what I was a father I wasn't completely sure.

Tentatively I let go of the dressing table and made my cautious way over to Valerie. She was smiling beatifically. At least *she* was alright. "Well done, sweetheart," I said.

She looked up at me and said, "Are you alright?"
"Fine," I lied.
"Go and make Valerie a cup of tea," said the midwife firmly. As I made my uncertain way out of the room, I caught a glimpse of my face in the mirror. Literally, I was as white as a sheet. It's a very good thing that men don't have babies!

A quarter-of-an-hour later I took Valerie and the midwife a cup of tea and was able to have another look at the baby. What a transformation. He not only looked human, he really did look a beautiful little boy. I was a father. This little Christopher John was part of our family. At that moment I caught a fleeting glimpse of how our heavenly Father might feel when additions are made to His Family.

* * * *

On 4th July 1959, two-and-a-half years after Christopher was born, the Daily Telegraph announced:

'On Independence Day, at home,
92 Redhatch Drive, Earley, Reading
To Anne Valerie (nee Hignett) and John B. Smith
a daughter (Kathryn Jane), sister for Christopher.'

Katie Jane was named after her two great grandmothers, Kate and Jane. Unlike her brother, she arrived at a civilised hour. It was 7:30 in the evening. With brown hair and blue eyes, Katie really was a beautiful little girl. By nine o'clock the nurse had left, Valerie was asleep in bed and Katie was asleep in a little cot on the other side of the room. At about midnight Valerie woke. There was no sound from the cot. She sat up in bed, straining her ears to hear Katie breathing. There was not a sound. Valerie slid out of bed onto the floor and crawled across to the cot and listened. Katie was fast asleep, breathing very quietly but steadily.

Katie Jane

Between the arrival of Christopher and Katie, Valerie had a miscarriage. Then after Katie was born, Valerie had another miscarriage and two still births. To say all this was traumatic is an understatement. Eventually we discovered that Valerie and I had incompatible blood groups. This was due to what became known as The Rhesus Factor, and the gynaecologist advised us that having any further children would run the risk of them being severely disabled. So much for Cheaper by the Dozen, I thought, but I hadn't reckoned on babies by mail order!

* * * * *

For some time both Christopher and Katie had been nagging us about them having a baby brother and sister. That may well have been the reason that Valerie attended a Ladies' Meeting at church to hear someone speaking on adoption. The speaker was the director of The Mission of Hope Adoption Society, located at a place called Birdhurst Lodge in Croydon. Valerie wrote to them for details. Later she said to me, "It's a pity that Christopher and Katie haven't got a baby brother and sister."
"Yes, it is," I said unguardedly.
"Do you really think so?"
"Yes, I do," I said emphatically, safe in the knowledge that we couldn't have any more.
"What do you think about adoption?"
"Adoption! What do I think about adoption? It's a very fine thing, especially for those who can't have children."
"That's us."
"Yes, but we have two already."
"True, but you yourself said it would be a fine thing for Christopher and Katie to have a baby brother and sister."
"Did I? When?"
"Just now!"

"So I did," and thus the decision was made, that was to bring Timothy and Penelope into our lives and with them immeasurable joys and rewards. In February 1967 we decided first, to adopt a boy and later a girl. We wrote to the Mission of Hope who sent us some papers to complete. In due course we had a visit from someone sent to assess our suitability. She was a delightful lady who attended Greyfriars Church in Reading. The process of assessment was extremely thorough. Not only was the interview very searching, but we also had to supply the names of a variety of people who were asked for references. After a number of weeks, we had a letter from the director of the Mission of Hope, advising us that we were suitable for adoption.

First the weeks and then the months passed, and we heard nothing until, by the beginning of 1968, we thought they must have forgotten us. We were about to contact The Mission of Hope, when we had a letter saying that, at last, they had a *suitable* little boy and would we like to collect him two weeks' hence.

Two weeks later we were at Birdhurst Lodge and met Joyce Muddiman, the director. We were enthusiastically received. "Mr and Mrs Smith, we know it has been a long wait for you, but we wanted a little boy who would be *suitable*."

Timothy Paul

There it was again. What did she mean? I was about to ask what she meant by 'suitable' when she went on to say, "This little boy's father is a 'Gold Medal Architect', *there!*" I had no idea what a Gold Medal Architect was, but from the way she said '*there*', I assumed it had to be something special. Before we could say anything, she continued, "But that's not all! This little boy's *mother* gained a Double First at Edinburgh University!" We never did find out what the Double Firsts were because Joyce Muddiman astonished me by saying, "We have waited a whole year to get a suitable little boy with an intelligence likely to match the two of you."

When I realised she wasn't joking, I said, "Miss Muddiman, I don't know about Valerie, but as for me, I can tell you, I have waited all my life for someone to say something like that!"

She laughed, obviously thinking I didn't really mean it. She was wrong but any further comment was cut short by her saying, "Now come this way and I will introduce you to him." From the depths of his little cot this prodigy regarded us very solemnly, while he sucked the first three fingers of his right hand, a habit he kept until he was at least five. His head looked very slightly lop-sided and one of his ears was crinkled. It was probably my imagination, but he looked formidably intelligent! Snugly wrapped up in the carry-cot we had brought, our new addition to the family slept all the way home.

A few months later Timothy caused us some concern. Valerie was the first to notice that something was amiss. We had a crowd of visitors in the house. Valerie was holding Tim who was being admired by the visitors when I cracked a joke, which, regrettably I forget but which caused a great shout of laughter. Valerie was looking down at Tim at that precise moment and was concerned by the fact that he hadn't even blinked at the sound of loud laughter. It wasn't the absence of Tim's sense of humour that concerned her, for he was only five months old. Was it possible that he could be *deaf*?

Valerie shared her concerns with me and we carried out some tests, all of which seemed to confirm her first fears. Timothy really was completely deaf. We made an appointment for him to see the doctor who, sure enough confirmed total deafness in both ears. The GP made an appointment for us to take Tim to a consultant about a week later. It was an anxious week, during which we were planning how we were going to help Tim cope with total deafness.

The consultant carried out a brief examination and confirmed that indeed Timothy was not hearing anything. We were still within the statutory time when we could change our minds about adoption. The consultant knew that Timothy was a potential adoptee and said to us, "What difference would it make to you adopting Timothy, if I told you that he is totally deaf?"

"No difference at all," Valerie immediately replied. "We believe that we should adopt him and we love him dearly. His being deaf doesn't change any of that."

"Well I'm glad to hear you say so, but in the event there's nothing to worry about, he's just immature."

"Immature!" I said. "He's only five months old!"

"I use the word in a technical sense," said the consultant. "This condition is not uncommon in young children. He is auditorially immature; what we call a Visual Baby. He just needs waking up emotionally."

"How do you do that?"

"Well, I can do it now. It will only take a moment." Saying which, he disappeared with Timothy, only to return in a matter of a few minutes.

"That should do the trick," he said.

"What should do the trick?" I asked.

"High frequency sound waves awaken dormant inner consciousness. I think you'll find that within a week or so Tim's hearing will be quite normal." Such was the case, and he certainly was very much more aware of what was going on around him. He's never looked back.

* * * **

Our fourth was Penelope Joy, and everything proceeded like clockwork. We knew our way around the adoption procedures, the authorities knew us, and we knew the Mission of Hope. A year after adopting Timothy, we had a letter from Joyce Muddiman saying that they had a perfect little sister for Timothy. We hoped Timothy would agree! When we saw her fast asleep in her cot at Birdhurst Lodge, she looked an exquisitely pretty baby. Her mop of jet black hair showed up against the whiteness of the pillow slip, and in her sleep she gave a little smile. She was truly enchanting.

Penelope Joy

Penny had amazing fortitude and a formidable determination. She obviously sensed that Valerie and I'd had far too easy a ride thus far, and consequently we had a completely false idea of what parenthood should be about! Single-handedly she intended to make good the deficiency! The first real exposure I had to Penny's self appointed role of Parent Educator came a little while after she had learned to walk. On Sunday afternoons Valerie ran a Mini-Crusader Class of three-to-five-year olds. Penny was too young for the class so when possible I would take her out in her pushchair for a long walk. On this particular Sunday afternoon it was bucketing down with rain, and so I had Penny with me in one of the bedrooms.

Penny was always very aware of what was going on, and she knew that downstairs some interesting things were happening of which she was not a part. I had given her some toys to play with and was reading a good book. Suddenly I became aware of the fact that I was alone. I caught up with her when she was half way down the stairs. To get there, she'd had to go through two closed doors. Surely she had not dragged a stool from the bedroom to reach the doors? Protesting violently, she was carried back to the room from which she had escaped. On my way back I had quietly locked the second door as a precaution, and picked up the stool. I deposited both Penny and the stool in the room and pretended to be absorbed in my book.

Giving surreptitious glances in my direction, she dragged the stool to the door, climbed up and grasped the door handle. Very quietly she climbed down, opened the door and, dragging the stool behind her, went out. Soon a corner in the corridor hid her from view, so I got up to see what would happen next. Puffing away less quietly now, she dragged the stool to the second door, climbed up and tried to open it. Finding it locked she turned and saw me looking at her. Her face went dark with sheer fury and, climbing down from the stool, she attacked me with both fists. Back in the bedroom, she sat on the floor glowering at me for the rest of the afternoon. Nothing could distract her from giving me that malevolent glare. About half-an-hour after tea that same day I said to Valerie, "Where's Penny?"
"In her room, I expect."

I was half way up the stairs when I heard a faint puffing and grunting. Creeping the rest of the way, I looked round a corner of the corridor.

266

On one side of her Penny had my now empty cuff links box; on the other side was a neat pile of broken links. Between the first and second finger of each hand was the last of the cuff links. Red in the face from her exertions, she was busy trying to break the chain by pulling them apart. To get the box of cuff links she had used the stool to climb up to my dressing table. It must all have been worked out while she was glaring at me earlier.

* * * * *

In the 1960s and '70s the Children's Special Service Mission became a significant factor in the lives of our children. The Children's Special Service Missions, known as CSSMs, are a feature of many holiday seaside towns where there are sandy beaches. Bude is one of the better known CSSMs. Run by the Scripture Union, CSSMs are staffed in the summer holidays by volunteers, many of whom are students from universities. The purpose of the CSSMs is to provide fun and games for children on holiday and at the same time to present the gospel and Christian teaching in ways that are understandable to children.

In 1954 the first Inland Children's Special Service Mission was started on Wimbledon Common by a local Anglican minister. It was the instant success of this mission that led three of us to consider starting a CSSM in Reading. My two confederates were Gerry Muldowney, from the Army Apprentices School, and a mutual friend named Peter Edwards.

The first mission was in Prospect Park and ran for two weeks. It was destined to continue for a number of years and attracted enormous crowds of children. Staffing the team was a group of dedicated workers, many of whom gave their entire holiday to help us. In the following years the mission expanded into Palmer Park, on the other side of Reading from Prospect Park, and also into neighbouring villages, notably Arborfield, Finchampstead and Mortimer. The Arborfield mission continued for nearly twenty years and was led by Gerry and Barbara Muldowney and continues to this day..

The Reading Inland Missions brought a different dimension to the image of CSSMs! It has to be said that up to this time, CSSMs wore a somewhat upper crust mantle. The kids attending our mission were of a different ilk. On one occasion, a small gang was creating a disturbance in the marquee where we were holding the meeting. Being the leader, it was my job to sort out the problem. Rather than discuss the matter in the tent I invited the gang to step outside. This was interpreted as meaning an invitation to a fight, so outside I found myself surrounded by a dozen or so aggressive- looking teenagers.

"Right," said one, pulling out of his pocket a length of chain, "who starts?"

None of my training in the Palestine Police or the army had equipped me to cope with confrontations of this nature. I was comprehensively out of my depth and stood helplessly as the gang moved closer. I just had time for one short prayer: "*Help!*" Immediately two extraordinary things happened. I was filled with an overwhelming feeling of compassion for this gang of thugs. God really loved them as much as He loved me! With that realisation my moment of panic left. The second thing that happened brought a high level of relief.

"Wait," shouted the leader. "What sort o' people do you fink you are? Here's this guy, tryin' to 'elp all them kids in there so's they don't grow up like us. 'Sides, there's gotta be somethin' in what they say. Look at 'im. There's twelve of us an' one of 'im but he 'int afraid, so come on you guys, from now on we 'elps this geezer, right."

Then he turned to me and said, "OK guv, anyone who kicks up a row, leave 'em to us. We'll sort 'em out good an' proppa." Here was a notable addition to our team, because some of the youngsters attending our CSSM were distinctly down-market. However a little basic instruction was necessary for our new Law and Order Team – like putting away bicycle chains and knives!

We were definitely different from our beach mission colleagues. Gerry, Barbara and I attended a Scripture Union conference on 'How to Run a Successful Mission'. One of the speakers was Quentin Carr, ex-brigadier in the Indian Army, Director General of the Scripture Union and leader of the Bude CSSM.

"Always make sure you wear a tie, your shoes are polished and your white flannels are pressed."

Gerry leaned across to me and whispered, "We're lucky to keep our shirts on our backs at our mission!"

But kids came to know the Lord. Fifty years on, I still meet folk who come up to me and say, "You don't know me, but I became a Christian at the CSSM in Prospect Park!"

* * * * *

Forty-four years ago during a CSSM Good News Hour, the Lord spoke very personally to our seven-year-old Christopher. Immediately after the 'Good News Hour' he went up to his mother and said, "Mummy, I want to ask Jesus to come into my life." When they got home they went up to Christopher's room, knelt by his bed and in a simple and straightforward way he asked the Lord to come into his life. It couldn't have been more simple. "Lord, thank you for knocking at the door of my life. I ask you now to come in to my life, take away my sin and help me to live my life for you. Amen." How true are the words of the Lord, when He said, 'Unless you change and become like little children, you will never enter the Kingdom of Heaven.'

It must have been a trial to Katie having a saintly brother who at the same time was such a helpful chap. To Katie's great frustration she found it very difficult to quarrel with her nice brother. She watched him like a hawk, and if he stepped out of line, she would instantly remonstrate. One day they were playing together, when Katie's treble voice was heard saying, "Cherrr-ristopher, *you* shouldn't say things like *that*! *You're* the one who's supposed to be a Cherrr-ristian!" We didn't ask what it was that Christopher had said to incur this censure, but we were interested to know that Katie, even at the tender age of five, was not drifting into the dangerous world of nominal Christianity. It was clear that if ever she did make a commitment to Christ, it would be a definite and distinctive decision. That was how it was to work out much later.

Katie was an unusually pretty little girl, but that seraphic countenance could change into a formidable face of thunder. When the Mock Turtle in Alice in Wonderland was describing his school curriculum, he said that he had lessons in the three branches of Arithmetic: Ambition, Distraction and Uglification. Unlike the Mock Turtle, Katie didn't need any lessons in Uglification, it came naturally, whenever she went into a strop.

It wasn't just looks that went with these episodes; they could be attended by action. On one occasion she was sent to her bedroom in disgrace. Fulminating loudly, she stomped up the stairs to her room. About fifteen minutes later Valerie said to me, "Katie's ominously quiet up there."

Hoping to see a repentant daughter, we crept up the stairs and quietly opened the door. The contents of every drawer, cupboard and wardrobe were all piled into a gigantic, muddled heap in the middle of the room. Standing behind this jumble was a diminutive figure of defiance, arms akimbo, Advanced Level Uglification patent, "Now, let *THAT* be a lesson to you!" she said.

Katie had a playmate in the daughter of our GP, Doctor Davies. Her name was Jane, and was born just twelve hours after Katie. There must have been something in the air when these two were born, for they were extraordinarily alike. Valerie was much struck to learn on her next visit to Jane's mum that during that same week Jane had similarly been sent to her room for some contretemps. This was followed by a suspicious silence and an investigation. Hearing a noise in their own bedroom, they went in to find Jane standing in front of an open wardrobe. Seeing them, she said, "I've *spat* on your new shoes! I've *spat* on your new dress, and now I'm working up some more *spit!*"

* * * * *

Something that constantly amazed me was the speed at which very small children learn to speak despite the vagaries of our English language. It wasn't so much that they got things wrong, but they could get so much right. Some of the invented words showed great initiative. When Katie was only three she was taken for a ride on a little pony. "Mummy," she said, "I can't get my feet in the puggles." She knew they weren't pedals, but 'puggles' is a much better description than 'stirrup irons'. Children have an insatiable appetite for knowledge and constantly ask the question, "Why?" All of ours were like that, but Tim was the most persistent enquirer. One morning, when out with Valerie in the car, he asked, 'Why?' 42 times in five minutes. Out of interest she had noted the time and counted the questions. He was perhaps the youngest to speak intelligibly, probably because of the influence of his older brother and sister. His vocabulary was certainly the most inventive. His little red rubber boots were waidie waiders. Seeking 'Wednesday' he called it 'half past week.'

Timothy and Penny could not have been more different. The difference is perhaps best summed up in their individual approach to receiving presents. Tim would examine a parcel carefully, looking for the sticky tape. He would then carefully remove every piece of tape, placing the pieces in a neat pile beside him. Then, again carefully, so that the paper was not torn, he would unwrap the parcel, folding the paper before turning his attention to the present. If it was in a box, that too would be subjected to the same treatment. In the meanwhile, this lengthy process would be driving Penny mad with impatience, even though the present was Tim's.

In contrast, Penny's method swiftly reduced any wrapping paper and box to waste paper, and she would know in a second or two what her parcels contained. Penny's approach to everything was bold and decisive. The cautious experimental approach was not her way. The day after we moved into Turnhams House, I had to fix a faulty tap in the water supply. The tap was sunk about two feet in the ground. My head and shoulders were deep in the hole when I heard a high pitched voice say, "Daddy! Look at me!"
"Yes Penny! I know you're wearing that nice little yellow dress. You look very pretty."
"No! Daddy! *Look* at me!"
"Penny, I can't leave this tap or we'll have a flood!"
"*DADDY! LOOK AT ME!*"

I looked, and an appalling sight met my stupefied gaze. Penny was covered from head to foot in black gloss paint, the open tin of which she had found on a shelf in one of the sheds. It was all over her face, in her hair, over her legs and up her arms. Imprinted all over her 'pretty yellow dress' were black hand prints. Out of her black face, two eyes and her white teeth were shining brightly! I gave the yell for help that was most appropriate, "*VALERIE!*"

* * * * *

Bringing up children is a tricky business. There is an over-riding need for consistency and fairness. I had read somewhere that threats were to be avoided at all costs if they were not to be followed up. One morning, just before leaving for the infants' school, Katie said, "Mummy, where're my shoes?"

"Mummy's not your slave, Katie," I said, "look for your shoes yourself."

"If you don't find my shoes, I'll go to school without them," said Katie.

"Your choice, Katie, but *I'm* not looking for your shoes."

She stood looking at me for about a minute, arms akimbo and uglification beginning to spread. Weighing up the situation, she decided to call my bluff. "Then I'll go in my *bare feet!*" she said. I opened the door for her and out she went. The school was about half a mile away. Pretending to ignore the discomfort, Katie threw me a defiant look and stomped off up the road. I went in and shut the door. A few minutes later Valerie came down with Katie's shoes in one hand and a pair of little white socks in the other.

"Where's Katie?"

"Gone to school," I said, trying to sound indifferent.

"What's she got on her feet?" asked Valerie, looking at the shoes in her hand.

"Nothing," I said.

"*Nothing!* You haven't sent that child to school in *her bare feet!*"

"*I* haven't sent her anywhere. It was *her* choice."

"Why, that poor little thing," cried Valerie, and ran out of the door and up the road, calling to Katie.

When she came back, Valerie said, "You wouldn't have let her go all the way to school, would you?"

"I'm afraid I would, and let her stay all day."

Valerie looked at me as if I was a heartless monster, then, just as I was beginning to feel like a heartless monster, she spoilt it by saying, "What on earth would the teachers have thought?"

"Probably think we were economising!" Nothing more was said about the incident, but the next morning Katie found her shoes without a word.

A thing that irritated Katie was that Christopher always seemed to have plenty of pocket money, whereas she was frequently stony-broke. This disparity in wealth is perhaps best explained by the episode of the toad. It all started when Christopher found a large toad in the garden. This toad was a decidedly indolent fellow, but Christopher pretended to Katie that he was going to coach him in the technique of the high jump, and enter him in the forthcoming Toad Olympic Games. He said that he had hopes of a Gold Medal. Christopher was so enthusiastic about his toad that, not surprisingly, Katie wanted a toad as well. She searched everywhere for a toad, but there wasn't even a tadpole to be found. When Christopher judged that Katie's desire for a toad had reached its peak, he offered to sell her his precious toad.

"How much?" she asked.

"Sixpence!" he replied. Sixpence was a great deal of money to a little girl in those days, but off Katie went to raid her piggy bank and soon she was the proud owner of a possible contestant in the Toad Olympic High Jump! I don't think I ever saw that toad so much as move a limb, let alone give an Olympic jump! Two days later the toad was back with Christopher.

"I thought this was Katie's toad!" I said.

"Oh it is," said Christopher, "but for a ha'penny a week I'm looking after it for her." The following morning I noticed a great deal of activity outside the front drive. A cardboard sign displayed the word 'ZO' with 'EN TRANS ONE PENY' underneath! On the edge of the drive was the hamster cage with a notice 'HAMSTA'. Next to the hamster cage was a glass jar with a sign 'STIK INSEX' which at least was intriguing! Tied by her lead to the gate was our little cocker spaniel with a cardboard sign 'TOFFY' and underneath 'SPANYUL DOG'. A label on a cardboard box containing Katie's toad read 'FAYMUS TODE'.

"What's he done to be famous?" I asked Christopher.

"He's not famous yet, I'm just getting him used to crowds!" said Christopher optimistically. Valerie joined me and we pretended to be an Olympic crowd. The Spanyul Dog wagged her tail and barked excitedly, thinking we'd arrived to take her for a walk, while the Faymus Tode just sat there, rhythmically puffing his throat in and out in his usual complacent way.

"Don't let your stick insect out!" I said. "Toad might surprise you and you'll lose a quarter of your Zoological Garden!"

Some amused neighbours came to the zoo, which was not to be wondered at, for Christopher stood on the pavement and stopped them as they passed with, "Would you like to visit our zoo?" The low overheads gave a good profit margin, but the zoo closed down at midday. There had been no visitors for an hour and the animals and keepers were getting bored. The total take for the morning was an astonishing two shillings and eight pence. When Valerie and I tendered our one penny each, we were surprised to find only sixpences in the box. Apparently the first visitor had paid sixpence and, keeping up with the Joneses, the other four did the same! This ability to make money has been an extraordinary characteristic of Christopher. Happily there is an attendant generosity.

A thing that I found particularly pleasing about all our children is the facility 'to walk with Kings yet not lose the common touch'. They appear to have an innate respect for everyone and this carries with it a poise and easiness that makes for quick friendships. On the other hand they have a very healthy disdain for any kind of pretension. Perhaps Penny was the one most exposed to snobbishness because, among some of her fellow pupils at school, there were significant levels of pretension. Some of the pupils came from very well heeled parents and would arrive at school in a chauffeur- driven Rolls Royce.

It was against this background that an interesting situation arose with the question of adoption. A discussion in class had arisen about adopted children and one of the chauffeur-driven girls said, disdain dripping from every syllable, "*Miss*, Penny knows *all* about adoption, because... *she is adopted.*"

The disconcerted teacher said to Penny, "Would you like to comment on that Penny?"
"Yes! Thank you," said Penny, "I would."

She went out to the front and stood looking at the class. Then she said, "Some of you are here because of an accident, but *my* Mummy and Daddy *really* wanted me, that's why they adopted me!"

With that, Penny smiled at the teacher, said "Thank you!" and walked back to her seat in the ensuing silence. It was the teacher who told us of the incident which seemingly, had made a profound impression on both the teacher and the class.

Chapter 31
We Move to Turnhams House

"I really don't think I can cope with another CSSM like this one," I had said to Valerie. We had completed the last of the children's missions for 1970 and all 72 workers had gone home. Valerie had catered magnificently, the budget showed that the really delicious meals had cost just over a shilling each. In today's money that is five pence.

When Penny arrived in 1969 we needed an extra bedroom, so we demolished the garage and built a tandem double garage with two bedrooms and a bathroom over it. The garage was designed to enable us to take a caravan right through it and on to a hard standing area at the back. Even with five bedrooms, a caravan, a large garden room and a number of tents, it was not possible to accommodate all the members of the CSSM team. Our house had been over-flowing with people for four weeks and we were exhausted.

"There's nothing for it, we'll have to move."

So we set about trying to find a house that would accommodate more people, but without adding significantly to the housework. Having looked at over twenty possible locations, we had come to the conclusion that there was nothing available. In desperation we had invited a builder friend, Philip Chandler, to visit us to see if there was any way in which we could extend our house any further to provide the needed accommodation. He had just told us that we had no alternative but to find somewhere else, when the postman delivered yet another estate agent's pull. This was a large property in Tilehurst, and the agent candidly admitted that it was 'urgently in need of repair'.

"That means it's falling to pieces," said Philip, "but it's cheap enough". The price was £7,950. We were expecting to sell 92 Redhatch Drive for about £11,000 so, financially it might work.

"Let's go and have a look at it." So we went. It had rained heavily in the night and everywhere was dripping wet. We were shown over the house by Mrs George. With her husband, she had lived in the house for nearly 25 years. Mr George had retired from the railways just four months earlier. He had attended a farewell party in London, and was intending to catch the last train from Paddington to Reading. He arrived on the platform just as the train was leaving. Running alongside the train, he opened a carriage door but slipped and fell between the platform and the train. He died instantly. A sad Mrs George showed us around a sad-looking house. Had it not been for the tragic death of Mr George, I would have found the tour of the house positively amusing.

We had approached the house via City Road from which the house looked depressingly dull and dingy. When we left I turned to Valerie and said, "*Well*, what do you think of *that*"!

"Perfect," said Valerie.

A Depressingly Dull and Dingy Turnhams House

I laughed. Then I looked at her straight face and said, "You *are* joking aren't you?"

"No!"

"You're not joking! How can it possibly be perfect? Tell me *one thing* that's right about it!"

After a few minutes' silence, Valerie said, "Well, it needs one or two things doing to it, but I believe this is where the Lord wants us to be!"

We had beef stew for lunch. It turned to ashes in my mouth as I thought about the place 'where the Lord might want us to be!' In the afternoon, armed with a drawing pad and pencil, I went back to the house, this time going up the narrow Pincents Lane. Framed in the arching boughs of two huge oak trees in Pincents Lane the house looked encouragingly different. By a curious coincidence, when I was writing this, a neighbour gave me some old photographs, one of which was of Turnhams House in the 1920s. It was taken in winter with a great deal of snow everywhere but it clearly showed the same view that I'd had on that day in 1971.

A surprisingly different Turnhams House when viewed from Pincents Lane. Photograph taken in the 1920s

In a slightly more encouraged mood I asked Mrs George if I could have another look around. I took a chair with me and sat in each room, pushing walls out here, removing chimneys there, enlarging windows and generally demolishing the house. I spent two hours there. When I got home I drew it all up afresh and two days later gave it to an architect. At the same time we contacted the agent, Martin and Pole and offered £7,500. The next day we were told our offer had been accepted. The legal work went through very quickly and thus we became the owners of Turnhams House in Tilehurst.

After some lengthy discussions with the architect, we eventually had everything ready to put the work out to tender. The *lowest* estimate for the alterations was £47,575! That would be equivalent to about £300,000 today! However clearly the Lord may have spoken to Valerie, He for sure hadn't told me to spend that sort of money on a house that was falling to pieces.

I went back to Martin and Pole and asked them to put it back on the market for £7,950, enough to cover our costs plus a little more. Martin and Pole gave it a great write-up under a large photograph in the middle of their main window. The photograph made it look a very attractive residence! They thought it would sell quickly. It didn't. A month later I went in to see Mr Pole. "Have you had any offers for Turnhams House?"
"Not one. I don't understand it?" he said.
"Drop the price to £7,500."
"You're giving it away," he said. They dropped the price and Martin and Pole thought it would sell very quickly. It didn't.
A month later I again saw Mr Pole. "No offers?"
"None. I simply don't understand it. I'm inclined to buy it myself."
"Done!" I said, but he wasn't serious.
"Put the price down to £6,950. That should do the trick."

But it didn't! After a month with not a single offer, it at last dawned on me that the Lord really did want us to have it! So back I went to Mr Pole. "No offers?
"Not a single offer. I simply don't understand it. It has been a mystery."
"Well, it's not really a mystery. The Lord told my wife three months ago that He wanted us to have it."

"Lord? Lord who?"

Here we go again, I thought, "No, not a peer of the realm. I mean God told her."

"*God* told her! God told your wife He wanted you to have this house!"

He stood up, came round his desk, put his hand on my shoulder and said, "Mr Smith, if *God* told your wife He wants you to have this house, I don't want to be responsible for selling it to anyone else! You'd better keep it! It'll mean loss of business for us but I'm taking it off the market!"

So now we were faced with making Turnhams House habitable at an affordable cost. I took the plans up to the house to see what alterations could be made and discovered that the work of demolition had already started. Vandals had got into the house and smashed everything that was breakable, even the banister railings. Fortunately, everything vandalised was what we were going to throw out anyway, and although we told the insurance assessor this, he insisted on us putting in a claim for all the damage. The total came to a formidable sum. We also had a splendid set of large photographs of the house supplied by the police who were investigating the vandalism.

Having reduced the scope of the desired alterations, we again submitted the plans for tender. This time the lowest quote was for £27,950. The alterations were going to cost nearly four times as much as we had paid for the house, but, it was where the Lord wanted us to be!

When the builder started, he spent three days putting up supporting wall jacks all over the house. These are six-inch diameter expandable pillars from floor to ceiling.

"What are all these for?" I'd asked.

"To stop the house falling down when we remove all the walls you want taking out."

They then set about taking out the three huge chimneys and the unwanted walls. Showing a friend round the site a few days later, she said in bewilderment, "But what have you bought, other than all this rubble?"

We move into Turnhams House – 1972

We realised that before we could move in there would need to be some extensive alterations. In the meanwhile we still owned the house in Redhatch Drive, which was just as well, for it was nearly seven months before Turnhams House was finished. My rough plans had been taken by the architect and the builder and between them they produced what was to be The Smith Family Home for the future. We have been here ever since and it looks as if we'll remain here until we make our permanent move.

* * * * *

When we moved into the house, the garden of an acre-and-a-quarter was a wilderness of trees, bushes, little gravel paths separating small allotments of vegetable plots. It was a totally neglected garden. Thistles and nettles stood five feet high. It was August and Christopher was on holiday. Always a willing helper he was very keen to sort out the garden; the problem was knowing where to start. Most fortuitously I had a visit from a client. He was looking at the garden and said, "What you need is a bulldozer. Would you like one?"

I thought he was joking, but he was perfectly serious. "I've got a JCB you can borrow," he said, and the very next day turned up with this massive piece of machinery, complete with various sized digging buckets and scrapers. He showed us how to work all the levers and how to refuel it from the boiler fuel tank. Within a very short time fourteen year old Christopher had mastered most of the manoeuvres and we started serious work. It is amazing how much work can be done with a bulldozer. I would be in the garden by 6:30 but Christopher would be ahead of me, having started up the diesel engine of the JCB. We had it for two weeks during which time we pulled up unwanted trees, dug up paths hedges and bushes, levelled the entire site and built a tennis court.

Twenty years later, when Valerie's father reached 90, it was considered prudent for him to come and live with us. In order to accommodate him with an acceptable level of independence and privacy we made some alterations to the house. The foundations under the garage and utility room were strengthened and we built over them a very attractive and spacious apartment. Valerie's father was a wholly delightful old gentleman and it was our great privilege to have him living with us for nearly eight years.

Although the house is undeniably large it never feels too large, for on occasions it is fully used. We are able to accommodate missionaries on furlough and waifs and strays who seem to gravitate to us. They all bring a dimension of life that is enriching and rewarding. In much the same way as the house, the garden of more than an acre may be large but never seems too large. Just when we thought it was all becoming too much for us, an angel in disguise arrived to help. This was Dave Tyrrell, a near neighbour, who rapidly transformed the garden and has maintained it ever since. Just when it looked as if it was going to be too much for both of us, another disguised angel arrived to help. This was John Turner, the brother of Brian, the neighbour who has been so helpful in checking the text of 'Threads of Destiny'.

The garden at Turnhams House, & Dave Tyrrell

Chapter 32
Sun Life Conferences

Among the many exciting features of working in the Sun Life Assurance Company of Canada our conferences were rated very high. These were held every other year for the top representatives. Much to the disgust of our children, especially our daughters, children were not invited to these conferences. In reality they were a highly successful means of motivating the entire sales force, sometimes to super human effort. The reward was lavish accommodation provided in five star hotels for five days during which there was a varied programme of recreation, relaxation and education. In order to attend these conferences a minimum amount of quality business had to be produced over a two year period. Production of double the amount of the required business entitled the spouse to attend.

My aim was to get Valerie's qualification first and add mine to that! It seemed to work for she qualified for every conference and I was able to go with her! Our first conference together was at The Imperial Hotel in Torquay. It was posh, posh, posh! When we arrived we checked in and collected our key to the room. Turning the key we went in and immediately turned round and went out again. Back at the desk we explained that they had given us the key for a suite of rooms.

"Very sorry, sir," said the young man and took the key. He was back again in a moment saying, "This is the key beside your name, sir." So back we went. This time we had a good look around. There was a huge sitting room with a patio and garden area all overlooking the sea. A spacious bedroom led off to one side with an enormous en suite bathroom.

"It must be another Smith," said Valerie "they've mixed up the initials!" So back we went again. This time we met John Kearsey, the conference organiser standing by the door of the concierge.

We explained the problem and he smiled. "It's the first time anyone has complained their rooms are too posh!" he said. "I allocated that room because you are the leading unit manager. You enjoy it!"

We did and we went on to enjoy a week of similar luxury at every biannual Agency Conference for the next 37 years. These were held in Torquay, Eastbourne or Brighton and always at the very best hotels. Wives were expected to attend the first and the last days of the conferences, but Valerie and her friend Meera Thomas were considered most supportive because they attended the other days as well. What the organisers didn't know was that they played an exciting word game during the parts they considered boring, although I think they will admit that most of the sessions were at least interesting and most were thoroughly entertaining.

In addition to the Agency Conferences we also attended a number of Sun Life Leaders' Conferences. Some of these were positively spectacular. One was at the Hilton in Rome. The main dining area was huge and it was in this magnificent room that the principal banquet was held. The theme for the evening was Ancient Rome. A guard of dozens of Roman soldiers lined the dining room walls. Just before the dinner, a splendid white stallion galloped in pulling a chariot in which was our top producer, dressed as an Emperor. The stallion had leather boots to protect the floor, but it was a dramatic entrance. This was followed by the chariot race sequence from the film Ben Hur, portrayed on the walls round the dining room. The 3D effect was sensational.

Robert and Meera Thomas with Anita and Aruna

Seated at the president's table for dinner that evening were Robert and Meera Thomas. Life with Robert was always exciting and this dinner was to be no exception, but there had been a time when life for Robert and his family had been a good deal too exciting! The Thomases, together with their two daughters, Anita and Aruna had experienced a devastating time in Bangladesh. Robert was a senior tea plantation manager, when he was arrested by the Bangladeshi authorities who suspected him of being a spy.

Robert had heard Christian broadcasts from Radio Manila but the reception on his ordinary radio was poor. In order to improve the reception signal he erected a tall radio mast. This certainly gave a good signal and Robert thoroughly enjoyed the broadcasts. Unfortunately, the tall mast gave entirely the wrong signal to the Bangladeshi authorities, who jumped to the conclusion that the owner of such a radio mast could only be someone who was intercepting military signals, and was therefore a spy. Robert was arrested but, unable to find proof to support the charge of spying, the authorities then changed the charge to cattle smuggling! They couldn't find proof of that either, but he was nevertheless sentenced to death!

Almost overnight Robert's situation had changed dramatically. One moment he was a senior plantation manager living in a luxurious house with his lovely wife and two enchanting daughters. Looking after them they had two butlers, two chauffeurs, four full-time gardeners and a houseful of other servants. To put it mildly Robert's position was one of affluence and authority. The next moment he was separated from his family and his luxurious home and was in a stinking cell with nearly 30 others prisoners all condemned to death and sharing hopelessly primitive and inadequate toilet facilities.

It was after a number of ghastly weeks that God spoke to Robert. Looking back, Robert is able to testify that God was using that terrible jail to bring him to his senses. He realised that in his previous position of privilege he had become proud and arrogant. From a situation where seemingly he *lacked* nothing God brought him to a place where he actually *had* nothing! No wife, no family, no home and, with a death sentence hanging over his head, probably no future! It was then and in that unlikely situation that Robert had an extraordinary revelation of the extent of God's love for him. In a specific act of repentance Robert asked God for His forgiveness and committed to Him every moment of whatever was left of his life.

Robert's remarkable deliverance is an epic story that hopefully one day will find itself into the hands of a publisher. Sufficient here to say that the deliverance involved the improbable presence of a respectable looking total stranger lingering at the door of Robert's terrible cell. Robert surreptitiously gave this stranger a message that he had been concealing in his shoe. Almost miraculously the stranger was able to find Meera and deliver Robert's message. Thus a chain of events was started that resulted in Robert's release.

It is a fascinating possibility to think that 'the respectable looking total stranger' lingering at the door of Robert's cell might in fact have been an angel, sent as Robert's deliverer. After all, an angel was sent to deliver the apostle Peter from prison! He too was due for imminent execution! To all events, through the faithful perseverance of this stranger and subsequently through the intervention of Meera's influential father and some high-powered friends, Meera was able to secure the release of her incarcerated husband.

It was subsequent to all this that Robert came across my advertisement in the Crusade magazine. Thinking that anything would be an improvement on their past few months Robert and Meera decided to write for more details. We regularly received a large number of enquiries and had instituted a system for selection which included aptitude tests. These were automatically sent to Robert, who duly completed and returned them. The selection papers threw up obvious problems. Robert was born near Kashmir when India was British India but now is Pakistan. He was working in Bangladesh as a tea planter and had no life insurance experience whatsoever. However the Personality Profile and other Tests also indicated that, on paper at least, he looked a promising applicant. So, ignoring all the obvious problems associated with a tea planter coming to work in the UK as a Life Underwriter, I wrote to him suggesting he looked into the possibilities of emigrating to the UK!

It so happened that Robert's reply arrived when I was on holiday and the office was being run by my colleague Arthur White. In his letter, Robert said that he was following up my suggestion and was looking at ways in which he could come to the UK. When Arthur read this, realising how absurd was the idea, he immediately wrote to Robert telling him that any offer of a job was completely out of the question

286

and there was no way in which he could be employed by the company.

I had been back from holiday a short while, when I was told there was a Mr Robert Thomas on the line. The name rang a bell but I couldn't place it! "Hello! Can I help you?"

"This is Robert Thomas here."

"How can I help you, Mr Thomas?"

"I'm ringing about the job you offered in the Crusade magazine."

At last the penny dropped. "Yes of course, er, Mr Thomas, it's good to speak with you! Where are you speaking from?"

"I'm in London."

"In *London*! What are you doing in London?"

"I've come to see you."

Well, if he'd travelled all the way from Bangladesh in order to see me, the least I could do was to see him, so I invited him to come. In due course he arrived. Everything about him indicated that he was tailor-made for the job. The problem was that the UK's employment laws prohibited us from offering him a job if he didn't have the all-important Work Permit. As Arthur had said, getting a job with us without a Work Permit was out of the question. Had he come all this way for nothing? Worse still, he had brought his wife and two daughters. Even worse was that they had all entered the country on holiday visas!

It was while I was chatting to Robert that I turned up his file. There was the copy of Arthur's letter, telling Robert on no account to come to the UK, but *also* in the file was the *top copy and the stamped addressed envelope!* The letter had never been sent!

As I looked at these, I had a growing conviction that God was in this. With that conviction there came the verse, 'When God opens a door, no man can close it!' From that moment I was engaged in a colossal battle to get Robert a Work Permit. The battle lasted four months, and cost a small fortune, but the sustaining refrain was 'When God opens a door no man can close it'.

Meanwhile the Thomas family came to live with us. It was fortunate that by this time we had moved for, quite apart from casual visitors, there were now ten of us living in Turnhams House! Every day

Robert and Meera's stay in the UK was hanging by a thread, but we redeemed the time, first by putting Robert on a training course, and then allowing him to accompany an experienced agent to learn how the job was done. Robert was a very quick learner and had an insatiable appetite for knowledge.

Over the following four months, during which the family were able to move into rented accommodation, Robert received three Court Orders for Deportation. In support of our successive appeals against the Orders, we enlisted the help of everyone we could.

Eventually we came to the final appeal and a Court Hearing was convened. The prosecutors were the Home Office and the Department of Immigration. In preparation for our defence we employed an Immigration Barrister who took great pains instructing us both what to say and how to say it. "This particular judge likes to write everything down," he said, "so don't speak quickly, have plenty of pauses and, above all *watch his pen*. Don't speak while he is writing." This was difficult for Robert, who is both a rapid and an impulsive speaker!

The case lasted all day, but at the lunch interval the chief prosecutors came to me and said, "Mr Smith, whatever the outcome of this case, and we fear it will go against Mr and Mrs Thomas, we just want you to know that never in all our lives have we more wanted to lose a case."

Towards the end of a most wearying afternoon, the judge arrived at his summary and conclusion. He expressed his sympathy for the plight in which the Thomases found themselves, and so on and so forth, but concluded by saying that the law allowed no loophole whereby he could grant Robert a Work Permit. This was the end of the road and my heart dropped into my boots. There was a deathly hush in the court. The two prosecutors looked at me and pulled doleful faces in commiseration.

I was already working out how we could get the family to Canada and enlist the help of our president to get Robert a Work Permit there, when the judge continued speaking. He was looking at Robert and Meera as he said, "Having carefully studied all the details of this unusual case, I have decided to exercise those powers vested in me, and

I hereby grant you and your family Political Asylum." I promptly burst into tears.

The Immigration Officers and Home Office officials cheered and, while the judge looked benignly on, they rushed first to the Thomases and then over to me, and soon they also were in tears. The precious Work Permit arrived by first class post the very next day. 'When God opens a door no man can close it.'

From the moment of his appointment Robert was an outstanding success, first as a representative, then successively as a unit manager, sales manager and branch manager. Their two lovely daughters have given Robert and Meera three enchanting grandchildren. Despite living for so long with us at that critical time, they remained and still are close and loving friends!

Although she was sitting at the top table in the poshest hotel in Rome that evening, Meera's enjoyment was tinged with a dreadful apprehension on account of not knowing what Robert would be up to next. 'Dinner with the president' had its own particular haunting memories for Meera. It was at the final banquet of the 1982 Agency Conference in Eastbourne, that Robert and Meera were among the ten guests of the then president, Alastair Campbell. Mr Campbell was a tall Scot who had emigrated to Canada when in his early twenties. His somewhat austere mien reflected the fact that he had been the company's treasurer and then its actuary. He had a formidable intelligence.

To Meera's dismay she was seated two chairs away from Robert. This was too far away to have any significant influence on what he did. Worse still, Robert himself was placed directly opposite Mr Campbell. Meera resolved to give her undivided attention to those sitting next to her, and pretend that Robert was nothing to do with her!

Robert was very clever at performing tricks at the meal table; one of the more spectacular of these was to balance a three-quarters-full wine glass on the edge of its base rim. Mr Campbell was not gifted in the art of small talk with the result that between the main course and the dessert there was a conversational hiatus. With the intention of filling this gap, Robert took his glass of red wine and, holding it in the middle of the table, tilted it towards Mr Campbell. After holding it steady for a moment he let go and, sure enough, miraculously the glass remained tilted on its rim. Everyone at the table watched in silent wonder as Robert performed this amazing feat. Meera was quietly having kittens!

Pointing to the tilting glass, Robert said to the president, "Mr Campbell, have you ever seen anything like that?" Before the president could reply, the glass fell forward emptying the entire contents all over the white damask linen table cloth directly in front of him. As the crimson stain rapidly spread, Mr Campbell picked up his napkin and, after mopping up some wine in his lap, looked at Robert and laconically said, "No, never!"

As if he was not sufficiently famous already, that little incident served to spread Robert's fame even further, for it supplied the president with a story which he frequently shared with fellow diners at special functions. Perhaps knowledge of that very incident resulted in Robert and Meera being at the table of our new president, George Clarke, during the banquet in Rome. Meera's anxieties were somewhat eased when she saw that Robert was nowhere near either George Clarke or his wife Elsa.

Towards the end of the meal Robert left the table. What none of his fellow diners knew was that he had arranged with one of the Roman soldiers in a magnificent Centurion's outfit, to lend him the uniform. In a few minutes a splendid fellow appeared at the table requesting a dance with Meera. Looking up at this helmeted figure, Meera politely declined. Robert moved to the wife of the president, who promptly left the table to dance with him, thinking he was one of the soldiers. Looking round for Robert, Meera was suddenly struck by the similarity between the Centurion and Robert. Suddenly the penny dropped and she cried out, "Why, that's *Robert* dancing with Mrs Clarke!" All eyes went to the couple on the dance floor. It must have been at that precise moment that Robert disclosed his identity, for they saw his dancing partner suddenly collapse into Robert's arms, helpless with laughter.

The banquet had been on the Saturday evening and, as no special arrangements had been made for a Sunday Service, Valerie and I thought we would have an informal gathering and communion in our room at 7:30 before breakfast. We had only told a few people about this, but by 7:30 the room was full. We were about to start, when there was a knock at the open door and Elsa Clarke walked in and asked if she could join us.

One of those there was John Hall, a representative from our Leicester Branch, who had become a Christian just a few weeks before the conference through the witness of his branch manager, Ray Pearce. John Hall shared his testimony with us and a very moving story it was. When he had finished there were a few moments of silence, broken by Elsa Clarke praying beautifully and thanking God for John's conversion. This was the background to a brief time of communion. The fact that it was in Rome made it reminiscent of the Apostle Paul being in his own hired room in Rome and having communion with those who gathered to pray with him. Afterwards Elsa Clarke asked if we would pray for her that she would be a faithful witness to folk she met.

It would have been a good thing if Robert had asked us to pray for him, for Nemesis was stalking his heels and would overtake him before our Rome holiday was completely over. By a stroke of Machiavellian misfortune, one of Robert's suitcases was identical to a suitcase of Richard Baker, our general manager. Wanting to get away early from the airport, Robert picked a case from the baggage carrousel, congratulating himself that within a very few minutes he would be on the motorway. Arriving home to a warm welcome from his two daughters, Robert had opened the case, and was beginning to wonder just exactly where he had put the little presents for his two girls, when the telephone rang. It was the general manager asking if Robert had noticed anything unusual about his suitcase! Robert rapidly repacked the case he had brought home and awaited the arrival of the general manager's chauffeur with a suit case that was identical to that of the general manager!

* * * * *

One of the most luxurious hotels we used for a conference was The Montreux Palace on Lake Geneva. Following the porter down a marble floored passage, Valerie and I came to an enormous apartment, beautifully furnished and appointed. It was number 90. The porter took us through this apartment with its large sitting room and bedroom, to an adjoining apartment, number 92, equally large and well appointed. Going through this the porter took our bags to the bedroom and turned to go.

"Which is our apartment?" I asked, "90 or 92?"
He smiled, "Both of them are yours."

Outside there was a huge balcony. It would have been huge for one of the suites but we had a double balcony. The far balcony rail overlooked the street below. We had been in the rooms about half-an-hour when we heard a great deal of shouting. Stepping out on to the balcony, we were astonished to see the wife of one of the delegates, three suites away from us, standing next to the rail, a suitcase at her feet, throwing armfuls of clothes over the balcony rail on to the street below! We looked over the balcony. Down below clothes were scattered all over the road and pavements. Pedestrians were looking up in amazement. A passing tram car had gathered up a pair of dress trousers and was sailing up the High Street flying them, most appropriately, at half mast! Our neighbour later told me by way of explanation, that he and his wife had had a slight tiff! I wondered what she did when they had a real row!

Various outings had been scheduled for us during the conference at Montreux, one of which was a splendid boat trip on Lake Geneva. One of the stops was the Prison of Chillon, the prison that held Francois de Bonivard for six years for refusing to renounce his evangelical faith. Bonivard is the subject of the well-known poem, 'The Prisoner of Chillon,' by Lord Byron. It will be remembered that it goes:

> *My hair is grey, but not with years,*
> *Nor grew it white in a single night,*
> *As men's have grown from sudden fears:*

There is a certain irony about some of the words Byron used:

> *Chillon! Thy prison is a holy place,*
> *And thy sad floor an altar – for t'was trod,*
> *Until his very steps have left a trace*

Worn, as if thy cold pavement were a sod,
By Bonivard! May none those marks efface!
For they appeal from tyranny to God.

The irony lies in the last couplet: *May none those marks efface!*
Wherever Byron went, and he was a great traveller, he left his mark
that none ever since have effaced! There, on a pillar in the prison of
Chillon, is his mark, *'Byron'*. There, in the Acropolis and the
Parthenon in Athens is *'Byron'*. There too, in The Blue Grotto on
Capri and in The Coliseum of Rome is *'Byron'*. He was a compulsive
graffitist. As the sixth Baron Byron of Rochdale, he inherited the
ancestral home, Newstead Abbey in Nottingham, and even there is
found evidence of his graffiti. On the glass window pane of one of the
toilets there is scratched:

'Oh! Ophelia! Goddess of this place,
Look on thy suppliant with a smiling face!
May his motions, soft and obedient flow,
Not rashly swift, nor obstinately slow.'

Athens was another venue for one of our overseas conferences. I have
two vivid memories of that conference, both associated with Valerie.
Thinking that it might be desirable to have a coffee now and then in
our room, she had packed a bag of instant coffee granules.
Unfortunately the bag had burst in transit and there was coffee
everywhere including all over my dress shirts. It wasn't really a
problem, for the valeting service went into action and I had a
beautifully laundered and pressed shirt all ready by the same evening.
The other reason I remember Athens, is because the company had
paid for 'Paragliding Experiences'. Valerie had always wanted to go
parachuting and this seemed the next best thing, so she put her name
down to go the next morning. Unfortunately a stiff onshore breeze
ruled out paragliding for that day, but the following day was perfect.

There was a very high jetty near the hotel, the sea being a good 150
feet below. When we arrived at the launching site, a very athletic-
looking chap of about 25 was putting on a harness, which had ropes
going to a parachute arrangement. Another rope led over the edge of
the jetty, and down to a speed boat on the sea below. An attendant

stood nearby holding the parachute. There was a shout from down below and, looking down, I saw the speed boat shoot forward at high speed. At the same time the chap leapt off the jetty into space.

"What a lunatic," I thought. The rope tightened, and first the parachute and then the man started to climb into the sky. The parachute climbed higher and higher as the boat, still travelling very fast, let out more rope. Within two or three minutes the parachute and the figure dangling from it were mere specks in the sky.

"So that's how they do it," I said turning to Valerie. She wasn't there. By this time another parachutist was being got ready, and another boat was down below with a rope. I looked round for Valerie and suddenly saw that she was the figure in the harness. I started forward intending to ask if she really, *really* thought she ought to do this thing that looked positively dangerous, particularly as only three months earlier she'd had a hysterectomy!

"Stand back, sir, stand back. Can't you see, the lady's about to make her jump?"
"She's only just had a hys..." That was as far as I got for Valerie ran forward and, to my horror, leapt off the edge of the jetty into space. Within three minutes she too was just a speck in the sky. The athletic chap came back first. As it neared the jetty, the speed boat stopped and the man and the parachute dropped out of the sky like a stone. A little later, I saw a flash of colour in the distance with a tiny figure dangling precariously in the harness. It was Valerie approaching on the end of her lead. She was very high in the sky and it looked a terribly long way to fall before she would hit the sea. Suddenly her boat stopped and I held my breath as she dropped out of the sky. The speed boat was quickly at her side, which was just as well, for I found I hadn't taken a breath for about a minute-and-a-half! I didn't think much of all the ruins and broken statues around Athens. It looked as if it had all been bombed, but I preferred it to watching Valerie jump into outer space!

* * * * *

A first for the Sun Life of Canada and for us was the Adriatic Cruise Conference in 1990. Our trip started at the Sheraton Skyline Hotel at

Heathrow with a champagne breakfast. Val had orange juice and I had her champagne! A coach took us to Terminal Two where we found everything was organised for us. It was bliss to put ourselves in the hands of a courier who piloted us through all the formalities and took us to the departure lounge.

For some unknown reason the plane was delayed for two hours. Arriving late at Milan meant that, after the coach ride, we were too late to see anything but the docks of Venice. We got off the coach and went straight onto our ship. The Azur was a luxury cruise ship and Valerie and I had a splendid cabin right at the front with two huge picture windows looking straight ahead.

The cruise took us first to Dubrovnik, the ancient and picturesque port on the Adriatic coast. Sadly, Dubrovnik was badly knocked about during the World War II. Following the end of the war, a major rebuilding project was begun, led by the Croatian authorities and UNESCO. They rebuilt the city in the ancient style to keep its sense of beauty and history. As well as rebuilding damaged buildings, surviving structures were strengthened against earthquakes.

A great deal of this rebuilding was in progress as we wandered round the Old City. There is a path on top of a wall that goes all round the town of Dubrovnik. Valerie and I walked round nearly all of this wall which gave a fascinating insight to the lives of ordinary people, because at times the wall was only a few feet from the houses and gardens.

The next stop on our cruise was in Greece so that we could visit Olympia, known, of course, for having been the site of the Olympic Games in classical times. The Olympic Games, dating back possibly further than 776 BC, were held every four years. Olympia is also known for the gigantic ivory and gold statue of Zeus that used to stand there, one of the Seven Wonders of the Ancient World.

The Olympic flame of the modern-day Olympic Games is lit by reflection of sunlight in a parabolic mirror at the restored Olympia stadium, and then transported by a torch to the place where the games are held. When Pierre de Coubertin, the founder of the modern Olympic Games movement, died in 1937, a monument to him was erected at ancient Olympia. His heart was buried at the monument. Now, isn't *that* exciting!

From Olympia we went on to the Isle of Capri, the unparalleled natural beauty of which was better than my imagination had conjured up. No wonder the Emperor Tiberias built his magnificent villa on Capri. Down below is the legendary Blue Grotto with Lord Byron's graffiti *'Byron'!*

Messina was our last port of call. We were given a coach trip to the town of Taormina. We strolled through the cobblestone streets to Palazzo Corvaia with its classic double windows and the fortress-like duomo that dates back to the 13th Century. The most splendid of Taormina's ancient relics is the 3rd Century Greek Theatre. Known for its unique acoustics, it is still used for concerts with a breathtaking view of Mount Etna in the distance.

It was all fascinating, but you need to be a committed tourist to take much in after five days of sight seeing. I was glad to get back on board ship for our last leg to Milan. Air Italia flew us punctually out of Milan and into Heathrow on time. All was forgiven. We'd had a splendid time, but I preferred the sheer luxury of The Montreux Palace.

We were not entirely dependent on the Sun Life of Canada conferences for our holidays but certainly they were a great deal more comfortable than the Do It Yourself holidays described in the next two chapters.

Chapter 33
A Sailing Holiday

One evening in a rare idle moment Valerie and I were looking through a holiday brochure and came across an advertisement for a sailing holiday on the Norfolk Broads. I had never been on a sailing boat in my life and said to Valerie, "It must be great fun to sail a boat."
"Oh it is," said Valerie. "I've actually been sailing on the Norfolk Broads."
"Wow! Can you really sail a boat?"
"Well, I've been on a course at Bisham which *included* sailing, but they were very small boats!"
"Well! Let's go for a sailing holiday." There and then we set about choosing a boat. Misguidedly, I thought we should have one that was reasonably spacious and we chose a craft from a boatyard on Oulton Broad near Lowestoft in Suffolk. Valerie's parents agreed to look after Christopher; the others hadn't arrived at that time.

In due course we came to Oulton Broad and our chosen boatyard. It was large and had any number of boats for hire, many of which were anchored out on the Broad. As we waited our turn to collect our vessel we stood together admiring all the sleek looking little boats. They all seemed to have a great many ropes attached to the masts, booms and spars, but I wasn't worried... I was with an experienced sailor who had been on a course! She'd be able to teach me what was what!

Looking out over the Broad I nudged Valerie and said, "Look at that great monster out there. I wonder how big a crew is needed to handle that?" The monster had a huge mast reaching into the sky and was positively festooned in ropes.
"Sorry to keep you waiting," said the proprietor, "it's Mr er...?"
"Smith," I said.

"Ah! Yes," and he looked at me very approvingly, as if he had something special for us! I nearly said, 'Don't expect anything from me, *I'm* not the sailor', but he was off to his office where we signed some papers.

"Right, I'll go and get your boat."

He got into a rubber dinghy and headed off straight for the monster. Tying his dinghy to the stern he brought this huge ship to the quay. It looked even bigger close up.

"Is this *our* boat?" I asked.

"Ah! 'tis'n'all. *All* yours! Now I suppose you'll have no difficulty with rigging it up so I'll leave you to..."

"No! No! What I mean is... well I've never actually rigged one of *these* before so perhaps you wouldn't mind doing it. Better to have it done properly!"

"No problem."

No problem to him! I inched over to Valerie. Do you know how to rig this?"

"No idea," said Valerie.

Fascinated, I watched the man haul out of a hatch what appeared to be about half an acre of sail, ropes dangling from every corner. Quickly this was attached to the front end. Goodness, all that sail was just the jib. The man then hauled out the main sail. It seemed to cover half the jetty, but in next to no time it was all attached and docilely giving a little flap now and then. "What do we do now?" I asked Valerie.

"I haven't the faintest idea!" she said.

"What!" I yelped. Then reducing my voice to a whisper said, "What do you mean, 'No idea'? You're the sailor."

"Not of anything like this."

"OK?" said the man.

"A lot of mishaps happen in the first ten minutes of taking on a new boat," I said, assuming a knowledgeable air. "Perhaps you could just give us a turn in her so that we get the right feel."

"No problem. You're right about mishaps, sir," he said. "It's always the first ten minutes where accidents happen. You're dead right."

I wasn't greatly taken by the final phrase but said nothing. "Better to be safe than sorry," he went on. "Now, sir. Those your bags? You haven't got much have you?" I nearly said we didn't think we'd have all this room, but got on with loading our stuff aboard.

"Right then. Cast off fore and aft." I ran to do his bidding, not so much out of enthusiasm, as not wanting to be left behind. "Watch out you don't get a gybe. With a boat this size that could be nasty."
"Indeed," I said, not having the faintest idea what a gybe was but determined to watch out for one none the less! Watching the man closely it all looked very simple. To go right he put the huge tiller over to the left and visa versa. In a few minutes we were approaching the quay again.

"All yours," he said and nimbly jumped on to the quay as we slid past. I adjusted the position of the tiller a fraction and we pulled away in a most sedate fashion. We were running parallel to a large wood at the end of which was the mouth of the river. We headed towards it, the gigantic sail now filled by the gentle breeze reaching us in the lea of the wood.

As we approached the end of the wood about 30 small yachts with blue sails came round the corner, all heading for a little yellow buoy just ahead of us. At the very moment that this flotilla hove into sight a positive gale hit our boat. It seemed to come out of nowhere but we had just left the shelter of the wood and we got the full brunt of a very stiff breeze. The boat now leaned over at an alarming angle as it quickly gathered speed. We were really galloping along splendidly when there was a shout.

"Put the tiller over," yelled Valerie, "we're heading straight for that race." But it was too late and amidst a great deal of both nautical and naughty shouting we galloped through the racing yachts. Belatedly remembering my instructions, I put the tiller hard over. The huge boat responded remarkably quickly. Too quickly for me. I was about to learn what a gybe was. Unseen by me, the boom came crashing across the cockpit, hitting me on the back of the head and knocking me practically senseless down the steps. Scrambling back up in a dazed condition, I was just in time to get the boom crashing back the other way and catching me on the forehead. Back down the steps I went again.

Valerie let out a warning cry, but it was too late. The wild manoeuvre had turned us completely round and we were heading in the opposite direction straight for all the yachts which had reached the buoy, turned and were heading back on the return leg.

In a few seconds we were back amongst the flotilla again. This time there was some *very* naughty shouting as by the tiniest of margins we missed running down a number of the little boats as they scattered out of the way of this menacing leviathan.

We did a wide turn and headed back for the river mouth. We were now going at a spanking pace, wires humming like a violin. Not knowing anything about spilling wind, and not wanting any more gybes, I shouted to Valerie, "How do you slow these things down? If we're not careful we'll be catching up with those little blue yachts!" As we reached the river mouth there was an extra strong gust of wind and the boat, leaning at a wild angle, shot up the river bank and lay there like a stranded whale.

A passing launch approached with an offer of help. Despite much churning of water the boat didn't budge an inch. Nor did we budge when two more large launches joined in to help. Eventually, with a small army of helpers on the bank pushing and heaving, the boat slid back into the water. Untying the ropes from the launches, I turned to give a wave of thanks, only to be thrown off my feet by the boat again mounting the bank! Back came the launches! This time we did what we should have done when we first went on board. We lowered the sail and, when once more we were afloat, we started the engine, much to the relief of the crews on the launches. Using the engine on a sailing vessel is considered very *infra dig*, but not as much as spending a week up a river bank!

* * * * *

We woke the next morning to a cloudless sky and a gentle breeze. We hoped to be in Great Yarmouth by lunch time. We hadn't reckoned on the treachery of Breydon Water. This is a huge stretch of water just outside Yarmouth about three miles long and more than half a mile wide. After changing tack every 50 yards along the river I thought I was beginning to get the hang of this sailing business. What I didn't know was that only a very narrow channel through Breydon Water is navigable. The rest of this vast expanse of water covers a horrible black clinging mud. We were on our third or fourth tack and about to turn again when we came to an abrupt halt. There was a long pole on board and thrusting this over the side I discovered that we were in only four feet of water. Our keel beneath the boat was over four feet deep but the sheer impetus of the big boat had carried us well out of the dredged channel into the mud.

The charts told us the tide was going out so we'd have to bustle about if we weren't to spend the rest of the day there. For an hour-and-a-half I wrestled with that great, heavy pole, inching the boat out of the sticky black mud. By the time we were back in the channel I was thick mud from head to foot to say nothing of our lovely yacht. Belatedly we could see diminutive buoys marking the channel. We had been a good 50 yards outside them.

We used the engine to take us the rest of the way over Breydon Water and into Yarmouth. Valerie piloted the boat while I washed myself and the boat clean of mud. It had been an exhausting morning and we decided to remain in Yarmouth for the rest of the day.

During the night we could hear the wind making the wires hum and slapping the ropes against the big mast. "If this wind keeps up it'll be a great day for sailing tomorrow," I thought. After an early breakfast, we stormed out of Yarmouth at a high rate of knots, rushing from one bank to the other as we tacked. By lunch time we were approaching Horning. On the banks of the River Bute, the sailing aristocracy have their very smart and expensive-looking thatched boat houses, each one with its own purpose- built inlet for anchorage. Immaculate lawns reached down to the river edge.

I now know that high winds outside a town can create sudden gusts of great velocity. We were ready to 'go about' when a savage gust of wind hurled itself at the boat. By this time I had learned to spill wind from the sail, and this I attempted to do, but the wind had taken possession of the boat and there was no holding it back.

Travelling at high speed we shot through a gap in the bank into the private inlet of a very posh-looking house and under the entrance to the adjoining boat house. We looked up and to our horror we saw that

301

the mast was wedged in the thatched roof. Bits of thatch descended on us and the boat.

Gingerly we lowered the sails, started the engine and put it into reverse gear. Slowly the boat extricated itself from the endearing embrace of the thatch. I knocked at the door of the house but there was no-one there. Coming back to the boat we looked at the thatched roof. It looked as if it had given itself a little shake and, rather like a chicken with ruffled feathers, everything had settle back in its proper place. It didn't look too bad at all! The further away we got the better it appeared. We decided that as we had escaped causing significant damage so far we'd let sleeping boats lie, tie her up and go into Horning for a bite to eat.

A short way up the river we came to a pub. The bar was crowded with men in thick Guernsey jerseys and dark blue felt peaked caps. We found a table and I went to the bar. Thinking of our narrow escape, I said, "Lovely day for sailing!" and laughed.
"You're right there, sir," one said and they all laughed in agreement. They thought I'd been joking.
"Only an idiot would try to sail in this," said another. I smiled rather lamely.
"Shame really. You're all tied down I suppose."
"Oh! Yes indeed. All tied down just outside Horning."
"Never mind," said another, "It's going to be a lovely day for you tomorrow."

So it was. Nobody came back to the posh house but close inspection happily showed no real damage to the thatch.

We had learned that our best route was to go back a mile and take the River Ant to Barton Broad, so first thing in the morning that is what we did. It certainly was a lovely route and we went all the way to Spa Common just outside North Walsham. The river was not navigable for our boat beyond Spa Common so we turned round and came back. On the last day as we were approaching Oulton we calculated that we had covered nearly 100 miles in the week. Our worst experience was on Breydon Water but we also had problems on Barton Broad when a rope got caught round the engine propeller and I had to dive down repeatedly to cut it away. However, our adventures were not yet over.

"We've brought the cine-camera all this way and haven't taken one film," said Valerie as we tacked across the Waveney.

"OK, you get the camera and on the next turn I'll go near the bank and you jump off. You can then take a film of the boat tacking first on the other side then on this."

Valerie, safely on the grassy verge on the bank of the river, had the camera ready for a souvenir shot of me returning towards her, then going about and finally going back on the other tack. The sun was in exactly the right position, perfect for photography. We'd had problems with our little golden cocker spaniel jumping off the boat as we turned near the river banks, so as a precaution I had shut her in the cabin. Half way across on the outward tack Toffee pushed open the cabin door and came up on the deck looking speculatively at the approaching shore.

Quickly I grabbed her, thrust her back in the cabin and slammed the door. Unfortunately I was not quite quick enough to bring the large boat about and we ended hard up against the bank. A cardinal rule in sailing is never to end up on a lea shore, that is, the shore towards which the wind is blowing. We were on a lea shore! Worse still, there was a fairly stiff breeze blowing.

I did some rapid calculations and set the sails in such a fashion that if the boat was turned into the wind, first, the jib would fill and pull the boat round so that the mainsail would fill and the boat would go forward off the lea shore. I felt quite pleased with myself.

I then took the long heavy pole ashore with me together with the aft securing rope with which I could steady the boat as I climbed back on. I then went through the motions of pushing the bow away from the bank. It looked as if it would work and give me time to get the pole, the rope and myself back on the boat while the jib pulled the boat round.

Getting a good foothold I lodged the pole against the bow and pushed. The boat was very heavy and there was a stiff breeze. I pushed harder and slowly the bow left the bank. I kept on pushing, all the time sliding my hands back on the pole until I reached the end of the pole. With a great crack, the jib filled with wind and at the same instant the heavy pole slipped from my hands.

My pausing to pick up the pole and fling it on to the deck gave that capricious boat all the scope it needed to give me the slip. I had done the job too well, for, with lightning speed the mainsail filled and the boat was rapidly leaving the bank. I pulled with all my strength on the rope but there was no holding it and I was yanked off the bank into the river and was being towed along behind the boat like a little rubber dinghy.

I was wearing very loose cotton trousers and as, hand over hand, I pulled myself along the rope, I could feel the trousers slowing retreating. As I started to climb up the rope to the deck I could feel the trousers retreating further but I daren't let go of the rope.

At last I fell on to the deck but by now we were very nearly crashing into the other bank on which stood, not just Valerie, but a small crowd of spectators. Yanking up my trousers with one hand, I put the tiller over with the other and most expertly adjusted the sail. It was a perfect turn worthy of being filmed. I looked at Valerie to see if she had filmed this spectacular performance only to see both her and all the other spectators doubled up in hysterical laughter.

After making a gentle turn I again approached the bank and helped Valerie aboard.

"Did you get a shot of all that?" I asked eagerly.
"No!" said Valerie, wiping her eyes, "I couldn't do anything for laughing."

Happily we were able to hand the boat, intact, over to the owner. It had been a most adventurous introduction to sailing.

Chapter 34
Caravanning

Deep in Valerie's psyche there is a desire to live in a tiny mobile box about ten feet by five feet by six. As these miniature homes were expensive they were quite beyond our post marriage budget so this desire on Valerie's part remained wishful thinking until she saw an advertisement in the local paper:

FOR SALE
Fully Equipped Four Berth Caravan Only £45
Apply Mrs Selbourne, 20 Peppard Road,
Caversham, Reading.

Arriving home from work one January evening I was shown this exciting news. It had been snowing heavily and there was about four inches of snow everywhere. I was glad to get home safe and sound.

"Could you go and have a look at it?"
"Sure."
"Well, do you think you could go now?"
"*Now?*"
"It'll be snapped up if you don't go now." I couldn't imagine queues of would-be buyers standing in four inches of snow outside 20 Peppard Road, but I got back into the car and drove the perilous four miles to Caversham.

Parked on a hard standing in front of the house was a large snow-covered caravan. I rang the bell, and the door was opened about three inches.

"Mrs Selbourne?"
"Yes."
"I understand you have a caravan for s..."

I got no further for she put her finger to her lips and hissed, "Sh, sh, sh!"

"Why sh, sh, sh?" I whispered.

With a jerk of her thumb behind her she said, "He doesn't know!"

"Who doesn't know?" I whispered back.

"My husband."

"Your husband doesn't know," I said in alarm, forgetting to whisper.

"Sh, sh, sh," she reminded me, shaking her head fearfully.

"Why are you selling it?" I whispered, back in a conspiratorial mode.

"I hate caravanning!" she said with savage emphasis.

"But you c..." again forgetting to whisper.

"Sh, sh, sh."

"You can't sell his caravan without telling him! Why don't you tell him you hate caravanning?"

"I'm scared to."

"Would you like me to tell him?"

Her face lit up and she nodded.

All of this was conducted through a crack in the door. "Well, let me in and I'll see what I can do."

"Of course, do come in."

I stamped the snow off my shoes and followed her into a sitting room where an enormous man sat in an armchair reading a newspaper. He was in his shirt sleeves that were rolled up revealing colossal biceps. He was in bedroom slippers and was sporting some bright red braces. On his rather large head was a tweed cloth cap. As I came into the room he looked over the top of the newspaper. "What's up missus?" he said. Missus gulped and said nothing.

"Mr Selbourne?"

"Aye. What's to do?"

"I'm really sorry to call on you so late, but I have some bad news for you."

He lowered the newspaper and stood up. He was huge. "Bad news?"

"Aye!" I said dropping into the vernacular.

"It's not Judith?"

"No! Judith's all right," I said hopefully.

"Robert, then?"

"No! Robert's all right too. It's nearer home than that. Your wife hates caravanning."

"My wife... my wife hates caravanning?" he repeated blankly.

"Yes. She really hates it, but she loves you so much she doesn't like saying so."

He turned to his wife, "Is this true?"

"Yes, dear!" she said.

He suddenly turned to me and said, suspiciously, "How do *you* know this?"

"Your wife told me just now." He accepted this without another thought.

"So you want me to sell it?" he demanded of her. She nodded.

"How much?" he asked.

"£45," she said promptly.

"What!" Turning to me he said, "It's worth at least £100." I said nothing.

"Please dear. Let's get rid of it. Mr... er! Oh dear!" she turned to me, "I don't even know your name."

Immediately the huge man looked less suspicious. "I can't imagine why you couldn't have told me yourself. But if that's what you want, so be it." Then to me he said, "Can you pay cash?" I nodded. "Now?" I nodded again. He held out his hand. I pulled out my wallet. I had £46 and counted out £45 into his great hand. Mrs Selbourne took me by the arm and pulled me towards the door. She couldn't get me out fast enough.

"I can't take it now. I haven't even got a tow bar."

"Never mind that. Just go. Oh! and thank you." she said.

I got a tow bar fitted the next day and, after knocking the snow off, towed the caravan home. It was exceedingly heavy but it was destined to become even heavier.

First I got it insured and we joined the Caravan Club. In the early summer of that year we offered to lend the caravan to a couple of friends, Roger Wales, a psychology student and Bill Hawes a theological student. I towed the caravan to a field recommended by the Caravan Club. When I visited Roger and Bill three days later the caravan had been nearly wrecked... by a bull only an hour earlier!

The caravan had an outside tent loo and, at the very moment that Roger was on the loo, Bill saw an angry-looking bull standing about

50 yards away from the caravan pawing the ground most theatrically and eyeing him in such a menacing way that Bill called out a warning to Roger on the loo. The moment that Bill shouted the bull charged. With commendable agility Bill climbed a nearby tree, just getting out of the reach of the bull as it shot past underneath. In the meanwhile, Roger emerged from the loo in a rather disreputable state of undress. As the bull turned it got a full view of Roger and, evidently offended at the sight, charged again. Roger promptly joined Bill up the same tree leaving his trousers at the bottom, so to speak! Thoroughly frustrated the bull set about the caravan, repeatedly butting it until the cabin parted company from the chassis.

Satisfied with his work of demolition the bull calmly wandered off and paid no more attention to the couple up the tree. About half-an-hour later they surreptitiously crept down from the tree and hid in the caravan, now tilting at an alarming angle. When I drove into the field I passed quite near the bull which paid no attention to me whatsoever. The caravan was no longer habitable and I took Bill and Roger home to finish their holiday with us. The caravan was insured for £250 and in due course it was repaired and delivered to our home looking practically new.

Two months later I towed it down to Hope Cove, in Devon, where we had pre-booked a place in a field, again recommended by the Caravan Club. It was our first caravan holiday and it was a great success – until we started to return home. Whichever way you leave Hope Cove there is a hill to climb. One is a winding lane with a few passing places and the other is a long straight climb with just two passing places.

The repairers of the caravan had given it a new chassis made of 4" x 4" oak beams. It was now very heavy. I reckoned that if we had to stop on the steep incline we'd not be able to get going again, so Valerie went to the top of the hill so that she could stop any vehicle coming down until we were clear. The road was quite clear when we set off, gathering as much speed as possible in the short run before the steep incline. As we went up the hill I could feel the clutch slipping even though we were in bottom gear. About 50 yards short of the top the car ground to a halt. We couldn't go forward so we had no alternative but back the three-quarters-of-a-mile down the hill. Reversing with a caravan is difficult at the best of times but when you can't correct a mistake by going forward it's a nightmare. Foot by foot we went down the hill. It took the best part of an hour. Fortunately no-one wanted to pass.

Once down we thought we couldn't risk towing with a defective clutch, so we decided to leave the caravan on the site. Having got the clutch fixed we thought we'd go back in the spring, have a holiday, and get someone with a tractor to tow us to the top of the hill to start us on our way home. This plan was forestalled by a telephone call from the farmer in November telling us that a hurricane had swept across his field and destroyed our caravan. It must have been a terrific wind for it lifted this heavy caravan in the air, twisting it over so that it landed on its roof. The heavy chassis then crashed through the body of the caravan rendering it a complete write-off.

We received £300 compensation, £250 for the caravan and £50 for the contents. With the proceeds we bought a smart, new, four berth caravan. It was a Fairview Indus, a feature of which was that it was mainly constructed of aluminium and consequently was very light and durable. It was well equipped with an oven, a four burner hob, a refrigerator and a complete set of matching Mellaware crocks.

It seemed a waste to have such an excellent facility that would only be used two or three times in the year so we had the notion of making it available to my colleagues in the branch. We looked up various caravan sites, including some on the Continent. There was one site in Brittany that attracted us. It overlooked a safe sandy beach just outside Dinard on the Brittany coast.

At the beginning of May Valerie and I set out on the first part of a saga that was to last five months and nearly end in catastrophe. The idea was that Valerie and I would go for a week, set up the caravan and then return in the car as far as Cherbourg. We would leave the car in the ferry car park ready for the next family who would have driven to Southampton and left their car in the Southampton ferry car park. Having crossed on the ferry they would collect our car and drive to Dinard for their two weeks' holiday, while we collected their car at Southampton to drive home.

Two weeks later, another family would arrive at our home, leave their car with me and take the car of the family still in Brittany to Southampton ready for them to collect on their way home. In August we had two weeks in the caravan after which the procedure continued to work well right through to October when Valerie and I went back to Brittany to collect the caravan and bring it home. When we arrived in Cherbourg there was a large notice in the car written by the previous user to say that there were problems with the caravan. That turned out to be an understatement. The caravan had been impounded by Customs Officials! We had to report to the site manager on arrival.

By this time we knew the site manager very well. As soon as he saw us he threw up his hands in a gesture of dismay on our behalf. Our caravan was sealed by the Customs Officials and he could only release the key if we handed over our passports. This we did and with due solemnity he conducted us to our caravan. It had some very pretty seals on the doors and windows all interconnected with some strong-looking twine. Later we were to discover what had happened.

The previous family was that of David and Jenny Winter. Towards the end of their second week they got into conversation with a couple of French men whom they took to be holiday makers. In fact they were Customs Officials dressed in holiday clothes.

"Are you staying long?"
"Only to the end of the week."
"You have a very fine position here. Is it expensive?"

Of course the whole holiday was incurring minimum expense. Instead of taking the car on the ferry there were just the passenger fares. We had obtained a very good rate for the site because we booked it for six months. When divided between twelve families the cost was derisorily small, so the enquiry about the cost struck David and Jenny as exquisitely funny.

"Oh this holiday is costing us a small fortune," said David and inadvertently dropped me in the soup. Apparently there was a strict law in France at the time prohibiting foreigners from hiring out their caravans to holiday makers. We had explained to the site manager what we were doing and he had thought it a splendid idea, as indeed it was, providing the caravan was not being hired out for profit. We assured the site manager on that score. We certainly weren't making a profit. In fact the opposite was the case. The car put on about 10,000 miles during that five months and we also had to have a new clutch fitted – one of the holiday makers kept forgetting the car wasn't automatic!

David and Jenny's friendly visitors then revealed that they were Customs Officials and no matter what David and Jenny said, the Customs men were sure they had rumbled illegal trafficking in caravan letting. Apparently an appointment had been made for us to meet with a Senior Customs Officer the next morning in Dinard.

Equipped with a French/English dictionary we arrived in good time for the appointment and were ushered into the Chief's office. He looked very important with loads of scrambled egg all over the peak of his cap and many gold braid rings on his sleeve. He also looked very stern.

"You break the law," he said.
"No, we haven't broken the law," I said.
"Yes, yes, *yes*. You break the law of France. The law say 'Not hire caravan' - you hire the caravan. You break the law. So we take the caravan."
"What! You take the caravan. Nonsense."
"You have the carnet?" he barked. The carnet is the travel document used for taking a vehicle overseas.
"Yes, I have it here."
"Give, give me the carnet. The carnet say you break the law."

It was a booklet with a bright red card cover. He looked through the carnet for three or four minutes, turning the pages back and forth. Then, triumphantly pointing to the back cover, "The carnet say *here* you break the law."

I looked and there on the back of the red cover, *printed in red*, was the almost invisible instruction: "*The letting of holiday caravans is illegal in France. Any infringement may result in the confiscation of the caravan.*" I was about to say how stupid it was to print in red on a red cover when I remembered our defence was that we were not letting it. We had not broken the law either inadvertently or deliberately.

Nevertheless things were getting serious. We had to bestir ourselves or we might lose our precious caravan which would have been a shame after the good service it had provided. Putting a great deal more emphasis than fluency into what I said, I told this official that we liked other people to benefit from what we had. I told him about the excellent holidays our friends had enjoyed at so very little cost other than to me! For good measure, I also told him that at that very moment we had about twenty people staying in our house at home at no charge. The scrambled egg man began to be less aggressive. He then held up a hand as if stopping traffic, and reached for the telephone with the other hand. "I ring the *Commissioner* himself," he said, adding importantly, "in Paris!"

There was a long exchange between him and the Commissioner in Paris while I riffled through the pages of my little English/French dictionary trying to pick up the gist of what he was saying. Every now and then he would look at us and either shake his head or nod. I whispered to Valerie, "He's just told his boss that we are either rich idiots or thorough-going villains. On balance he thinks we are probably rich idiots!"

Eventually he put down the receiver and stood up facing us. "You break the law of France. You take the caravan and leave France today." I held out my hand for the carnet and he gave it to me. I thought we'd quit while we still had the caravan, but at the door I couldn't resist turning and saying, "We have *NOT* broken the law of France!" He waved us out! We left Dinard that day but we stopped at Mont St Michelle on the way to Cherbourg, boarding the ferry the following day. The whole notion was a good idea and it worked well, but we didn't do it again.

We had a number of holidays in the Fairview Indus but when it began to leak we traded it in for a Monza. It was when we had the Monza that we started going to Bude so that the children could attend the CSSM, but after a while I began to think that caravanning was a trifle over-rated. I was forever bumping my head against cupboard doors, but it was going to the loo in the middle of the night when it was raining that used to bug me. At first there was an element of novelty attached to donning Wellington boots and a mackintosh and then splashing across a muddy field in the dark. The second time I did it I found the novelty had worn off. Deliverance was at hand.

The children were enjoying the CSSM and Valerie was enjoying the children enjoying the CSSM! They would leave early in the morning, we'd then pick them up at about twelve and take them back again at two and not see them again until about five.

One day we were on our way to pick them up when I said to Valerie, "It would be very handy to have a house down here." As we approached the CSSM house we saw a FOR SALE notice on the house nearly opposite. Within half-an-hour the agent was showing us over the house and within another ten minutes we had agreed to buy it for just under £15,000. It was a well built four bed-roomed semi-detached house and we loved it. It was called Tresco after the Scilly Isles Island and it became our holiday home for the next eight years. Christopher and Katie, who were twenty and eighteen respectively, were on the Bude CSSM Team, Timothy was nine and Penny eight. There were special classes in the morning geared to particular age-groups and the children loved every moment of it.

For Valerie it was a complete break. Immediately after breakfast the whole family disappeared and weren't seen again until lunch time. After lunch there would be various games down at Crooklets Beach just 300 yards away, followed by 'The Good News Hour', which was great fun. For the older children there were evening activities. For an hour each morning there was a teaching time for adults in the house across the road from us and we heard some excellent teachers.

This was the programme for a whole month and the children never tired of it. I would drive down to be with the family for the first weekend and drive home on the Monday or the Tuesday, going down again on either the Thursday or the Friday and staying for the next two weeks. I would then come back to Reading for three or four days and go back for the final weekend. The Bude house was a great success in every way. At this time we had a couple of cars so, on the first trip down, we were able to drive in tandem, which was fun for the children and meant Valerie had a car in Bude for the month.

We also used the house for the occasional holiday at Easter or at half term, but for much of the year we made the house available for ministers, missionaries and other full time Christian workers. Selwyn Hughes and Trevor Partridge, of Crusade for World Revival used the house as a retreat. Not only was the house easy to look after it was an exceptionally well built house and needed virtually no maintenance during all the eight years that we had it.

On Sundays we went to the Anglican Church at the village of Poughhill which was about two miles away. Poughill Church used to be the parish church of the Guerney family. It will be remembered that it was Sir Henry Guerney, the High Commissioner in Malaya who was murdered on the way up Fraser's Hill. Over the door of Poughill Church there is a plaque commemorating Sir Henry and the tragic event of his murder. Sir Henry's father was Sir Goldsworthy Guerney. He was a notable engineer and claimed, against all engineering practice, that it was possible to build on sand. He was deliberately raising an engineering controversy and not a theological one! To prove his point he built Bude Castle down by the beach. It is still there as sound as the day it was completed; now it houses the Bude Council Offices.

Poughill Church was a staunchly Evangelical church and was usually packed out during the summer holiday period. One year my mother came down to Bude so that she could be with us on her 90th birthday. She stayed for a week in the house next door, where our neighbour made a great fuss of her, giving her breakfast in bed every day!

Mum's 90th birthday was on the Sunday. She had become a Christian just three years earlier and during the morning service at the church the minister spoke about her conversion at the age of 87, stressing that it was never too late to turn to the Lord.

After we had sold the Bude house we once more ventured into the world of caravanning, first with an Award Day Star, which we traded in for a Swift Corniche. This was caravanning with a difference! The Swift Corniche had every conceivable mod con from hot air heating ducts for the winter and air-conditioning for the summer, double glazing, automatic water pumps, fly screens, shower room *and* an electric flush toilet complete with cassette removable from the outside. In some ways it was better than home from home. Our house didn't have an electric flush toilet system!

Chapter 35
Holiday Property Bond

For a number of reasons we sold the house in Bude and so had to look for alternative holiday venues. We had heard of the Holiday Property Bond and, without a doubt, as far as holidays are concerned, it was one of the best discoveries we have ever made. We all look forward to holidays but often there is a concern about the accommodation. Will it be clean? Will it be comfortable? Will it be expensive? Will it be *built*? The Holiday Property Bond solved all these concerns and over the years has delivered beyond expectations.

It is so good and has been so much part of our lives that it deserves a special mention in this narrative. This is how it works. In effect all the Bondholders collectively own a large number of first class holiday properties. One becomes a 'co-owner' by investing in the Bond. There is a minimum investment: when we joined it was £4,000, though the average initial investment was about £7,000. Points are then issued which can be used every year. The more invested, the more points there will be available and the number of holiday points held determines the extent of the holidays taken.

There is an annually published comprehensive brochure which shows the properties available for holidays. Having made the investment, which is then up-graded annually automatically in line with inflation, a rent-free holiday is secured for life. Not only so, but it can be passed on to future generations. In the meanwhile friends can use the holiday allocation of points if for some reason the owner is unable to use them. There is a modest non-profit user charge to cover local costs.

We have been using the HPB for over twenty years and have always experienced the very best in choice, value and service. The Bond properties are fully furnished and equipped to a standard that can only be described as luxurious. Facilities such as swimming pools, tennis courts, video libraries, billiards, bowls, croquet, table tennis and a host of other games are all provided free of any charge.

If all that wasn't enough, Bond holders can benefit from the extra dimension of being able to rent privately owned villas, cottages and apartments at very special prices without using their allocated points. The Bond also organises special Theme Weeks, also points free, where an organised group of Bondholders get together and pursue particular hobbies or recreations. A Tours Programme gives special holidays selected from a world-wide itinerary.

Above all, we have invariably found that fellow Bondholders are the kind of people we would want to choose as friends. The locations are characterised by an atmosphere of friendliness and Old World courtesy. This is not surprising for bad behaviour incurs the risk of the Bond being withdrawn. It will be seen why the Holiday Property Bond is rated so highly by our family.

Every other year we would have family reunions at one of the Bond locations. As the wider family grew so we would require more accommodation with numbers increasing by the year. One of our family reunions was at Duloe Manor in Cornwall. The manor is located just outside the village of Duloe three-and-a-half miles inland from the delightful village of Looe. That holiday was the occasion of a booking miscalculation on my part. In defence I can claim that booking four or five different apartments that more or less coincide is very demanding! To all events when we got down to Duloe Manor we discovered that we were a property short for a night. It was the height of the season so accommodation was at a premium, however the HPB manageress at Duloe had a friend who owned a local pub and she got us in there.

It was during the night at that pub that I got a nasty fright, but nothing like the fright Valerie had. I woke up at about 2:00 in the morning and, looking round, saw a man's close-cropped head in the bedroom silhouetted against the faint light of the window. Feeling my way round the large room, I cautiously approached this intruder and was just about to launch myself at him when I stumbled over a low stool and, with a mighty crash, fell against a dressing table. The noise was appalling and the intruder gave a loud wail and disappeared out of the window! The close-cropped head was the arched back of a moggie sitting on a ledge inside our window! I don't know who I frightened most, Valerie or the cat. Certainly the cat didn't return that night.

One of our latest HPB family reunion holidays was in 2005 to celebrate our 50th wedding anniversary. We all went to Brittany to the Manoir du Hilguy. This magnificent 18th Century chateau stands at the bend of a small valley, near the picturesque village of Plogastel St Germain about fifteen miles from the city of Quimper. The main entrance to the Manoir is through an impressive monumental archway leading to a large, gravelled courtyard. Several steps lead up to the main house with its elegant and graceful rooms.

Over the years we have had HPB holidays in Florida, Portugal, Madeira, Lanzarote, Austria, Majorca, Tuscany, Isle de France, Constant in the Dordogne, Javea in Spain as well as numerous places in the UK. We have also been on HPB Theme Weeks, one of which was to Turkey when we visited the sites of the Early Churches.

It was said earlier that one of the joys of the Holiday Property Bond is that you meet folk you would choose as friends. On holiday we often meet folk and say we must meet again but in practice this seldom happens. Our Theme Week in Turkey has been a notable exception. Predictably we met some delightful folk sharing the Theme Week but for six successive years eight of us have met for a Turkey Reunion. Perhaps that is the most eloquent comment on HPB members that can be made.

PART SIX
A Missionary
(1950...)

Chapter 36
The Borneo Evangelical Mission

Many times my mind has gone back to that 'proper breakfast' in 1956 when Valerie asked, "What would be your reaction if the Lord wanted you to be in an ordinary job?" and my reply had been, "I'm pretty sure He wants us to be missionaries..."

Since then it has been brought home to us that whatever the job into which the Lord calls us we are all missionaries. What then makes a missionary? Rather than being a matter of crossing the sea it is more a matter of seeing the cross! A missionary is someone with a mission and the fact is every Christian is someone with a mission. It may indeed be across the sea, but on the other hand it may be across the street.

The astonishing thing is that God made us the way we are precisely so that we could do those things that He planned in advance for us. It's all there in chapter two of Paul's letter to the Ephesians. God has planned specific "good works" for us to do. Not that by doing them we'll be saved (verse 8 & 9) but, having been saved by grace we then do these "good works" and thereby "show the incomparable riches of His grace."

My being called by God into selling life insurance seemed bizarre at the time. What on earth was God up to? But we stepped out in faith and step by step God did reveal what He was up to. Countless numbers of clients were blessed through the members of the growing team of life insurance salesmen; each one called to be a missionary! At the same time many were Bible teachers in their churches and others were heavily involved in supporting missionary societies and countless other "good works." The job leant itself legitimately to these 'extra' activities.

Despite a busy life in the Sun Life the Lord led me unmistakably into an association with the Borneo Evangelical Mission, an association that lasted for over 30 years. For eighteen of those years I was the British General Secretary, which job I did in an honorary capacity. The point is that I was just as much a missionary in the one as I was in the other, the criterion for each being the call of God.

The reader will recall that I first heard of the BEM when I was on holiday with Bill Lees at Fraser's Hill, in Malaya in 1950. Gordon Blair had joined us for part of that holiday. Gordon was a New Zealander who was attached to the British Army in Malaya as a Scripture Reader. He was a real 'man's man', being a very successful amateur pugilist. Whether preaching or boxing, he carried a hefty punch.

There on Fraser's Hill, surrounded by the jungles of Malaya, Gordon told us about a tribal people living in the jungles of Sarawak and Sabah, the two northern states of the island of Borneo. Gordon gave us some background to what was happening.

The Anglicans and Methodists had been involved in church work in the principal towns and had made an attempt to reach the animist and tribal peoples with very little success. Then, in 1928 the Borneo Evangelical Mission was founded in Australia with the express objective of reaching the tribes in Borneo. They tried to reach the powerful Iban tribe with the gospel but met obdurate resistance from these proud and arrogant people. There was another tribe, the Lun Bawang who were deep in the interior. When the BEM asked if they could work amongst this tribe the Government was hesitant to give permission. The problem was that chronic drunkenness and attendant disease made them a liability and the Government was anxious to limit the contagion.

Gordon then went on to tell us that it was this very tribe that God was using to bring salvation to all the other tribes in Sarawak and Sabah. It was an amazing and thrilling story and we listened, spellbound. Strong 'Threads of Destiny' were being woven in that holiday home on Fraser's Hill in Malaya.

Back in the 1930s the Lun Bawang tribes-people were completely dominated by spirit appeasement and attendant drunken feasts.

Harvests were left un-gathered, malnutrition was universal and disease endemic. Large amounts of the rice that was harvested was used to make rice beer that kept the entire population, men, women and children paralytic for up to four days on end. Frequently only the dogs were sober. All of this was in a futile endeavour to placate the spirits who had complete control over the lives of the people.

There is a passage in the New Testament that is a telling comment on the wisdom and power of God when compared with what we call wisdom and power. It is in 1 Corinthians 1:18-31. It is so apposite to the Lun Bawang that I'll repeat some of it here:

> *For the message of the cross is foolishness to those who are perishing, but to those who are being saved it is the power of God... For the foolishness of God is wiser than man's wisdom, and the weakness of God is stronger than man's strength... God chose the foolish things of the world to shame the wise; God chose the weak things of the world to shame the strong. He chose the lowly things of the world and the despised things... so that no-one may boast before Him.*

In an amazing way a group of three Lun Bawang tribesmen encountered an American missionary working with the Christian and Missionary Alliance in Indonesian Borneo. From this missionary they learned that there was One greater than the spirits. He could not only deliver them from their fearful bondage to spirits, but could deliver their whole tribe. These young men decided they wanted to know more about this Deliverer, so they stayed in the village with the missionary and in due course they made a commitment to Christ that was to be momentous, not only for them, but for all the tribal people in Borneo.

They decided to go back to their own people with the Good News that they had both learned and experienced in their lives. Back in their village they encountered fierce opposition from the witch doctor, but their changed lives spoke volumes to the head man and other village leaders. Eventually, after much discussion, but more importantly, much close observation of the lives of these young men, there was agreement in the village that they should turn their backs on the spirits and trust in this Jesus who was claimed to be more powerful than the feared spirits. Not only did they do so, but parties of them went to neighbouring villages with the Good News. The result was the eventual turning of the entire tribe.

From a condition of third degree drunkenness and abject submission to spirit omens they turned to worshipping this God who had delivered them. This turning probably didn't mean that the entire tribe was instantly born again. Some undoubtedly would have been born again at the initial turning, but the collective turning led to many more coming to know the delivering power of Jesus, and eventually to thousands of individuals being truly born again of the Holy Spirit. Such collective turning is somewhat foreign to our Western individualistic mind set but in the Acts of the Apostles Chapter 16 verses 31-34 we read that the Philippian jailor 'turned, together with his whole house'. In Borneo a house can be half-a-mile long!

Prior to this dramatic turning, the BEM missionaries were again seeking permission from the Government to work amongst the Lun Bawang, but the decadence of the tribe was perceived to be so deeply rooted that again there was hesitation to grant this permission. The Government's attitude was not so much punitive as protective of the other tribes who could be adversely affected by the depravity of the Lun Bawang. It was not long after the turning that bemused government officials came across a completely changed Lun Bawang tribe. Perhaps these people were worth helping after all.

The government officials suggested to village leaders the advantages of growing tobacco as a cash crop, but the Lun Bawang associated tobacco with drinking and spirit appeasement and would have none of it. They would do nothing that might estrange them from their Mighty Deliverer, who already was bringing about vast improvements to their lives.

This was the background to the Government actually approaching the BEM missionaries asking them if they would investigate the extraordinary change that had taken place in this tribe. When the mission carried out a survey of the Lun Bawang they got a shock. As soon as the village people realised that here were people who knew their God they immediately declared: "Oh! We've come to know God too. We're glad you've come because now you can tell us what we need to know!" Endless questions followed:

"What does God want us to do when we gather in our harvest?"
"What does God want us to do when one of our women has twin babies?"
"What does God want us to do when...?"

In the spirit dominated days they consulted the spirits about anything and everything. Even when they were sober, which was only about two thirds of the year, they wouldn't gather in the already overdue harvest until the spirit in a particular hawk caused it to circle anticlockwise instead of clockwise. If a mother gave birth to twins it meant the spirits were angry and had sent a demon baby. The mother would walk a prescribed distance from the communal long-house; there she would dig a shallow grave and bury both her babies alive.

All that had changed. Now they wanted to know how God wanted them to behave in the everyday situations of life. A visiting missionary declared that he was flabbergasted. "When is your next beer feast?" he asked.

"Beer feasts! We gave those up long ago. Now we want to know what special things we can do to show God our appreciation for all he has done for us."

It was the same in every village. Here were a people who didn't need evangelists. They needed disciple makers and the mission responded immediately. Soon missionaries were hard at work, learning the language, translating the Scriptures into Lun Bawang and teaching the people the wonderful truths of God's love and His ways.

All of this happened just prior to World War II. When the Japanese invaded the coastal regions of Borneo, the missionaries in those areas simply retreated into the interior where the Lun Bawang lived. The tribe that was once denied any missionary help now had the entire mission force working amongst them!

A great deal of language learning, teaching and translation was achieved by the missionaries before the Japanese caught up with them and put them in prisoner of war camps. But that didn't stop the progress in translation work, which could now be continued even in the prison camps. If a search was made, the precious manuscripts were hidden in all manner of places, even hung out under clothes on linen lines! By the end of the war huge progress had been made, both in translation work and preparing teaching aids for literacy.

After release from the prison camps the missionaries were again able to make contact with the Lun Bawang. Had they kept the faith during the war years? Not only had they done so, but God had given them a tremendous missionary zeal to reach out to neighbouring tribes, their previous headhunting enemies. Seeing the change in the Lun Bawang, other tribes were asking for the delivering Good News. Entire villages from other tribes had been turning to this God of the Lun Bawang.

In this scenario what was the role of missionaries? Clearly the priority need was translation and Bible teaching. This teaching needed to be directed at those who could teach others also. This of course was precisely the instruction that the apostle Paul gave to Timothy 2,000 years ago. Villages were asked to select able men and women who could attend a Training School, learn to read, and learn how to teach others also. This was the amazing news that Gordon Blair shared with Bill and me when on that holiday in 1950. Strong Threads of Destiny were being woven for both of us.

On his way home from Malaya Bill went to Australia in order to meet Harold McCracken. Harold, an astute lawyer, was the Chairman of the BEM and a mission visionary. Bill was impressed both by Harold and all that he learned of the BEM. By the time Bill arrived back in the UK he was sure that the Lord wanted him in Borneo but there was a problem. The mission policy determined that they wanted single men on the field. Bill fitted that category but before he had left for Malaya the intention had been that on his return he and a Miss Shirley Johnson would be married. Bill had met Shirley at a wedding where she had been the bridesmaid and he was the chief usher. Each was convinced that the Lord meant them for each other but Bill's National Service had intervened and now this bachelor issue had arisen. If the BEM wanted him only as a bachelor that was the way it had to be. As a result he and Shirley agreed to put their romance on hold. Still convinced that the Lord wanted Bill in Borneo, Bill and Shirley agreed that, if God wanted them to work as a couple, then He'd have to resolve this issue, failing which they would go single.

Meanwhile Bill got a job in the surgical department of a Birmingham hospital. At the end of six months the BEM changed its policy about bachelor candidates. "Thank you, Lord," said Bill and he and Shirley were married in Westminster Chapel by Doctor Martyn Lloyd-Jones.

Six months later, in 1951, the couple set off, not for Borneo, but for Australia where the mission wanted them to attend a linguistic course run by the Summer Institute of Linguistics, an organisation associated with Wycliffe Bible Translators. After completing the linguistics course in Melbourne and then doing some deputation work, Bill and Shirley left for Borneo. They arrived at the mission headquarters in Lawas in Sarawak just in time for the Mission Conference where they were able to speak about new linguistic techniques in translation. What they had been taught proved enormously helpful to the team as a whole.

In due course Bill and Shirley were assigned to the Tagal tribe and made their operational base in a village called Meligan. There they set about the business of language learning, translation of the Scriptures, and the associated teaching and training of prospective church leaders. Places such as Meligan in Sabah were destined to become household names in many homes in the UK where prayer partners were now praying for Bill and Shirley, Valerie and me among them.

Chapter 37
BEM in the UK

When Valerie and I were married we felt sure that the Lord wanted us to have a BEM monthly prayer meeting in our home, and this we started in 1957. Despite having been with the Sun Life for only six months, we felt that we could be doing more for the mission. We didn't know what, but thought we could perhaps take the occasional meeting. Bill and Shirley Lees had arrived in the UK in 1957 in order to help run a linguistic course similar to the one they had attended in Melbourne. As this was being held in Merstham near Reigate, we thought we would visit them and see if there was anything we could do for the mission.

While having tea with them we raised the subject of being of some kind of help. Bill and Shirley exchanged looks and Bill pointed to an envelope on the mantelpiece. It was addressed to me.

"Open it," said Bill. The letter was an invitation by the mission for me to be the UK General Secretary of the BEM. In the event that was nothing like as grandiose as it might sound. For one thing there was precious little of which to be general secretary. A lovely couple, Eric and Sis Pearson, had been responsible for receiving and forwarding to the field any donations to the mission but in all conscience this hadn't amounted to a great deal. It was obvious that the mission was thinking of my appointment in honorary terms! Gradually it became clear why the Lord had led me into a job where my time would be my own, legitimately to use as I chose. The Threads of Destiny were coming together. Everything seemed to fit and Valerie and I had no hesitation about me accepting the appointment.

Two weeks later Bill and Shirley came to stay with us for a week. Although Bill gave me a crash course on how to run the home end of a mission, clearly I would need someone to whom I could turn for help and advice. Just fifteen miles from Merstham, Rev Ralph Morrish was the minister of the Cranleigh Baptist Church. Bill was a friend of Ralph's and during his time on the language course he had been able to visit Ralph and discuss the need for a BEM UK Council. Ralph was delighted to be part of it and, in particular, to make himself available to me if problems arose.

So it was that I met Ralph Morrish. As well as being a notable Bible teacher in a large church he was also a recognised missionary statesman in the evangelical mission world. Above all he was a kind and delightful man. He was a splendid choice by Bill and over the years Ralph and I became very close friends.

It was decided that Eric Pearson and Jim Lees, Bill's brother and a qualified accountant, should also be council members. Later they were joined by Roy Stillman, the headmaster of Crosfields School in Reading and by Jim Graham, the Minister of Highgate Road Chapel, in London. As a council of reference we had Doctor Martyn Lloyd-Jones, the minister of Westminster Chapel and the Rev John Stott, the Rector of All Souls Langham Place in London, both exceptionally prominent and respected churchmen.

Later Hugh Thomson joined the council. Hugh's company had been Malaysianised and he found himself out of a job. Returning to the UK, Hugh and Jean initially came to live with us in Redhatch Drive. Their stay in Reading was intended to be a temporary one but discussions with Hugh had an interesting consequence. My business activities in Reading revealed a possible niche that Hugh could fill. I was constantly being asked to recommend to clients an estate agent and valuer who was a really committed Christian. To fill this need a first step was to buy a company through which businesses could be sold. For a year I worked with Hugh finding businesses and clients, putting them together and generally getting this new company off the ground. It was interesting and rewarding work, but coupled to my Sun Life and BEM work it was all extraordinarily arduous!

At the end of the first year I concluded that our business agency needed a first class qualified surveyor. We found one in Douglas Chilvers who was the Berkshire County Surveyor. This was a well paid job, but we offered him terms that he couldn't refuse and the result was the creation of an estate agent's firm which we called Campbell Thomson and Chilvers; Campbell was Hugh's middle name. Within a very short time it was one of the leading estate agents in the town. So Hugh's temporary stay in Reading became permanent; he and Jean bought a house in Tilehurst and Hugh joined the BEM council.

All of this was further evidence of the weaving together of the Threads of Destiny. Starting back in Taiping in 1950, the intervening years were revealing an emerging pattern, the purpose of which was support for an exciting work that the Lord was doing in Borneo. It is often only retrospectively that we see God's guiding hand. The demanding thing for Valerie and me was to walk by faith when the way ahead was unclear. Now we were beginning to see how the Lord had led us to the very heart of the development of the BEM in the UK.

The work was not going to be easy but it was immediately obvious that I would need a secretary. In fact I needed an organising genius and the Lord sent me one in the person of Barbara Attfield. A lovely Christian girl, Barbara was engaged to be married to Paul Chandler, the son of the builder who had visited us when we were looking for a house.

Barbara Chandler with Ray Main and me

I had told my Sun Life manager that I needed a secretary. "You'll have to pay her yourself," he said.
"Of course," I replied.
"How much are you thinking of paying her?"
"Ten pounds a week," I said promptly.
"Ten pounds a week. Don't be absurd. My secretary only gets £3.17.6 a week."
"Well *you* only need a £3.17.6 a week secretary because you are highly organised. *I* need a £10 a week secretary because I am highly disorganised!" That ten pounds a week was one of the best investments

I ever made in my entire business life. Barbara Chandler, as she became, worked for me for 35 years apart from the time when she was a full-time mum. She was still with me when I retired and there is no doubt that she made a significant contribution, not only to the BEM but also to my very survival!

The Sun Life occupied a prime site in the centre of Reading. One or two other organisations rented accommodation in the building, but tucked away on the top floor was a vacant office. I negotiated with the landlord a very economical rent and Barbara turned it into a splendid office. There she was to handle all my Sun Life work, our Children's Special Service Missions work, the work of the BEM and for a time the work involved in the new estate agency. It was a perfect arrangement.

As far as the BEM in the UK was concerned we were really starting from scratch but we had a great message. What God was doing in Borneo He could also do in the UK. The power of God at work in the transformation of the Bornean head-hunter was equally available for the transformation of the West End barrister.

In order to get this message across I accepted every opportunity that arose to speak in churches on Sundays and take mid-week meetings. Through invitations from our steadily growing number of prayer partners I would find myself speaking at two, three and sometimes four meetings on a Sunday. More and more frequently I would be asked to take a whole Missionary Weekend. Mid-week meetings were less well attended than Sunday services but they provided greater opportunities for deeper and more personal discussions. It was from these smaller meetings that the majority of our future BEM missionaries came. University Christian Unions requested visits and I found myself regularly attending prayer groups from Oxford and Cambridge Christian Unions as well as many of the provincial universities.

The whole programme of deputation was significantly challenging, particularly as I was also fitting in my demanding Sun Life work. However, soon new prayer meetings were being started throughout the country and folk became interested in the work of the mission. We ran a biennial conference and up to 150 people came to learn more about the mission and to pray. At the beginning Bill and Shirley were the only UK missionaries, joined later by Jean Davis, a talented linguist and teacher, but the numbers gradually grew until we had sent out 23 from the UK, each one extraordinarily gifted. Every valedictory service meant an increase to the workload, and gradually the BEM correspondence, coupled to my Sun Life work, became too much for Barbara to handle. The Lord again came to the rescue with another organising genius in the person of Lesley Hobbs.

I will always remember my very first contact with Lesley. It was in the early seventies and occurred during one of those times when Barbara was not available and chaos reigned in the BEM office! Lesley had been recommended to me as a possible secretary for the BEM work, an appointment that was desperately needed! She had telephoned to fix an appointment for us to meet and I was greatly struck by her *beautiful* voice. I use the word deliberately because it was a voice that conjured up a vision of elegance and beauty. I made the appointment and eagerly looked forward to meeting her!

In due course she arrived. She wore a Harris Tweed jacket and skirt, ribbed woollen stockings, strong brogue shoes and tan leather gloves. In her left hand she carried a briefcase – not a handbag, I observed, but a business-like briefcase. Her hair was swept back in a severe bun and on her head she wore a felt hat.

Lesley was significantly less than average height but she had a remarkably long, mannish stride. She looked the very image of a terrifying French teacher I used to have who repeatedly told me I was a congenital idiot. As this vision from the past held out her hand with: "Mr Smith, I presume," my heart dropped into my boots and I all but stammered: "Yes, Ma'am"! That was my first meeting with Lesley Hobbs.

While I was trying to reconcile this austere-looking lady with the dulcet tones of the telephone call, she asked if she could see the mission office. "Of course," I said, remembering too late the shambles in which I had left the office early that morning. As we mounted the stairs in silence, a dreadful foreboding gripped me.

I should explain that we were in the throes of producing an 87 page mission prayer diary. It was an ambitious multicoloured affair with different colours for the various tribes in Borneo. It was being produced on an old Gestetner duplicating machine that was for ever going wrong, resulting in an appalling waste of A4 paper. The office had become a nightmare. Cravenly I thought of pretending I had left the key at home, but after a sidelong look at Lesley I changed my mind!

The office was worse than I had remembered. There was a colossal pile of screwed up multicoloured paper against one wall. On an overflowing filing cabinet there were two cups of cold coffee – no saucers! Under a mountain of papers on the table was a tray, attached to which was the somewhat appropriate label 'Fi...' Somehow the '... ling' had got torn off but I hadn't noticed it until Lesley came in to the office.

I was trying surreptitiously to hide the dirty coffee cups behind some books when, pointing to a pile of unopened letters on the floor, Lesley asked: "What are they?" I had been in a hurry that morning. A client was waiting for me downstairs and there hadn't been any room on the table for the morning's letters, so I had temporarily dumped them on the floor.

Feeling more and more like a guilty schoolboy, I showed her where everything was and explained what we were trying to do with the prayer diary. I was to discover that Lesley never needed to be told anything twice. "Is there a deadline for this prayer diary?"
"Yes," I said, "two weeks, I'm afraid."
"Then I think I'd better be getting on with it", she said.

I was groping behind the books for the dirty crockery when, without looking up, she said, "Leave the cups. I'll wash them later"!

Bill and Shirley were in the UK on extended furlough from Borneo at the time and were actually living in Reading. That afternoon Bill came in to my Sun Life office to see me and I thought I'd take him up to Lesley. When we walked in I thought I'd got into the wrong office because it looked at least twice as big. The table had been cleared of rubbish, and neatly laid out were numerous pages of the prayer diary. Lesley was hard at work on a typewriter while the Gestetner machine, predictably subdued, was now churning out faultless sheets of neat typing.

As will have been gathered, Bill was our mission guru. Brilliant ideas just tumbled out of him. Unfortunately he'd just had some new ideas about the prayer diary and, after a brief introduction, Bill set about explaining to Lesley how the prayer diary and most of our systems could be improved. For a while Lesley listened in silence while I retreated to the door. Apprehensively I watched Lesley building up a head of steam. Then, in a voice that would have put my French mistress to shame, Lesley said: "Dr Lees, I know *exactly* how to organise this office and I will get on a good deal better if you would kindly go away."

Never before had I seen Bill so confounded! He opened his mouth to say something but I hustled him out and shut the door. We met the janitor in the corridor who told us that he had taken six loads of rubbish to the bins. Then he said: "I'll tell you what, guvner, that there 'secatry' you got is straight out o' the top drawer." That was an apt description of Lesley. The prayer diary, beautifully produced, was ready on time.For nearly twenty years Lesley was the mainstay of the BEM in the UK. She was an ultra efficient office secretary. The first time I saw her typing I couldn't believe the speed at which she did it – and never a mistake. But she was also a born organiser, and from the moment she joined us, she managed all our conferences. Later, when the BEM merged with the Overseas Missionary Fellowship, which used to be the China Inland Mission, Lesley was responsible for the Malayasian news and prayer letters, and she continued with that responsibility until illness intervened. Lesley was a treasure.

Lesley died from cancer in 2002 but, because she was so loved and appreciated by my family and friends alike, this is a good medium to express a tribute to her. When she first joined us I believe she was motivated by a sense of gratitude to the Lord. That of course is understandable. How can there be anything other than gratitude towards a creator God who loves us so much that He actually became a human being in order to die for us. Lesley knew why Jesus had come to this earth. She knew that God had become Man for the express purpose of living a perfect life *for her* and then to die on a cross *for her* in order to take away *her sin* – for ever. It was a very personal thing. Lesley had a crystal clear grasp of the fact that her salvation rested, not on her undeniably faithful work, but on the perfect life of Jesus, His death and resurrection.

It was out of gratitude that she had given her life in service to the Lord. But there was a sternness about that service. Then something quite wonderful happened. Lesley went on a week's retreat to an Abbey. There she met with the Lord in a new way. From that moment she was just as efficient, but there developed in her an understanding compassion, a lovely grace and a deep, deep beauty. That beautiful voice was now matched with a lovely face and manner.

Lesley became the epitome of 2 Corinthians 3:18 where Paul says, "... and we, who reflect the Lord's glory, are being transformed into His likeness with ever increasing glory, which comes from the Lord." The Message paraphrases it like this: "Nothing between us and God, our faces shining with the brightness of His face. And so we are transfigured, our lives gradually becoming brighter and more beautiful as God enters our lives and we become like Him." It was indeed a great privilege to know this lovely lady.

The Lees Family at Redhatch Drive. From left to right: Valerie, Bill, Ruth, Shirley, Heather

Knowing the Lees family has been another of our privileges. Bill and Shirley had three girls, Ruth, Heather and Valerie, each of them enchanting. Through the prophet Isaiah, God reminds us that His ways are different from our ways. They certainly are different. In moments of perplexity we find ourselves thinking that we could have organised things a bit better than the way God has done it!

I am bound to admit that the thought occurred to me quite frequently when I reflected on Ruth Lees, for it transpired from a fairly early age that she suffered from cerebral palsy. I say suffered, but perhaps that is not the right term, for she was a happy child, although fearfully handicapped both physically and mentally. The consequence of this was that Bill and Shirley found it needful to return to the UK from Borneo when Ruth was about eight in order that she might receive specialist treatment and education.

For the first months the family lived with us in Redhatch Drive. All nine of us lived together in a three bed-roomed house for nearly nine months. As Ruth had a behaviour pattern of a child of about two, it is a significant comment on the grace of God that we all lived in an atmosphere of total harmony and love for each other throughout the whole of that time. If medals were awarded for that then it is the mums who deserved them most, for by any normal standards there must have been some pretty trying moments! In all honesty I can say that never once did I hear a negative comment from either Valerie or Shirley. The fact is they had a deep love and respect for each other, something that has persisted over the years.

Providentially there was a sympathetic Education Authority in Reading which recognised Ruth's need for specialist education and this was provided by a local school. However it became increasingly clear that Ruth's handicaps were not going to become less, and Bill and Shirley decided to rent a house so that they could function more normally as a family unit.

They found a delightful home in Peppard on the Caversham outskirts of Reading, and in due course moved in. The Lees lived in this rented house for a period of nearly eighteen months, by which time there was a remarkable provision for Ruth which enabled Bill and Shirley to return to Borneo for another full four year term.

One Sunday morning Bill was preaching at Wycliffe Baptist Church in Reading. At that service was the Morris family, Mum and Dad and four children. By an extraordinary sequence of events it was borne in on Joan Morris that the Lord may be wanting her to look after Ruth, so that the Lees family could return to Borneo. This was a fantastic notion. Joan had her hands full with four children, on top of which she was struggling with a bad back which seemed to preclude looking after Ruth, who was quite heavy and needed a lot of lifting.

Even so the notion would not go away, so Joan said to the Lord that if He wanted her to look after Ruth, He would have to organise things so that on the next day, the Monday, she would unexpectedly meet up with this Doctor Bill Lees. It so happened that Joan needed to visit the pastor of Wycliffe, and while she was there Bill called as a locum GP to the family. When Bill knocked at the door of the pastor's house it was Joan who opened the door! The Lord really was speaking to her about Ruth. In due course Ruth moved in with the Morris family and stayed for four happy years. In the meanwhile the Lees family returned to Borneo for a very fruitful four year term.

Joan Morris with Ruth Lees

When the time came for the Lees to return to the UK they had an SOS from Joan Morris to say that Ruth was seriously unwell. Instead of returning by boat they flew home. Ruth's condition gradually deteriorated. With her simple love for Jesus, she was a great blessing to many in the wards at Borough Court hospital. Ruth's severe respiratory infection failed to respond to treatment and she died. In her fourteen years Ruth had been an enormous blessing to a huge number of people in a variety of ways and, even now, after 40 years, folk still speak warmly of her and her love for Jesus.

During the time that Bill was in the UK we did a great deal of deputation together and I learned a huge amount from him. It was rather like old times. Nevertheless it became increasingly clear that if I was to represent the mission adequately, to say nothing of accurately, it was high time that I visited the field personally.

Chapter 38
We leave for Borneo

One of the great advantages of Lesley joining us was that I could now more easily take extended time off to go to Borneo. The estate agency business was working smoothly and successfully without further input from me. The Sun Life was totally comfortable with the notion of me being away for a number of months. As a matter of fact they temporarily provided an assistant branch manager who was responsible for looking after my affairs. In fact Barbara would have done that perfectly well but one doesn't look a gift horse in the mouth!

It is perhaps relevant to mention another issue related to my being able to leave my Sun Life work for such a lengthy period. The general manager had given his personal blessing to my visits to Borneo but this particular trip was to last over four months. As I was on a commission-only contract no-one would suffer financially from that absence other than me. I have said earlier that God is no man's debtor. In a way that was nothing short of miraculous, during the six weeks immediately prior to our departure the business simply poured in. Then immediately on my return the flood of business resumed to such an extent that in just over seven working months I produced more business than anyone else had produced in the entire year.

Unsurprisingly both Valerie and I needed a holiday so we decided to go by boat. Thus it was we found ourselves at Tilbury docks in London on the SS Orsova, a liner bound for Australia via Penang. It was a cold and drizzly day but soon we'd be in glorious wall to wall blue skies and rising temperatures. We couldn't wait to be off. The Bay of Biscay was unusually calm, which was a blessing, for Valerie had proclaimed herself to be a rotten sailor. In fact at no time during the three weeks' voyage did she feel in the least queasy.

Every morning a ship's bulletin was delivered to the cabin. When we were half way through the Mediterranean the ship's bulletin carried an invitation: "CAMEL RIDE. Arrangements have been made for camels to be available in Benghazi for those who would like to travel to Cairo by camel. There the journey on board ship can be resumed. Would those passengers desirous of disembarking at Benghazi and rejoining the ship in Cairo please contact the ship's bursar."

"Look at this," said Valerie. "I'd *love* to ride a camel!"
"Not to Cairo you wouldn't!" I said.
"Why not? It would be a great experience."

I had ridden camels in Palestine and found it a very unpleasant experience. "Let me see what it says. They can't be serious. Everyone would be so sore at the end of the first day they'd want to be back on board." The invitation was genuine but it was a facsimile of a bulletin given out to passengers on board a ship exactly 100 years earlier! Life on board then must have been pretty terrible if folk would actually prefer a 500 mile camel ride!

It was a long haul from Aden to Malaya but in due course we arrived safely in Penang, our port of disembarkation. We were due to attend a linguistic conference in Thailand so we had arranged to fly straight away to Bangkok. We had two free days before the conference and we decided to spend them seeing the Royal Palace and the Floating Market in Bangkok. The palace was nothing like as good as the one in the film, 'The King and I' and, while The Floating Market was certainly different from any other market we had seen, we didn't buy anything.

One of my clients was in the Diplomatic Service and had been appointed as First Secretary in the Thai Embassy in Bangkok. A few weeks earlier he had been on leave in the UK and we were given strict instructions to visit him in Bangkok. Nothing could have been a greater contrast than Peter Scanlon's accommodation with some of the Bornean longhouses where a week or so later we would be sleeping.

The linguistic conference was held at a tiny coastal village called Banglamung just outside Pattaya, about 60 miles south of Bangkok, on the Coast of the Gulf of Thailand. The journey there was extraordinarily gratifying. By a happy coincidence, Prince Philip was not only in Bangkok at the same time, but was taking the very same route as us. Quite unknown to us, his cavalcade of cars was following about five minutes behind. Police cars and motor cyclists were at every corner waving us on and all along the road we saw people waving Union Jacks. When we came to a village, the road was packed with cheering crowds all waving their little flags. In many of the villages bunting was stretched across the road from house to house. Enthusiastically we waved back to the delight of the crowds who cheered even louder.

Although surprising, it was thoroughly heart warming to see the crowds, to say nothing of the efforts the police were making, seemingly for our security. It all made us feel very welcome and important!

In Banglamung we met up again with Shirley Lees, who was able to introduce us to the Field Chairman of the BEM, Alan Belcher and his wife Madge. We also made friends with a number of Overseas Missionary Fellowship missionaries with whom we are still in contact over 50 years later. A large number of Bible translators were attending this conference run by the Summer Institute of Linguistics (SIL) an organisation which partners with Wycliffe Bible Translators. It was thrilling to be with so many talented people. Many of them were the only ones in the entire world who would be able to give to the people, amongst whom they were working, the Scriptures in their own vernacular language. To do that of course, they had to learn the language with its own particular idiom and grammar. They would have to reduce that language to writing. Only then could they translate the Scriptures. The translation would have to be checked and rechecked before a Bible Society would be prepared to print the work.

In addition to translating the Scriptures the missionary would have to produce learning aids and teach the people to read. All of that takes enormous effort and application, more often than not, in an isolated environment where disease is rampant and extreme discomfort the norm. Translators are the heroes and heroines of the church and deserve support. The joy of the work is that they place into people's hands the Scriptures that make them 'wise unto salvation'.

Of course linguistic problems are encountered, some of them seemingly insurmountable. For example, how do you translate The Parable of the Pearl of Great Price for people who have never seen the sea, let alone a pearl. While having a pearl described to him, a translation assistant said, "Oh, yes! That's like the gallstone of a monkey."

"But a pearl is very valuable," said the missionary.

"Ah, but the Chinese will give anything for the gallstone of a monkey because it is used for medicine!" So in those Scriptures it is 'The Parable of the Gallstone of a Monkey'! As we listened to some of the problems that translators face, I was heartily glad the Lord hadn't called me to be a translator, but at the same time I praised God for bringing into being Wycliffe Bible Translators who, all over the world, run courses and conferences similar to the one we were attending.

Wycliffe Bible Translators was started by a young American by the name of Cameron Townsend. In 1919 he was a missionary in Guatemala where he was distributing Spanish Scriptures, because they were the only ones available. A man from an Indian people group asked him, "If your God is so great, why can't He speak my language?" That was Cameron Townsend's 'aha' moment. He immediately set to and started work to reduce that language to writing and give those people some Scriptures. By 1934 he had completed the entire New Testament. It had taken fifteen years of hard work, during which he learned a great deal about translation work; so he returned to the States and founded the Summer Institute of Linguistics and Wycliffe Bible Translators.

Twenty-first century missionaries involved in translation owe a great deal to Cameron Townsend being called into this work, and a great work it is. Languages having an adequate Bible number 451. Another 1,185 have an adequate New Testament and 845 others have at least one book of the Bible. Worldwide, a new translation project starts every five days and work is going on in over 2,000 languages.

Nevertheless the fact remains that nearly a billion people do not have a single Scripture in their own heart language. Of those, more than 196,000,000 people in 2,393 language groups are waiting for work to start on their language. That number was vastly bigger back in 1965 when we were in Thailand. Since then Scriptures have been made available to thousands of people by the very folk attending that course.

At Banglamung most of the lectures were given by the celebrated Eugene Nida, author of 'Customs, Culture and Christianity' as well as countless other books. We found him to be a most delightful man but most of what he said went right over my head. Taking a break from the lectures a number of the delegates went out in a sailing boat to an island a few miles away. Valerie and I were invited to join them and we had a splendid picnic on a beach and a swim in a lagoon. It was like swimming in a huge tropical fish tank. The water was positively warm and so clear that all around us we could see hundreds of brilliantly coloured fish.

The conference over, we returned to Bangkok and the same day flew back to Penang where we picked up a hire car to make a whirlwind tour of North Malaya. Our first destination was Kampar, which is between Ipoh and Kuala Lumpur. In Kampar we met Doctor Samuels who had prayed for me in Taiping back in 1949. It was a great reunion. While we were with him he said he had a surprise for us. We set off in his Land Rover and, quickly turning off the main roads, we were soon making our way along tracks, heading straight for the jungle.

It had been twelve years since I was last in the jungle and a highly dangerous place I had found it to be. As we moved along the track some kind of preservation instinct was screaming at me that we were making far too much noise, and we should either be moving much more stealthily, or a great deal faster.

While I was trying to tell myself that the terrorist threat had disappeared at least five years earlier, I nevertheless found myself trying to pierce the dense undergrowth on either side of the track, and was constantly looking for possible escape routes from an ambush. It was only with a great effort that I was able to relax and chat normally with our genial host.

After travelling about twenty miles deep into the interior we came to a clearing. Scattered around were some very small huts on stilts. As we approached, little figures appeared at the doors of the huts and came down to greet us. Dr Samuels, speaking to them in a language very like Malay, introduced Valerie and me to the headman who greeted us with a wide albeit toothless smile. These were Orang Asli, people of the jungle. They were all Christians who had been brought to know the Lord through the life and testimony of a young Orang Asli who had met a missionary a few years back. Now there was a large community of them, and a delightful crowd they were.

The day was a Sunday and they were about to hold a service together. Dr Samuels preached, and although we couldn't understand a word of what he said, his beaming smile was a sufficient benediction. We had communion with them. The 'bread' was rice cake and the 'wine' coconut milk. When we left, the headman gave me a strong hug. He then shook Valerie's hand, holding it in both of his he gave it a kiss. There was grace and love in the gesture that was curiously moving. These primitive people, mostly dressed in clothes made from bark, were our brothers and sisters in Christ. It was a humbling and yet thrilling experience to be with them and certainly it was a memorable surprise.

From Kampar we returned north to Taiping to visit old friends and haunts before going to Penang where we stayed at the P&O Hotel. There were people we wanted to visit in Penang, particularly a Chinese by the name of Wilson Wong. Shortly after I became a Christian, I would go with Wilson Wong on weekend evangelistic tours to a number of villages around Taiping. He had an amazing ability to catch the attention of people and an almost folksy way of speaking about the truths of the Bible.

I recall him speaking about different ways of getting clean. In his delightful Chinese clipped accent he would say, "If you have been gardening, then soap and water gets the dirt off your hands. If your bicycle chain comes off and your hands are greasy, soap and water is no good! You need petrol. But there's something inside us that neither soap nor petrol will clean. It's the heart! Only one thing cleans the heart. It is the precious blood of Jesus that was shed for you!" I was amazed at how people responded to such a simple message.

During a visit to the UK Wilson stayed with us at Redhatch Drive. I recall him preaching in our church. It was a riot of laughter. He started by introducing himself as a big family man. He had one-and-a-one-half-dozen children. Actually, he had seven, not eighteen children! He told us of his wedding day in a Christian church. He was not at all sure what he should do so he resolved to watch what others did. But that didn't help very much for when it came to praying, some of the congregation closed their eyes and some kept their eyes open. He decided to close one eye and keep the other one open!

When we visited the Wongs we were disappointed to learn that Wilson was in Australia but Mrs Wong insisted that we returned the following evening for a meal, and what a meal it was. She had prepared a fantastic spread of the most delectable Chinese food imaginable and we spent a delightful evening with her. When we said goodbye, little did we think that we would meet up with Wilson when we went to Australia, but that comes later.

The fabulous meal with Mrs Wong

BORNEO

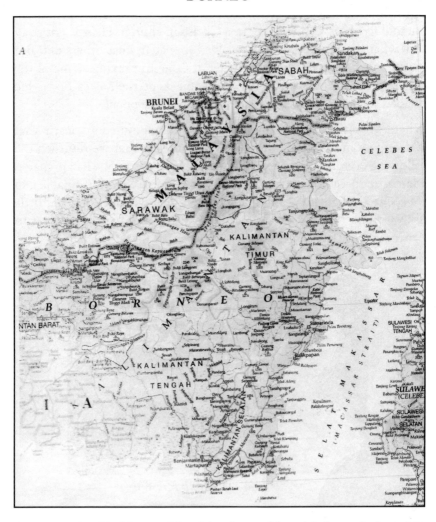

Borneo is the third largest island in the world and is located about 500 miles East of Singapore. The island is divided between Indonesia (Kalimantan) in the South, Malaysia (Sarawak in the East, and Sabah in the North) and Brunei (next to Sarawak's North Eastern border). Malaysia's region of Borneo is called East Malaysia or Malaysian Borneo.

The Borneo Evangelical Mission worked among the tribal peoples of both Sabah and Sarawak and it was in those areas that our travels are recorded in the next chapter.

Chapter 39
Borneo

From Penang we flew to Singapore where we caught a plane to Kuching, the capital town of Sarawak. In Kuching we met up with ex-Apprentice Lance Corporal Jamieson who had been at the Army Apprentices School back in 1954. He was now a senior NCO. With a beaming smile he told us how he was serving the Lord in his army unit. It was a great encouragement to see him going on with the Lord and I wondered how all the other apprentices were doing in their various spheres of service, both military and spiritual. From Kuching we flew to Lawas civil airport. As we came in to land we could quite clearly see the airstrip and buildings of the mission headquarters on the other side of the river from the civil airstrip. The mission planned to take Valerie and me round the entire mission field covering the whole of Sabah and Sarawak. Because of the little plane this was going to be possible. The Piper Tri-Pacer carried three passengers and the pilot. It was a classic STOL plane. STOL is the abbreviation for Short-Take-Off-Landing. It could land on the metaphorical pocket handkerchief, which was just as well because some of the strips on which we landed were positively diminutive.

It is worth recording how the mission came to have this Piper Tri-Pacer. After the war, a bush doctor in Australia read about the Borneo Evangelical Mission. Because there were no roads in the interior of Borneo much of the valuable time of missionaries was being taken up with walking from one place to another, journeys

The Piper Tri-Pacer

that sometimes took three to four weeks. Being a medic, the bush doctor also appreciated how vulnerable were the missionaries in their isolated locations with no hope of help reaching them for two or three weeks.

The doctor had an Auster monoplane which he used to visit his outlying patients and, figuring that the missionaries' time was more valuable than his, he decided to give the plane to the mission. He had a close friend who was a trained and experienced pilot who, learning of the need promptly asked to join the BEM. While the plane was being crated up and despatched to the field, the search was on in Borneo to find areas that could be turned into landing strips. With life generally being lived on the perpendicular this was not an easy task but gradually little airstrips were being carved out of the jungle-clad mountainsides near to villages. In some areas it proved quite impossible because of the proximity of swift-flowing rivers or mountain cliffs, or indeed both! The plane project was a great success and the little plane transformed the work of the mission.

One of our prayer partners in London was an 85 year old lady who suffered from crippling arthritis and was permanently bedridden. She was totally committed to praying for missions and the Borneo Evangelical Mission in particular. She received a number of mission publications regularly through the post and used them as her praying schedule. A BEM supporter in Melbourne was a newspaper publisher and he had the notion of printing a quarterly newspaper for the mission. As well as giving up-to-date news it also carried feature articles. One such article was about the plane project.

In the UK we had arranged to receive a large supply of these quarterly newspapers which we sent to all our prayer partners including our arthritic supporter in her London flat. She had a friend who regularly visited her and one day this friend arrived in a high state of excitement.

"My dear, what do you think? Arthur has agreed to go with me tonight to hear Doctor Billy Graham at Haringey." Arthur was her wealthy brother.

"Then we must pray for him."

And so they did, most earnestly.

The next day the friend arrived, even more excited and delightedly announced that her reserved brother had not only gone to the Billy Graham Crusade meeting but had gone out to the front to make a personal commitment to Christ. The name of the brother was Arthur Drysdale.

"Get him praying for missions," was the spontaneous response, and reaching across to her praying schedule she picked up the piece of literature on the top of her pile and gave it to her friend to give to her brother. The paper happened to be the BEM newspaper featuring the plane project. About three months later I received a letter from Arthur Drysdale containing a folded cheque. In his letter he said how he had recently come to know the Lord and that he had been given, by his sister the BEM newspaper. I assumed the folded cheque was to cover the cost of us sending him the quarterly newspaper. He went on to say that the Auster was not entirely suited for Borneo because it had a comparatively long take off requirement. He had been researching the industry and discovered that the most suitable plane was a Piper Tri-Pacer and recommended that the Auster be replaced with one of these.

This was very sound advice but a new aeroplane was financially completely out of the question for a mission which had no surplus funds whatsoever. The Piper Tri-Pacer would be wildly expensive. At the bottom of the letter was a cryptic comment that the enclosed cheque was intended to help achieve the replacement. Unfolding the cheque I saw the figure one and so many noughts after it that at first it didn't sink in that Arthur Drysdale was actually funding the purchase of the plane. A little later we received a cheque to cover the cost of crating and despatching the plane to Borneo.

This was the little plane that was to take Valerie and me all over Sabah and Sarawak during the time we were there, but Arthur Drysdale had not finished with us. Shortly after my return to the UK I received another cheque for a similar amount in order to pay for a second plane! His comment was, "As the mission becomes more and more dependant on the plane programme, so the work will be disrupted by periods when it is not available because of maintenance and airworthiness tests. A cheque is enclosed to cover the purchase, crating, despatch and insurance of a second plane." Still he was not finished with us! Later we received a cheque to cover the cost of a spare engine! In Luke's gospel Jesus, speaking about the Father, says: 'A good measure, pressed down, shaken together and running over will be poured into your lap.' What bounty.

Arthur Drysdale was elderly in 1965. He will be in heaven now, not because of his generosity, but because of the generosity of God! But the plane project was one of the best investments he ever made. The rapid growth of the church in Borneo continually brought great joy to this faithful servant. Another faithful servant was our 85 year old prayer partner who, despite her desperate physical limitations, shared her great vision for missions with her friend's brother. They were true missionaries!

* * * * *

Our first trip in the Piper Tri-Pacer was to Ranau deep in the interior of Sabah. On our way to Ranau, we flew past the majestic Mount Kinabalu. With its peak at 13,400 feet, Mount Kinabalu is the highest mountain in South-East Asia. The sheer height and ruggedness of the mountain has earned it considerable attention in myth and legend as well as in geography, and the mountain has for long been revered as a sacred spot. The hundreds of square miles encompassed by its slopes, from sea level to the jagged stone edge marking its summit, now form the Kinabalu National Park. Within this area is found some of the richest flora in the world.

According to a fable, the name Kinabalu comes from Cina Balu which means 'A Chinese Widow'. Due to the linguistic influence of the Kadazan Dusun of Sabah, the pronunciation for the word was changed to Kina Balu. The fable tells of a Chinese prince who was cast upon the shores of Borneo when his ship sank in the middle of the South China Sea. He was subsequently rescued by the local natives from a nearby village. As he recovered, he was gradually accepted as one of the local village people. Eventually he fell in love with a local girl and they got married.

Years went by and he started to feel homesick, so he asked his wife's family if he could go back to China to visit his parents, who incidentally were the Emperor and Empress of China! He promised his wife that as soon as he had reassured his family of his safety, he would return to Borneo to take his wife and their children back to China. After building a simple sailing ship, he went back to China. When he arrived, he was given a grand welcome by his family but, to his dismay, his parents told him that he was already betrothed to a princess of a neighbouring kingdom and he would have to marry her. Having no choice, he obeyed with a heavy heart.

Meanwhile, back in Borneo, his wife, growing more and more anxious, decided to climb to the top of the mountain near her village, so that she could have a better view of the ships sailing around the South China Sea, and thus get early news of her husband's return. At every sunrise she was seen climbing up the mountain, only returning at night to attend to her growing children. The effort took its toll and she fell ill, eventually dying at the top of the cold mountain.

The spirit of the mountain, having observed her for years, was extremely touched by her loyalty and out of admiration turned her into stone, facing the South China Sea, so that she could wait for her husband's return. The people in her home village were also deeply touched and they decided to name the mountain Kinabalu, in remembrance of her. To them, the mountain is a symbol of everlasting love and loyalty. To this day, some of the older village people around Ranau believe that St John's Peak was the stone into which her body was turned.

* * * * *

In Ranau we were welcomed by Wes and Doreen Battle and Jean Gollan from Australia. Sam Gollan, Jean's husband was some miles away doing some translation checking on the Dusun New Testament. We decided to pay him a visit. Apart from very few roads in Borneo and a short length of railway, visits meant going by Shanks' Pony. That doesn't mean walking; there is very little walking done in Borneo. You *climb,* or at least you climb up one side of a mountain and slither down the other. Where our muscles ache after a lot of climbing, the Borneans' muscles ache when they do a lot of walking on level ground! Their muscles aren't used to it!

Our walk to Sam was a good deal more arduous than can be imagined. Our guide was a very strong young Bornean who carried a gigantic pack of stores on his back. I had a small satchel and my camera. After the first four or five miles I was really beginning to flag. Seeing this, our guide removed my satchel and put that on his back. Two or three miles later he lifted my camera off my shoulder and carried that too! I was too exhausted to protest!

We eventually came across Sam in a little leaf hut about five feet by five by five. With papers strewn across a table he was working on the translation. The curious thing about him was that his feet, encased in huge Wellington boots, were in a large cardboard box. He explained that it was to keep the leaches off his legs.

We found Sam to be a delightful, if somewhat diffident, man. He and Jean had been in love with each other for a long time but it seemed to Jean that Sam could never pluck up the courage to pop the question. In vain his colleagues contrived situations where he and Jean would find themselves alone but Sam was always tongue-tied. Eventually, when Jean was in Lawas and Sam in Ranau, Jean, out of sheer desperation was persuaded to send a telegram to Sam asking if *he* would marry *her*. A day later a telegram arrived at Lawas for Jean. It contained two words: 'Agreeable. Sam.' Thereafter he was known as Agreeable Sam!

After a fairly strenuous week in and around Ranau, we took the celebrated short rail ride from Kota Kinabalu to Tenom where we were met by a Doctor Peter Graham. Peter was a government medical worker who later spent three months of every year in Nepal training young medics to perform cataract operations. Through his work, literally hundreds of thousands of people have been given back their eyesight. We spent a delightful evening with him.

The next day he took us by jeep along some tracks to a place where we were to meet Shirley Lees. We were now in Tagal Country where Bill and Shirley had been working. At the time of our visit Bill was doing deputation work in New Zealand and Australia but Shirley was there to meet us and to take us on another walk!

Our destination was the village of Sugiang where Agong was the pastor. Eventually we arrived exhausted and unbelievably thirsty.

Most of the tribal people in Borneo at that time lived in long-houses. These consisted of a number of fairly small rooms, one room to a family, all connected to each other and separated by flimsy partitions. The rooms were all in a straight line with a connecting veranda running the length of the long-house. The whole thing was built on stilts lifting the house about five to six feet off the ground. During tropical downpours it was better to have flood water going under your house than through it. You could tell the size of a village instantly by the length of the longhouse; the larger the village the longer the house. We came across one long-house that was half a mile long!

In the village to which Shirley had taken us the villagers had built Agong a separate house to give him some privacy in his role as their pastor. This house was to be our accommodation for the night. It was small and built of bamboo. The pastor and his wife and other church leaders met us and during a very convivial evening plied us with copious amounts of condensed milk mixed with water. The arduous journey had made us ferociously thirsty and we must have drunk at least two pints of this liquid refreshment. Borneans go to bed fairly early and we had no objections to this for Valerie and I were ready to drop after the exhausting journey. Earlier we had been shown a bedroom which I assumed was for Valerie and me but when I came into the room later Shirley and Val were already in the bed.

"Where do I sleep?" I asked Shirley.

"With us!" was her nonchalant reply.

Looking at the size of the bed I said, "Wouldn't it be better if I slept on the floor?"

"Not if you want to get any sleep," said Shirley. "You'll get eaten alive."

The room had just two articles of furniture. One was a sleeping platform, now pretty fully occupied by Valerie and Shirley and the other was a huge round tin can about two feet high.

"What's that?" I asked Shirley, pointing to the can.

"It's an old kerosene tin," she replied with a straight face. When I asked her what it was for I wished I hadn't!

Putting out the candles I got ready and quietly slid on to the bed making sure I was on Valerie's side! Hardly had I lain down when the two pints of liquid refreshment started to make insistent demands. As I lay in the bed pretending to be fast asleep I saw in my imagination with ever increasing clarity that enormous kerosene can and I quaked with apprehension. I soon discovered that I was not the only one simulating somnolent sounds, for in turn, first Valerie and then Shirley, left the bed and made extensive use of that noisy container. The reality was even worse than I had imagined! Diffident before this demonstration I was now utterly determined that come what may I would renounce the provided facilities and seek an alternative.

I waited while the adjoining breathing deepened and soon I reckoned they were fast asleep. Creeping surreptitiously towards the door I stumbled over that wretched kerosene can. There was a mighty crash that should have awakened the dead let alone my companions. Happily, I caught the can and stopped it from going over. As I stood in that frozen position I listened. There had been what sounded suspiciously like a snort but even deeper breathing followed on its heels and I put it down to a snore and continued to make my way to the door. It opened noiselessly. 'This is going to be easy,' I thought.

Crossing to the exit door I gave it a gentle pull. It didn't budge so I gave it a gentle push. Again it didn't budge so I gave a harder pull and then a harder push. It didn't move. I could see no locks so why wouldn't it open? I gave it a violent pull and push in quick succession. Although the whole of that bamboo house shook to its foundations the door remained obstinately shut. What I didn't know was that small holes had been bored through the bamboo door edge and the adjoining bamboo door frame. Small rods were then pushed thought these apertures to make an effective lock.

I looked at the three foot square opening that served as a window. The sill was about four feet from the floor. I gave a jump and my bare feet nearly went through the bamboo slatted floor. Feeling around for some joists, I positioned myself on them and gave a mighty leap, pulling myself up as I jumped. I came up on to the sill but the impetus of my jump kept me going and I sailed on right through the window landing on the notched log below. The notched log serves as stairs. One way of 'locking the door' is to turn the log round, securing it at the top.

I bounced down the log landing on the rather squelchy ground beneath. As the village pigs were free-range I discovered that what I landed on was not all 'ground'! In my semi-stunned state I thought I heard stifled cries from inside the house but assumed it must have been me.

Having achieved my exit I now attended to the object of my exertions, and not before time! While I was thus engaged, a loud-high pitched noise sounded in my ear. It was the cicada I had heard while lying in bed. That creature will keep me awake all night I thought and threw a stick at it as an encouragement to find a more appreciative audience. The moment I threw the stick the sound started coming from a bush behind me. It was even louder now. I retrieved the stick and threw it again. Exactly the same thing happened. I spent a good half-an-hour determined to dislodge that cicada but with no success. Either there were two of them in a conspiracy or the one was a ventriloquist. I yielded defeat and went back to the house.

A nasty thought belatedly crossed my mind. *How was I to get back into the house?*

The window sill was a good ten feet from the ground. I climbed the log to the door and gave it a savage push and an equally savage pull, to no avail. No need to turn this log round. Eyeing the distance to the sill from the different notches of the log I thought that if I made a fairly spectacular jump I might just be able to reach it. Whatever happened I mustn't miss the sill! I had good reasons for wanting to avoid another fall! Rather like a chicken going to roost, I moved up and down the notched log eyeing the sill and trying to decide which step gave the greatest advantage.

Eventually I launched myself into space, desperately reaching for the sill. I caught it with one hand and hung on for dear life. The house swayed alarmingly and for an awful moment I thought I would pull it over on top of me. I am not very strong but I pulled myself up onto that sill with such velocity that again I overshot the mark and tumbled right through on to the floor. It was at that point that I discovered the earlier cries were not mine but Shirley's and Val's. They had both been in near hysterics from the moment I stumbled over the kerosene can!

We were hugely impressed with the Tagals and took away some fond memories that we were able to share with praying friends back in the UK. One thing I was not going to tell them was that I had spent a night in bed with one of the UK's most respected and beloved lady missionaries! But there was a great deal more to see and learn before going home.

* * * * *

The following three weeks was a very busy time for both Valerie and me. Wherever we went we were asked to speak or preach, or lead this that or the other meeting. 'Wherever we went' really means everywhere. Of course this was the object of the exercise but we ended up seeing more of the mission field than many of the missionaries who had been there for decades.

One unscheduled visit was when we had to make a forced landing in the Piper Tri-Pacer as unexpected bad weather closed in. Flying in the un-charted interior of Borneo was hazardous at the best of times but it was definitely ill-advised to fly through clouds. More often than not they would be stuffed with a mountain! On this occasion, as the weather suddenly and unpredictably deteriorated, our pilot, Bruce Morton was anxiously looking for a hole in the clouds below us. Suddenly the little plane banked sharply and spiralled down through a tiny gap at the bottom of which he had caught a glimpse of a small clearing in the jungle. It was a diminutive football pitch. The arrival of the plane at this small village was an unprecedented event and caused great excitement, calling for a celebratory feast. We were to be introduced to a Tagal delicacy – jarok.

Cooked rice and heavily salted raw fatty pork is stuffed into a four inch diameter cylinder of bamboo about three feet long. This is then sealed at both ends and buried about two feet deep in the ground. There it is left for two or three months depending on how well hung you like your raw fatty pork! Shortly after our arrival the village elders went off to their jarok larder and returned bearing three cylinders of this delectable delicacy. At a distance of about 50 feet we could almost hear it humming! Valerie and I were seated with Bruce and the village elders while liberal helpings of jarok were sluished out on to our enamel tin plates. The smell was appalling enough but the taste positively defies description. A twelve month dead donkey preserved in mothballs and chopped green chilli peppers would be an inadequate description.

Suddenly we were in the front line of mission work. When you are a guest you eat what you are given. It was matter of "Where He leadeth I will follow; what He feedeth I will swallow", so we prayed: "Lord, I'll get it down if you'll keep it down!" The first spoonful exploded in our mouths making it feel as if scalding steam was coming from our eyes, noses and ears. Happily there were wide slats in the bamboo table and the bamboo floor through which, undetected, we fed the pigs below. Nearly 50 years later we can still taste that jarok when we think of it.

In the afternoon the weather cleared and with consummate skill Bruce used a diagonal run across the football pitch to get the little plane into the air. There was no margin for error but anything was better than another meal of jarok!

Towards the end of our time in Borneo we made a two week tour of the south of Sarawak to visit some more of the interior villages. Again Bruce was the pilot and this time his delightful wife Ruth joined us for the whole of the trip.

The first leg was to Bintulu, one of the coastal towns. From there we went on to Sibu, where we left the plane securely tied down and took a boat down the River Rejang, first to Binatong to see Keith Napper and then to Pakan to see Colin Reasbeck, who later married Margaret Bradley.

The next stage of the journey was considered too primitive for Valerie and Ruth so they were left at Pakan while Bruce and I were taken in a dug-out canoe up some narrow rivers to Rumah Empali. Primitive was a good description. I reckoned the way the tribes people were living in the long-house we visited probably hadn't changed much in the last 5,000 years. We were in Iban country. These were the proud and arrogant people who years before had contemptuously refused to turn to Christ.

"Don't come to us with your God," they had said. "We'll gladly drink beer in hell with the devil!" Lun Bawang missionaries had also approached them with the Good News of the gospel. Traditionally the Iban had despised the Lun Bawang. This was with good reason, bearing in mind the previous state of the Lun Bawang tribe. Whenever an Iban even mentioned the Lun Bawang he would spit. However the Lun Bawang had changed so radically that beneath the arrogance a number of Iban were beginning to ask questions of visiting Lun Bawang:

"Why are you no longer frightened of the spirits?"

"Why are you interested in helping us when you don't get paid for it?"

Among themselves they were asking questions. "How did the Lun Bawang get this personal authority, yet remain so helpful and compassionate?" So it was that here and there in Iban communities there were those who were turning to Christ.

In the long-house that we visited there were no born again Christians. The signs of spirit worship were everywhere. That night I tried to get some sleep lying on the veranda outside a room over the door of which hung a cluster of human skulls. It wasn't the skulls that bothered me - it was the hard floor, the bugs and the fighting cocks. The hard floor was of thick unforgiving timbers, but it was what they concealed that caused the most problems. As soon as I lay down to sleep an army of bed bugs came out of the woodwork and within a few seconds were sitting down to the first course of their dinner. These were not microscopic creatures; these bugs were *big*. I could feel them running all over me and they felt as large as mice.

I shared the veranda with about 40 fighting cocks. They might have been very good at fighting but they were very poor at telling the time. From about midnight they started crowing. First one would crow and then another, and within fifteen seconds the whole lot of them would be hard at it for half-an-hour. There might then be ten or fifteen minutes silence before first one would crow, followed by another, then they'd all be going at it again hammer and tongs. Attached to the cocks' legs were thin cords by which they were tethered to the veranda at about twelve foot intervals. I was sleeping between two who were in exceptionally good voice. The problem was that each thought the lump on the veranda was their private dunghill on which to stand and crow. They couldn't reach each other but they could each

358

reach me, one at one end and one at the other. What with the fighting cocks and the bugs, I had a fraught night and itched for a fortnight!

The next day we returned to Pakan, where we picked up Valerie and Ruth who in due course picked up some of our fellow travellers, so much so that by the time we arrived back at Sibu and the plane we were all scratching furiously. It wasn't long before we were sleeping on Kelabit floors, so I imagine we may have introduced some cross breeding in the bug world.

Bario was our next main destination. This was 600 miles away in the Kelabit Highlands, right in the interior of Sarawak and near the Indonesian border. En route for Bario we stopped at Long Bedian and Long Atip where we saw Phil Webster from Australia. In Bario we stayed with Tama Galang, the pastor of the Bario church who was hosting an Easter Convention held during the week we were there. The Borneans call these conventions Iraus; they are a throwback to their pagan days when they held beer feasts. Now, instead of getting filled with rice beer they gather together to be filled with the Spirit of God.

Over 1,200 came to this Irau, some having trekked over the mountains for as long as three weeks to be at the convention. At five o'clock we had an early morning call so that we could go to the prayer meeting where we joined about 1,000 others gathered for the prayer meeting which lasted nearly two hours.

Valerie and I had 'afternoon tea' with the conference leaders and the head man of the Bario village. There we were given Bornean names. Valerie's was Sigang and mine Munan. We were also given presents – Valerie was given a beautiful Bornean necklace and I was given a genuine ceremonial head hunting sword.

One of the most lasting memories I have of that convention was when I was sitting next to Mein Ribu, during one of the Bible readings. Mein Ribu was a Kelabit. Enormous bangles hung from his earlobes and sticking out from the top of his pierced ears were two great boar tusks. He wore very little by way of clothes but he had in his hand a copy of a newly acquired New Testament in his own language. The message was on 2 Corinthians 5:17, "Therefore, if anyone is in Christ, they are a new creation; the old has gone, the new has come." As the speaker commented on this verse, my neighbour drew from somewhere in his scanty clothing a stub of a red pencil and with infinite care he underlined the verse in his precious New Testament. I thought that he was the very epitome of that verse. Every now and then he would nod in agreement at what was said by the speaker and then he would turn to me and give me a beaming, toothless smile. There have been many revivals in Borneo and a significant number have started at an Irau. It was tremendously thrilling to have been part of one of these gatherings.

All too soon it came to an end. Most of the delegates were faced with a very long walk home lasting anything up to three weeks. We had a short walk to the airstrip and we were soon back at Lawas. We had a few more days of meetings but the time had come for us to leave Borneo. We were flown to Brunei where we caught a plane for Singapore.

Chapter 40
Home via Australia and India

The plane taking us to Australia was a BOAC Comet. It looked big enough for our little Piper Tri-Pacer to fly around the cabin. The purpose of our visit to Australia was so that we could meet up with my brother Fred and his family, meet BEM council members and incidentally do a little deputation for the mission. In fact we were given so many deputation meetings that, although we did meet up with Fred and Betty and with the council members, we were unable to spend as much time with them as we had hoped. We had a splendid barbecue out in the bush with Fred and his family, and Valerie spent a pleasant day on her birthday doing some shopping with Betty. Unlikely though it may sound, Valerie and I spent the afternoon of her birthday going to the cinema! We watched My Fair Lady which had just been released. That evening we spent a delightful time with Harold McCracken and council member Ralph Davies and his lovely wife Dulce.

We also had an entertaining evening with all the council members and their wives. We had been warned that they were rather serious and a trifle austere and at first they looked a formidable lot. One was actually wearing a wing collar but that was probably part of his professional uniform because he was a barrister. After a very formal welcome I was asked to comment on our visit to Borneo. I made the point that they were all much more experienced with field visits than we were but we had learned one or two do's and don'ts that they might care to hear about. They obviously thought I was going to share some profound cultural issues especially when I started by saying that I was about to give some really serious advice.

The top priority was, despite how thirsty they might be, on no account were they to drink too much, especially as the men would probably be required to sleep with a lady missionary! At first there were a few rather anxious looks but I went on to tell them that the drink would be condensed milk and water. By the time I had finished telling them about the sleeping and toilet arrangements they were wiping their eyes, probably from relief. We were subsequently told that future council meetings would never be the same again!

After a great number of meetings in schools and churches we found ourselves on a plane bound for Sydney where we had the delightful surprise of meeting up with Wilson Wong. At that time Sydney had the world's largest congregation of Chinese Christians and Wilson Wong was there taking a series of meetings. It was good to meet up with him again.

The following day Valerie left for Singapore en route for home. She had an overnight stay in Singapore which was spent at the famous Raffles Hotel. She was given royal treatment. Created in 1887, Raffles Hotel is one of the world's last great 19th Century hotels. It positively exudes its unique charm and grandeur and Valerie thoroughly enjoyed every moment of it. In the Raffles you are able to relive the old days at the museum featuring memorabilia from a bygone era, and then go shopping in the hotel's ultra-modern shopping mall where the retail shops include brand names like Tiffany's and Louis Vuitton. Happily Valerie just went window shopping.

The next morning Valerie was courteously escorted from the hotel to the airport and to the plane bound for the UK. To say that she would be glad to get home to the children would be an understatement. She arrived at Heathrow at 11:00 am and was met by some very excited children.

Meanwhile I continued with a heavy programme of deputation in Sydney, Brisbane, Adelaide and Melbourne. It was at this point that Bill Lees arrived from New Zealand in order to attend the Australian Annual Conference. Bill was the main speaker and he had the audience spellbound. It was a very good conference and I was glad of a rest from deputation. The conference over, Bill and I continued with the programme of deputation, some of which we did together. We then left for Perth and more deputation meetings. We were there for nine more strenuous days after which I left Bill in Perth and caught my plane for Singapore, the first leg of my journey home.

On our way out from Southampton, Valerie and I had met on board ship, Doctor Peter Snell and his wife Margaret, two delightful Canadian missionaries working in the very north of India in a little hospital in Menali. We had many talks together and agreed that on my way back to the UK I would try to call in to see them. Of course it would be a big detour but it seemed right to do it. It was for this reason that my return flights from Singapore were first to Calcutta and then to Delhi from where I could get a flight to the Kulu Valley in the Northern Punjab.

I had to spend a night in Calcutta where the airline had booked me in at the King George V Hotel. Having taken my bags to my room I thought I would go for a walk around Calcutta and so set off, leaving the hotel by a side door. I had been going about fifteen minutes when the sound of running feet caused me to turn round. Racing towards me was the concierge and two assistants from the hotel. Completely breathless and consequently unable to speak coherently, all three stood in front of me wagging remonstrating fingers for all the world as if I was absconding with the day's takings from the till. Eventually, when he had regained his breath, the concierge, who incidentally looked as if he was an Admiral in the Indian Navy, told me that under no circumstances could I be allowed to walk unescorted through the streets of Calcutta.

"Why ever not?" I asked.

Dramatically the concierge drew his fore finger across his throat. As if to brook no contradiction he then took me by the arm and led me back to the hotel. The general manager was standing on the steps and he too wagged a remonstrative finger at me. He had been berating the staff for allowing me to go out on my own but I was able to explain that I had left by a side door that automatically locks after being closed. This occasioned another severe wag of the finger.

It seemed as if the whole hotel staff regarded me as a delinquent so, with condemnation on every face I decided to go to bed early. Bearing in mind the security consciousness of the staff I thought I should lock the bedroom door but the lock didn't seem to work. I didn't give a lot of thought to this but, wearing only my underpants, I hopped into bed and was soon fast asleep. At about 2:00 am I sat up in bed, completely wide awake. I had not been able to work out how to switch off the light and I couldn't remove the bulb because the ceiling light was about twenty feet from the floor. I had no alternative but to leave the light on.

What had awakened me? I looked around, and as I did so I saw the knob of the door being turned. I slipped quietly across the bedroom floor to the door and stood watching the knob still being turned! When it stopped turning I snatched the door open and a most villainous-looking man nearly fell into the room. Holding him by his shirt front I demanded to know what he wanted. He immediately went down on his knees and let out a high pitched wail. I was only wearing underpants or I would have marched him up to the concierge but I couldn't face any more wagging fingers so I pushed him out of the door and shut it. I then did what I should have done earlier and wedged the back of a chair under the door handle.

The next day I flew to Delhi where there was an almost immediate connection with a flight to Kulu. Having checked in for the flight there was an extraordinary crowd waiting to board the plane. It wasn't the people who were so extraordinary as the things they were carrying as hand luggage. A great number had live chickens in cane cages and one man had a little goat in a cage. As soon as the official gave the word for us to board the plane there was a stampede for the steps. Not wanting to get knocked down in the rush I took my ordinary turn in the queue. When I got on the plane there were no seats left. I showed my ticket to the steward, a huge Sikh with a dark blue turban and a thick black beard. He then went round asking everyone for their tickets and came across a man who didn't have one. Lifting him up by his coat front, the steward promptly boxed the man's ears, frog marched him down the central corridor and literally threw him off the plane. I was then conducted to the vacant seat with a contrasting courteous bow.

No sooner had I settled into my seat than a message came over the Tannoy for us all to get off again. Men, women, children, chickens and the goat dutifully disembarked and returned to the departure lounge. This time I stood by the door. After a delay of about fifteen minutes an announcement was made that owing to the fact that the plane returning from Kulu had crashed at Chandigarh airport our plane would not be landing there and Chandigarh passengers should not board the plane. The starting gun then went for us and there was another stampede. This time I was the first on. I noticed that, despite having no Chandigarh passengers, every seat was occupied so there must have been a large number of standby passengers waiting to board.

The plane was an ex-war time Dakota and it looked as if it had been attacked by a squadron of Japanese Zeros. Our pilot was another powerful-looking Sikh and he got the plane off the ground without any problems. Later, as we flew over Chandigarh we could see the wreckage of our sister plane on the runway. One wing was completely detached from the rest of the plane. It was a sobering sight.

Our destination was Kulu up in the Himalayan foothills and even from the air the scenery was spectacular. As we came in to land a herdsman was frantically trying to round up his recalcitrant cattle and get them off the airstrip. They looked as if they were not interested in moving. Our pilot put the nose of the plane down and roared over the herd at not much more than four or five feet above horn level. The herd scattered in all directions tails held high in protest. It certainly got them off the grass airstrip.

The plane banked sharply and quickly came in to land. The pilot was laughing as the plane touched down about half way down the airstrip. From where I was sitting I could see him pushing hard on the back of his seat and for a while I thought we were going to run out of landing space. That would have been a pity because at the very end of the strip there was a steep drop into a fast flowing river. Two strands of barbed wire was the only barrier at the end of the landing strip. When the plane came to a stop the twin propellers were on the wrong side of the barbed wire.

The cockpit on a Dakota is further forward than the engines so the pilot must have given himself a nasty fright. When he looked down he would have been looking straight into the frothing river beneath him. We were all told to disembark where the plane was. I stopped to watch what they'd do. Soon a fire tender and two Land Rovers came up.

They attached ropes to the Dakota and dragged it back away from the barbed wire. The pilot started the engines again, swung the plane round and taxied over to the control tower, which was a little wooden hut.

I asked the pilot where I could find a taxi to take me to Manali and he called to the driver of one of the Land Rovers. The driver grinned and nodded. The pilot leaned towards me and told me how much should be charged. I thought I'd settle the fare before we started. The Land Rover man wanted precisely double what the pilot had said. I pretended to walk away. Eventually we agreed about ten per cent more than the figure given by the pilot. He shook his head reprovingly. It could have been a rip-off if the two of them had been in cahoots but it transpired that it was a very reasonable fare. The reason for this became clear later. The driver lived in Manali and was going there anyway.

Manali is north of Shimla in the beautiful forested Kulu Valley. With its flowing rivers and flower strewn walks it is known as the Valley of the Gods. It is virtually on the Himalayan snow line and the climate is essentially temperate. On one occasion it was to become a bit too temperate for my liking. Manali is famous for its orchards and, when I was there, delicious apples were on sale in the local market. In 1965 Menali was still a comparatively small village but Pandit Nehru, the then Prime Minister of India, set a trend by building a holiday home there. Today Manali is a huge tourist resort changed out of all recognition.

Doctor Peter Snell ran the Lady Willingdon Hospital, established in 1935 as an adjunct of the Amritsar Diocese of the Church of North India. As well as his wife Margaret, who was a trained nurse, there were two other nurses. The hospital was the only clinic in the whole of the area and therefore served a vast number of people. Adding to their numbers were many thousands of Tibetan refugees who had fled from the communist regime and were living in tented villages. The result was that the hospital was inundated with patients.

The entire hospital was crowded, and by crowded I mean there wasn't a square yard of floor surface not occupied by someone. At the back of the hospital an astonishing sight met my gaze. Winding its way back from the hospital was the waiting queue. It was about five to ten people wide and wound a tortuous way up a hill at the end of the valley and then disappeared out of sight over the brow of the hill. Later I discovered that every day a number of patients died whilst moving slowly towards the head of the queue. Perhaps the most depressing fact was that although the four members of staff started work at six in the morning and worked virtually non-stop until nine or ten at night, the queue was actually growing longer every day. One day I walked to the end of the queue. It was nearly two miles long consisting of well over 3,000 people. Not all of them would be needing treatment, probably half being attendant relatives. Even so, it was going to take at least a month before those at the end of the existing queue would be seen by the doctor or a nurse.

The articles of the foundation stated that the main purpose of the hospital was to declare, by works and word, the love of God so that those coming to the hospital would receive Christ into their lives. The unimaginable workload and the constant medical crises of every description certainly gave scope for the 'works' but didn't leave much time for the 'word'.

As I walked among that throng of needy people I wondered how Jesus would have handled that situation. Very quickly I concluded that He wouldn't have got into it in the first place. What *did* He do? His healing ministry was extensive but He was constantly on the move, so if a crowd gathered one day He was gone the next. Moreover His wasn't exclusively a healing ministry. His healing certainly caught people's attention but His priority ministry was teaching and disciple-making.

Here at the hospital there was hardly time for a bite to eat let alone teaching. Perhaps the best thing would be for them to close the hospital and for the team to move around from village to village, there to set up a clinic for part of the day, preach for part of the day and then teach those who responded.

Such a programme would give real opportunities of showing the love of God through meaningful personal relationships. Having done that in one village one day they could move to another the next. Five different clinics could be held in a week. Really serious cases could be brought back to the hospital but the staff wouldn't see patients there as the first port of call. It was a bizarre thought but it might be better than what was happening at that time.

Later I had the further idea that if they got their supporters in Canada to supply them with a long wheel base Land Rover it would be possible to convert it into a mobile clinic. I shared with Peter and Margaret the thought I'd had but it seemed to go down like a lead balloon.

The day before I left, Peter took some time out from the medical work to go on a walking climb with me so that we could discuss the mobile clinic concept in detail. After discussing the issues for about an hour we had looked at a number of possible problems. Peter confided that he was beginning to think that there might be something in the notion after all!

Suddenly we realised that it was growing very cold and getting dark even though it was only midday. With no warning we found ourselves in the middle of a blizzard and visibility dropped to about five feet. The terrain over which we had been walking was distinctly dangerous but Peter felt sure that if we continued to climb we would come across one of the Tibetan tented villages. After about half-an-hour of struggling on in the blizzard I was feeling frozen to the marrow and wondering how much further I could go. Marvellously we stumbled on a village. We shouted and a man came out and took us into his tent. A brazier was giving off some welcome heat. We took off our wet coats and sat round the brazier while our host became very busy. It was an education. He had a huge can of boiling water on the brazier and this he poured into a canister that looked like a World War I shell case. He swished the water around and poured it back into the can waiting a moment for it to boil again. He then dipped his hand into a sack, withdrew it and threw a handful of black stuff into the canister. When the water was bubbling again he poured it back into the shell case. He then pulled towards him a large bowl of greenish-yellow glutinous-looking fat. He dipped a tin lid into this terrible-looking mess and scraped it into the shell case. Peter leaned across and told me the stuff was rancid yak butter!

The man next got a rod about a yard long, at the end of which was a round disc with half-a-dozen holes in it. He squirted the contents of the shell case up and down using the rod like a plunger. It all gurgled and bubbled away in a most ominous fashion. I had realised for some time that he was in the process of making us a nice cup of tea, but I wasn't looking forward to drinking it!

He then fished out of a sack three cans that looked a bit like large Golden Syrup tins, except these were blackened with soot. Into these receptacles he poured his witch's brew. Globules of green and yellow rancid butter floated on the top of the liquid as he handed each of us a tin. As my fingers closed round the hot tin I realised how frozen my hands were. I took a tentative sip. It was like nectar. Never before or since was I to experience a cup of tea like that!

During the next hour Peter shared the Good News of the gospel with our host. He was very interested and asked a number of questions. Perhaps it was that opportunity of taking time to talk about the Lord, compared with the rest of his frenetic life that convinced Peter that they had to do something if they were to bring the gospel to villages like this one. The blizzard had blown itself out by late afternoon and we were able to make our cautious way back. It had been a useful day.

We didn't learn just how useful until about twelve months later when we had a letter from Peter saying the church had supplied them with a Land Rover that had been converted into a mobile clinic. They were visiting five strategic villages in turn during the week and holding literacy and teaching classes. Village folk were responding to the gospel and in three of the villages there was a group of believers. They were now teaching them to take the gospel to neighbouring villages. God moves in a mysterious way!

Back at Kulu airstrip I made sure of a seat on the plane. Once bitten twice shy. We were in the air long before reaching the barbed wire perimeter. Soon we were looking back at what must be the most spectacular scenery in the world. It was a cloudless day and we could see right to the top of the Kulu Valley with the Himalayas in the background.

There had been cloudless skies both before and after the experience of the Tibetan tented village. I wondered if God had sent that sudden and intense blizzard especially to provide Peter with that opportunity of sharing the gospel with the man in the tent. God does things like that!

Soon we were circling Chandigarh airport which had a proper tarmac surface to the runway. We could see the wreckage of our sister plane which had been towed well out of the way. As we circled the airport the captain told us that there were unusually strong cross-winds at ground level and we should make sure we were using the safety belts.

Just as the plane touched the ground there was a great squeal of tyres and for the next 200 yards the plane lurched from one side of the runway to the other, tyres squealing at each turn. Inside the plane there was complete pandemonium. Some of the passengers hadn't fastened their safety belts and were being flung from one side to the other. The cabin was full of flying packages, including a cage containing a couple of ducks. To add to the pandemonium the cage broke and the ducks took to the air, shedding feathers galore and dropping unmentionable debris on some of the passengers. I was at the back of the plane and wondering whether we would end up keeping the other plane company. However no damage was done, at least none to the plane, which taxied back to the terminal building. When the plane stopped the pilot appeared and with a broad grin on his bearded face said, "A little bit rough." I supposed that if it was very rough the plane would have been a write-off!

As I came out of the plane on to the steps a great gust of hot air hit me and I ran down the steps to get out of the way of the exhaust of the engines. Then I realised that the engines had stopped. The hot air was the wind, boiling hot and incredibly strong.

We waited at Chandigarh for about an hour by which time the strong wind had somewhat abated and we re-embarked. The ducks had been captured and were back in a new cage but their feathers were everywhere. Soon we were safely airborne. I wasn't sad to be leaving Chandigarh behind. At Delhi we made a safe landing and I had a fairly quick connection with the plane to Heathrow. Soon I was with the family again. It had been a full but fascinating three-and-a-half months.

* * * * *

In the seventies the Malaysian Government's open door policy for missions changed and one by one the missionaries' visas were not renewed, but the 150,000 strong Sidang Injil Borneo, the Evangelical Church of Borneo, had been prepared for precisely this contingency. The BEM missionaries were able to leave a legacy of Bible translations in the local ethnic languages; nearly all the tribes had their own Bible School and training establishments; there were indigenous pastors in nearly all the Lun Bawang churches, and in most of the other tribal churches. A number of the church leaders had been to the Melbourne Bible Institute and taken theological degrees. This did not of itself help the development of the church but it did give theological status to those who took part in those trans-national conferences and discussions that would result in further missionary outreach, something in which the SIB was vitally interested.

In 1975, when the Borneo Evangelical Mission merged with the Overseas Missionary Fellowship, my work-load dropped dramatically. The OMF has a UK National Headquarters in Sevenoaks in Kent, six Regional Offices with full-time Regional Secretaries in different parts of England, Scotland, Wales and Ireland. I had been covering that entire area on my own as well as doing my job with the Sun Life of Canada. No wonder I was busy. With the merger of the two missions it was a great relief to hand the work over to an organisation that was not only highly efficient but thought and worked along precisely those lines that characterised the BEM. The efficient Lesley Hobbs became a co-ordinating prayer secretary for the OMF and continued to work for some time from the BEM office in Reading, but we were both exceedingly glad to hand over to the OMF the work of deputation, candidate selection, finance and a host of other things. Prior to the merger of the two missions I was appointed to the British Council of the OMF but the work that was involved was a comparatively easy burden.

Handing over my Borneo Evangelical Mission responsibilities to the Overseas Missionary Fellowship in 1971 meant that for the first time in fifteen years I was going to be consistently free on a Sunday. Coincidental with this was our move to Tilehurst. Our first need was to find the church in which the Lord wanted us to be involved. We decided to visit all the local churches and discover which subscribed to the basics of the Christian faith and refused to allow denominational affiliation to make it exclusive.

One of the privileges of being the UK Secretary of the BEM was that I could take the challenge of mission to churches. Whatever the denomination I never refused an invitation to visit a church and I always found a positive response to the amazing things God was doing among the tribal peoples of Borneo. The challenge to the church was very straight forward: What God can do among the tribes of Borneo He can do in the cities and suburbs of the United Kingdom. The Holy Spirit who gives victory to the pagan Bornean can give victory to the most sophisticated Briton. But that victory comes through the gospel and the gospel has to be preached: "Faith comes by hearing and hearing by the Word of God." My experiences at the Arborfield Apprentices School were a telling example of this.

One of the great blessings of moving amongst churches of different denominations was that it gave the opportunity of emphasising the inherent unity of the Christian Church. This lies in the basics of our faith: a Christian is one who accepts Jesus Christ as Lord and Saviour, is willing to make known to others the Good News of the gospel and seeks to live out, in the power of the Holy Spirit, the character of Christ. These are the basics of Christian unity. Of course there will be other emphases and these can lead to disagreements. There is nothing wrong with healthy discussion over points of disagreement. It has been characteristic of the church ever since the days of the Acts of the Apostles. They are inevitable in a church where the members are encouraged to think. Thinking is not forbidden in scripture! What is forbidden is argument that descends into acrimony and unloving relationships leading to division and separation. The testimony of a church hinges on the extent to which the members commit themselves to loving one another. When outsiders see 'how these Christians love one another' even, or perhaps especially, when they disagree, then the power of the gospel is revealed because it is nothing less than miraculous. This is the miracle that attracts people to Jesus.

We were not looking for the perfect church. If we found such we would have done well to stay away! But we were looking for a church that placed emphasis on the basics and refused to get hot under the collar about inessentials. The first church we attended was Tilehurst

Free Church. It was a church where the gospel was preached in the power of the Holy Spirit and where men, women and children were being saved. Moreover, the members had a deep love for one another. We never got around to visiting any other church and we have been committed to it ever since. For three years I was a Deacon and for thirty years an Elder. Nowadays Valerie and I are regarded as a mother and father in the church – which is not surprising as, together with a couple of very dear friends we are the longest serving members. We couldn't be in a more loving "family" which incidentally has changed its name to Reading Community Church and is under the leadership of Yinka Oyekan.

PART SEVEN
A Father-In-Law &
A Grandfather
(1955...)

Chapter 41
Here Comes the Bride!

'Where does the family start? It starts with a young man falling in love with a girl – no superior alternative has yet been found.'

(Sir Winston Churchill)

As we look back over the 54 years of our eventful and wholly delightful married life we recognise that some of the most rewarding memories are those associated with our children. We acknowledge that we have been singularly blessed in having four children who love us dearly and who love each other. At strategic locations in our house we have photographs of the family's weddings, reminders of immensely happy occasions, and the addition of two delightful daughters-in-law and two extraordinarily competent sons-in-law, all harbingers of an expanding wider family.

The first of the weddings was Katie's on 21st June 1980 when she married Robert John Smart. Never was a surname more apposite. A sharp wit and an exquisite sense of humour is allied to an immensely lovable character. He was head boy at The Lord Williams Boarding School in Thame and at college he captained the rugby team. Nor was a husband more suited for Katie for they are both extraordinarily adventurous. It is hard to grasp that at the time of writing this the wedding was nearly 30 years ago for sometimes it seems like yesterday! With a lot of help from friends we had a 'Do It Yourself' celebration. The day before the wedding was frenetic. Valerie cooked twenty chickens, the first batch going into the oven at 6:30 am and the last coming out at 3:30 pm. In addition she made seven trifles. The actual reception was being held at the Sue Ryder Hospice in Nettlebed which, incidentally, used to be the home of Ian Fleming. Gerri

Katie's Wedding – From left to right: Me, Valerie, Dad, Mum, Penny, Bob, Katie, Tim, Valerie's Dad, Christopher

Andrews was a great friend of ours and the Night Sister at the Sue Ryder Hospice. She had been able to arrange for the reception to be held there. Half way through the afternoon before the wedding a phone call from the Home advised us that a general panic was under way. They had made a miscalculation and there wasn't room for about a quarter of the guests. This was about 25 people. By re-arranging where the top table was situated, we could use an adjoining area, which meant we could accommodate everyone and the panic subsided.

The weather on the day was perfect. Compared with the day before, everyone was remarkably relaxed. Bob and Katie had both just learned of their successful graduation from Exeter University and that contributed considerably to the relaxed atmosphere. Valerie had a blissful time helping Katie and Penny get dressed. The bride, the bridesmaid and the bride's mother all looked beautiful! I am bound to admit that I felt very proud of my daughter as we walked down the aisle together. John Dart, the minister at Tilehurst Free Church took the service, during which Katie's and Bob's responses to the wedding vows were so moving that Valerie was in tears! It was a very happy occasion!

They left for their honeymoon in a little white Austin Mini which had so many balloons tied to it that the car was barely visible. The car was still beautifully decorated when they returned from the honeymoon just in time to celebrate Katie's 21st birthday. After the birthday celebrations they left to go to Exeter where they had bought a delightful house, which, thanks to many generous friends, was completely furnished. They both had teaching appointments at The Priory School in Exeter. There was much for which to be thankful.

We had to wait six-and-a-half years for our next wedding in the family but, when Christopher rang to say: "This is the *real* thing," we knew that he had been smitten! When we met his Penny we could see why. They had been members of the same church for a number of years but only recently had Cupid been letting his arrows fly. Miss Penny Willis was a much-loved deputy head of a local primary school quite near to her charming Olde Worlde Cottage. On 22nd October 1988 Christopher and Penny were married in the beautiful and historic local Parish Church, which was packed to capacity. The bride looked incredibly lovely, as did her eight bridesmaids, two of whom were our daughter Penny and our grand-daughter Kerry. A vast crowd gathered afterwards in Sudbury Town Hall to a superb wedding reception, thanks to the generosity of Penny's parents, Ken & Maureen. It was a truly memorable day.

Christopher's Wedding. From left to right: Tim, Me, Valerie, Penny, Christopher, Penny, Bob, Kerry, Katie, Jonathan, Valerie's Dad

379

My mother frequently referred to any one of her three sons by a random selection of the names of all three, sometimes even including the dog in the confusion of names. Her problems were nothing to those of Penny's mother, Maureen. Before her daughter married Christopher, Maureen already had a Penny, a Christopher and a Timothy. Her Timothy in turn has a Timothy and a Penny. As if the potential for confusion was not enough, her Penny married a Christopher who had a brother called Timothy and a sister called Penny. You really would have thought it was impossible to add to that confusion, yet Christopher and Penny have done so by naming their youngest son Timothy. Yet Timothy is a splendid name. No wonder it is so popular.

When our Tim introduced Sharon (Shash) Rault to us we were hugely impressed. Pretty, lithe and graceful it was obvious why she was the senior dancing instructor and choreographer at Guildford's most élite dancing academy. She seemed just the partner for Tim and when they visited Gene and Lynne, Shash's parents in South Africa, they felt much the same about Tim.

On 24th July 1995 the wedding ceremony and reception were both held at historic Great Fosters, Henry VIII's magnificent hunting lodge

Timothy's Wedding – Back Row: Jonathan, Timothy in Tim's arms, Shash (Sharon), Kerry, Katie. Front row: Danny, Joshua, Ben

near Epsom Forest, and the last word in royal luxury. For Gene and Lynne only the very best was good enough for their daughter and the very best they had. The ancient baronial hall seemed such a perfect setting in which to hear the bride's father conducting 'labola', South Africa's traditional tribal bartering over the dowry.

In realistic style Gene was producing pigs and horses from the pocket of his morning suit as a demonstration of the seemingly high regard in which he held his new son-in-law, but in reality, his objective was to get from Tim a large proportion of Tim's herd of cows! He pointed out that 'any plain Jane' was worth a minimum of four cows. If she could cook that would certainly be worth another couple of cows. But if she was a veritable stunner *and* could cook... solemnly he adjured Tim to take a long look at his new bride... how many cows was she worth - twenty?

By what seemed an extraordinary coincidence to everyone except Shash's mother, Tim also came to the wedding with a similar but different collection of dowry live stock in his morning suit pockets in order to conduct 'labola'! Watching her father and her new husband playing farms, Shash was left wondering whether her net worth was two horses more or three cows less as a daughter than as a bride! Someone was heard to remark that they had never heard more brilliant speeches at a wedding. They were totally in keeping with the spectacular setting, a cloudless day, scrumptious food and delightful guests.

We then had to wait nearly nine years for our next wedding, but it was worth the wait. On 1st May 2004 our youngest, Penelope Joy was married to Paul Gomersall. They had met ten years earlier on a kibbutz in Israel, and had been friends ever since, which is not surprising for Paul is one of the most charming and good natured people we know. Valerie and I had liked Paul from the moment we first met him, and when they told us of their engagement we were delighted. Paul is the very epitome of the Do It Yourself expert, seemingly there is nothing practical to which Paul cannot competently turn his hand. This was especially pleasing to me because I am a great believer in the truth that there is nothing a man can't do around the house if he is handy... with a cheque book!

Penny's Wedding. From left to right: Katie, Bob, Valerie, Tim (R-S), Me,
Shash, David, Katie, Paul, Penny, Joshua, Jonathan, Timothy (S), Ben,
Kerry, Danny, Matthew, Penny, Christopher

The wedding was a great occasion. Christopher married them, Bob gave the wedding service address, Tim played the organ, Katie Smart read the lesson, and Katie Smith and Kerry Smart were the bridesmaids. The bride looked simply lovely in a stunning long white dress and veil. The two pretty bridesmaids wore delightful dusky pink dresses, while the bridegroom, his father and brother looked nearly, but not quite as pretty, in their splendid Scottish Clan full dress kilts!

Over 50 guests enjoyed the wonderful hospitality of the White Hart in Great Yeldham, one of the oldest inns in Essex. Founded in 1505, and famous for its cuisine, they certainly did us proud. After the celebrations the bride and groom left for their honeymoon at Tigh Mor Trossachs in Scotland. Not surprisingly they had a marvellous time.

The opening paragraph of our 1983 Christmas Letter ran: "As we write this letter we are in the middle of a wedding in the family. The weather has been very unkind, for it is dark, cold and raining. As weddings go it was a very quiet affair. No bridesmaids, no ushers and only four guests. This didn't seem to bother the bride or the bridegroom as they were too intent on each other. It had been an 'arranged' wedding and this was the first time they had met! Immediately after the ceremony, the bridegroom, who is as black as the ace of spades, left and hasn't been seen since; which is deplorable because the bride is now expecting triplets!" For the sequel to this event you will need to read the last two paragraphs of the next chapter.

Chapter 42
"They have their entrances..."

"Grandparents can't spoil grandchildren!" (John Smith!)

I have one or two definite views about being a grandparent. It is my considered opinion that God knew what He was doing giving children to young people! That is why, as a general principle, wills should not be drawn up that make grandparents guardians of their grandchildren in the event of those children being orphaned. Well chosen contemporaries of the parents are a much better choice. Grandparents are for visiting!

Another opinion is that grandparents can't spoil their grandchildren. Only parents can do that. Of course it is perfectly legitimate for grandchildren to spoil their grandparents; in fact it is obligatory! For 27 years we'd been waiting for the opportunity to put our theories to the test, when in our Christmas letter of 1981 we were able to write: "We are so glad that we delayed writing our Christmas Letter, for now we are able to share with you the latest hot press news received today – *Katie is going to have a baby!*"

Because Valerie looked so young, we thought no-one would believe she could be a grandmother. In comparison, they would have no problem believing I could be a grandfather because I had looked like a grandfather for the previous twenty years!

It was on 23rd July 1982 that we achieved the great ambition of becoming grandparents. How splendid of Jonathan Paul Smart to arrange his arrival on our wedding anniversary. I recall that he looked very small and at 5lb 13oz he certainly wasn't very big. A fortnight after his arrival he made the journey down to Bude. His Great-grandmother Smith had also made the journey so, for the first time we

had four generations together. Jonathan's Great-grandma celebrated her ninetieth birthday during that time together so there was great rejoicing and celebrations all round; but Great-granny Smith rejoiced most at being able to hold her great-grandson.

90 years old Great-granny Smith with Jonathan

Kerry Jane Smart put in an appearance on 19th July 1984 at three minutes to midnight. We had been in Germany for the Oberammergau Passion Play, and on the 19th we travelled to Igles in Austria for a further week's holiday. That evening Valerie telephoned home but had to conclude the entry in her diary with: 'No baby yet.' At 12:25 am we had a call from Bob with the news of Kerry's arrival. At 1:25 we had a further call to say that mother and baby were both doing well. At breakfast time we had yet another call to say that mother and baby were *still* doing well, so we sent a telegram to Kerry from Innsbruck: 'Austria Welcomes You.' Because we were in Austria, it was a few days before we saw our little granddaughter, but as soon as we got back to the UK we went down to Bude, where the Smart family joined us. Whenever we think of Austria we think of Kerry.

Incidentally, the Oberammergau Passion Play was very good. The background to the play is interesting. During the Great Plague of the 19th Century the frightened population of Oberammergau prayed that they would be spared from the plague. They made a solemn vow that if they were spared they would present the story of Christ to the world every ten years for evermore. The vow would be fulfilled, not by a few, but by the whole community, rich and poor alike. The town was spared, and a tradition was born. The play is now performed at the start of each decade. Since 1860 the German text has remained virtually unchanged. The production is performed in native German, but an English translation is available. Though the cast has 1,700 parts, it is a requirement that all the performers must be Oberammergau natives, or have lived there for 10 years, or been married to a native who has lived there for at least ten years.

Born in the posh new Maternity Unit of the Royal Berks Hospital in Reading, Daniel James Smart arrived at 5:47 pm. He weighed 6lb 7oz. Bob had brought Jonathan and Kerry to us and then spent all day at the hospital with Katie. The impending event had a catastrophic effect on Valerie who suffered a series of disasters. Her diary read: *"Was sick in Penny's car on the way to Rivermead. Then I crashed my beautiful car. Had a picnic in the park and set the grass on fire."* What on earth would be Danny's effect on Valerie when he's grown up?

We have a lovely permanent reminder of Danny as a baby. Katie took him to see his Great-grandmother Smith, and while she was holding him they had their photograph taken. That was the last photograph taken of my mother and, as it is in a prominent position in the house, we have a constant reminder of both her and Danny. Nearly a century separated his birthday from that of his great-grandmother and one wonders what kind of world it will be when he reaches 97!

Great-granny Smith – now 97, holding two weeks old Danny

There was great rejoicing over the arrival of Kathryn Elizabeth Smith, Christopher and Penny's first. She weighed 7lb 12oz and arrived at 2:30 in the afternoon. Her mother had been working hard for fourteen-and-a-half hours to bring this about. When Valerie and I saw Katie, she was fast asleep and looked as if she had been the one working hard! It may be imagination, but Valerie and I think Katie looks like us, and her maternal grandparents thinks she looks like them! Certainly Katie was a very pretty little baby. Come to think of it, she's now a very pretty teenager!

These modern mums! Benjamin Joel Smart was born at 1:50 in the morning and Katie was home at 11:00 that same morning. They must need the hospital beds really badly! Ben wasn't going to hang around - he only gave his mother 45 minutes' notice. Valerie and I went round to see this family of six. They were rehearsing the song 'Welcome to the family.'

Welcome to the family,
We're glad that you have come
To share your life with us
As we grow in love and...
May we always be to you
What God would have us be to you,
What God would have us be
A family always there,
To be strong and to lean on.

May we learn to love each other
More with each new day,
May words of love be on our lips
In everything we say
May your Spirit melt our hearts
And teach us how to pray
So we may be a true family.

We were having an anxious time prior to the arrival of Joshua John Smith. With 1992 being a leap year it would have been a great shame if he'd been born on that rare Leap Year Day and thus only have one birthday every four years. That catastrophe was avoided with five days to spare.

Valerie and I went to see our newest grandson and as I looked down at him in all the miracle of his tiny humanity, I marvelled afresh at the wonder of creation reflected in this little life:

Furthermore, he was fully equipped;
fingers and toes with nails were tipped;
He'd great big eyes, and a mouth clear cut;
when the mouth was open the eyes were shut!
A baby to stagger and flabbergast;
stupendous, miraculous, unsurpassed.
Born into the world with many dozens,
he's only equalled by his sister and cousins!

Valerie and I had a jumpy morning on 18th October 1994 waiting for news, but it was nothing like the jumpy morning that Timothy Joel

Smith spent, eventually jumping out through the sunshine roof! After her Caesarean Section, Penny and Tim were doing fine. Tim weighed 7lb 1oz and arrived at 11:00 in the morning. Grandparents are notoriously biased, but by any standards Timothy Joel was a remarkably beautiful baby.

We nearly felt as exhausted as Shash by the time Tim had finished his blow by blow account of the arrival of Matthew James Rault-Smith. Shash's ordeal started at 7:00 in the morning and went on until 8:30 in the evening. With dark skin and dark hair contrasting with blue eyes, Matthew was already a lady-killer, not so much because of his looks, but because he was putting on seven ounces of weight in a week! Matthew was dedicated on 6th August on the shores of Loch Achray, in Scotland's Trossachs. The dedication involved all the family, including the four grandparents, for Shash's mum and dad had travelled from South Africa. Shash and Kerry performed a spectacularly beautiful symbolic dance.

We were in Derbyshire when the news came through that Matthew had a little brother – well actually, not so little. David Daniel Rault-Smith weighed 9lb 13oz, definitely in the heavy-weight league. Predictably Shash had a difficult time. How thankful I am that God chose the woman to have the baby. I am certain that had it been the other way around, men would have opted out to such an extent that, within a couple of generations there'd be no-one left! One advantage of being born in the year 2000 is that David should have no problems telling his age, unlike Violet Conti who said, "I can lie quite convincingly about how old I am because, at my age, I can't always remember what it is!" The whole family of nineteen gathered in Kent to celebrate David's arrival. Actually, with our miniature Schnauzer Schnooky there were twenty of us.

Penny went into labour at 3:00 in the morning and 'labour' is the right word, because she was still at it at 4:10 in the afternoon. It wasn't until then that it was decided she should have a Caesarean Section. Valerie had carried the phone around all day expecting a call at any moment. Penny phoned at 6:30 and was really happy, relieved too I should think! When we visited the hospital everyone was saying that Samuel Arthur John Gomersall was a lovely-looking baby, and certainly he has grown into an enchanting little three year old.

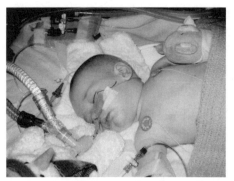

Jamie on Intensive Care

Born on 28th August 2007, our youngest grandson James Andrew Gomersall was destined to give his parents and his grandparents more anxiety than all the rest of the family put together. When he was just over four months old, Jamie became seriously ill with double pneumonia and only survived with the aid of a life support system. There followed a roller-coaster of life threatening conditions lasting two months with Jamie being whisked into High Dependency Units successively in Halifax, Leeds, Reading, Oxford and, finally, into the celebrated Great Ormond Street Children's Hospital in London.

Throughout this time we were all profoundly impressed by the compassion, care and dedication of folk in our National Health Service. The UK is extraordinarily blessed by this institution and daily we thank God for it. The clever and dedicated medics involved not only kept our precious grandson alive but wonderfully succeeded in diagnosing a chronic disorder. Jamie has what is clinically known as 'CD 40 Ligand Deficiency', which means that his immune system is seriously compromised. It seems that this is a congenital disorder requiring Immunoglobulin treatment. This is the infusion of a blood product, given as a replacement for those antibodies that Jamie is unable to make for himself. This infusion involves the insertion, into each thigh, a needle through which the fluid is pumped via a contraption that is strapped to his back. It can be imagined that this operation, performed every two weeks by Penny and Paul and which lasts two hours, is not regarded with any marked degree of favour by any of the participants – least of all by Jamie! What really excites him is the sight of

Jamie's wonderful recovery

the back pack in which he is taken for walks. Penny hit on the notion of producing the back pack just before the infusion operation. Jamie is now more inclined to tolerate the pain of the treatment because he knows it will be followed by a two hour walk, but it is vital that his immune system is topped up every two weeks.

As for the future, the immediate need is to find a compatible donor for a bone marrow transplant. That in itself is a high risk operation, even if a donor could be found, and Jamie's bone marrow definition is sufficiently rare to make that possibility significantly unlikely. A possible solution could be Paul and Penny producing a sibling for Jamie with a compatible bone marrow definition. Another ray of hope may lie in work being done in Nottingham, where a medical team is carrying out research on umbilical cords and stem cells, precisely for the purpose of solving intractable conditions such as Jamie's; but such a resolution of Jamie's problems is likely to be some way down the road. In the meanwhile we think this little family is positively heroic.

A heroic family

The following paragraph appeared in our 1981 Christmas Letter: *"The news of the prospective arrival of Katie's baby quite overshadows another 'happy event' about which you may not have heard. Another happy event? Yes indeed! We have had an increase in our family. Born on 3rd March, she was desperately underweight, six ounces to be precise, but intensive care and round-the-clock feeding brought her through and she survived to be a much adored member of the family. We had difficulty with her name – but Valerie had the final word since, after all, she was the one most involved with the arrival! On account of her dark skin and black curly hair, Valerie decided to call her Lucinda... and that's her name - Lucinda Smith. It's a bit awkward, but it suits. A recent visitor wrote to say that Cinders was quite the most adorable thing she had ever seen."*

With her weighing only six ounces it will be guessed that Lucinda was not another grandchild. In fact she was a puppy of our poodle Liquorice. When Jonathan was born one of our friends rang to ask if his parents would appreciate a hand-knitted woolly jacket. Of course we said they would be delighted. Our generous friend then went on to ask after Lucinda:

"Now we mustn't forget Lucinda."

"Er – no, of course not."

"How big is she?"

"How big? Well she's about fourteen inches long, and about thirteen inches tall."

"My word, she has done well. What does she wear?"

"Wear? What does she *wear*? Well she doesn't actually wear anything."

"She doesn't wear *anything*? You mean you let her run around with nothing on!"

"Hang on. Who do you think Lucinda is?"

"Why the little piccaninny you adopted of course!"

Chapter 43
"...and their exits"

Valerie and I were greatly blessed by seeing three model grandparents in action: Valerie's parents and my mother. "What about your father?" would be a reasonable question. Indeed it would. In response I would simply say, "My father was a butler." In fact he was a very good butler. As butler to Sir John Ramsden he was responsible for the smooth running of two castles and four other large houses, all with a full complement of servants. But, he was 'In Service' and the problem with being 'In Service' is that The Family is not the flesh and blood relations but the family for whom those servants work. It is an all consuming, all demanding way of life, and my father was an archetype of the genre.

He was astonishingly unacquainted with the most basic happenings in his own family. On one occasion when Dad was giving us one of his rare visits, Mum said to him, "Sydney, you haven't asked John how he's doing at school!"
"School!" said Dad. "Don't tell me he's *still* at school!"

The only family wedding he attended was Katie's, and that was because he had retired and was living across the road. He enjoyed every moment of it, and all the guests enjoyed his being there, simply because he was such great fun to have around. He hadn't come to our wedding because he was with The Family in Scotland, and he didn't come to any of the other children's weddings because by then he was in heaven.

In response to *that* comment the question might well be asked, "How can you *know* that he is in heaven; particularly as his performance as a father was so questionable?" Let me preface the explanation by saying that none of my father's unusual behaviour has ever generated negative reactions on my part. I believe I have understood my father, and certainly I have loved him with very real affection. Moreover, by the grace of God, I was able to honour him for the simple reason that he was my father. However, there is no doubt, that he was not a good model, either as a father or a grandfather.

At the age of 85, and much to his regret, my father had to retire. Sir John Ramsden had died, but Dad had continued as butler to Lady Ramsden, who had moved to a house near Ascot. Dad would not have retired at 85 had it not been for a ferocious accident that all but killed him. He was cycling to the library. It had been snowing during the night and the road was treacherous. Cycling along with six library books under one arm, Dad saw a friend approaching in a car, took his hand off the handle-bar to wave, lost control and fell, hitting his head on the curb-stone. Fortunately the friend saw the accident, and quickly ran to a nearby house to summon an ambulance from Ascot Hospital which was only five minutes away.

Dad suffered a colossal fracture of the skull, resulting in the loss of a great deal of cerebral fluid. Unconscious, he was put in the Intensive Care Unit but he was not expected to live. The next day I took Mum to see him. He was still unconscious and she was only allowed a few minutes. "It didn't look like Dad at all," she said.

Three days later I had a telephone call from the hospital to say that he had recovered consciousness and Mum could visit him again. Mum had a bad cold, so that evening I went on my own. Leading me down the ward, the matron said, "Your father must be as strong as a horse." Stopping by the bed of a stranger she added, "We never expected him to live through this."
"Where *is* my father?" I asked, looking around.
"This *is* your father."
"No! There's been some mistake. That's not my father." Just then the figure in the bed opened one eye, closed it and opened it again in an unmistakable wink! "But he doesn't look anything like my father," I said.
"You should have seen him the night he was brought in. He's made an astonishing recovery physically," said the matron, "but his mind is all over the place. Don't worry if he talks a lot of gibberish. He's been saying some amazing things about the Resistance Movement."

Just then Dad beckoned me with a finger. I drew up a chair as the matron smiled and left us. Dad beckoned me closer, put a finger to his lips and whispered, "Now pay attention. This is *very* important. We must find a dossier with the list of Resistance Workers. I know where it is but they've tied me down to this bed and I can't move. Will you go for me?"

"Tell me where it is," I replied. This was much better than The Gang of Revenging Spies.

"Take care you're not caught," Dad whispered. "You get caught, curtains," and he drew a finger across his throat in a dramatic gesture. "The dossier is in the large house at the end of this road. The Gestapo have taken it over as their local HQ. On each side of the entrance there're two brick piers with eagles on 'em. Just inside the gate there are some rhododendron bushes. It won't be difficult to get into those bushes. There will be two sentries on guard at the front. Being Germans they always do exactly the same thing. They'll stand side by side for a few seconds then they'll do an outward turn and each will march slowly to their end of the building. It'll take them 65 seconds exactly. They'll pause for five seconds and then turn right about and slowly march back. OK so far?"

"OK" I said. Despite being safe in Ascot, I was feeling quite nervous.

"Right. In the middle of the forecourt, about ten yards in front of where those sentries stand, there's a manhole cover. It will take you five seconds to get from the bushes to the manhole cover, five seconds to shove a lever under the edge and lift it and another five seconds to slide it *towards the house*. That's important. It'll slide easily on the ice and snow. About a foot down on the house side of the manhole there's an iron ladder fixed to the wall. Get down the manhole and pull that cover over the hole. Don't let it drop in position. Lower it gently. All of that shouldn't take you longer than 30 seconds. OK?"

"Won't the sentries see or hear me?"

"They won't see you if you wait 30 seconds from when they start their outward walk. Now, listen. There are eighteen rungs to that ladder. You'll have already gone down six so you'll go down another twelve."

I was thinking, how on earth does he do this? He nearly died three days ago! But where was this all important dossier?

"Now the dossier," said Dad as if reading my thoughts. "When you climb down the ladder, facing it, turn left. You'll be in a tunnel. There'll be plenty of headroom but you'd better use a torch, no-one will see it. Five yards down the tunnel on the right is another tunnel leading towards the house. Follow that for 25 yards and you'll find another wall ladder on the right. It's got eighteen rungs. That leads up into a long corridor in the house. You'll be at one end of the corridor. You want the fifth door on the left. The door leads into a big room with a door in the far opposite corner. Through that door is the room you want, but take care. There may be a guard." He didn't tell me what to do if there was a guard. I was feeling more nervous by the minute!

"At the far end of the room is a large mahogany cupboard with three drawers at the bottom. You want the middle drawer." I was thinking, if this was for real, I wouldn't be wanting anything of the sort!

"In that drawer you'll see a brown manila file. *That's* what we need. Now listen to me. We don't want any heroics. We want you out of there safe, with that dossier. But... just in case of mishaps, take a grenade with a five second fuse. If you're seen and you're likely to get caught, put the grenade on the dossier, preferably round a corner from you, pull the pin on the grenade and scarper. If you are caught with the dossier on you, you'll just have to pull the pin on the grenade anyway, *but the dossier must be destroyed.* You understand me? You still want to do the job?"
"Dad, listen! This isn't really happening. You... !"
"Don't waste time arguing. They may be back any minute. Don't forget. You'll need a lever, a torch and a five second grenade. Good luck," and he held out his hand. I took it and we shook hands. Goodness me. Did they really do things like that? I thought it only happened in books.

At the end of the ward I met the matron. "Did he ask you to go and get a lot of papers?" she asked. I nodded. "He's tried that with all of us. It's really bothering him. There's nothing we can do to convince him there are no papers."
"Well, he thinks I'm on my way to get 'em!" I said, making her stare.
"So I'll go for a bite to eat and then come back and say the dossier's

been destroyed. That may give him a little peace. You go and tell him that I told you to tell him not to worry. The job will be done." "That might work," she said and I left.

An hour later I was back. The matron was watching out for me. "I'm glad you've come. He's been really worried and keeps asking if you're back. It's all so real to him. It is amazing."

I went down the ward. Dad was watching out for me. I raised my thumbs in a gesture of success and his poor damaged face lit up like a light. He raised a delighted thumb. "Success?" asked the matron, who had followed me down the ward. Dad raised his thumb again.

"Do you think we should celebrate with your special medicine?" she asked him. He put his thumb up again. She went off, coming back a little later with three glasses, one half full, one a quarter full and one with a drop in the bottom. She kept the latter, gave the quarter full one to Dad and the half full one to me. It was whisky and water. I looked at her questioningly. "The doctor said he could have it," she replied. "It's mainly water." What a doctor! What a matron! What a hospital! What a patient!

I stayed with Dad a while. He was looking very relaxed and was soon fast asleep. The matron came up. "That was a good idea," she said. "He'll do alright. But what an amazing man he is." I agreed. She was an amazing woman too.

Dad was discharged from the hospital but the accident had taken a fearful toll on him. More often than not he didn't know where he was. Regretfully both he and Lady Ramsden agreed that he should retire and, for the first time in 30 years, Dad came home to live!

Mum was so used to living on her own that she found this new life quite difficult. We had moved to Turnhams House and had so organised things that the completion of the work there would coincide with the completion of the new house we were having built for Mum. Unfortunately the company building Mum's house went bankrupt so there was a long delay in getting the house finished. Just at the time when Mum most needed us, we were not across the road. I seemed to spend a lot of my time going to and from Redhatch Drive.

"John, can you come over? Dad thinks the door to the bedroom is a horse and he can't get out!" Mum and Dad shared a large bedroom in which there were two single beds. One morning she had got up leaving Dad in bed, but he surprised her by appearing in the kitchen a little later, fully dressed with his coat on.

"Well, I'll be off," he said to her.
"Off? Off where?" she asked.
"Off home. I should have gone long ago."
"Home? *This* is your home."
"No! I mean back to Norah."
"Back to Norah? *I* am Norah!"
"*You* are Norah! Oh my goodness! Then who was I sleeping with last night?"
Mum gave him a big hug. "You were sleeping with me, silly."

Eventually they were able to move into the new house opposite us and life became less traumatic for Mum but not for us. One day I arrived home to find twelve policeman and two police dogs outside. "What's going on?" I asked the inspector.
"Your father's gone missing."
"He's probably in one of the pubs."
"We've tried all those."
"But why are there so many policemen?" I asked.
"Oh this is just the change of shifts but the six others decided to stay on to help. We're just off on another tack."

The police didn't find Dad, although I was hugely impressed by the efforts they were making. Two railway workmen found him on the side of the rail line from Tilehurst to Goring. It seems that Dad had walked the two miles to Tilehurst Railway station and asked for a ticket to Norwich. He probably thought he was at Thetford in Norfolk and the fare to Norwich what it had been 40 years earlier. Shocked by the price he said to the ticket clerk, "Humph. It's cheaper to walk."

The ticket clerk hadn't thought any more about it until he was asked the next day. In the meanwhile Dad had walked down the platform and just continued walking! It was January and getting dark. After stumbling over a number of railway sleepers Dad thought he would join them, so he curled himself up beside the line and fell fast asleep, wrapped up in his thick coat. During the night it snowed heavily, covering everything, including Dad, with three or four inches of snow.

The next morning, using a little maintenance trolley, two railway workers came down the line and found Dad. They got him on to their little trolley and took him on to Goring. There they phoned for an ambulance and Dad was admitted to the Royal Berkshire Hospital. Dad never much liked hospitals and he kicked up such a fuss at being taken to one against his will that by 2:00 in the afternoon they had sent him home in a hospital car, none the worse for his adventure.

At tea time he said to Mum, "Well, I'll be off!"
"You won't," said Mum, and promptly locked the door!

* * * * *

It was about this time that the Lord spoke to Valerie. "I want you to share your faith with Dad."

Although she thought Dad eccentric, she had a real affection for him. Even so, it is quite intimidating to share the gospel with an 89 year old, especially when that 89 year old is your father-in-law. Nevertheless Valerie went over, having sent up an urgent prayer for help. Instead of Mum answering the door, as expected, Dad did. "Hello! Have you come to see Mum? She's upstairs having a lie down."
"No, I've come to see you," said Valerie.
"That is an honour," he replied. "Come in."
Sitting down in front of Valerie, Dad said, "Right! What can I do you for?"
"I've come to talk about my faith," Valerie began.
"Your face, what's wrong with your face? It looks all right to me."
"No, not my face! My *faith*," said Valerie, wondering where this was going.
"Oh, your faith. Well, fire away," said Dad.

Valerie, noticing that Dad was looking more *compos mentis* than he had looked for months, 'fired away' with a very simple presentation of the facts of salvation. After a while Dad held up his hand. "Just a minute. Are you telling me that the reason Jesus came to this world was so that he could take all the punishment for the wrong-doing of *everyone?*"

"Jesus will take the punishment for the sin and wrong-doing of all those who trust in Him. That's what I'm saying," said Valerie.

"And are you really telling me that by trusting in Jesus, *everything* that *I've* done wrong is forgiven because *He* was punished for it?"

"Precisely," said Valerie. "I couldn't have put it better."

"Well, that's not right is it?"

"In what way, not right?"

"Well it's not fair! Not fair on God! I ask you. Is it fair?"

"Of course it's not fair. But that's the wonder of it all. It's called grace."

Dad sat thinking about this for a few moments. Then he said expressively, "Well, I'll go to our house."

"Dad, do you want Jesus to take all your sins away?"

"Is it really as simple as that? Don't you have to do something?"

"You just have to accept it. Jesus has done it all."

"Do you know, I've never understood that before. It's amazing!"

There and then Valerie led her 89 year old father-in-law to the Lord.

When I got home that evening Valerie said, "You'll *never* guess what's happened. Dad has come to the Lord!"

I went straight over to see him. He himself answered the door. His face seemed to be radiantly luminous. It shone! The extraordinary thing was that he'd had a period of complete lucidity, but about two weeks later he again began to forget where he lived, and he was for ever getting lost. Always friendly, affable and entertaining, we would find him in a house somewhere down the road. We could usually find him from all the laughing that he was causing. He had an endless supply of anecdotes and experiences and folk loved to listen to his unusual Norfolk accent.

Eventually his disappearances became so worrying that he had to be admitted to Fairmile Hospital near Moulsford. The first evening he was there I called to see how he was getting on. "I've come to see Mr Smith... " I started.

"Oh! Sydney!" said the receptionist. "You'll find him in the main hall."

Sure enough, there in the main hall was a large crowd of residents, all standing around Dad, who was sitting in a chair telling yarns and quipping away as if he had been there all his life. About a week later when I visited him, he told me what a great place it was and how kind all the staff were to him.

"Why, they even take me down to the pub each evening and buy me a Guinness."

I asked the warden about that. "A Guinness is nothing?" said the warden. "That's the least we can do for him. Ever since he arrived there have been no problems. Everyone wants to hear Sydney. The ultimate threat is to say they won't be able to listen to Sydney if they don't behave!"

That evening Dad took me on one side. "John, I know it's very good of you to pay for me to be at this posh hotel, but the cost must be huge." In vain did I try to explain that it was costing me nothing.

Later he caught a chest infection and he developed pneumonia. It is general policy in establishments such as Fairmile, that infections are not treated with antibiotics, and it was not long before we got a phone call to say that Dad was not expected to last the night. I took Mum to see him, and although he was sleeping, it was obvious that he was dying. The matron took Mum and me into her office. "Mrs Smith, I'm sorry to tell you that there is nothing we can do for your husband."
"You mean he is dying?" said Mum.
"I'm afraid so," replied the matron.

Mum reached across the desk and took the matron's hand in both of hers and said, "My dear, you mustn't be distressed. You have done all you could, and we appreciate it." They both stood up and Mum gave the matron a hug and a kiss. When we left the office it was the matron who was in tears! Dad died that night but thanks to the grace of God he went to a place even better than a Five Star Hotel. Dad may not have been a good model, but he made a great exit.

* * * * *

After I joined the Sun Life of Canada Mum lived just across the road from us, both when we were in Redhatch Drive and shortly after we moved to Turnhams House, so over the years there had been a very close contact between her and our whole family.

I have mentioned elsewhere how Mum went to Bude to be with us on her 90th birthday. For her age she was remarkably alert. One evening I went across to see her and found tables laid out for a whist drive. She had made refreshments, the cards were on the table and prizes on the sideboard. She had fifteen guests coming.

The next day I asked how the whist drive had gone. "I'm so cross!" she said.
"Why? What happened?" I asked, fearing some kind of disaster.
"Would you believe, I won first prize! I didn't try to win, but I had the best cards ever in my life."

There was one 'No go' area in my mother's life. Evangelical Christianity was anathema. Billy Graham and all his works was a monstrous racket. "Don't try to tell me that he isn't making millions out of all those crusades," my mother would say. In vain we'd point out that he lived very modestly and the money from crusades all went to Christian charities. Eventually Valerie and I decided that it was best to keep off every subject that was in any way Christian.

Relationships between mothers and their daughters-in-law can be tricky, but despite Mum's antipathy towards anything remotely evangelical, she and Valerie always had a deep love and respect for each other.

One morning Valerie was in the kitchen at home when the Lord spoke to her. He wanted her to go across to Mum to share the gospel with her. Valerie promptly burst into tears. "Lord, you know what happens when we talk to Mum about You, and we have such a good relationship together!"

But the Lord pointed out to Valerie that Mum had no relationship with Him whatsoever and that was what He wanted. So Valerie dried her eyes and went across to speak to Mum. Valerie didn't normally go to see Mum in the mornings, so she was greeted very warmly with, "Valerie! What a nice surprise! Do come in. Is everything all right?"

"Yes," said Valerie, jumping in at the deep end, "I've come to talk about Jesus."

"Well, that's lovely! What did you want to say?" Valerie was not expecting that reaction at all but, recovering from her surprise, she produced the booklet, 'The Four Spiritual Laws', and asked Mum if she could go through this with her. Mum drew up her chair and together they went through that very excellent presentation of the gospel.

"So what do I have to do?" asked Mum.

Valerie emphasised that salvation was not through doing good deeds, but came through repentance and faith in Jesus. To Valerie's astonishment Mum said that she really wanted to receive Jesus into her life. Mum then took the little booklet and prayed the prayer of commitment that is printed at the end. They then prayed together. When I arrived home and Valerie told me what had happened, I went across to see Mum. She had a hymn book open, and was reading one of the hymns. Never did I expect to see my mother reading a hymn book! "Some of these hymns are wonderful aren't they?" were her first words. Thus it was that after praying for over 25 years for my mother I saw her, at the age of 87, take Christ as her Saviour.

She went on to live a further ten happy years retaining all her faculties, good humour, friendliness and compassion. One day Valerie had gone over to see her early in the morning and left her chatting and joking. It was later that she had a massive stroke. She was taken to hospital where she died peacefully and painlessly without regaining consciousness. There were many people at the funeral including my brother Bill and his wife Dorothy from Canada. Of course there was grief, but not the grief of 'those who have no hope'. Mum knew Jesus as her personal Saviour so there was also a real note of triumph. She too made a glorious exit.

* * * * *

Never was a man more blessed than me by his in-laws. My mother-in-law was my Pin-Up-Girl, lovely in every way. Children are not easily deceived, and it is a fitting tribute to my mother-in-law that her grandchildren, Christopher and Katie simply adored her. She was one of their most favourite people. It was a great tragedy that the rest of the grandchildren and great grandchildren never knew her. She always

*My wonderful
Mother-in-law*

managed to give the impression that the person she was with at the time was the most important person in the world!

Our very small daughter Katie had the notion of setting up a shop stocked with exotic seeds. She collected every imaginable seed from the garden and the nearby meadow, laid these out at the back of the house and then announced to a large assembled company of visitors that she was opening her shop. The only adult to respond was her grandma. Taking her by the hand, Katie led her to her market stall where she proudly exhibited her wares.

Her grandma was enthralled, and after inspecting all the seeds, proceeded to make a comprehensive purchase. "I'll have four of those, three of those, oh, eight of those, six of those and two of those. How much does all that cost, let me see, sixpence, nine pence, one shilling and fourpence, oh! I can't afford eight of those, I'll just have six, that's two shillings and two pence, and just two of those, that comes to a total of two shillings and sixpence. That's half a crown. There you are my dear. What a splendid little shop you've got. These were just what I wanted. Thank you, and... Good afternoon!" Katie looked in astonishment at the shiny half crown in the palm of her hand. This was wealth beyond the dreams of avarice.

When she was only a little bit older, Katie was staying with her grandma together with her similarly aged cousin Caroline, the daughter of Valerie's brother, Bernard. Both Katie and Caroline found themselves on a nearly vertical learning curve. One evening when their grandma had settled down to read a book and had lit a cigarette, Katie asked what smoking was like. "Would you like to try one?" was the seemingly innocent reply. Soon these two youngsters were holding a lit cigarette and, having watched their grandma, they each took a long draw. There was an instant explosion of coughing and spluttering during which the offending cigarettes were handed back with great alacrity! Neither of them have smoked since!

On another occasion during the same holiday, Caroline asked if she and Katie could use some of grandma's lip-stick. "Of course, my dears. Come up to my room." There she handed over her posh make-up case. "Help yourselves!" she said. An hour later the two presented themselves before their grandma. "They really looked a couple of tarts!" reported their grandma to the respective mums later.

She was an excellent cook and a great hostess to the many visitors who gravitated to her home. Sadly, this was to come to an end when she was diagnosed with advanced and inoperable cancer. Before being admitted to hospital, the last weeks of her life were spent at Turnhams House.

The evening before she died I was by her bedside at the hospital, and she asked me to read Psalm 23. "Thank you," she said, "that is a lovely Psalm!" She was only 67 when she died.

* * * * *

My poor father-in-law was devastated by the loss of his beloved wife. Their lives together had been characterised by hospitality, and in a heroic act of will, my father-in-law decided to continue the practice. The problem was that his culinary ignorance was total. He bought a number of cookery books and immersed himself in them. A friend of his once said to us, "Harold is the only person we know, who has bought cookery books out of necessity and now buys them as a source of entertainment!" When we visited him he would have drawn up a complete schedule of menus for the weekend. These would not be your ordinary run of the mill meals but 'Cordon Bleu' specialities such as boned stuffed duck preceded by a prawn cocktail covered with his own recipe of delectable sauce.

One of his passions was music. He had a highly sophisticated system for playing music through a couple of gigantic loudspeakers. After a rather soporific evening meal Valerie and I would be departing into a state of semi-consciousness when my father-in-law would put on some music. He liked to hear music as if he were part of the orchestra. Many of the more famous musical pieces start with a tremendous crash of instruments, so the somniferous silence of the room would suddenly be rent by an explosion of sound. As one, Valerie and I would rise vertically about two feet out of our easy chairs, only to realise that the end of the world hadn't come after all; it was only our host playing some music. It usually took the rest of the evening for us to recover from the shock.

My father-in-law had told us that Prague was one of the most beautiful cities in Europe, the food was good and inexpensive, and it was a city for wonderful music. So in 1993 we arranged to spend a week there in the September.

The first of our musical feasts was to be held on the second evening of our stay. It was in the Hall of St Nicholas. It was a string quartet which, despite some excellent rendering of Mozart and Beethoven, I found quite difficult to appreciate, largely because the seats were solid concrete. By the interval I was positively numb, and as Valerie and her dad had suffered in the same way, we went off to a posh restaurant, where we had an excellent meal at a very modest cost.

We were not overly sad at missing half of the musical recital for we were going to hear Don Giovanni the next evening. I had gone on ahead to make sure we had some soft seats only to find they were all very solid wooden ones. I saw the manager and, after some considerable negotiation, persuaded him to put some padded chairs in the aisle for us. The presentation of Don Giovanni was with marionettes and was great fun. Unfortunately, Val's dad considered it an indignity to watch marionettes, and at the interval decided he would opt out of the second half. We couldn't let him go back to the hotel on his own, so that was the second musical treat of which we only saw half!

Never mind, we still had tickets for The Marriage of Figaro. Before going to the theatre we had a splendid dinner at the Golden Goose in Wenceslas Square. Approaching the theatre entrance I noticed that there was no-one around. Entering the foyer I called out to the attendant, "Where is...?"
"Sh...sh...sh..." she said fiercely.
I went nearer and whispered, "Why sh...sh...?"
"The concert, she is began!" she said.
"Began, er... begun? Why did it start early?"
"She begins right. Harss pass siss," nodding vehemently.

"Hass pass s... !" I exclaimed, forgetting to whisper.

"Sh...sh...sh...", she put her finger to her lips and looked fierce again.

"Half past six? I was told half past *seven!*" I complained.

"Hass pass siss she begin! Hass pass *siss,*" she insisted. I'm glad she wasn't subject to spoonerisms! "You vait," she continued, "I listen. Ven I open ze door, you go. Ze seats is zere."

So she stood with her ear to the door and suddenly snatched it open and pointed to three seats just inside the door. We scuttled in and sat down trying to look as if we'd been there for the whole performance. Alas, yet again we only heard half of the programme! The next day we returned home so we had no opportunity of hearing the halves we missed!

Val's dad was a highly regulated individual, seldom departing from his own set routines. Any provisions bought by my mother-in-law, if not part of his routine diet, remained untouched in the larder. When asked by his visiting great-grand-daughter Kerry, if he had any cornflakes, he said he thought he had some in the loft. There were indeed a number of packets in the loft and presently he returned with one of them and breakfast was resumed. After a few moments Kerry whispered, "Mummy, there's something odd about these cornflakes." Close inspection of the package revealed that they were 'best before' eighteen years earlier!

We had been urging him to sell his bungalow and come and live with us, but he always insisted that he was doing fine. He even assisted with delivering Meals on Wheels to the elderly. It was this service that got him an invitation to one of Princess Diana's 25th

Birthday Celebrations on 16th July 1986.

It was the 25th Anniversary of The Pre-School Play-Group Association that prompted the invitation. Valerie read in the Pre-School Play Group magazine that they were looking for a family with four generations of involvement. Valerie contacted them saying that she, her daughter and her grandson were all involved in Pre-School Play Groups. "What a pity there isn't a fourth generation," said the secretary.

"Well, my father delivers Meals on Wheels."

Princess Diana's 25th Birthday Celebration on 16th July 1986.
Speaking with Diana is Valerie's father, Valerie, Katie and
four years old Jonathan. The basket of flowers was presented
to Princess Diana by Jonathan

"That's simply wonderful 'cos Meals on Wheels is also celebrating 25 years along with us. That fits in perfectly."

So Valerie, her father, daughter Katie and grandson Jonathan all went to this posh, posh hotel to celebrate these 25th anniversaries. The hotel was the Carlton Towers in London, which was also celebrating 25 years.

Four year-old Jonathan was chosen to make a presentation to Princess Diana and as they chatted together they made a charming picture. The other guests all had to pay a huge sum to one of the charities for the reception and lunch but Valerie's quartet were guests of honour and went free.

It had become a tradition for my father-in-law to join us for Christmas Day each year, and then stay for a few days, before returning to his home in Boxgrove near Chichester. His routine was to go to the morning service at Boxgrove Priory, and then drive to Reading, arriving in time for Christmas lunch.

On Christmas Eve of 1995 I had a strange compulsion to ring him and urge him to allow me to go down to Boxgrove and bring him up to us for Christmas. He wouldn't hear of it. The following morning, Christmas morning, we were just about to leave for church, when I said to Valerie, "I'm just going to ring your Pa-pa to see if he would, after all, prefer me to go down and pick him up."

This I did and his reply was, "Perhaps that would be best, if you don't mind." All the way down, I was wondering what on earth had happened to bring about this change of mind that was so uncharacteristic of him. I was soon to discover. When I rang the door bell, it was opened by a figure whose hair was matted with blood.

It transpired that he had decided to go to the midnight service on Christmas Eve, thus giving him a little more time to get ready to drive to Reading on Christmas morning. Just before leaving the house to go to church, immaculately dressed, he went in to the kitchen where he fainted and, in falling, struck his head against a counter top.

He came to at about one o'clock, which meant that he had been unconscious for just over an hour, during which time his head wound bled copiously. Struggling to get up, he found himself now covered from head to foot in all the blood that was on the floor.

Taking off his suit, he mopped up the blood and, carrying his shoes and socks, he took all his clothes to the bathroom, ran a bath and, with his clothes in his arms, he got into the bath. It took him until four in the morning before he had got rid of all the blood, but in the process he forgot his hair.

Dressed in a sports jacket and trousers, he then took an alarm clock to the lounge and set the alarm for 10:15, at which time he planned to leave for Reading. I rang him at 10:10. If I had rung just five minutes later, I might have missed him. I parked him back in his chair in the lounge, made him a cup of coffee, cleaned him up and the mess in the kitchen and in the bathroom, and together we set off back to Reading.

He was extraordinarily chirpy on the journey, made a great fuss of everyone when he arrived, had a glass of champagne and a good Christmas lunch, listened to the Queen at three o'clock and only began to fade at about seven in the evening when we were going to play 'Murder in the dark'! However it was a salutary indication that steps should be taken to accommodate him in our home.

We got Tony Horne, a member of our church and a competent architect, to draw up the plans for an integral apartment, principally built over the garage and utility room and taking two of the bedrooms of the house. A stair lift made the apartment easily accessible. Another church member and close friend, Phil Baines, was given the job of carrying out the building work.

Building the apartment for Valerie's Dad.
He and Valerie are in the foreground

The result was a really splendid apartment. It had a 35' x 17' lounge with three large windows providing spectacular views of the surrounding area which has been classified as an AONB – Area of Outstanding Natural Beauty. There was a most elegant 15' x 10' bathroom, and a bedroom and dressing room that had previously been part of the house. The large kitchen was the last word in appearance and equipment.

After selling his bungalow my father-in-law moved into the apartment at Turnhams House and was delighted with it. He lived with us for nearly eight years throughout which he was his usual courteous and friendly self. He died peacefully in his sleep in the early hours of 21st July 2004, less than six weeks short of his 98th birthday. It was decided that I should pay a tribute to him at his funeral, but he was the kind of man who transcends any tribute. Nevertheless it was my honour to do it and for the record it is reproduced here:

Valerie, Valerie's Dad and me

In his letter to the Corinthians the Apostle Paul says: "Consider your calling brothers and sisters. Not many wise and not many noble are called." I'm glad the apostle said 'not many' rather than 'none' because my father-in-law was both wise and noble – and he certainly was 'called'. To me he epitomised the proverbial fount of wisdom. I knew that when I shared a problem with him he would carefully consider it and then come up with a really helpful insight. Invariably I'd say to myself: 'Now why didn't I think of that?'

He was immensely knowledgeable. He was a Fellow of five Institutes – not just a member, but actually a FELLOW of five institutes: the Institute of Chemistry, the Institute of Physics, the Institute of Metallurgy, the Institute of Management and the Institute of Directors. His speciality was metals – in fact he was a world authority on nickel alloys – so he was in great demand on both sides of the Atlantic during the Second World War and subsequently in the early stages of space exploration.

Yet, with all that, he was a very humble man. I once told him that every year I read the Queen's Honours list fully expecting him to have received a peerage.

"Get away with you – bother," he said.
"But aren't you proud of all your achievements?" I asked.

411

I'll never forget his reply: "Proud of my achievements! The only achievement I'm proud of, is being the father of Valerie."

I am certainly grateful for that achievement! Yet – peerage or no – he was a 'noble' man. Like Nathaniel, he was a man in whom there was no guile. 'Wise' and 'noble' – and, even more significantly, he was also 'called'. In his highly organised and disciplined way he served the Lord. At The Priory in Boxgrove near Chichester, where he lived before coming to us, he was Warden to a succession of ministers, holding the fort during interregnums. Since it's Harold we're talking about, I should get it right and say interregna.

In the light of all this, you will appreciate why I can say that it has been both a privilege and a joy to have had this very special man actually living with us for the last eight years. Well, now he's in glory. He knew that one day he would be with the Lord. This was an unshakeable conviction based, not on his undeniably faithful service, but on a simple and confident faith in Jesus as his Saviour... and that is such an encouragement to the rest of us, isn't it?

That was five years ago, but my father-in-law is still greatly missed. When facing a dilemma I frequently find myself asking, "Now what would he have done in this situation?" Valerie and I are so grateful to our Heavenly Father that we are blessed with fond memories of our parents.

Chapter 44
Health, Healing and Hope

Increasingly during 2004 I had been having fierce pains in my tummy and I was beginning to wonder whether there were unwelcome things growing down there, so I went to the doctor who sent me to see a consultant. She was an exceedingly large lady. After telling me to sit down in a chair placed immediately in front of her desk she took a sheet of paper and rather forcefully slapped it down in front of me. It was a printed map of the hospital.

Without any preamble she took a red felt pen and started drawing all over the map. "This is your digestive system," she said. As I saw the thick red lines emerge from her pen I felt my stomach muscles contract, sharp stabs of pain shot through me and I began to feel distinctly unwell.

"This is your Small Intestine," she continued, as she traced a lengthy organ that seemed to go all over the place, at one point passing briefly through the Maternity Unit next door. She then came to the Large Intestine. The Small Intestine was apparently over twenty feet long and I wondered how an even larger organ could fit in to what I persist in calling my trim figure! In the event the Large Intestine is significantly smaller, being only about five feet long.

With great enthusiasm the consultant told me that they now had an ingenious device which combined a miniature television camera with a swivel-headed searchlight and something that sounded alarmingly like a tiny plumber's blow-lamp. This device she intended to shove up my backside – not just a few inches as I had blithely imagined... but all of a number of feet! The television camera then sent movie pictures down these yards of cable winding their convoluted way through my insides back to a television screen which the consultant could sit and watch.

Up to that time I had bravely pinned to my face a look of interested appreciation. At the same time I was holding tightly to the front of the desk to prevent me falling out of my chair! She then went on to explain that it might be necessary for me to stay on at the hospital. It seemed that on occasions her little gadget ruptured the intestinal wall. The resulting flood of faecal fluid would then cause peritonitis unless dealt with expeditiously. By this time, simulating a relaxed mode, I had my elbows on the consultant's desk and was holding my head in my hands. Up to then I hadn't realised how ill I felt!

I left the consultant's office with a sheaf of papers containing instructions and a prescription for a special laxative that turned out to be exceptionally powerful. She also gave me a date when Valerie had to deliver me into her hands at the hospital where she would carry out a so called colonoscopy but which she speciously described as "a little peep!"

On the day before my colonoscopy, in accordance with my instructions, I began my preparation. I had no solid food all day; all I had was some anaemic fluid from a stock-pot Valerie boils up every day for Schnooky, our Miniature Schnauzer. That evening, when I was beginning to feel the pangs of hunger, I took the consultant's "Special Laxative." The instructions must have been written by someone with an exquisite sense of humour for they read, "a loose watery bowel movement may result." What actually resulted more resembled a NASA space exploration launch. The toilet seat could have done with a safety belt. I spent pretty much the whole of the night in the bathroom spurting noisily. The next day Valerie drove me to the hospital – which was very brave of her for I had been experiencing occasional return bouts of "Special Laxative" spurts. No catastrophe overtook us; had it done so there would have been no alternative to us getting another car! In the event I was safely delivered into the hands of the lady plumber relatively intact.

I cannot describe what it is to experience a colonoscopy for I was blissfully asleep throughout the whole of the procedure. Evidently it turned into an extremely lengthy exploration and gave rise to my lady plumber bringing in a number of plumber's mates with whom she could share the exciting discoveries that were new in even her long experience.

It seems that she couldn't wait to share these exciting discoveries with me for I was still in a fairly muzzy state when she came to see me. From what I could pick up it seemed I no longer had what could anatomically be described as a functioning colon. Instead I had a multitude of festering pouches all strung together along the length of this long-suffering organ. The consultant was extremely animated and I half expected her to break into song when she said, "She'd never seen anything like it in her life." Decidedly I should have it all out. However, in exchange she offered to give me a little bag.

Despite her assurances that such an operation would not present a problem I decided to keep my defective digestive apparatus. By all accounts its dilapidated state was the cause of no little interest amongst those who are paid to look into these dark mysteries. With my diminishing claims to fame, I thought I should hang on to this part of my anatomy which was apparently unique.

The consultant warned of severe and increasing pain and prescribed some powerful painkillers. Being fairly dopey at the best of times, I thought the painkillers would make me even more dozy and in fact I never took them. The consultant hadn't exaggerated about the pain, so much so that more and more frequently I found myself reviewing her offer of a swap for the little bag.

Then, in February of 2006, about eighteen months after the examination, I was scheduled to preach in our church. I'd had a particularly bad week, and was in severe pain in addition to which the festering colon had given me a high temperature. Feeling distinctly wobbly, I thought I might not survive the whole service, so I asked Yinka Oyekan, our senior minister, to get me on early so that I could go home after the sermon. He duly obliged but first prayed for me. He prayed that my 'internal system would be completely renewed'. I appreciated the prayer and the attendant compassion, but I added a rider to the Lord that all I really wanted was an hour's strength and the ability to get home.

Early one morning that same week Christine Wiltshire, a very close friend of Valerie's, had called and told us that the Lord had specifically said she must pray for me that I would be delivered from these terrible pains. There and then she prayed for me most fervently and lovingly.

I can solemnly assert that in the three years that have elapsed since Yinka and Chris prayed for me, I have not had so much as a twinge of pain from my dilapidated tummy. Like salvation, healing is undeserved grace!

That experience was both real and very personal. If I am asked if I believe in miraculous healing, I can do no other than gratefully raise my hand. Of course, in a very real sense, all healing is miraculous, whether it is through the ministry of surgeons, physicians or the humble aspirin. Occasionally God short circuits the medics and we have a 'miraculous' healing.

Why this should be so is a mystery. We can and should *pray* for those who are sick, but it is *God* who not only *does* the healing, but inscrutably it is He who decides *who* He will heal and how He will do it. That is His prerogative. He happens to be God Almighty! For our part we do well to accept Him for who He is, a God who loves us unconditionally and who has a wonderful plan for our lives. His priority is that we focus on Him and get to know Him better. We are infinitely better off knowing Him as a personal loving Saviour, than receiving any gift of healing, no matter how dramatic. Of course, the two are not mutually exclusive!

However, occasionally God lets us in on what He is going to do. That is when we can pray with a confident hope that is not presumption. The imminent conversion of my friend Bill Deane, recorded in Chapter 24, is an example, but I have to confess that my experience of this is not as frequent as I would like. The humbling fact is that such confidence is the result of increasing intimacy with God and explains why my friends Yinka and Chris could pray the way they did. It also explains the persevering approach to prayer by others.

About seven years ago I was having difficulties with sleeping. By difficulties, I mean I wasn't getting any. I went to the doctor who sent me to see a consultant. I was given an appointment for a test which involved staying overnight at the hospital. Through the courtesy of the National Health Service, I had real five star treatment with a private en suite bedroom.

After getting into bed I was brought a mug of hot chocolate. The consultant then arrived and wired me up to a contraption that, throughout the night, would measure everything that was measurable: pulse, blood pressure, breathing rate and so on. A camera was positioned to record my every move. Having wired me up I was wished a good night and left to myself.

Early the next morning I was brought breakfast in bed! 'This really is the life,' I thought! Later I went to see the consultant and he told me that in all his experience he had never encountered a worse case of insomnia. During the eight hours that I was 'asleep' it seems I dozed off 87 times, or, to put it another way, I woke up 87 times. The longest period of 'sleep' was for seven minutes and there was only one of those.

After all that research, all the consultant did was write out a prescription for some nasal drops for me to use. It seemed very prosaic after that five star hospital treatment. The results were anything but prosaic. Immediately I had violent headaches, terrific nose bleeds and constant vomiting. I went to my own doctor and told him about the nasal drops. He pulled a long face and unsurprisingly advised against them.

I had survived two years, so I decided to soldier on. Six months later I was getting really desperate. Everything was a dead weight. Even my bedroom slippers felt as heavy as a deep sea diver's boots and any activity involved a colossal effort.

One Sunday morning, in the middle of the service in church, my friend, Tony Horne came up to me and said, "Margaret feels she should pray for you." I was up for that and went with him to the back of the church where his wife, Margaret was standing. They had known for some time that I was struggling with sleep problems and had been praying for me, but now there was a new sense of urgency and, without preamble, this loving couple started praying.

The praying went on and on and eventually I opened my eyes. Both of them had tears pouring down their cheeks. After about ten minutes they stopped praying but suggested that they should pray with me the next day, and the next, and every succeeding day, until I was healed. They were quite confident that healing would come.

That night I thought I should give their prayers a good head start by going to bed as late as possible! In fact, it was exactly eleven o'clock by

417

our illuminated clock when my head went on to the pillow. Almost immediately I woke up and looked at the clock. It said four minutes past the hour. "Well that praying didn't do any good!" I thought. Wait a minute. Four minutes past *what hour* was that? I looked again; it was four minutes past *four*. I had been asleep for five hours. Almost instantly I dropped off again and the next thing I knew it was half past seven. I'd slept for a further three-and-a-half hours. Ever since then I have had more problems with staying awake than going to sleep!

* * * * *

As I write this I am 80 years old so, if 'the span of a man's years is three score years and ten', then I have already been in the departure lounge for ten years, and inevitably getting nearer and nearer to the exit! Does that thought dismay me? Not in the slightest. The Bible speaks of a *certain* hope. The Christian lives with the *certainty* of that hope being realised. Before I was born again, I didn't have that certain hope. There was not only the fear of death, there was the uncertainty that went with it. In Palestine as well as in Malaya, where death was a constant and distinct possibility, I carried a dreadful fear of dying. After I became a Christian, although I had a highly developed sense of self preservation, that awful dread of death had gone.

This deliverance from the fear of death had been brought home to me very forcibly in 1961 when I was 32. I had been working very hard for an extended period getting to my Sun Life office very early and then going to the mission office and dealing with the work there. By 2:00 in the afternoon I might be on my way to take a meeting for the mission in some distant city or town. Later, motorways would transform travelling by road in the UK, but in 1961 there were only very short stretches and none anywhere near Reading. In those days a one-way journey to, say, Norwich could take six hours or more. The result was that I wouldn't be home until the early hours of the morning. This routine had continued for some time when it was abruptly interrupted.

One morning I was in the office, very early as usual, and was working at my desk, when suddenly I found myself on the floor. It was as if I had been kicked in the chest by a shire horse. I was quite unable to move, not even to reach for the telephone wire to pull the telephone off my desk. I was utterly helpless, and there wouldn't be anyone else in the office for another hour-and-a-half at least. With a massive pain in my chest I guessed I'd had a heart attack. With that realisation came the thought that I was about to die. I did a quick radar scan of all my relationships. There was nothing outstanding. If ever I thought anyone had a problem with me I would go to them and try to sort it out. As far as I knew there were no outstanding problems.

All my life insurance premiums were up to date! After selling hundreds of thousands of pounds worth of life insurance, I was about to become a life insurance *claim*! Was that stuff worth selling or was it worth selling? I knew that I had made ample provision for Valerie and the children, but suddenly I realised *I wouldn't be seeing them again.* That was very hard, and did nothing to ease the excruciating pain in my chest. Then I had another thought. Oh my goodness! I was about to meet God! *God! GOD!* God the creator! God, the *Judge!*

Now, *this* is my reason for sharing that experience. Instead of being terrified at the prospect of meeting God, I was really excited about it. I lay on my office floor and at any tick of the clock I was expecting to meet, face to face, this amazing Saviour who loved me enough to become Man and then die for me. If I had been able to move my arms I would have stretched them out towards Him.

I had a clock on the bookcase in my office and, one by one, I watched the minutes tick by. Half-an-hour passed, still I couldn't move and still I hadn't gone to be with the Lord! Well, that was nearly 50 years ago and, while I fully recovered and enjoy every day of my life, if the real thing is anything like the dummy run, then I'm looking forward to it! That little episode served to bring home the wonderful truth of Hebrews 2:14, put so clearly in The Message: *'Since we are made of flesh and blood, it's logical that the Saviour took on flesh and blood in order to rescue us by His death. By embracing death, taking it into Himself, He destroyed the Devil's hold on death and freed all who cower through life, scared to death of death!'*

Death, really and truly, need not be feared. No wonder God says: "I know the plans I have for you... plans to give you hope and a future."

Chapter 45
Retirement and the Future

I retired from the Sun Life of
Canada nearly eighteen years ago
and, as I look back on the 37 years
that I spent with that company, I
can truthfully say that I cannot
remember a day I did not enjoy.
Throughout the whole of that time
I was accountable to men for
whom I had the deepest respect and
great affection. In the later years
this was Vice President Agencies,
Paul Littleton and my General
Manager Richard Baker, whom I

Paul Littleton, me and Richard Baker

counted and still count as personal friends. From the very earliest days
my colleagues were enormously supportive and I grew to love them
most dearly. I don't think I am being pretentious when I say that I
believe they loved me too!

In all of that I realise that I was extraordinarily privileged, yet, despite
the joys and enormous satisfaction gained from my work, I am bound
to say that retirement is the best job I ever had! It started with our
General Manager, Richard Baker and his lovely wife Vanda treating all
the family to a simply splendid dinner.

My retirement has been an incredibly busy life, not least because I no
longer have my amazingly competent secretary, Barbara Chandler.
However retirement has not been so busy that I haven't had time to
enjoy friendship with delightful neighbours, reunions with colleagues
and friends, fellowship with lovely church members, more contact
with my growing family and, best of all, the day by day love, support
and friendship of a simply wonderful wife.

421

Left to right: Bob, Katie, Tim, Penny (neither were married at that time),
me, Valerie, Vanda Baker, Richard Baker, Penny and Christopher

The Managers and wives in the Sun Life of Canada Reading Region.
Left to right, back : Barrie Machin, Ray Pearce, Arthur White,
John Smith, Ray Main, Douglas Austin, Robert Thomas.
Front : Valerie Smith, Mildred White, Pat Machin, Nancy Pearce,
Linda Main, Joy Austin, Meera Thomas

*A miracle of
God's grace and
goodness*

Our marriage was a miracle of God's grace and goodness and our married life has been quite marvellous. Wonderfully my retirement became the occasion for a second honeymoon that has now continued for eighteen years and seems to get even better day by day.

My retirement must have come as a massive disturbance to Valerie's busy and well regulated life. For one thing I was at home during the day. She had married me for better or for worse but not for lunch! Retirement enabled me to see afresh what a truly amazing person was the wife God had chosen for me. She holds the family together as well as me. She copes with unexpected visitors, some of whom come for weeks. Day by day, regularly and without any fuss, she prepares delicious meals and can carry on an intelligent conversation at the same time.

Observing all this, when I retired I decided that I would lend a hand and duly announced to the family that on a particular day I was going to prepare a meal. It was going to be a retirement celebration meal for the whole of the family. I decided to cook a goose – in some ways an unfortunate choice, particularly when combined with a selection of starters and three rather elaborate desserts. My abysmal ignorance made it highly likely that I would be 'cooking my goose' in more ways than one.

I started to prepare for this operation two days in advance. On the day, sensing impending crises, the entire family decamped and took shelter in my daughter Katie's house about two miles away. They figured the fall out would be less at that distance!

The first set-back came early on. The recipe told me to 'dress the goose with seasoning'. Valerie has about 50 jars of different herbs and spices and I searched through all of these looking for one marked 'Seasoning'. There are degrees of ignorance but it will be evident that my culinary unenlightenment was absolute. In desperation I rang Katie to ask where Valerie kept her jar of 'Seasoning'. I could hear the noise of my assembled family and heard Katie call across the room. There was a great shout of laughter which eventually subsided sufficiently for Katie to inform me that seasoning was another term for pepper and salt!

Despite my abject ignorance I am able to record that the meal positively astonished my family who were all prepared to settle for Kentucky Fried Chicken after throwing away my creations! It was rated an outstanding success, and so it ought to have been, for it cost the equivalent of three weeks' housekeeping. That probably accounts for the fact that while meals prepared by me may be exotic they are infrequent!

Valerie, Schnooky and me – Courtesy of The Mail on Sunday

Some time after my retirement I had a telephone call from an editor at The Mail on Sunday. Seemingly he wanted to send a photographer to get a photograph of Valerie and me to go with an article that was to appear in a coming issue of the paper. This sounded distinctly ominous for the only tributes that I had read in newspapers were featured on the "Obituary" page! I forget what the article said but unfortunately it wasn't libellous! However we did get some splendid photographs, one of which is Valerie's all-time favourite of the two of us.

Incidentally that photograph has met a pressing need. Ever since I started writing this autobiography I have been repeatedly asked when a photograph of our miniature Schnauzer was going to appear. It was reported by the members of the family that her requests were becoming increasingly importunate! Well, there she is. It is not every little dog who gets its photograph in an autobiography *and* in a National newspaper. I should add that Schnooky is a joy. She's a challenge too for one of my prayers is: "Lord, help me to be the kind of person Schnooky thinks I am!"

In the different Parts of this book I have commented on our children. They have been a constant joy. They are our best friends and the best friends of each other. We are proud of them too; not merely because of their scholastic achievements, although they are all extraordinarily talented. Nor does our pride lie in their post graduate industry, although they all have worked prodigiously hard which has brought attendant success. No, we are proud of our children because, as the years pass, they are all becoming more and more like Jesus. I rather suspect that He is proud of them too, and that is enormously pleasing because, as I was told 60 years ago by Dr Samuels, why else are we here.

As I write these closing words, I am with most of our family in South Wales. Some of them couldn't be with us. Katie was at university taking exams, Danny was in Canada and Shash had a teaching programme. We are in St Brides Castle, which is about fourteen miles beyond Haverford West. My 80th birthday was a wonderful excuse for extended celebrations that have run from early March to May. Here we will have a final celebration banquet, which seems a most appropriate thing to do when you are staying in a castle.

*At St Brides. Left to right: Priya, Jono, Tim (R-S), Paul, Sam, Penny (G),
Jamie, Tim (S), Matthew, Christopher, Stefano, David, Joshua, Kerry,
Schnooky, Penny (S), Katie, John, Valerie*

*View from St Brides Castle. Left to right: Tim(R-S), Bob, Katie, Jono,
Priya, Stefano, Kerry, David, Matthew, Christopher, John, Valerie, Tim
(S), Ben, Penny (S), Joshua*

St Brides Castle

Having the children and grandchildren around has prompted me to look back on the tapestry of my life. Something of a pattern and purpose emerges; but that was not always the case. There were times when life appeared to be a tangle of loose ends. It is at such moments that we want to 'turn the tapestry over' to see what is designed for us. But life is not like that. It has to be lived 'a stitch at a time'. The secret is having confidence in the One who has already made the plans... plans that give us all hope and a future.

THE END

APPENDIX A
Some Wonderful Friends

Adrian and Diana Whittaker
Alan & Eve Jones
Alan & Muriel Lloyd
Alan Sumner
Alex & Veronica Mitchell
Alf and Rose Waller
Andrea Baker
Andrew & Valerie March
Andrew and Rose Miles
Andrew & Penny Mowll
Anita Bettle
Anita Hawthorne
Ann Thatcher
Anne & Jimmy Rutherford
Anne Long
Anne Wells
Arthur and Mildred White
Arthur and Pat Allchin
Barbara Davis
Barbara & Gerry Muldowny
Barbara & Paul Chandler
Barbara Myatt
Barrie and Pat Machin
Barry and Bunny Kirk
Barry and Lisa Ramsay
Beatrice Clayre
Ben Smart
Ben White
Bernard & Prudy Hignett
Berry family
Betty Pedley
Bill and Liz Hunter
Bill and Shirley Lees

Bill and Val Hawes
Bob & Belva Foster
Bob and Jean Shorney
Bob and Katie Smart
Bob and Pat Brown
Bob and Sally Moore
Bob Sadler
Bob Stroud
Brian and Julie Turner
Brian Trew
Britt Bjoro
Bruce & Margaret Thomson
Bud Abbott
Carolyn Hignett
Carolyn Morris
Charles and Betty Tucker
Cherry East
Chris & Pauline Michell
Christopher & Penny Smith
Clargo family
Clive & Liz Grantham
Colette Bridges
Colin & Margaret Reasbeck
Daniel & Beccy Susanbach
Danny & Rachel John
Danny Smart
Dave & Angie Wheatcroft
Dave & Grace Turner
Dave & Steph Tongeman
Dave and Maz Wraight
Dave and Sheila Masters
Dave and Steph Tongeman
Dave and Teresa Stillman

Dave and Vron Tyrrell
David & Jan Dixon
David & Yvonne Neville-Rolfe
David and Jenny Winter
David and Lynn Stevens
David and Valerie Green
David Fulbrook
David Hignett
David & Helen Putley
Dev and Jaya Matadeen
Don and Iris Mills
Doris Whelan
Dorothy Forchuk
Dorothy Lim
Doug & Rosie Sadler
Douglas and Joy Austin
Eric & Almuth Lockerbie
Ernie and Ruth Bowden
Fiona Lindsay
Frank Gregory
Fred & Betty Smith
Gail Eiloart
Gareth and Rachel Owen
Gary and Sue Bowden
Gene and Lynne Rault
George and Ann Lindo
George and Dora Lear
Gerald Coates
Gerri Andrews
Gill Stedford
Gladys Riley
Glenda Povey
Graham & Angela Bates
Graham & Jo Bennett
Hannah Putley
Hanni Griffiths
Hasel Kisiala
Haydn and Ann Burnham
Hazel Clargo
Heather Errington
Helen Burslem
Helen Macintosh
Henry Stockwell

Hilary Stoneman
Huw & Marian Davies
Iain & Beatrice Clayre
Ian and Mabel Boyd
Ivan Cavell
Jane Smart
Janet Parke
Janet Parkins
Jean & Hugh Thomson
Jean Davies
Jean Nanney
Jean Thomas
Jenny Russell
Jeon and Sheila Kwang
Jeremy & Ros Muldowney
Jim & Julie Lees
Jim and Liz Andrews
Jim Graham
Joan Day
Joan & Jack Morris
Joan Tresidder
Joan Wales
John & Lindsay Bishop
John & Anne Lawley
John & Anne Marcham
John & Kate Arkell
John & Kath Pady
John & Kathleen Wallis
John & Marion Marett
John & Virginia West
John & Vonne Kearsey
John and Aruna Whetter
John and Joyce Murdoch
John and Kathleen Wallis
John and Margaret Dart
John and Marj Lewis
John and Pat Madge
John Brown
John Hall
John R W Stott
John Rawcliffe
John Roper
John Turner

Jok and Long Wan
Jon and Judy Eastwood
Jonathan & Matty Thurley
Jono and Priya Smart
Joshua Smith
Julia Wilcock
Julie Noble
Katie Baker
Kay Carswell
Keith and Audrey Ternent
Keith and Brenda Hester
Ken & Pam Annal
Ken and Chris Wiltshire
Ken and Maureen Willis
Ken McSherry
Kerry Smart
Kevin & Alison Hallowell
Kevin and Linsey Potter
Kwang and Sheila Jeon
Leanne & Dale Holzer
Linda Clargo
Liz and Alf Davis
Liz Legg
Luke Baker
Maeve Edwards
Malcolm and Julia Horne
Margaret Scott
Margot Dart
Marianne West
Mark and Ann Penson
Mark and Jane Eddison
Mark and Lucy Malcolm
Mark Boshier
Marsden and Kathy Baker
Martin Higgins
Martin & Moira Sheppard
Martin and Diana Symons
Martyn Lloyd Jones
Mary Baxter
Mary Cook
Mary Older
Matthew and Lynn Shaw
Matthew Stubbs

Matthews family
Maureen Boshier
Maureen Fairbairn
Maurice Garton
Maurice Houghton
Michael & Valerie Griffiths
Michelle Sexton
Mick & Liz Lear
Mick and Sophia Penson
Mika Karwal
Mike Burmingham
Mike and Mychelle Oke
Mitchell-Baker family
Mowll family
Nathan and Sue Winyard
Netta Bernard
Niall and Nina Gurrey
Nick & Lesley Whelan
Nick Crowder
Nigel and Kathryn Tolson
Noel and Margaret Brien
Norah Joyce
Oyekan family
Pamela Hathorn
Pat and Bob Brown
Pat Baines
Pat Herbert
Patrick le Dily
Paul & Geraldine Witcher
Paul and Ann Littleton
Paul and Brenda Howard
Paul and Heather Garratt
Paul and Meg Wraight
Paul and Penny Gomersall
Paul and Wendy Bevan
Paul Boshier
Paul Philippa McMurrain
Paul Podesta
Paul Shepherd
Peter & Barbara Chapple
Peter & Gwen Graham
Peter & June Drew-Clifton
Peter and Gwen Graham

Peter and Jean Smart
Peter and Ruth Cornforth
Peter and Val Taylor
Peter and Val Thomas
Peter Braithwaite
Peter Flynn
Peter Watts
Phil & Carolyn Baines
Phil & Sue Simmons
Philippa McMurrain
Phyl Peskett
Putley family
Quentin de la Bedoyere
Ralph Morrish
Ray and Linda Main
Ray and Nancy Pearce
Raymond Head
Rene Brown
Richard & Shirley Harbour
Richard and Vanda Baker
Rob & Jane Goodwin
Rob and Lesley Carter
Robert & Meera Thomas
Roger and Alison Grant
Roger and Faith Forster
Roger and Tony Wales
Roy & Monica Stillman
Sammy Horne
Sandy and June Penman
Sean & Jayne Stillman
Sheila MacLeod
Shirley & Tony McCall
Simon & Julie Carruthers
Stefano Pisola
Steve & Désirée German
Steve & Maureen Rocker
Steve and Mary Walton
Steve and Pauline Lye
Stirling and Donna Foster
Stuart Lovegrove
Suzanne Prescott
Sylvia and Alec Talbot
Sylvia Eedle

Sylvia March
Sylvia Webb
Terry & Doreen Halewood
Thelma & Kenneth Hearn
Tim & Shash Rault-Smith
Tim & Tricia Barrow
Tim and Phil Clewer
Tim Pearce
Tom and Aileen Stanley
Tony & Alexandra Mercer
Tony & Margaret Pitkethley
Tony and Carol Carson
Tony and Margaret Horne
Tony and Toni Davey
Tony and Wendy Heath
Tony Cooper
Tony Gray
Tony Horsfall
Viola Taeni
Wolfgang Fernandez
Yoder family
Yomi & Valerie Oneayemi

APPENDIX B
An Open Invitation

In chapter 28 I record an interview I had with my bank manager during which the following exchange took place:

"So, you're on chatting terms with the Almighty are you? How long has this been going on?" He said it as if I had some dread disease.
"About six years."
"You've been chatting with God for six years! How did all this start?"
"It's quite a long story," I said.
"Oh, I've plenty of time." So I started at the beginning...

The outcome of that conversation was that, despite having no income, my bank manager gave me an unsecured loan of £3,000, the equivalent of about £150,000 in today's value. Another outcome was that the manager became a personal friend. The loan was repaid in a miraculously short time and I never had to resort to a further loan but it was very comforting to have a personal friend in my bank manager! What was even more comforting was to have "the Almighty" as a personal friend!

We have sung "What a Friend we have in Jesus" so frequently that the words sometimes fail to make the impact they should; but the more we stop to think about it, the more staggering is the fact that our Lord Jesus Christ – our Creator, Lord and Master, Judge, Redeemer, Saviour and a great deal more – wants to be our friend! Even more staggering is the fact that He **actually wants us to be His friend.**

In the Old Testament we can see that Noah, Moses, Job, Enoch and David all had a very close relationship with God BUT **WE HAVE**

BEEN CALLED TO BE **FRIENDS** OF GOD! Stop and think about that – and marvel!

Verses such as Philippians 2:6-8, Hebrews 12:1-3 and many others, bring home to us the fact that our friendship with God has cost Him dearly. When Jesus paid for our sins on the cross, the temple veil that symbolised our separation from God was split from top to bottom, indicating that direct access by ordinary people to God was available. We can approach Him at any time. *"Now we can rejoice in our wonderful new relationship with God – all because of what our Lord Jesus Christ has done for us in making us friends of God,"* Romans 5:11. *"All this is done by God, who through Christ changed us from enemies into His friends,"* 2 Corinthians 5:18.

It is all so staggering that it is sometimes difficult to imagine how a really intimate relationship with the Creator of the universe can be possible. In 1666 a little book was written called "The Practice of the Presence of God." It's still in print and is the classic book on learning how to develop a constant conversation with God. The treasures in this little book come from Brother Lawrence, an eighty year old humble cook in a monastery who confessed that he "was a great awkward fellow who broke everything." But Brother Lawrence was able to turn everything he did, even the most commonplace and menial task like washing dishes, into acts of praise and communion with God.

"The key to friendship with God," he said, "is not changing what you **do**, but **changing your attitude** toward what you do." What we normally do for ourselves we begin doing for God, whether it is having a meal, having a bath, working, relaxing or emptying the waste bins. Brother Lawrence found it easy to worship God through the common tasks of life; he didn't have to go away for special spiritual retreats!

Another of Brother Lawrence's helpful comments was that we pray short conversational prayers **continually** through the day. He said: "I do not advise you to use a great multiplicity of words in prayer, since long discourses are often the occasion for wandering." The context was a wandering mind! In an age of attention deficit, this 350 year old suggestion from an eighty year old to keep it short and simple is particularly relevant!

Church attendance, a regular quiet time, reading and learning Scripture are all important but **friendship** with God is built by sharing **all** our life experiences with Him. He wants to be included in *every* activity of our lives. God is a "talkative" God. We constantly read the words: "And God said..." but He is also a good listener. Involving Him in everything is what Paul meant in 1 Thessalonians 5:17 when he said *"Pray without ceasing!"* Practising the presence of God is a skill we can develop. We need to train our minds to remember God. It is helpful to create reminders such as using a pocket alarm - or anything that reminds us that God wants to be brought in on everything we do.

Back in 1956 my bank manager asked: "So, you're on chatting terms with the Almighty are you? How long has this been going on?" At that time my reply was: "About six years." Today I would be able to say: "About 60 years"! Sixty years ago I had a great deal of help from others and that is why I would like to close with an open invitation to contact me if by any chance you think I could be of help to you.

Turnhams House
Pincents Lane, Calcot
Reading RG31 4TT
Tel 0118 9422227
jbs@turnhams.org

Bearing in mind that I am 80 years old it might be helpful to give an alternative contact! You would find the Christian Enquiry Agency, enormously helpful and at the same time completely confidential and unobtrusive. They work on behalf of all the major churches in Britain.

The Christian Enquiry Agency
FREEPOST WC 2947
South Croydon
London CR2 8UZ